My Resilience

A Dinka girl's true story of civil war in Sudan, growing up in Cuba and making it in Canada

By Sarah Gabriel

Fifth Edition

To chris, many thanks!

sarahachuoth@yahoo.com
ISBN 978-1-105-76977-1

Table of Contents

Dedication

This book is dedicated to my beloved brother, Agor, whom I truly miss and wish were here with us in this life. My brother had a big heart! He was a giver and he sacrificed his life for the freedom of his people.

During his life, he always put others before himself. Agor dedicated his teenage and early adult years fighting to bring peace to his people. He fought with courage for his country in the Sudanese People's Liberation Army (SPLA) during which he lost his life. Agor will always be alive in spirit as he occupies a special place in the hearts of his family.

He was to us the one and the only Agor who can never be replaced by anyone. He was Resilient! Despite the hardships he faced in his young life, he always had a big smile on his face and was still the most happy and caring person I have ever met.

I will remember him as the big brother who was always there for his family and his people.

Acknowledgments

I would like to give special thanks to my loving parents, Gabriel Achuoth and Rebeca Acuch Gabriel, and my siblings for their support during my book research. Without their help this story, and the wonderful life I have now, would never have been possible.

Thank you Jok Mach Nai and my cousin Achick Jok for giving me information on my life in Cuba. I also want to thank Darcy Bomford, Allan Gee, Deborah Joell, Maria Luisa and Ruy Romano and all the Sudanese students I knew in Cuba. They lived through this with me in Cuba and were known as the Lost Children of Sudan.

Thanks to my dear beloved best friend Anne, who has became like a sister to me, and her husband, Julius Ruechel. It was such a blessing to have their help and encouragement. Thanks to all my friends and co-workers at the Canadian Food Inspection Agency for believing in me during the writing stage.

A special thanks to Linda for her encouragement to begin my project and to her brother, Rory C.J. Frankson, who kindly lent six months of creative writing advice. He drew out the information that needed to come out to make My Resilience real.

Another member of the Frankson family, Kokie Elisondo, was a big help with the arrangement of my story and in naming the book. Much thanks to Dave Dandell for his photography and the fun photo shoots he organized for our 'team' project. He got just the right photo for my wonderful cover.

Thanks to Amy Hyson for her advice and contribution at the beginning of the editing stage.

Finally, I'd like to give a very special thanks to my editor Frank Hilliard and his wife Pam for their hard work in polishing, editing and publishing my book. I have learned a lot from you both and will be forever grateful for your help in turning my dream into a reality.

Chapter 1
Back to Africa

Back to Africa; this is where I was going, flying back to my past. Africa, where my life began, held little of my collected memories. Most were from a world away as an adult living in Canada, having settled in British Columbia's beautiful Okanagan Valley and its small city Vernon. Now I had the dawning reality I would soon be on my native soil. It caused many mixed emotions; a dreamt-of-moment almost impossible to imagine. Most of the work to organize what I knew would be yet another major life changing event had been done. The ticket was paid for with money saved from months of study and unfamiliar work. The planning and numerous international phone calls to family were finished.

It had taken me thirty two years, but I was really going home; home to put together the pieces of the puzzle that was my life journey; to understand the frustrations, the constant imaginings of my life, the life that was, and my life in the here and now in 2008. My wanderings had shaped me so differently from the family I was now going back to find in the Africa I'd been torn away from in 1986. With so many years and countries between, my mind was reeling with memories and emotions coming to the surface. They were mixed in with all the details of my final travel plans and the combination was very close to overwhelming.

This was my Africa, where I hoped to find answers to a lifetime of questions and deep feelings of loss. To see my family for the first time in over 18 years made me very nervous. They were living in Nairobi and would pick me up at the airport. I was to stay with them at my brother's or my step mother's house. I was nervous but I was also really very excited that we were finally going to meet. I asked myself how I'd recognize them; I had never met most of them before. The only one I knew was my younger brother Chol, who was also meeting me at the airport. It had been twenty years since I had last seen him and the only picture I had of him was one he'd sent me five years earlier. There they'd be, this family of strangers at the airport waiting for me, and I wasn't even sure I'd recognize my own brother... such strange things to think of continually.

Sometimes my weird and silly thoughts became nightmares. I imagined my family might be a bad family that might catch me and carry me off to some forgotten village and sell me for cows. Or I thought I might be captured in enemy raids by other tribes who might only do the same. There are a million ways tribesmen can keep a Sudanese woman captive in their country. I might never see Canada again! That dream really got me going; to the point that it became a very real idea. I told myself I'm now a

9

Canadian Citizen. I have found the place I chose to call home. I'm safe coming back as a Westerner. And yet Africa is such a big place. My real friends and family might never find me, and oh man. *Lions!* For some reason lions are a very large primal fear for me. Imagine, being eaten by a pride of hungry Lions!

I could see me, kicking and screaming all the way. 'Chomp, chomp, chomp... *oh dear, Sarah Gabriel. Just gone!*',

I had to giggle to myself at those, at times, funny, nervous thoughts.

As my travel date came closer, many more hours were spent in this kind of anxious state. I would have pictures rise up in me from my past; visions so strong I could almost smell the great heat that comes off the soil of my homeland. Dusty days of childhood play, Mama calling us children to dinner through the kitchen door, the buzzing hover of bugs; it all filled my mind. I lay tossing in bed trying to sleep while these thoughts and feelings travelled through my head, a flood, of rapidly changing memories. When sleep would finally come, I'd have dreams that would wake me in a panic shivering. I would curl into a ball to hug and rock myself back to groggy slumber. Real sleep was almost impossible to come by because I couldn't shut off those feelings. I would get up in the morning tired and carry on, put on my face and keep my world moving.

I tried to bury these emotions, to only show a smiling face to my friends, to be the Sarah they knew. Really it wasn't a difficult thing for me to do I'd been shutting down my true feelings for so long. It was second nature. I had my running, sports, Latino friends and an engaged social life with boyfriends, music and dancing. These were all things I loved to do with many different kinds of adopted families, cultures, responsibilities and work. I filled my world full to overflowing by adopting a stream of seemingly never ending new culture. Yet, in private, the hiding times would come and I would feel these thoughts and feelings. They wouldn't leave me alone. Me, Sarah...

Sometimes I'd ask my mirror: *'who am I really? Am I this image I see? Am I the dress I wear everyday?*

This Dinka child...of Africa. Me!"

This identity was part of me, though I could only be alone with her, keep her to myself, share loneliness with her that haunted me. It was an emptiness that could not be filled, no matter how active I was. There was a building pressure like a dam I knew was about to break. I couldn't think of Mama and not cry, not come so close to losing it. No, I could not break down. I had to go back to Africa. It was time to settle this conflict in myself. I had to dig even deeper and find the strength to face the nightmares, the visions of a lost family, a child's past... confused visions that haunted this soul, visions of a girl called Acuach Cor, of the Dinka Tribe.

There was so much I just couldn't share, or maybe even face. I had to be strong. For a long time I had drummed into my psyche, be brave for others, buoy them with my easy laughter, and forget the inner pain; move on. Work, enjoyment and fun; these things had saved me; a smooth seamless circle of learned public faces that hid the pain and kept it in its place. So I could live. Survive. Search over the next valley, the next hill, down another long road and find the means, the resources to build a home, a house of sticks. And all the while I had these memories that would crawl into my baggage and move along to the next place with me. At times, I felt they threatened to break me to tiny pieces.

There were other things that came along that weren't personal in nature, but which affected me just the same and added to the building pressure. At the time I'd chosen to go back home, Kenya was beginning to have violent protests connected with its elections and I began to keep track of the news of these events on TV with very mixed feelings. I wasn't sure I wanted to face more hard times, to be reminded of bad memories from the past. At the same time, I didn't want to delay my trip. I couldn't because I still had to deal with my dreams. They were always there, always a part of me.

Before I knew it, it was time to go. Outwardly I was ready. I had shopped for gifts for everyone in my family. But mentally I wasn't ready. I was excited but at the same time I wasn't sure what to expect. All I knew, was I was missing my family achingly despite all the years that had gone by. I had my fears but my family were always with me in my memories and they were drawing me home.

A dear Kenyan-Canadian friend, Anne, was very happy for me because I was finally living out the dream I had so often shared with her in confidence, of going back to Africa. She insisted she take me to Kelowna airport to see me off. It would have been Anne I would have chosen for this anyway, if she hadn't offered. Her consideration made me glow with real love for her as a sister, which is what she'd really become.

And here I have a confession. I had no definite plan as to what my final destination would be. Would I return or would I stay in Africa? I didn't know, As a result, it was like saying goodbye for possibly, a very long time.

There I was, leaving Canada and friends behind I might never see again...

While we waited at the airport, Anne tried to comfort me, to tell me not to worry and that everything was going to be just fine. She said when I came back I would be fulfilled, having finally seen my family. She wanted me to have a memorable trip and a deserving visit. It was a blessing having her with me and having her see me off. Her reassurance made me feel better and more confident it would all work out. Finally it was time to go and with a tearful hug, Anne left me at the departure gate.

For reasons I didn't really understand at the time, I was very sad to leave Canada and at the same time, very happy to be going back to Africa.

Another reason I suffered a lot of confusion was that I really didn't know what kind of reception I was in for. I knew under Dinka family law my Father, as the head of the Family, could force me to stay in Africa whether I wanted to or not. At the same time, I had made a promise to myself many years ago that if at any time Mama needed me I would be there for her. Because of my phone calls, I knew she wanted to see me. There was another issue; money. I didn't know the situation I would find my family in, when I got there. Were they comfortable and well off, or were they struggling and in poverty? Would I, their little girl in Canada be considered an asset or a burden? These were some of my thoughts as I left to board my flight and my first short hop to Calgary before going on to Britain. The time there, seemed to drag on forever.

While waiting at Calgary airport I tried calling my brother Anyuon, who was working in Brooks, Alberta to find out if he'd managed to get hold of my cousins who lived in London. I wanted to meet them and have their company during my stopover in England. Anyuon told me they weren't able to. It was heart breaking news because I really wanted some family support, given all the revelations and emotions I was going through. Not having anyone to console me made me feel completely alone. I felt even more alienated, on my own, travelling through this whole wide world of strangers.

On the plane on the long flight to London, I spent most of my time trying to sleep so I didn't have to think about things. When sleep didn't come, I tried to read or look through magazines to kill the time. No matter how hard I tried, I couldn't relax. My mind was constantly going over all the things I'd been through since I left Sudan on the run into Ethiopia and all the following years I spent in Cuba. Always I wondered about the fate of Mama and Baba in our war torn country since I had no news of their welfare. Now I would finally come full circle, find the truth about things that had plagued me for many years. I didn't want to think of all the horrors we had lived through, not just me but all the students who were refugees with me in Cuba, nor about the Sudanese people and the conflicts that were still happening in Sudan as well as the countries around it. Yet these thoughts drifted endlessly through my mind, as if they had a will of their own, keeping me from much needed rest and the release of sleep.

When I arrived at London's Heathrow airport, I had to wait nine hours for the last leg of my journey to Kenya. At first it seemed a lot of time to wait, but Heathrow was very big and there were a lot of shops and things to see. So I started to get the feeling it wouldn't be too bad after all spending some time experiencing new things in a terminal the size of a small city. That in itself was a kind of novelty, once I got over being intimidated by it and feeling I might get lost. That this huge place might just up and swallow me whole, was my first very real feeling, what with my rather raw emotions, but eventually I got over it.

I found myself interested in watching the people and travellers from all over the world, being entertained with all the hubbub going on around me. I realize a lot of people were travelling alone, just like me. I did a lot of walking through the shops and not buying anything. I wanted to, as a few items caught my attention and I really liked, but good God, everything was so very expensive! I didn't want to spend too much of the limited travel money I had with me, too soon. Even the food was very expensive! I enjoyed it though and ate a lot. I think it was a kind of a nervous reaction; food and the action of eating took away some of that nervousness I felt. It took my mind off things.

While I was eating and drinking some yummy tea, I heard a lady talking on her cell phone in Spanish. I waited until she finished and went over and said, "hola," It was great to hear her say back, "oh wow, you speak Spanish!" I asked her where she was from and she said she was from Spain. I told her that I was from Sudan, but grew up in Cuba. We kept on talking while waiting for our planes and even walked around checking things out. I was so happy and relieved to no longer be alone. More and more of my nervous loneliness began to fall away. I had made a new short term friend and even though we would have to go our separate ways, it took some of the sting away from not being able to see my family in London.. Well then, I thought, I could be a part of a make believe family of travellers since it was not hard to strike up a social conversation in Latin culture.

Another couple heard us talking in Spanish and they joined us. It was great fun being happy to have met others who spoke Spanish. It had been a long time since the woman had spoken her native tongue. She was from Colombia and her husband was British. They lived in Kenya and they were going back to what they described as a lovely home. They went on to talk quite a lot about their two children born in Nairobi. They loved living in that part of Africa. They now considered it their home. These acquaintances, having the Spanish language in common and with their natural type of honest openness, really helped the time go by quickly. I had also been attracted by a gentle look and a brilliant smile to a young black man like me called James from Kenya. He had been on business to the States and was returning to his home in Nairobi. It gave me the opportunity to find out what he knew of Nairobi and what was happening in Kenya and on the African Continent.

Even though I'd just met him, he seemed a person I could trust and so I told him a bit of my story and about how my family had left Sudan. I began to pour out; that I was still more than a little worried by the news and the recent upheavals taking place in Kenya. I'd overheard some people in the airport earlier talking about the current news and was shocked to hear there were gun battles going on between rival factions in Kenya. This had frightened me a lot, had made me feel that familiar shaking inside, because of the memories they brought to the surface. Knowing I couldn't handle a repeat of being trapped in the middle of a conflict all over again was a very real fear for me.

James could see that I was quite upset by these developments and in a very straight forward, compassionate manner, painted a different picture. He said, in his view, Africa as a whole was very stable and it was just a matter of knowing where to go and how to get there. He patted my hand and told me there was no need to be scared. Really I was more confused than scared. Under it all I knew what he was telling me was true and he went on to smoothly change the topic. He spoke about his love of Africa and the goodness he'd seen the people held in their hearts. He said good changes were coming to Africa. Yes there were still conflicts but they seemed to be getting fewer and fewer.

I could see there was an underlying feeling to the way he talked, and after a while it came to me a regal sort of noble hope. James projected a real love for his country and admiration for all her long, and at times violent, history. He respected those who were trying to bring peace to a troubled land. We covered so many different kinds of topics. Most of my worries fell away while we exchanged sometimes funny banter, shared personal stories, or while I listened to his very African political concerns. For me it was refreshing to be immersed in talk with an obviously intelligence and optimistic individual. For example, we talked about Obama becoming the U.S President. It was really interesting to find out he knew Obama's family back ground on his father's side since he was from the Luo tribe in Kenya. Yes indeed the world we knew was changing. I also realized it was going to take great personal changes for my country to grow with those leaps to peace, prosperity and a better way of life.

We had so much to talk about, even though it was only a short while, I felt I had known him for a long time. The things that were brought up were of such a personal nature, the way he handled himself with a comfortable confidence brought out something in me, but I didn't quite know what it was right then. It was like a planted seed that I knew would grow, a feeling that yes. Great changes were coming...coming for me.

I believe that seed was hope and the belief my Africa, my country and my life could be changed! The confusions I sometimes experienced and couldn't really share with anyone just might fall away. My visit might open a different part of me to share, a part that felt locked away and before was almost unreachable. These feelings were now flowering in my breast and I held that flower close to my heart. It was so delicate and precious, it needed to be nurtured. I felt I could water it forever with my tears if it ever came to the surface.

It had been a real surprise to me, this time between flights with my adopted little group and a beautiful mixture of cultural diversity, with these flowers in my garden of hope. My new found African friend and the Spanish speaking friends were helping me; lending me strength and making time seem to fly right by. Then all too soon, the departure time came around and I had to say good bye to my friend Carmella from Spain and give her a hurried thank you and a hug at her departure gate. The others were on the same flight as mine and I gave them shared warm hugs as well because we had different seats and our time together was at an end. We held different lives to be travelled into, different families awaiting our arrivals, different histories that had brought us together for this short period of time shared. I was separate again, alone with different concerns that were piling up in me and more with each passing second to take off. As I felt again this growing anxiousness, the familiar tightness in my chest, a tear rolled down my cheek. This was it; it was all so real, so present! My destination was actually happening, growing through me. This seed was alive, planted in my heart.

'Oh boy!' I thought, 'now I have to fill in this time alone. Without going totally crazy.'

I watched London out of my window shrink into the distance. My heart was racing as I saw the clouds pass outside, so soon I would have my heart's desire. The plane banked to leave English airspace. All my thoughts were drawing me back to where all of my hopes had begun... Africa!

Chapter 2
May 16, 1983 - Revolution

Baba and Mama both came from big families in Dinka villages in South Sudan. When he was a young man, Baba dedicated himself to studying and work and tried not think about the opposite sex despite family and friends who told him he should get married. Then he met my Mom and fell in love right away.

According to Dinka culture, he had to pay a bride price in cattle to my mom's family in order to marry her. The cattle were produced, the couple married, and they moved to the city where Baba was a clerk in a veterinary clinic. He was also, on the side, involved in politics as a Communist. The marriage was a happy one. My dad even asked Mama if she were ready to start a family, a thoughtful gesture since most Dinka men automatically expect their wives to give them children.

My parents started their big family of ten children, in 1969. We were born in different provinces, but according to Dinka culture, we are all from Kongor town, because that's where my dad's from. The first born was my brother Deng Did, then came Agor, Anyuon, Deng Ti, Abany, and me; Acuach Cor which means small color or little tiger. They baptized me as Sarah Gabriel, my Christian name. All my brothers and sisters have Christian names as well as Dinka names. Yong was born after me, then Majok, and Chol, the last born. Also part of the family was my cousin Achol Tarif who was more of a big sister to us.

As is typical in Dinka families, we had a lot of relatives living with us, most of them children my parents brought from the villages so they could go to school. We had a big family, a big house, and life was very good for everyone. Baba was a very busy man, working all the time. When he was off work, he would still be surrounded by many people. He was always having company over for dinner or lunch. Everyone wanted to talk to him. He was a very well known and important man. Because of this, I didn't spend much time with him, but that was OK. Mama was always at home taking care of us. My older brother, sister and cousins went to school. I stayed at home with mama and my younger brothers, since we were too young to go to school. My mother would play games with us and I remember it as a happy time with loving moments.

Each time Baba went off on a long trip he would come home with gifts for everybody. On one such excursion, he come back with his friend Peter and a surprise. We were happy to see him but also waiting for our gifts. My dad could tell we wanted the gift so he told us to go look in the car. When we got to the car we found a monkey! It was so amazing we all liked it but at first I was very scared of it. Once I got used to it, I became very close and friendly to our Monkey. We never named him; we just called him Makako, which means Monkey. He was very smart and would copy everything we did at home.

One day I was fighting with my brother Yong and I was winning the fight. The monkey didn't like that. Makako started to spank me with a stick, the way Mama used to! We also had a dog and a cat. It was a lot of fun having all these animals we truly loved. It was a peaceful life. Outside town, Baba had some land where he grew peanuts. He also had some cattle he kept at his friend's farm not far away. Our dog, besides being our playmate, would take care of our cattle.

Now a date I'll never forget, May 15, 1983. I was eight years old and living with my family in a small town called Bor in Southern Sudan. My whole world was about to change dramatically. I was at home with my family except for Baba and my two older brothers, Deng Did and Agor. In the evening, a visitor came who looked extremely nervous and in a big hurry. Mama took him into the library so they could talk without interruption. After they had a long conversation and he'd left, we could see this mysterious visitor with what ever they had talked about...

Had made Mama, obviously upset.

My siblings and I had no idea what was about to take place, but Mama's change of humour was obvious; she couldn't hide it from us. I was puzzled and anxious and just watched her without saying anything. Right away, she left to have a quick meeting with the elders of our family. When she got back, she started to pack our stuff like a crazy woman. This was not like packing for a normal trip. I knew something was very wrong but I didn't want to ask what it was because Mama was very busy. I had been told by my parents many times not to interrupt when somebody is busy, so I kept quiet. My brothers and sisters between us were murmuring, guessing about what was going on. We tried to figure out what all the frantic rush meant, but we couldn't. It was not something we could have guessed, not in a 100 years!

Mama, with help from the other family members, packed everything that needed to be put away. They put some mattresses on the bedroom floors, and then Mama came and told us we were all going to sleep on those mattresses. She didn't explain too much, only that it was an emergency. I imagined she didn't want us to worry.

That night when Baba and my older brothers came home, they closeted with Mama and the other family members. We smaller children had no idea what was going on, or what was about to happen. All we could see was that all the adults were very serious and nervous, not acting like we had ever seen before. This made for a very anxious evening for us children, trying to understand what this might mean for us.

The next morning on May 16, 1983 at about 6:00 AM, I heard something that sounded like thunder. It woke me and my sister Abany. Abany said, "Oh, Oh, I have to pee and its going to rain!" I was just sitting on the mattress wondering about the thunder, wondering if it was really going to rain. I thought it might be fun. Even though Abany didn't like hanging out with me, maybe my sister and I could sneak out later to play in the rain. I told myself I would try to convince her to do this with me, even if I had to give her my meat at dinner time because Abany liked meat. Especially, if it was mine! I was really very happy with my plan; it sounded like a great way to spend our coming morning.

Bor was a small undeveloped town. Its dirt roads were in very poor condition and in the dry months, they would become very cracked and full of pot holes. This meant when it rained, the roads became very slippery. I remember the school teachers telling us to slow down when playing outside because we would fall down. Of course, we didn't listen very well and laughed a lot watching others fall into the mud. African kids learn to laugh at anything, even if it's falling into the mud. We would think it great fun to go sliding in the muck and would make it into a kind of a game.

Usually when it rained, my parents would send a driver to pick us up from school. Otherwise, we would get home soaked, dirty and muddy. I preferred it when he didn't pick us up, so I could have fun walking home in the rain with my friends.

Abany was still sitting on the mattress, repeating the same thing over and over again. "I have to pee, and it's going to rain." My brother Anyuon told her to just go and stop going on about it. They were always quarrelling and it was still so early in the morning, I didn't pay much attention to the two of them. I was having too many good thoughts of the rainy day of play to come with new and interesting things to be done, with real gooey mud. Like making mud pies and such things an eight year old would think up.

Mama called us and we found her preparing our morning meal looking very worried. She told us to eat quickly and we did, nervously and in a rush. She told us it wasn't going to rain and we couldn't go out to play. It wasn't thunder that we'd heard upon waking, it had been a bomb that had exploded. Mama and the adults just couldn't keep it a secret from us any more. They had to tell us what was happening.

There were now people running around everywhere screaming in panic. Mama swallowed and took in a deep breath, to have this announcement fall from her lips.

"Children. Our country has entered into Civil War!"

I could see she was trying to appear brave for us little ones but her whole being was shaking. Whatever the heck Civil War meant, it was bad and Mama followed that up by bursting into tears. Would we now have to leave our home? It was all so bewildering. What did this mean? Leave our home and everything that we knew? This was all too scary to comprehend, and, anyway, there was no way I wanted to leave our home. No ... no way!

My heart was racing. It just could not be true. I felt tears forming in my eyes and a tightening in my chest that turned to a sob. I could no longer see the rest of that morning's meal and the remainder stayed uneaten. My mind just felt too numb and confused. I wandered through our home in disbelief wondering, 'what would be coming next, Sarah?' My eyes were leaking blurry tears as I stared at all the familiar things around me; a home of family, learning and the happy playful noise of the banter of brothers and sisters. To think of leaving this, to go where? My young mind couldn't grasp the concept. The rest of that morning passed in a fog ... of sheer panic.

Like the screams outside, my heart was filled with a fearful dread you could almost taste. All of us were suffering through a day we would remember, forever ... burnt into our lives! Sudan was at War with itself, us at war within ourselves.

Around about noon a very official-looking man appeared at our home and had a rifle in his hands. He told Baba that Kerubino Cuanyn, who was a party member, had been shot and that things in our area would soon get much worse. My younger brother Yong and I were beside this brave, serious man with the rifle. We were wide eyed to hear such things and intrigued at this wicked looking firearm because we had never seen one before. Mama shouted at us almost angrily, "move away from the rifle, it is very dangerous." We were to find out all too soon just how dangerous these automatic rifles were!

With Kerubino having been shot, we had to move quickly because government troops were coming for Baba and anybody who was seen to be part of the uprising. We had to literally sneak out the back door and run like crazy to my Uncle Izack Kot's house nearby. There was something wrong with Baba's car, so we all had to ride in my uncle's truck. Unfortunately, it was a small pickup and, with it already loaded with his family, not all of us fit in. Baba and my two elder brothers bravely said to go on ahead; they would catch up with us later. My heart fell when I heard this and it felt hard to breathe. The whole family was now running for our lives. The decision had been made. Everything was just happening so fast. I could do nothing but cry.

Mama had packed as much as she could, but because we left in a panic, we only had what we were wearing. Mama had made a pot of porridge for us to eat earlier and that was the only thing she'd grabbed to take with us in the way of food. Everyone in Bor was going crazy around us; people screaming and running every which way, rifles firing, smoke and fire all around. Mama put the pot of porridge in the back of the pickup where we were sitting, but it was still so hot some of us were burned. The thing I admired most about Mama was that she always had something for us to eat. Even now in the midst of the uproar her first thought had been for her children's' stomachs!

Most of the roads out of Bor were blocked by the army and many friends and family we could see were being killed. Everyone was in a panic to get away from this boiling madness and slaughter all round us. We were very lucky as our driver remained calm. He had figured a way to leave town without being in too much danger from the army. He prayed that God would be with us and guide us to a safe place. Mama, being a Christian, also prayed with him. Then she told him in a forced calm to, "go for it!"

He drove very fast, like a madman, around trees and scrub brush, while we held on to the bouncing, swaying vehicle. As we got further away from home, the noise from the bombs and gunfire began to fade into the distance.

God must have been with us because there were no soldiers on the roads we took. It was a miracle that the driver knew those back-roads so well. Everybody in the back of the truck was very quiet as we got further and further away from the horror. There were numb unbelieving looks on our faces. What were we going through? What was actually happening? My brother, Deng Ti suddenly screamed as his shirt got hooked by a tree branch which almost took out his eye. The driver wouldn't stop. He didn't want to take any chance the soldiers were following us. It was all we could do to avoid branches from the trees alongside the road and still most of us were scratched by passing whipping tree branches. God, having saved us, seemed to be punishing us for some unknown wrong.

There was a feeling of death and misery on the roadside that night. We huddled in fear and confusion in the back of the truck. It was the first of many nights on the run for me and my family. It was also the scariest and worst day of my childhood, one I would re-live over and over again through out my life. The scenes of sudden explosive violence stayed burnt into my mind. I thought the horror of it all would never end. I was in shock. I had never seen so much death, misery and bloodshed. I was so upset I couldn't even outright cry. Instead I found myself shaking and whimpering, fearing the soldiers would find and kill us too.

I wasn't the only child cowering in terror in the back of the pickup that night. There were many of us crowded into its bed, curled up, clinging to one another. It was very difficult for Mama and my Aunt to calm us all down. They struggled to keep us quiet, fearing our crying and fussing might be heard by a passing army patrol in the night. Somehow, they managed, moving from the youngest and the most terrified to the next, cuddling and murmuring soothing words so we would fall into an exhausted sleep. I don't think they got much, if any, themselves.

At dawn the next day, I was woken by the truck starting and we were off again, down bumpy back-roads being bounced around and into one another. We didn't hear any screaming, any bombs going off, or rifle fire. The tension we all felt began to lessen the further we got away from Bor. This was even more so as the truck pulled into Yalee where my Mama's Mother, my Grandma lived. It felt safe there because there had been no bombing and there were no dead and mutilated bodies, something I had dreaded to find in this village as well. I could see immediately in its calm daily routines it was a much different kind of life here than in the town where I'd grown up.

The next day Baba and my two brothers arrived in Yalee. My heart filled with joy to see them and I ran to them with watering eyes and hugged them hard. I felt as if my life depended on feeling them physically, knowing they were in fact real. With all the death on the road the day before, I had imagined Baba and my brothers among the dead, lying there with sightless eyes. I had already imagined a lifelong sense of insecurity; a feeling life would never be the same again for me. I knew what were feelings for me were already facts for many other families after just one day of what would be Sudan's long Civil War.

So when I saw them safe there came a feeling of joy and relief all at the same time, a feeling so strong it was painful. I had been sick with worry; my worst nightmare had been a reality. And now it was over. I was seeing them again! It is something, even today, I can't truly describe. Even though we were in strange surroundings, we were a family together and whole. In those horrible times of sudden traumatic change, it was enough. We had survived while sadly, so many others had not.

Chapter 3
Naked Shaman and Tribal Dentists

My uncle and his family didn't stay with us, but after visiting friends and family, drove on to Kongor their tribal village, believing it safe to do so. Meanwhile, to our surprise, life in Yalee went on as normal, unaffected by the war. The change for us was that we were not in our own place; we were crowded in with Grandma's people, refugees from a war that hadn't arrived in this mostly agricultural region of southern Sudan.

After four months, we had basically eaten our hosts out of house and home and Mama decided she had to do something. Since the fighting appeared to have moved, she figured it was safe enough for a trip back to Bor to get essential food and other supplies such as sugar, rice, oil, salt, cloth, and what was needed for a large family. In her place, Mama left us in the care of our eldest sister, Achol.

I didn't feel good about Mama leaving us and didn't think it would be safe for her to go back. She said there were many things we had left behind that we needed, and anyway she was leaving us in very capable hands. Mama assured me she'd heard through tribal gossip Bor was safe to go back to since the army was no longer in the area. She told Achol to take care of us and to try and keep us out of trouble while she was away.

Still, as I waved goodbye, I was afraid both for her and for myself. Tribal 'gossip' had been wrong before and might be this time. I ran away from the others and began to cry. Thoughts and feelings of dread, visions of slaughter and the burning of Bor ran through my mind. I pictured Mama caught by soldiers and something dreadful happening to her. I knew I could never live in a world without Mama in it and cried all the harder. She had only gone for a few minutes and I was missing her already! Finally drained, I made my way back to the others, resigned to my fate, and maybe to fill my grumbling tummy . . . and play.

Back then I was a fussy and a picky eater, but my sister really knew how to manage me, just like Mama. She could make me eat anything by saying that the food was tasty and good for me. I fell for it every time. This was especially true that day. After crying myself out, I found myself ravenously hungry and dinner to be very tasty. Convinced that it was all very good for me, I gobbled it right up. Then I ran from Grandma's hut to find some other children and involve them in some new games.

At first I was shocked with village life. I was used to having clothes on and most everyone here was running around half naked. There was no school to attend and no reason to dress up. It was a primitive kind of lifestyle; the people, houses and the food, absolutely everything was different. We didn't like it much but we weren't about to go back to Bor and get ourselves killed so we tried hard to settle in and not complain. The hardest part was having so much time to ourselves. At times we were very bored and had nothing to do. All the others in town would go to work in the morning, even the children. But since our adults were away, and we had no land or cattle, we were left to make our own entertainment. We didn't have any toys either, so we invented games and played with anything we could find to make into toys to make it more interesting and fun.

All the same it was very hard to live within this village life. Before this forced and prolonged stay we had no comparison between country life and city. They were two totally different worlds and very far apart. As a child I didn't have words like 'primitive,' or 'culture shock.' We only described it as 'different,' or made a distinction between 'country people' and 'city people.' There weren't all that many miles separating the two, but the gulf was enormous. City people stayed in the city and these simple country people never strayed too far from their cultivated tribal lands and precious livestock.

The huts the people lived in were quite small with a thatched conical grass roof and a very small entrance way. The only way to get into one was by crawling in. Even though I was very small, it was still very tricky to get inside and I was always hitting my head against the entrance. I discovered that the small entrances are meant to keep the family safe from invaders. If someone tried to attack the family, he would have to crawl into the hut. It would be difficult for the invader to attack anyone when he is crawling on his hand and knees, making it possible for the homeowner to hit them on the head.

Also the way that people dressed was very different than we were used to. Some of them didn't wear any clothes at all! To me, a proper little schoolgirl, it was rather shocking. One morning we were having tea at Grandma's hut when a very tall man announced himself and came into the hut naked from head to toe. He had short curly deep red hair. I was intrigued with the colour and Grandma told us later it was a cow pee treatment that made it that way.

I noted this Dinka man didn't have any bottom teeth and I wondered at the chicken feet marks on his forehead. It was explained to me these scarred tattoos of five lines were to distinguish him as a member of his tribe. In his hands he was carrying a stick and machete as well as a stick in his mouth which he used to brush his upper teeth. I thought he looked kind of cute, with his tight curly red hair. I thought it suited him very well even if it was made with cow pee!

As he got closer to us, we became very quiet and were staring at him as he spoke. Abany looked into my eyes with an expression of rolling her eyes to mean 'look at this crazy guy,' so I would laugh. But at that first introduction to a naked man, I held it in to not appear rude. Then Chol, who was two years old, went closer to the tall man, stood in front of him, and grabbed the man's penis. He said in Dinka, our tribal language, "Your pee pee is not covered, ha ha ha. You're naked!"

At that point everybody started laughing which felt good, because I couldn't hold it in any longer. I laughed so hard I actually peed myself. I will never forget that day. Abany and I were rolling on the ground with tears of laughter, so much so, our tummies hurt. We continued to laugh even after the tall man left, just to think of it and we said silly things to each other about it to keep this ridiculous, strange event going.

Some days later the same tall redheaded man passed by the hut again, but this time he had his clothes on and, to me, he looked much better! He told everybody in the village there were city folk staying over at arongdit's (grandma's), that they wear clothes and expect everyone else to do so too. Otherwise, he said, they will laugh at you like there is something wrong with being naked. I realized then we had offended the poor man and the event was not quite as funny as we'd thought.

In other ways, the people of Bor had a few lessons to teach us, including a united sense of community and strong principles. For example, it wasn't considered disrespectful to spank other peoples' children. If children were found misbehaving or behaving in a disrespectful way, using bad language or fighting in the streets, locals would go out of their way to correct those behaviours, sometimes with a very firm hand! The child's parents, far from complaining, were grateful to them for looking out for the welfare of all the children of Bor. This helped the children be respectful to others, especially when they knew all the adults of Bor had permission to discipline any child. Baba was very proud of his children because there were very few times we had to be disciplined by other adults for getting into trouble.

In Yalee there were many different ways to get into trouble with out knowing we were, or really understanding why. One day Abany thought it would be fun to take the village drums and start playing on them. She had us dance while she played. It was great fun. Yong and Chol and I were happily jumping up and down trying to dance Dinka traditional dances when we suddenly heard a lot of screaming. We looked towards the uproar and saw everybody in the village running and screaming: "Bahre are here, Bahre are here!" People were coming from everywhere; from the fields and huts running around frantically. We were totally shocked watching this take place. All we could do was to hold each other's hands with our mouths gaping frozen to the spot. Then one of the villagers saw us with the drums and was really upset. He shouted, did we realize we had set off drums that were an alarm for the villagers?

'Oops!' I thought; we're in trouble now.

The villager who had come out to find what was going on, right away stopped the others from running around in a panic and explained it was just us crazy city kids playing the drums. Then they came and told us very angrily, we weren't to play with those drums... *'ever!'* We were very upset because we didn't understand at the time how important the drums were to the villagers' safety and their very lives. This was just one of many village rules we just didn't understand or know about. The result was that we became known as village troublemakers.

As much as we thought that they were weird, they thought we were weirder than them. Later we were to find why the drums weren't to be played with. It was to be a very sad and violent awakening.

Fortunately to my joy, Mama arrived back from Bor in time to save the situation. Hearing of the ruckus we'd caused, Mama thought we needed some separation from village life, specifically that we secure a more modern dwelling with better conditions than Grandma's tiny hut.

That sounded good to me because I really missed my home. Our house in Bor was huge by comparison, considered one of the nicer houses in the city. The Dinka people are very well known for looking after their large families if they have the resources. Since Baba was a respected, educated, and influential man in town, he was also responsible for his numerous relatives as well as his immediate family. Our home reflected this and contained a compound type living area.

The furniture in our living room was made out of braided bamboo wicker, with colourful floral cushions. The adjoining library was where Baba spent most of his time and where he had a grand collection of books, a very nice wooden desk and a comfortable sofa and chairs.

We had six very large bedrooms with four to five beds in each to take care of the many relatives who were always coming and going. All our bed posts were very tall and the beds had a lot of space underneath for storage. The mattresses were filled with cotton and over time would become really lumpy and not very comfortable at all to sleep on. Compared to what we slept on in Yalee, those lumpy beds were sheer Heaven!

The kitchen of our Bor home was very spacious and was separate from the main living area. Since there were many extended family members who lived with us at any given time all the women shared kitchen duties. The shower rooms and toilets were all in separate buildings made of concrete blocks with tin roofing. The shower room was very big and usually had running water. Sometimes when there was no water, we had to carry water in buckets to bath. The toilet was really an outhouse and was separated from the bathroom like most other homes in Bor. For those who didn't have one, there was a common outhouse anyone could use.

With that description, you can see why the small huts in Yalee were very cramped for us and that conditions were primitive and unbearable. In thinking about this it dawned on me that Mama was in fact, a very resourceful person. She was always striving to make a bad situation a bit more bearable and so now she organized the construction of a small house. With the villagers help it was made of stick walls and mud, had a grass roof and was secured with doors. Which even had locks on them, which for sure wasn't normal at all! *Our house of sticks.*

As the months wore on, our lives in Yalee became better, more tolerable. Or, maybe we were just getting used to having and dealing with less. Mama's positive attitude helped us fit into this unstable transitional world. As the Civil War in Sudan deepened, it began to affect more and more people and more of the tribal territories were involved in turmoil. For us children, it just didn't seem to matter as much. We were adapting and the younger the children, the easier that seemed to be. For the older ones and some aspects of tribal life of Yalee... not so much.

According to Dinka traditions, males must have their bottom teeth removed when they reach a certain age. When we got to that point, we began to spend a lot of time trying to avoid having my brothers' bottom teeth yanked out. And not by any dentist!

One day I was playing outside with friends and saw a group of tribal men coming toward our place all decked out in tribal gear with painted designs on their bodies. They had their cattle with them that were also painted up. As they walked, they were singing loudly and looking oh so serious. I was told these were a group of Dinka Clan Elders who had come to perform a tribal manhood ceremony on my older brothers. According to their traditions they were the right age for these Elders to remove their four lower teeth. Thank Heavens my brothers weren't home at the time and were out visiting friends!

These very serious elders didn't believe Mama when she told them her boys were not around. I was scared because they didn't accept her word and started looking everywhere, throwing things around and even looking under the beds to see if my brothers were hiding there. My friends knew I was scared and that I didn't understand what was happening. One of them said to me, "don't be scared, these Elders are not bad. They only want to make your brothers into real men Acuach Cor!"

I thought, *'hey, my brothers may be grown up but they still need their bottom teeth,'* and I didn't say anything back to her. Mama said to Achol in Arabic, so the tribal men wouldn't understand, "go find the boys. Tell them not to come home until things calm down." Off she went to warn them.

Two days later, the Elders came back again looking for my brothers only this time they were at home. Very quickly Mama put them in the bedroom and locked them in. She told them to be quiet and not to come out for any reason, even if they tried to break the door down. Mama was sitting cutting vegetables when they arrived. She stood up and told them with some force, "If you are looking for my boys again, you will not find them, because they are not around. You don't need to ransack the house again because you will not find them! Even if you tear the house down, it will be a waste of your time!"

Mama had been ready for a big fight, but they told her they'd come back for them, that they'd get them sooner or later, and then they left. Mama was relieved. At least the problem was done for one day. But unknown to her, the elders met one of their leaders at the street corner who told them they had to return to our place and search it better. As a result, they came back and started looking. Mama told them the boys had left the village and would never return. But these determined 'Elders of Purpose' didn't believe her for a second and kept right on searching to complete their dreadful mission of enforcing manhood rights.

At one point in all this, they found they didn't know how to open the locked bedroom door. It wasn't that they didn't have a key, it was that they'd never seen a lock before. Now, on account of Mama, modern life had come to the simple country people of Sudan. It was really very comical how they looked at the door and no matter what could not open it! They stuck around for little bit, and not finding the boys, finally gave up and left all in a huff, full of frustration. We can laugh about it now, but at the time it was a very traumatic event for the boys. One small lock had come between them and having those manly four teeth yanked out of their heads!

A week later Mama and Achol left to go to Bor for more supplies, leaving us with Grandma. As always we never had much to do and as usual we got into trouble with the villagers. Grandma would entertain us by telling stories sitting around the camp fire. Grandma's traditional stories were usually pretty scary. This particular night she told us a story that was also a song about a girl and a lion. Grandma, in her telling, was very descriptive, so much so we were too scared to sleep in the house alone without an adult. Grandma, for her part, didn't like sleeping in what she called those city people's rooms. As a result, we all had to go sleep with Grandma in her Hut. Getting there meant walking through the dark with a full moon and light clouds and more than usual shifting shapes and shadows. It made my hair stand up on the back of my neck. The scariest parts of Grandma's creepy story played over and over in my mind leaving me trembling in fear in my blankets.

In the middle of the night I woke up and had to pee really badly. It was a need that just couldn't be ignored. I tried to wake Grandma so she could come with me because the moon had set and I was even more scared in the dark. The hut had very round small windows shaped like a ball. Right then I saw something move in one of the windows. I gasped. In my imagination it was a lion's head and it looked to me as if the head was trying to break in through the window. Well I did what I knew how to do best, I started to scream. I had a very vivid imagination and I guess because of the story about the lion earlier in the evening, the movement had to be a *'Lion that was trying to get in, and really eat us up!'* I imagined those great big teeth and razor sharp claws Grandma had described ... all too well, around the camp fire light.

Well, I opened right up and just kept on screaming, "the Lion, the Lion is going to eat us!" over, and over. That woke up my sister and my younger brother who began screaming in fear right along with me. There was a regular choir going on with poor Grandma trying frantically to calm us down. Finally she went to the window and removed what was hanging there. It was nothing scary, just some decoration. After she brought the decoration over to show us up close, this did settle us down. Afterward we all started laughing when I told them I was going to wait to go pee in the morning. I still didn't want to go out into the dark so badly the pee urge calmed right down!

Not long after the evening of grandma's story of the girl and the lion, the big rains came and flooded everything. There was so much water on the ground, the land couldn't absorb it. It was usual to rain very hard, and that's why the province was named, *'Bor'* meaning in Dinka, *'flood plains.'* It was not the first time that it had rained since our arrival, but then it was not like the rain I could remember in Bor that I loved to play in. It just rained and rained to the point where there was no dry land to walk on and the floods took over. There was flooding and mud everywhere. We heard people in the Village screaming and crying in very real fear.

The village drums we had mistakenly played with now began pounding, mixed in with the alarm of panic that ran like a wave through Yalee. With it came the dreaded announcement, *"Murle Bahre!"* We were about to learn about the dreadful meaning, of those warning drums.

The Murle Bahre are a tribe in Sudan that are fierce warriors, and for centuries beyond memory they would come to raid and plunder the neighbouring villages. I had heard many frightening stories of the Murle people; that they were ruthless warriors capable of many horrors. I was told the Murle Bahre were too lazy to grow their own crops or raise their own cattle but instead turned to plundering, stealing, robbing and killing. What they wanted were the other tribe's cattle and children. They wouldn't hurt the children, but would raise them as their own to swell the numbers and strength of their tribe. The Murle Bahre warriors would plan their raids when the families were at their most vulnerable; when most of the men were away hunting and their children, women, and grandparents were taking care of the cattle and crops.

The memory of that morning, with everyone screaming *"Murle Bahre!"*, still makes me shiver and shake. Mama wasn't around and my cousin Aya was taking care of us children with the help of Grandma. My brothers and I didn't know what to do. All we knew was that we were in much danger. I remember my cousin trying to calm us down, telling my older brothers she was going to need their help with us younger ones. As the ground was flooded, and it was raining harder than ever, we would have a tough time getting away.

To escape this brutal raid we would try and reach the safety of the Cape. The Cape was where village people would go when they were in danger. It's a place where a lot of trees and vegetation grow together creating a walled clearing. When you get inside, it looks like it was made by nature just for safety. It's dark and no one would ever guess there could be people in it.

Before the warriors got much closer to where we were, I was so scared I fainted right away. All I can really remember is my brother Deng Ti pulling me though the flood waters. I was floating and sliding over the top of things as he dragged me along. Finally we reached the Cape and hid there all day with nothing to eat and only dirty rainwater to drink.

I remember my brothers and I were both bleeding badly. I'd been cut by something hidden under the water. My brother had been pulling me along, I'd felt the pain of a cut on my knee and then more pain when I hit something else. There were a lot of sharp things under the water which kept opening the wound even more. Even with these pains, at least for the time being I felt relief we were safe in our hiding place from the fearsome Murle Bahre.

Our worry now was for Grandma who had been left behind. She said she couldn't run with us because she was too old and didn't want to slow us down. She told us hurriedly it was going to be a long run and that she was speaking from experience because she'd had to do the same thing in the past. All she cared about was that her grand children were safe in the Cape. She said if anything happened to her, it wouldn't matter, because she was old and only wanted her family to escape. We prayed and wept for Grandma's safety as that's all we could do. We would simply have to wait it out and then go back to see if she survived. This nagging worry only added to our misery.

There was water all around us and we stayed hidden all day trembling from the cold and rain that kept coming down in buckets. The day dragged on and on as we huddled together in weary wet discomfort, worried not only about Grandma but the whole village of Yalee. Finally, someone came out to the Cape to tell us there was no more danger. This meant again wading, tired and miserable, back over the flood plains we had fled through and facing the violent aftermath.

When we got back to the village there were a lot of people injured and poor souls crying for loved ones who were killed in the attack. There was a lot of smoke, because some of the huts had been burnt down. We frantically searched through the ruined village looking for Grandma, but we couldn't find her. We thought she was lost to us, forever! Finally we found her hiding in her chicken coop and were relieved she was indeed alive. This meant we were all safe, even though the Murle Bahre had taken quite a lot of Grandma's cattle.

In a short period I'd experienced the attack on Bor by the government troops and a raid on Yalee by the Murle's! From that moment on, I felt our lives were always in danger. No matter where we would go, or try to hide, it felt to me our lives were over. There was no safe place or any happy place for us anymore. It felt as if it was the end of all the good things. Little did I know that things would get even more dangerous as the war went on and, that life for us would be far more terrifying than I could ever have imagined.

It was a couple days before Mama and my sister came back. They'd heard about the brutal attack by the Murle and were extremely worried for us. Back then, there were no telephones or proper communication between villages, but word of mouth spread news of the events. Thanks to these reports, Mama and Achol had learned about the attack and came back to Yalee as quickly as possible.

So when she saw us, she ran to embrace us, elated we were all right. Mama was concerned for us and felt that we had gone though too much in our young lives. We would have to move from Yalee. She wanted us all to go to Baba's village Kongor as it was larger and safer from Murle attacks.

Grandma refused to come with us. She didn't want to leave the home were she was born and raised. Mama didn't want to leave my Grandma, even though we knew she was a very tough old lady. But Grandma was insistent. She told Mama "go, take the children and go to Kongor. I will be just fine here!" We were sad she was not coming with us. I knew I was going to miss the time we'd spent together, especially her story telling around the camp fire at night.

The truly hard part was that we were leaving her there knowing she was still in much danger. Our lives were so upset and in turmoil, changes seeming to be taking place so quickly. I was afraid when we left I would never see my beloved Grandma again. Again came the unsettling and uncertainty, the pain of separating from that which had become familiar. I had lost another home to violent events I had no control over. I felt we were abandoning Grandma, abandoning Yalee, all for some unforeseen future. It was one more loss; like leaving shattered pieces of my heart

31

behind, this ache of missing those I loved, those that would become *the ghosts of memory.*

Chapter 4
Pythons and Child Soldiers

The next week we packed up the possessions we had and were off on another new experience and, what seemed to me, the long drive to Kongor, Baba's village.

Boy was it different! Where Yalee was mostly agricultural and grazing land, Kongor was lush green jungle with many kinds of wonderful tropical plants. I'd never seen a place so beautiful, never noticed a sky so blue, or witnessed such brilliant red sunsets. To hear the chatter of monkeys playing in the trees and see the different colourful tropical birds with their beautiful songs was almost magical to me. It was Heavenly. I was in awe in the presence of the jungle and all its bounty and beauty.

Mama didn't want us living in huts with very small entrances any more. She knew how much we hated being cramped into those traditional dwellings. To find something better, she went to another part of town where there were better houses that had electrical generators. There she found us a place to stay until our own home could be built. It was nice to be able to sleep in a regular house again. Although every night at about 10:00 PM the generator would be turned off, it wasn't a big deal because we were always ready for bed before that time, anyway.

While we stayed in that house, my brother Agor and Mama built us a new house in Mayak on the outskirts of town. She said she didn't want to wait for the war to finish because that could take a very long time. She was right, it did, and we were better off considering Kongor, Baba's home village, our new home.

When we moved in we all thought it was the most beautiful place on earth. Already our old home in Bor seemed like a distant part of our family's past. And, after what we'd become used to living in at Yalee, well, it was a great improvement. Mama said, Kongor with its beautiful jungle and maybe dangerous surroundings, was to be our home and we accepted that and settled into finding new routines. While we were accepting our losses and adjusting to life, the country was being torn apart. We overheard murmuring, concerned adults talking of the spreading civil war and the effect dug deeper, like pale sick worms, into us and the soil of Sudan.

Not long after helping build our house, my favourite brother Agor went off in the night to join the Sudan People's Liberation Army (SPLA) without telling anyone. Agor was only fourteen years old at the time and, as you can imagine, Mama was very upset because he was just a boy. She moped about feeling resigned because there was nothing she could do to bring him back. All she could do was to pray for his safe return, which she did almost every day.

Many Dinka boys left their homes throughout the war to join the SPLA. I remember more then half of the townspeople going to church to pray for the boys who had gone off to an uncertain future. Many never did come back to their families. We hoped and prayed this would not be true for our Agor. These concerns added to the tensions of everyday family life.

In settling into our new home, and trying to make a new life in Mayak, I wasn't happy about where the house was situated so far from the other houses. There were a lot of trees and dense bush in between the houses. I'd heard many stories about children who were eaten by wild animals. That was always in the back of my mind. When I walked though the trees I was constantly spooked, looking into the shadows of the jungle, wondering what beasts might be lurking. My imagination ran amok on me. I pictured some huge predator jumping out to devour me and drag me off into those shadows ... to be eaten!

Our life in Mayak, which was really a subdivision of Kongor, was very simple but we had what was necessary to keep us going. We still had no school to go to and in many ways I missed that the most. At times I would tire of making up games and was really bored. Going to school in my past city life had filled up time and I missed the steady routine. It was when I'd run out of things to do that my memories of the different life I'd had in the city came back to bother me. I thought of my friends left behind and wondered what they might be living through in Bor. I remembered my teachers and felt sad at all that had been lost and was now clouding over.

I had turned nine years old and my sister Abany was eleven. She used to get up early in the morning every day to make tea. She got so many compliments from Mama and my brothers for this, I became jealous. One day I got up earlier than her to make tea so I'd get some compliments too! The problem was; I didn't know where to find matches to light the fire. Without matches, there was nothing I could do. I told myself nothing was going keep me from making tea for my family! I knew Mama had matches in her bedroom, but I didn't want to wake her. So I decided to go to a neighbour's house about a block away to borrow some from them.

It was 5:00 AM and the sky was beginning to lighten so I decided to just go ahead and walk over there. I don't know how I got the courage to even try leaving the house so early in the morning and make my way though the jungle all by myself. My thoughts were more about the complements I was going to get and I just forgot to be scared. I was singing quietly and thinking how this feat would really put me ahead of my sister for a change. Yes, this was going to be ... just delicious!

34

About half way along the trail I suddenly heard a strange scary noise that sounded like, "*uf vu, uf vu!*" coming from in middle of the trees. It was such a weird sound; it stopped me in my tracks and sent shivers up and down my spine. I looked around and all I saw was this big rounded thing that looked like a tree root. It didn't make any sense to me. A tree root couldn't breathe and make a sound like that.

I was curious, I went closer and there was this very, very, very big python that was rising up to strike me, squeeze me and swallow me alive. Yet Sarah knew how to save herself. I had always been a very scared little girl, so it was so easy for me to do what I knew from experience. I screamed as loud as my little lungs could manage and ran as fast as my young legs could carry me. I had never screamed so loudly in my life. While shouting things like: "*hey, hey, Mama! I am going to get swallowed by a very big snake ... help, help, help! I am not going to make it to my house any more, I am going to get eaten alive ... and die!*" I screamed these things repeatedly and in less than two minutes, many people came running from their homes to save me from this monster.

Mama rushed up and hugged me saying soothing things: "*hey Acuach Cor it's OK; you are just dreaming.*" Maybe she thought I was sleep walking or something, so she asked, "how come you're not in the house, child?" I told her I was going to the neighbour's house to get matches so I could light the fire and make tea and surprise her. In my relief and shock I was like a chatter box as I told Mama what I wanted to do, all because I was jealous of all the attention Abany was getting.

That day I learned that it was OK not to get compliments all the time. I told Mama I was not going to make tea anymore. My sister rolled her eyes at me and said nastily, "How could you make tea when you don't even know how to light up the fire?" I answered right back with my hands on my hips. "Achol showed me how to work in the kitchen some time ago. I learned very quickly!" I added haughtily,"mama said so too!" I would have stuck out my tongue at her, but Mama was right there and wouldn't stand for such behaviour. In reply Abany smirked and said, "oh yeah, right!" She was always badgering me about every little thing I did and would roll her eyes at me and make faces. I guess it was because I was a bit annoying; a squeaky kid always bugging her to play with me.

I was upset with Abany because I'd almost been gobbled, and certainly scared half to death, and here she was acting snotty about tea and the fire. It hurt me that she wasn't more concerned about that, not me taking over her precious breakfast service. After that I gladly left her that job and didn't complain.

The experience made me realize I'd been thoughtless about my own safety. Neighbours who had lived in the area longer than us told us to be more careful. Children shouldn't walk in the area without an adult because the jungle was full of Pythons. They said a lot of their chickens, sheep and even young cattle, had been eaten alive by the huge snakes. It was pretty scary hearing them talk that way. I decided to 'not ever' try going anywhere on my own again in the surrounding jungle. Mama also forbid walking there alone after finding out I wasn't sleep walking and there really was a giant snake!

A few days later we saw a chicken swallowed alive by a python. It was not a nice thing to see, a very ugly part of nature. I didn't even recognize it was a chicken because the python's mouth was elastic and covered the entire chicken's body. We could see the poor chicken struggling inside the snake, fighting for its life. I wish I hadn't seen this because Mayak was a very beautiful place and I really liked living there. If it hadn't been for giant pythons and other wild animals, I would have been very happy living there.

One day we were having tea and there was a knock at the door. Mama called out, "hey kids, can one of you answer the door please!" I was very quick and ran to open the door. Standing there grinning with some of his SPLA buddies was my brother Agor! I recognized him right away even though he was dressed in a baggy military uniform. They all had assault rifles and looked very young. I didn't even say hello, I was so excited. I ran right back to Mama and yelled to her that Agor was back from fighting and had a big rifle with him!

My brother walked in with his friends and Mama was so happy to see him she started wailing in the Dinka tradition. Outside you could hear other neighbours wailing too. Tribal women do this when their men come back from war alive. Some of the parents were not happy as their sons did not return. The community thus was a contrast of wild rejoicing and utter silence.

Mama began preparing food with other mothers of Agor's unit because they were all very hungry. They told us they hadn't eaten any really good food for a very long time. My brother told us many stories about life in the rebel army and what they did to survive. I didn't understand how they could go through so much and still want to fight. They said they were doing it for a free country and for their families. Mama tried to convince them not to go back, but they refused. They said they didn't want to wait for somebody else to bring peace to the country. It was their obligation to protect us!

As Mama went on making them dinner, they took out guitars and started singing. This was their way of passing time around the campfire. Agor and his buddies were strumming their guitars and singing lovely sad songs. I could feel their sadness deep inside of me from the expression in their eyes and the tone of their voices. They sang in Arabic and also in Dinka. I especially remember their last song in Dinka. It was very touching. It was dedicated to their mothers; they would name each and every one in their song. Most of them had their mothers in the house with us, helping Mama in the kitchen, so there were many tears shed in there over that song! I especially remember the tears in Mama's eyes. It was very touching and made me cry too, right along with them.

I'd always felt close to Agor. It was like he was my best friend. Seeing him all grown up and singing these sad songs, it scared me. I didn't want him to go back to the war. I was afraid I'd never see him again. It was a short time spent with them, but at least it gave me good memories, and sad ones. All too soon off they went. Agor left before dark to report back to their Unit, to do what they felt was needed to protect us and liberate their country from tyranny.

After Agor left, my brother Anyuon, who was only 13 at the time, and some of the other boys in Mayak, were excited by the stories told and wanted a piece of the action. They got together in secret to make plans to follow the others to Bilfam where the SPLA was training. They had dreams of becoming great warriors and fighting for the liberation of South Sudan. They wanted to be part of the revolution.

Anyuon and Deng Ti were an inseparable pair and normally did everything together. But Anyuon kept his ideas to himself because he wanted Deng Ti to stay and take care of the family. Because Baba and my other brothers weren't around, he felt Mama needed at least one of her boys at home to help with things. On their way to Bilfam, one of Baba's friends recognized him. At first in a nice way, he tried telling Anyuon it wasn't a good idea to run off to the war. It was too dangerous and anyway Anyuon was far too young. That didn't work, so Baba's friend got a bit more aggressive. He threatened that if he didn't return home he and some others would tie him up and return him by force. Anyuon gave in, knowing it was not an idle threat; that they'd do just that, and returned home. Mama was forever grateful to Baba's friend and all of us were relieved to have him return home to us safe.

Chapter 5
My Father's Story

Baba was born Gabriel Achuoth in 1936 in Kongor village, now Kongor Payam. He went to what was known as a bush school in Kongor in 1947 and to Malek Primary School in 1949. In 1953 he left for Khartoum in search of further education. There he enrolled in a two-year Clerical course at the Khartoum Technical Institute (KTI). In 1957 he went back to Malakal where he got a job as a clerk in the Veterinary Department. That same year he was arrested and detained by the security forces for eight months after which he lost his job. After struggling to get by, he went back to Khartoum in 1960 to continue his education. He took courses, became a journalist and joined the Journalist Union. Baba went to jail many times as a result of his membership in the Union. His paper was finally closed down by the government of Mohammad Ahmed Magoub.

In 1967 he went to Bor to contest a by-election. It was a risky decision because the Magoub government of the Umma Party had already declared war on the Southern people. His arrival in Bor coincided with the arrest of 23 Tribal Chiefs who were rounded up and killed on the same day and in the same place and then, instead of being buried, were burned to ashes as an insult. The elections were now extremely risky because the government candidates were northern merchants who had participated in the killing of the chiefs and were determined to win. The opposition, however, kept on campaigning as a matter of principle. The results of those elections were as follows: in Bor North constituency a Jallaba of the National Unionist Party won. Bor Centre went with another Jallaba of the same party and the Bor South constituency was won by Elijah Ajith Mayom of the Liberal Party.

As the candidates were preparing to leave for Khartoum, they received warnings from the remainder of the chiefs and citizens of Bor they'd be in danger from the security people if they left Bor. They told them sometimes the security people got out of control and fired at crowds when politicians were around. Baba decided to remain to see if he could bring some safety to the township. The following day he started making contacts with the security people and the civil authorities and asked for a meeting to discuss how to bring peace to the area. They all welcomed the idea and a successful meeting was held, followed by the formation of a strong peace committee. The committee drew up a peace programme. Baba then left for Juba to establish a second committee and to make Juba the centre of the peace movement in the South. A national organization for peace and rehabilitation was established in Juba led by the late Rev.

Amusa Gama Provos of Juba Cathedral as Chairman. Gabriel, my Father, became the secretary.

By mid 1984, Baba was in Malakal north of Kongor on the Nile. Baba worked for the SPLM party and because of his activities it got pretty dangerous for him. The party ordered him out of Malakal and sent him down to Juba and Bor for his own safety. Baba boarded a ship that ran along the Nile from Malakal to Bor but the ship didn't make it to its destination. The SPLA, the military arm of the SPLM, was misinformed about the ship and laid an ambush at Wathkee thinking it was a enemy ship. As a result, many women and children on board were killed. It has been documented that over 2,000 passengers died as a result of the hastily planned ambush.

It was 1:00 AM and Baba was sleeping when the ship was attacked. He was able to jump clear before it sank and swam to the east bank. Many others weren't so lucky. Some died in the ship fire, others in the river because they couldn't swim, and some who reached the shore only to be devoured by crocodiles. Still a lot of passengers did get safely to land where they became disorientated and wanted to carry on going inland. Baba is a very good talker and people tend to take his counsel. He convinced them to wait till daylight because they were all exhausted from the shipwreck and it was already 5:00 AM. They didn't have that long a wait. At 7:30 they saw small boats coming from the west bank. They were manned by SPLA solders who took them to the west side of the river where the SPLA was camped. There they were attended to and given condolences and apologies for the mistaken sinking of a civilian ship. The survivors camped at a Nuer village overnight and the next day a small group decided to go on to Bor while the majority returned to Malakal.

Baba had injured his right leg when he jumped clear of the ship into the water. As he was swimming to shore a lot of fish were attracted to the blood in the water and feasted on his flesh causing a big gaping hole in his leg. The nearest village to get any medical assistance was the village of Duk Padiet.

For three days he walked towards the village despite very severe pains from his injury. After six days he couldn't walk any more because his wound was now badly infected.

They were then in the Akuacdeng area where they found the help of two SPLA units (104 & 105) whose commander gave orders to a dozen solders to carry Baba to Duk Padiet. From there SPLA leaders would give orders to carry Baba on to his home town, Kongor. Baba told the others who were with him to go on ahead because he was being looked after. Unfortunately it turned out the SPLA couldn't help because they had to leave the area. Before going, the Captain assured him he would send some soldiers back to get him to Duk Padiet.

He was delirious from the infected leg and was slipping in and out of consciousness but somehow he got word to Mama to come and get him. She arrived five days later along with his eldest brother. There was nobody who would carry him to Kongor so his brother sold one of his steers and hired porters to carry him back to Kongor. Baba is forever grateful for the assistance and care he received from the Nuer Family who stayed with him throughout his ordeal.

Through Baba's many contacts he was flown to Khartoum, the capital of Sudan, where he was admitted to the army Hospital and was put in an intensive care unit. After an operation on his leg and rehabilitation treatment he was discharged from the hospital. Two months later he still hadn't completely recovered from continuing medical complications.

Family members put their resources together and managed to send him to Europe to receive better medical attention. My uncle Panyagor decided to kill one of his bulls for a blessing to send him on his journey, a Dinka tradition. Some days later, Uncle Panyagor came to Mama and asked her to pay him for the bull he'd killed for Baba's blessing party. Mama was surprised that my uncle had the nerve. After all Baba was his younger brother! Even though Mama didn't have a bull to give him, she was determined to pay him back; Mama not being one to be indebted to anyone.

Some days later, Mama bought a beautiful, healthy longhorn cow and asked Agor and Deng Ti to take it over to Uncle Panyagor's place. My brothers, only fourteen and twelve, left early in the morning to walk the cow to Uncle Panyagor's house. On their way, Agor told Deng Ti it wasn't fair that mama should pay their uncle back with this beautiful cow, as cows were much more valuable than bulls. They gave much needed milk and this longhorn was much too beautiful he thought. He had a better idea. They should take it to the auction and sell it and then buy a bull for their uncle. It just wasn't right for Mama to be more or less giving away this beautiful cow.

Deng Ti thought it was a dandy plan and off to the auction they went to sell their beautiful cow for an excellent price. The two of them were really happy with this result, jumping up and down for their victory over uncle. They decided to buy the cheapest, skinniest, ugliest black bull for uncle and continued on to his house where he received it gracefully. You couldn't wipe the grin off their faces about what they'd done. After all their uncle was just being mean; taking advantage of Mama in Baba's absence. They were more than excited to return home and give Mama the money and tell her what they'd done. The cow had cost Mama a pretty penny and they were going to give it all back to her, wiping out the debt.

Mama was truly surprised and wanted to know where all the money had come from. They told her of their decision and their feeling it was unfair of Uncle to take advantage of her in that way. Then, with relish, they explained what they'd done; bought the cheapest, skinniest, ugliest black bull they could find. With huge grins, they told how gracious uncle was on receiving the bull. Mama roared with laughter and with tears in her eyes pulled her boys into her arms. She felt so proud and protected by her right thinking and very young sons.

The cow sale was a small bright spot in what would become the beginning of the end for us in Kongor as the political situation in the country was deteriorating. We really didn't know the core of the problems involved, just that it might affect us. We knew from gossip and village telegraph where the war was taking place and the people of Kongor were nervous it would come their way. All the adults could feel the building tensions, but we children went on about our business, playing and for the most part, being happy.

Baba didn't come back to Kongor from Europe but rejoined the SPLM/A in Itang, Ethiopia. There in 1985, because he was an educated and respected intellectual, he was appointed the Southern Sudanese Ambassador to Cuba. The first step in the move was to get his family out of Sudan. He asked uncle Arok Thon to go back to Kongor and help us all escape. The Civil War was escalating and more and more areas of Southern Sudan were becoming unstable. My uncle was the commander of an army unit of one hundred soldiers called Zindia. Because of his connections it would be possible to get us those many Kilometres to the refugee camp in Ethiopia.

Mama knew Baba would get us out of Sudan and somebody would come for us but she had no idea it would be Uncle Arok. She had no idea what would follow or that life for all of us would become so complicated. Leaving would begin a chain of events that would irrevocably alter our family for many years to come. I realize we were only one family among many in all of Sudan who would suffer through the 22-year Civil War, but it was ours; Baba's, Gabriel Achuoth's family.

In February 1985 Uncle Arok came back for us with part of his force to escort us from Kongor to Duk Deng and from there to Itang, Ethiopia. He explained to Mama that because of Baba's political allegiance and appointment by the SPLM as Ambassador to Cuba, it wasn't safe for us in Sudan. Mama got all us children together and told us what she thought we could understand and we prepared to leave. We were to take very little with us.

I remember being sad to be leaving yet another home as the preparations went on around me. Already I had good memories of this house and my friends here and now I was leaving them behind forever. The only thing I could be happy about was that I was going to be with Baba in this far away land of Ethiopia. Being again with my Baba! It brought some excitement to all the painful activity of breaking apart our home. I could see by the way my brothers and sisters were responding, they felt the same way I did. We had overheard some of the talk between mama and uncle and knew fighting was taking place rather close to where we were. So there was a feeling of 'hurry hurry' added to the work of packing before leaving for Duk Deng.

When people heard we were leaving Kongor to join Uncle Arok's SPLA unit at Duk Deng, many women and children joined us. They too wanted to escape to the refugee camps in Ethiopia. Because government troops were patrolling the roads, we had to move through the jungle and be very quiet. I don't remember how many we were, I only remember there were a lot of us.

There was fierce fighting going on between the army and the SPLA along the Jonglei Canal between Kongor to Duk Deng. We could hear gunfire, mortar shells and bombs in the distance. They hadn't detected us, thank God, but we could see the fires and smell the smoke. Every time a bomb went off, we would run and hide in the brush we were so scared. I really figured they were shooting right at me! At this point of our adventure our SPLA protection wasn't even with us so we tried to reassure ourselves that we were just civilians. But even so, our level of insecurity and fear was that much more.

Our journey went on for hours and hours as we made our way through active warfare and then bedded down for the night in the jungle. I didn't like it much, being in that jungle, because it brought back my worst fears over lurking predators and snakes! Even our escape from the Murle's raid months earlier didn't seem so bad compared to this!

Everything was such a blanket of confusion and fear I couldn't think anymore. Yet I watched Mama's strength; how she kept forging ahead with determination. If I followed her example, it didn't appear so bad. I began to get a feeling deep inside, a little voice telling me, we would be OK. As long we were all together, and as long as Mama was there with us, I could handle it. I had to be like Mama, be strong and brave. I had to believe we would survive this trial.

In the morning we had to move on because we were afraid of being spotted from the air. Even more people had joined us through the day because it was better to go to the refugee camp than to stay in Sudan. They had chosen the hardships and dangers of walking this road to Ethiopia. But it was going to be much more dangerous for everybody because we were now such a large group of displaced civilians fleeing madness. It made our chance of being caught all the more likely.

Finally, after a long day and hot muggy slogging, we met the SPLA waiting for us in Duk Deng. It made me feel a lot more protected now that we were in the company of my Uncle Arok's Unit. I admired them, these brave soldiers who had travelled this distance on my father's wish to bring us out of Sudan.

What we were greeted by was disturbing news. The way we had planned to go was blocked by the fighting we had just passed. In addition, Uncle Arok had to make a decision about the Zindia unit he commanded. Ten thousand Government troops had entered the Province of Jonglei in a major push toward the area around Bor. To meet this offensive, he said we would have to turn back to Kongor while he would add the Zindia Force to the SPLA units already fighting. It just wasn't possible to get us through to Ethiopia the way things were. The group which had followed us had to decide what to do. Most came back to Kongor with us, but some smaller parties went on and tried to make it to the border.

The route we took back to Kongor was safer and we didn't run into any fighting, but it was longer and we arrived back at our house exhausted. It was a very nervous time in Kongor. The news about these battles was all a buzz through the village since they were only one day away. It was very unsettling. Before too long news arrived that the fighting was moving away and was now centred around my poor loved Bor. Time stretched on and Mama made us keep our travel things ready to go at a moment's notice if the Zindia came back for us, as Uncle promised they would.

That month I had nightmares about Bor, again seeing people gunned down in the streets. Sometimes it was about hiding in the jungle with bombs going off seemingly everywhere and the cracking of automatic rifle fire. Sometimes I was being surrounded by lions and snakes and a host of other wild animals trying to eat me. I would wake up the whole house with my screaming panics. When I did, Mama managed to calm me down and stay with me till I could fall asleep again.

One month became two and still the Zindia did not come for us. Our travel bundles had to be opened so could use the clothes in them. There was a lot of news about how the SPLA was pushing back the larger Government Forces. The people were proud of this but also worried as many of their men and children were there right in the midst of the fierce fighting. We never heard any news about the Zindia and how they were doing in the battle, nor from Uncle. Mama prayed every day he would return to us. What we couldn't know was that in that two month period Baba was no longer in Ethiopia. He had been called to represent the SPLM in Cuba and had already left.

When three months had gone by and there was still no news about the Zindia, or from Uncle, we began to settle into a more normal routine in Kongor. Because the fighting was moving even further away, I stopped having nightmares even though I was still troubled by our jungle encounter. Friends and the normal sort of play time, regular meals and family routine, begun to take the sting out of the adult worries and fear of the war affecting us. I stopped feeling like a bomb was going to fall out of the air right on top of me or that there were enemy soldiers hiding behind every bush, even though the young boys of the village continued running everywhere imagining themselves SPLA shooting at these our enemies with their stick guns. Near the end of the third month, all that routine changed, overnight.

Chapter 6
We run to Ethiopia (300 Miles)

I was awoken just after dawn by a commotion in the yard outside the sleeping room our family shared in our house of sticks. I heard a door slam and booted feet cross the floor, followed by hushed, serious sounding voices. I tried to wipe the sleep from my eyes, leave behind my dreams, and understand what this might mean. My heartbeat increased as I realized the people milling about outside were the Zindia. They'd come back for us! I heard Uncle Arok's stern voice, almost bark to Mama: *"Wake the children, now. We must leave, just as soon as you can make them ready!"* I missed the last part said somewhat quieter in my hurry to jump out of my bed and into the clothes I'd worn the day before. My sisters were up and doing the same.

Mama didn't really have to fulfil Uncle's orders as we children were popping out of rooms wide eyed at the number of soldiers packed into our small house. They held rifles at the ready and looked totally dusty and deadly serious. The front door opened and more of Uncle Arok's Zindia could be seen in the yard looking even more intense and much harder than those who had first arrived. I could tell by the way they scanned the area in the growing light they were ready to battle whatever might show up out there in the jungle. I shivered to think just what terror that might have followed them here to our home.

What would follow in the coming days could in no way be foreseen. Again our family was about to be on the run; again it would have to leave another home behind. The danger this time was so far beyond our imagination as to be totally incomprehensible. It would be like a whirlwind of unexpected events storming through our lives. My brother Chol had been ill and Mama wanted to get medicine for him and some food and supplies for us. But Uncle told her there was no time; the government army was right on their tail. We would all have to move fast.

There was just no time!

Mama understood we were all in extreme danger. We couldn't stay in Kongor without Baba's protection; we'd have to go with Uncle and his unit. Mama had no idea we were to walk to Ethiopia until Uncle Arok explained we'd have to walk many days. Mama then tried to prepare us children, telling us to be strong and that we would unfortunately be walking a very long way to get to the refugee camp in Ethiopia. She did her best, but there was no amount of preparedness that would even come close to what was in store for us. We children, having no idea of how far Ethiopia was, innocently told her not to worry. It couldn't be that bad, could it?

Mama was worried about me and my two youngest brothers because we were very young to make such a long trek. I told her with confidence not to worry about me.

"I walked from the school to our home many times, with my friends!" I stated.

Mama laughed at that and answered seriously, "OK Acuach Cor, I know you are a very strong young lady, but we are going very far away to a different country. It's good that you're thinking positively, but you have to be prepared for the worst!"

With that she patted me on the head with a look that showed she still wasn't sure about how all this was unfolding. She also showed the pain of losing the home she had worked so hard for; a house of sticks, now falling down. It was lucky Mama always had an emergency food supply on hand or we never would have made it. She packed all the food she could find and put it in one big bin which she would carry on her head. My sister and I ran back to the bedroom to get some of our belongings to put into our travel bundles, but the solders stopped us. We couldn't take anything with us because we would be on the run and wouldn't be able to carry much. I started to wonder about this trip. I couldn't understand why they said it wasn't going to be easy. I really thought they were exaggerating about all the walking and effort. I really had no experience to compare it with, other than our first trip to Duk Deng which was bad on account of the fighting we'd encountered, but didn't seem that hard a journey. I was about to find out just how hard life could get!

We had to congregate quickly in the centre of our village and everyone was worried. Were the government troops close and would they see our large and growing group of civilians? The SPLA soldiers were nervous too because many had their own family and relations living in Kongor. As they said they were ready to move, many locals decided to leave with them. The Zindia were known and trusted fighters while their homes were now threatened.

It was a strange transfer of authority. The adults were now taking orders from the fighters who were mostly young men just like my brother Agor. These men, boys really, held our trust and never let us down. They lent us their confidence and their spirit and we were very grateful. When they gave orders to me, I instantly followed whatever directions were given as if they had come from Agor himself. They were our hope and faith. They were trying to stop the killing of the Dinka people, stop the northern troops from shooting us, stop innocent people from being slaughtered, being wiped off the face of the earth because we held to a different religious belief, were of different race. It was a world I found far too complicated to understand. I just stuck to my family, knowing we would follow wherever these determined serious warriors led us, out of Kongor.

They knew the goal of the military operation that had begun three months earlier. They had to get these people moving toward Ethiopia. Among them they had to deliver the Achuoth family to the UN Refugee Camp where Baba had arranged a place for his family. All this was now Uncle Arok's responsibility. He had to deliver all his kin to waiting UN assistance. If he succeeded he would be forever A Hero in the eyes of our family. Arok Thon would be known as a principled Commander, a leader who served his Party, his tribe, his people with honour and distinction, a man we trusted. All this was our hope and speculation, but the safety of the border crossing was many miles down the road. We still had to get away from the northern troops and open warfare where we civilians were even more likely to die than the forces protecting us.

The soldiers began to organize the trek by putting some men in front, which they referred to as 'on point,' some at the back, 'the rear guard' and those that flanked us civilians, their 'detail.' The children were put in the middle of the group. Though at times hard words of obvious worry were spoken, they kept this very large group moving fast. We overheard the solders suspected there was danger ahead. We could feel the building tension. The unit's scouts detected footprints in the grass. They were hunters and expert trackers and knew how to read the brush. What was useful for hunting was now being used for being hunted. It looked as though others were following us. This news moved down the line and through us. At first it was a murmur, then like a wave we responded and moved in unity like an ancient tribal memory; a survival memory as old as Africa . . . flight, fight. *Or perish!*

We are running for our lives!

We are sharing the terror and the long and brutal history of so many tribes and nations fleeing conquering invaders.

These movements, like the wind waving the grasses, shaped our continent, our motherland. Where we fled to, where we stopped our flight, created the boundaries and borders through the centuries. We were doing now what was done then, striving to preserve our lives, our families, our way of life. Our civilization was what we were doing at that moment. It boiled down to just me with my aching legs and burning feet, me trying to find air for my lungs, me running, fleeing from those who wanted to kill us with their rifles and bombs.

The family, of man...

At times I still weep to think of this panic, the madness that had us in its grip.

I see us now terrified shadows, silent in memory flitting across the earth because someone, somewhere else had an appetite for that same land. We fly like the wind over the land, almost ghosts. When I look away, we are gone, even our footprints.

The road to a country that would accept us, a way called many things to different wayfarers, travellers, traders was to us 'the punishing road.' We were fleeing to find refuge in a burgeoning camp already full to overflowing with the miseries of displacement, the loss of homes and homeland, tribal areas and way of life.

Ahead were many miles leading to an uncertain future, and all around us an underlying vibration of a mass panic, a metallic taste of fear. Fear of that which would pursue us, run us down, take away the only thing we had left to us, life! To stop us reaching the edge of insanity, end this misery, to not let go, we had to plumb the depth of the well of human hope and love of life, family and home. We felt love too for Ethiopia; how it had the dignity to open its borders to us, the new homeless, now trekking to a country with as long a history of tribulation as ours. They too had their trail of tears, their famines, the wailing for lost children, brothers, sisters, mothers, fathers, husbands, wives. They had wars of their own making! We moved on, as a unit, knowing some with us would not arrive, would not have the benefit of UN assistance.

The first leg to Duk Deng was done at a brisk walk and was mostly uneventful. It took the whole day. Then we settled in for the night, had a hot meal, and sat by the fires to visit, gossip, and drink tea. All along the way, people had found us, alerted by the bush telegraph that flew head of us somehow, and now as we sat, more new fires sparked to life. The camp was growing through the night as more border runners came to join the Zindia. They would appear out of the dark, build their courage by the campfire, tell whispered stories, and listen to the soldiers not on guard duty tell of past victories. They, in turn, spoke of the pitched battles and campaigns of the past three months, fighting ten thousand Government troops, trying to stop the Muslim conquest of South Sudan. Their stories bolstered us for what was to come. They gave us what we needed most, a way to look beyond the madness.

For my family they gave hope, a future in Ethiopia! They showed us the way to find our strength, to find the stamina of the African Heart.

How can I explain how important this was, this journey into our own souls? The way ahead also was a road of personal discovery, a road to self that had to be faced and conquered. Our bodies had to be possessed! We had to control our lives! We would be formed by the trials at hand; the need to keep running, willing away the pain, the anguish, till fear no longer made us stop. We must never give up! This road we began would show each of us that. This growing group of people would show me its many faces; give me a sense of honour and dignity, and hope. It would show the lengths we would go, for the love of children and family, and from Mama, the strength of her love. We would run that road.

And then it began...

Our road to safety was not a proper road through South Sudan that could be used by vehicles. It was a trail used by hunters and trackers and known to them to be the fastest way out of the area. To get to the Ethiopian border we would go directly east from Duk Padiet and purposely avoid all the small villages in that area. We hoped by doing so we would not alert the 'village telegraph' to our passing. There was a real road to where we were going but it was well covered by patrolling Government troops. So, as the crow flies, all of us would be travelling approximately three hundred and twenty kilometres with what was, by then, about two hundred men, women and children. With the Zindia Unit, this made easily three hundred souls.

The wild, uncharted terrain would add another hundred kilometres of side tracks and detours, skirting heavy bush lands, rocky outcroppings and a few wide open grassy plains, all to be hustled through at double time. The goal was to arrive at Akobo close to the border. This was Uncle Arok's plan. With military maps and a compass, he was confident his scouts knew the area well enough to get through in his scheduled time of four days. He knew his Military could do it. Could we?

The soldiers, looking firm and resolved, forced all of us into a distance-eating trot that was to go on for the duration of this grinding trail. That first day we jogged for a straight ten hours. Subsequent days were the same. It was to become a four day, mostly non-stop trot to Ethiopia and safety. What awaited us were masses huddled in a lost, nowhere place; a holding pen. There we would spend day after day in conditions that would eat away at our humanity. Our speed was a curse and a blessing. It was so hard, but later, in the refugee camp, I heard stories of others who had taken 15 days, or even a month, to make the passage, to cross the border trail of no name, because they had no protection as we did. Later, in that refugee camp, I heard others tell stories of taking 15 days to a month to make the journey because they had no protection from the Nyagats. Here I have to explain a bit.

SPLA/M was founded in Ethiopia in 1983 by a group of South Sudanese freedom fighters. John Garange de Mabior was elected the SPLA Commander-in-Chief and Chairman of the SPLM. The vision of the movement was to liberate all the marginalized people of Sudan from the dictatorial regime of Khartoum. SPLA/M stood for justice, equality and the separation of state and religion, among other objectives. Other elected members were: Kerubino Kuanying, William Nyuon, Salva Kiir Mayardit and Arok Thon Arok.

51

A splinter group of founders disagreed with the vision of the SPLA/M and with John Garange as leader. They claimed they wanted to liberate the people of South Sudan from Khartoum, but their real objective was to gain personal advancement by working with the government. This group was led by Akuot Atem and an individual with the single name, Gaitut. When their opportunistic plan was revealed, they split from the main group and went to the villagers and tried to convince them the SPLA was an exclusively Dinka-based organization and that the Nuer people would be discriminated against.

From that point, they formed a military organization known as the Nyagats, which killed thousands of civilians trying to escape South Sudan to join the SPLA.

We were very lucky to be protected by the SPLA because our military was a lot better prepared. Many groups had come this way before us who did not have protection. They had tried to hide from those butchers in small villages along the way. Many, many poor souls didn't make it and lost their lives at the hands of the Nyagat. The Nyagats didn't care about attacking and murdering women and children either. To those mercenaries, we were all the enemy and killing us is what they were getting paid to do. They considered us traitors from the south, even though we were fleeing persecution. If they could rob our bodies of booty, all the better.

We practically ran every day for those four days in a constant state of extreme anxiety knowing we had to dodge more than just Government troops. Well the adults knew; we children only picked up the mass feeling of jumpy hysteria. With wild eyes, they scanned the horizon and the ample scrub brush for any kind of suspicious movement that was not a wild animal. They looked for where the Nyagat could be waiting to attack our rag tag group. The most likely places were where we had to stop to give us Border Runners some needed relief.

The SPLA soldiers knew if the Nyagat attacked they would have a true fire fight on their hands. Uncle's Unit were well trained and veterans of many real battles and in this our group was truly blessed. They had Russian made AK-47 Assault Rifles, grenades, mortar rounds, pistols and they were led by Uncle Arok Thon, a well known crack commander of the SPLA Military Force. Most of those who had joined this human convoy didn't know why it had this protection and it was not something we shared. It was not unknown to have enemy pose as Border Runners and then sneak off and report their location to whoever would be pay for the information.

It really wasn't the Nyagat that Uncle's Unit was primarily concerned with.

These people were under the protection of what was an honour guard really, fulfilling Uncle Arok's personal pledge to my Father to get his family to safety. The Commander's concern was that Government Security Agents might get wind that Gabriel Achuoth's personal family was amongst this particular group, one of many attempting the crossing. Just that fact that it was being escorted by a Unit of one hundred soldiers made it stand out, let alone its size of almost three hundred people.

If this knowledge of Baba's family was learned by the Government troops, fighting in major battles so close, the hunt would be on.

They would try to wipe out Gabriel Achuoth's family!

This act would be considered a major coup, as would the destruction of Commander Arok Thon's Unit. This was because it had already made a name for itself in helping hold off the northern forces in the battle at Bor. There the SPLA combined forces had stopped the northern advance almost entirely.

It could not have been an easy time for Baba either, knowing his family was making its way to the Border. He had all the pressure of his roll as Ambassador in Cuba of a country at war, but he had no specific information on our progress. All he knew were military reports of the intense battles going on in the area we were running through. His only hope was that the promise made by Uncle Arok would be enough and that he would be reunited with us at some future point.

Till then, there was only hope and reliance on Arok Thon's talents and dedication.

The intrigues and stratagems of war, we knew nothing about. I didn't really understand at the time what my father represented. To me, he was only my Baba. Through time, and research for this book, I learned more. Yes, the war had come to our doorstep, its front line moving up from Bor where Uncle had come to get us after that battle. But it was more than that to get Gabriel Achuoth's family out of harm's way, it was to keep us out of the Government's hands. There was a standing eradication order by the Security Forces on SPLM/A officials and their families. This is why there was no time given and why we had to just leave everything and run.

We were Gabriel Achuoth's family!

So this group of Border Runners under this unknown umbrella of protection was not given much time to rest. We only had time to eat and get a bit of a breath, then off we would go again continuing down that punishing road, trying to spend every resource we had.

Did I say already, it was a total nightmare?

My little brother Chol was very ill when we left Duk Deng. Well into that ten hours of fast paced trotting he started vomiting and developed a high fever. Mama didn't know what to do because there was no medicine available to give him. To make matters worse, the soldiers wouldn't let us stop for anything. We were all scared to be caught by the government troops and it was made plain there was to be no rest. We had been running for what seemed forever before Uncle saw what was happening to Mama and Chol. He stopped everybody on account of Chol being sick, and there at his command we spent the night. Luckily Mama found some medicine among other members of the group and the next morning everyone agreed Chol looked much better.

According to my uncle's calculation we were one day behind his planned schedule. He was worried the enemy would catch up to us. He got us organized and we all started running again. There were many small children who just couldn't keep up and the soldiers helped by carrying some of the littlest ones. As we passed the morning and got into the heat of the mid-day sun it was unbearably hot; sweat just poured off our bodies, soaking through our clothes. People stripped down to basic coverings which only exposed more of themselves to the ever present clouds of mosquitoes and biting black flies.

Bugs, bugs, bugs, and more bugs. It made you crazy as you tried to run away from them.

Run, run, hurry, hurry!

The dreadful rhythm of trot, the soldiers put us into; I felt it went on for hours and hours. My feet and legs were burning in agony. Many times I thought I would just drop to the ground, but I worried they would just leave me there, so I would catch up to Mama swiftly enough. To challenge myself, I would run better, faster and farther than my sister, who I thought by far looked in worse shape than me! Any game I could dream up in my mind, anything to keep my legs moving, helped my aching feet pound through the dust. I would pick a point, go past a point, and did so with so many, I lost count. I would pick something like a noticeable tree far ahead and go for it. Maybe at that tree we would stop for shade, water and a chance to pee! And at some points ... we did!

We couldn't stop for long because the scouts knew there were others who were not far behind. In these short rests we could eat a bit of uncooked food and recuperate as much as possible, but never for more than four hours. At some stops Mama would say, "go help the other children to keep quiet, maybe sing Sunday school songs with them." On this second day's rest, after I'd rubbed my poor aching feet, I told mama I knew one of the girls my age in the group who used to walk with us from school in Bor. I went over to where she was resting in the shade. She looked just as wore out as I did. We both got the other children together as Mama was preparing something to eat and started to sing Sunday school songs. I knew a lot of them and I could teach the others. We played a bit too. It was good to hear the children laugh. Even if we were very tired, the sound relieved a lot of tension and reduced stress for our families.

There were several reasons I remember that day very well. The first and happiest was that it was my birthday. I had just turned ten. After singing and playing with the children, I talked with Mama about planning a birthday party when we arrived in Ethiopia. She'd said, "of course we will celebrate your birthday as I promised you long ago Acuach!" Of course this made me very happy and I couldn't wait to get to Ethiopia. I knew there wasn't much time left in the rest period as the soldiers had got up and begun to nervously move about. They were going among the people, getting them to their feet, and I felt the dread taking over my special happy moment with Mama. Because of my aching feet and legs, I thought I wasn't going to run a step further. I groaned with the knowledge it was about to start all over again.

Again I got that feeling I had earlier of all the good things being wiped out. My muscles were being stretched, but on the inside I think it was worse. I was always scared and screaming on the inside, never knowing what to expect next. There was no room even to find a small moment of happiness. It was then I felt a ripple of anxious fear go through our gathering. Heads snapping this way and that, eyes wildly looking into the surrounding bush. A real flush of fear went through me; this didn't feel good at all. The realization came to me in a rush of heat and panic strained sweat . . . *the enemy, had caught up to us!*

That second day out the Nyagats staged their attack.

First there was a single shot.

I heard a sound like a sharp bark and my head turned to where the sound came from in the tree line. That very same instant, I felt and heard a whizzing go right by my chest. I realized a bullet had zoomed past. It had gone right between Mama and me and hit a commandeered cow from a nearby village that had been right behind us. It gave out a low, deep moan of pain, rolled its eyes round in its head and dropped to the ground, dead! It was like everything froze for a moment and just hung there; Mama and me staring dumbfounded at the poor downed cow. 'Pop,' 'pop,' 'pop,' came more rifle fire into the milling and now outright panicking people, trying to figure out which way to run. Mama grabbed me by the arm hard and the bubble of my moment burst. I couldn't even do what I was best at and scream out loud any more; this terror stuck hard in my chest.

"Run Acuach, run!" Mama hollered and pushed me from the back to get me moving.

Everyone was now running away from what was a growing fire fight. I will never forget those moments of my life. Even though it was more than 20 years ago and I was just a child, I remember it like it was yesterday. The gunfire and screaming seems to linger in the distance and, later in life, haunted my dreams. I remember the exhaustion of running ten hour days, the hunger and the soreness and my bone bruised feet. I remember running over rocks, the pain of sharp thorns and my body getting scratched to pieces by weeds and the brush. I remember running in utter panic. It was very hard. I didn't completely understand the situation at the time, so it seems even scarier as I think back to those horrific events now, how truly life threatening they were. I was shortly to have that point driven to the very bone in a nightmare happenstance I can't believe I witnessed. Most people could never imagine the horror of what we were charging headlong, into...

After an eternity of mindless running, I remember seeing a difference in Mama when I looked into her eyes as well as the faces of many others expressing the same thing. There weren't all that many casualties from that attack, but it had put us all on edge, always looking and waiting for another worse attack. We knew it would make us all run again without thinking of our afflicted bodies, or the constant wailing of the little children, or for those who were lost. It was heart breaking, this look that was shaping our Africa, that was opening the place deep down inside where trauma lives. It showed you life in a very base way. It showed you what human beings just like you are truly capable of, from the most heroic of acts, to the most inhuman atrocities imaginable.

We saw the stuff we are made of ... what we may contain.

Most of Uncle's Unit had turned and gotten into position to fight the Nyagats in a rearguard action to let us escape, while other soldiers guided us away from danger and kept us together. So we would not just scatter everywhere in panic, they ran with us, protecting us from being ambushed from the sides.

The ensuing battle didn't last long. The Nyagats soon learned that although they were not outnumbered they were out gunned. They lost the will to continue and ran. We had no way of knowing this until afterwards. Time has no meaning in a place of rapid movement that seems like slow motion. There are fragmented pictures of captured seconds that hold you breathless; seeing all these soldiers like my Brother Agor, the fear, yes, but also determination. Brave actions were called for and they were delivering it, putting their lives in harm's way for women and children. In those times between the running, I looked upon these men; I held a love for these soldiers, I admired them as warriors. Brothers.

They were fierce men who did what was brave because they had to.

At times those same fierce warriors of the SPLA did wrong and made decisions that harmed people just like us. They would go into villages hungry, sometimes starving, and demand food, would take away precious cattle. Like the poor cow right behind us we didn't even get to eat who had to be abandoned in the attack. It was such a sad waste and a loss of milk taken from that village's children. Sometimes they took their crops and in some cases this resulted in famine for those villagers. If they resisted, it wasn't unknown for the soldiers to just shoot them!

Sudan's civil war did this to good hearted men and boys. It turned them into beasts.

Well of course I had always respected Mama, but I respected her even more seeing how she kept her children with her through that attack. Even when she was running she lost only a small amount of food from the bin and on her back she carried my little brother Chol. How we all stayed together through it all was a small miracle. Well Mama was no small miracle. Even in the worst situations in the wilderness, not knowing when the next danger would strike, she was a strong woman physically and spiritually, always looking out for her seven children on her own. I would follow any direction she would guide me to with a trust so complete it was an ache. I so admired Mama for that and I decided, if we survived, I would always look out for her as she had for us so selflessly. Without a second's thought.

Mama, a Lion... with her Pride!

She was always there for us and always with something to eat. She provided food for us from what she carried on her head the whole time. Those horrific four days, Mama never rested until we were settled, always keeping an eye out and protecting us. Fear? Well, fear was contagious. It would run through our group like a herd of gazelles. Mama showed it as I said. Forever after, in the depths of her eyes, you couldn't help but feel it. Yet Mama always kept her focus, always showed us a cool kind of reassuring calm. We would live; we would get beyond this and most importantly, get to her husband.

"Your Baba will hold his children in his arms again, wait and see!"

Her bright eyes shined when she made that commitment, right into our hearts. If Mama said it, it must be true!

In those fragmented moments I had a new respect for Achol as well. I saw she had learned from Mama. When it got tough, she followed Mama's lead. She would lend a needed hand to make some food stuffs and not complain, even once. When Chol was sick, and Mama couldn't be there for some reason, Achol was! She would wipe his face of sweat and give him a drink of water and stare into his eyes with such a pure love it set my heart on fire for her. Not that I would then show it, as it was that way with us even in that situation. In some ways, we are still like that. Yet, in that all out run for our lives from killing rifles, Achol showed a courage and grace I'd never seen before. She was like Mama!

Achol made the second best tea ... on the planet. I could grant her that.

In my heart that day I held my older sister a hero and my Mother a saint! It's strange that I remember so little of the first part of the run. Really it's just fragments; the first shot that almost hit me or Mama and killed the poor Cow, then the running with a herd of madness and the sounds of insanity. I remember the island around our family, a bubble that could not pop. It kept me sane! Here was strength, something I could hold onto, something that was more real than what was going on around me. I, Sarah... I ran for this... person, Acuach Cor. I became a gazelle for a time, so fleet of foot over the ground we covered and the bush we ran through. I was part of the herd in a wilderness of predators. We ran through Africa; the Africa that taught us the tribal ways, that gave us the woman the giver of life and the primal ancient order of things.

Like the family.

I found my stamina through long standing tribulation. Africa's teachings!

We were soon to be shown the opposite, a change that was sudden and startling. It instantly shifted the whole course of events and the way it was experienced. To this day the placement of these events is remembered differently by each one of us. We hold to our scars in different places so they differ greatly in the telling of them. Some will not talk of it at all. They are dealing with it in their own way and maybe in a lot of ways. There is no getting over it. Maybe eventually we will learn what it means to our humanity, our dignity, that we hold family values, teachings of the heart. Baba, who we were running to, granted us that vision from the time we could crawl. We learned of the love for our Family, our People, our Africa. He showed us the way, his vision, which was for him like breathing...

For me, I only see Baba.

I learned of his beliefs by watching the way he lived his life. His love for Mama, a woman of a different Sub-tribe than his, showed that a unity of the tribes could exist. He believed all this needless bloodshed between Brothers and Sisters need not be our future. We were in a war of ideals, North and South, Religion against Religion, Tribe against Tribe. To Baba, peace was possible; peace was the belief you raised your family with. Knowledge was the key, right thinking came from knowledge. Love of the family, the tribe, the people, the world, came through the heart. This was the foundation we grew up with as children in Bor; what our compound represented.

It was a unity of ideals. *Baba's world!*

It was a safe world, a world that crashed down to this. What Baba had fought to try and avoid was coming to pass. The peaceful world was burning down around our ears. Nothing could prove this out more than what I was to see that day. It was the opposite of peace, the most base aspects of war. It showed how men can be worse than animals. It brutalizes the soul, to think of doing those things to other living human beings. Our world was being stripped by layers: Bor, Yalee, Kongor; each was a blow. Each experience knocked notches away from our old reality. Now it came to the very bottom of the muck and mire. We were to face the ugly truth.

The heated stench of rotting death came on the wind. The herd shivered with a low moan. We had been running in crazy terror and something ahead smelled worse! We felt dread. Were we running right into some horrid trap? Were there more Nyagats hiding in wait ahead of us? It was a visible shiver, a shift in the way we ran. We were trying to turn away from the rotting smell but the lay of the land made it impossible. Suddenly we were right there, on top of an unimaginable hell.

It was a killing ground.

As we continued running from the attack we came out of the bush onto a trail across a wider opening covered with dead decayed bodies half eaten by wild animals. They had been like us, Border Runners, people who had come before us escaping to Ethiopia. We couldn't help stepping on these squishy, bloated corpses of our own people. We were having to run right through their final tragedy. While running I thought of the day Mama called to us sharply, "*back away from those rifles children. They are very dangerous!*" I could see now what the end result was from all those rifles. They were dead people who could have been my neighbours. They were staring up at me, trying to scream: "*What's happening to me!*" as, *Africa, Killed them* . . .

It was chaos; everybody was yelling and screaming and running without direction. I don't know what was worse, the attack or stumbling on those mutilated bodies and the smell of it all. No, it was the severed head. That was the worst of this nightmare. I can see it still as I write. It was by a big rock. Like the big snake I told you about, at first I couldn't understand what it was I was seeing. The feeling of curiosity like, 'what's that?', was like a magnet. I was drawn to this misshapen thing and its reality came into focus. The shock of it ran through me like electricity as I recognized it was a man's face. A mans face without its body? Ugly white worms were coming out of the eyes and the dung beetle bugs were just everywhere. Because it had been there for a time, it was terribly deformed and decayed. It was the worst thing I had ever seen. It was beyond gross.

There wasn't even time to throw up, although in that putrid moment I did gag, and then we were past and still running. The heaviness of the air with its horrid smell was retreating. But still the smell of death stuck to us, soaked right into our sweat. Because we had stumbled over them, their decay, their bodies coated our feet and stuck to our clothing and shoes. I have no recollection of what came after that, only running past and getting beyond that nightmare. I was in shock after seeing a severed head.

It was as if a switch had snapped shut in my head. I was running and running through a landscape of the impossible, running to get away from a scene I could see over and over.

'*Oh God, why couldn't this just stop?*' I felt the inner scream rising in me.

The rush of passing air just over my shoulder, the lighting all dimmed and the slumber of travellers on long flights, hung in the cramped cabin. My eyes flashed open. I was nodding off and this vision, the beginning of that familiar nightmare, had begun to take over. I felt a very real panic to be jolted from this ugly vision to the reality of a 747 in flight, making its way through the night, with the rapid beating of my heart. I felt my insides shaking and tried not to wake the passenger next to me by fussing in my seat. I tried to concentrate on where I was and what I was doing. My eyes were filled with tears and, in the background I saw that head. It was like a movie, the camera zooming in to reveal its every gory detail. I suddenly felt the plane was too small to contain this. I needed out! I needed to run fast, run away . . .

as far as I could.

I was trapped. I couldn't get away from that vision. Never before had I recalled that tenth Birthday of mine with such vivid details, feelings, emotional shock. I wanted to do what I did best . . .*start screaming, and never stop!* I wanted to run up and down the aisle and scream, "*it's not fair. It's just not fair,*" to have to live like this, to see such things and have this reality. Is there no getting out of this?

It took some moments for the panic to subside and to start feeling close to normal. I hadn't wanted to dig this deeply into what was and, should maybe, *just stay buried!* For reasons I couldn't understand, I needed to go through them then and there, during that flight. I was half the way to realizing this dream of mine, flying across an ocean. I knew there was nothing beneath us but water.

Water!

Water is so precious to Sudan. With so many things wrong in my Country and so much fear in me, so close to those memories; thirst won out! I have to have water with me always, it is almost a compulsion. I drank my fill from a water bottle and it felt so good. It soothed me as it always does. Water is the giver of life. To have a terrible thirst and no water to take it away is a torture no one should have to live through. I thought again of the past, of those trials, with half an ocean to pass before I could try to fill the missing hole in my heart. Tears and more water from my inner well came again. I saw Mama's face before me, those eyes of shining confirmation. '*Sigh*' they seemed to say, as she waited endlessly for Sarah. She was waiting for Sarah to fulfill her pledge and look out for her. My Mama... I gave her my tears.

It was all I could give to Mama right then; my precious water.

I was dying inside; all my anxious fears collected in one tight bundle. My courage was like food in a bin that was running out. Why could I not find courage? Why couldn't I face what I needed to see? This was something about my Africa that I needed to cope with before I arrived. *Even before I landed?* I wished I didn't have to do this. From past experience I'd found it takes a very long time for wishes to come true. I'd had a lot and few had come my way. *'Yet, if Mama said it, it must be true!'* There it was that small glimmer of hope. It began to glow within my chest; it would all be all right. I had seen Mama smile, as she used to say... about, my heart.

"See, Acuach Cor. There, you have courage!"

I thought, it's so long to wait and I have so little to hold onto. I needed to be brave. All my hopes and dreams were now at a crossroads. Ten years, one eighth of my life, were what I held so close to me; a memory of a happy life with my family all together in a place called home. It was a half a life time now, and still I remembered all those family teachings and values. I had tried to live by most of them; it was the ones I was missing that bothered me. Some part of the unfolding story in my memory was waiting, awaiting recognition. There was a part of me I needed to know; that part of me that told me, Sarah! What was I made of, this person made my two parents? That is me! This life time of waiting would be over. I was finally going to get my long held wish. Sarah Gabriel's time had finally come, to be at home in Africa...

To find myself, within my family.

I sat there with that glow for awhile and listened to the noise an aeroplane creates. It lulled me to sleep and just as I nodded off, more memories of those days of running came. It filled me with a new shiver. Knowing what is coming next doesn't mean it isn't spooky. Sometimes what you know is right there scares you to death, especially that face that can't be faced. How many other beliefs and values would fail, fall apart like a house of sticks? How many other things you believed in would be proven untrue? My faith and my fear, all in one basket, all together... I owned them both.

If only I could throw the fear away!

It comes on me just like that; a series of events comes bubbling up from my past. There is no end of sorrows I must bottle up inside and not blow up like a bomb. I'd felt this way many times over the subsequent years; felt frustration waiting for this flight home to eventually happen. I've had to wear many faces to get me through every day, and all the time I'd be working through these underlying fears, mostly without even knowing I was living through them.

Only they would still come out in my everyday routine.

Living was surviving!

My life was like my run for the border, running from one place to the next hoping that just over the next hill I could rest awhile and catch my breath. I was hoping I could build a home and not have it turn into a house of sticks, a collection of lost dreams. I was hoping I would find a place where I, Sarah, could put down roots to my tree. Where was it? They were always just over the hill; my hopes and dreams and most of all. *Freedom* . . .

There was always that need to be me, no matter what! No matter what, I had to live up to my pledge to look out for Mama, and my need to be me, to be a free woman. I had to find and hold dignity for the entire world to see. I'm Sarah Gabriel, my Mother gave me this life to have and own. She gave up so much of herself to get me to where I am. I sit in my seat and consider my life. With all its past hardships, it's a good life. Why was I so sensitive? For the most part I've always been a pretty happy person. Why is it so easy to just break down, into tears? I suppose I wasn't really finding much comfort right then, much to laugh about or make fun of. I had worked my way through different worlds and cultures, worked hard at my jobs to get me on this plane. I worked hard to be educated for Baba! To live the Ideals of my family; yes, I'd earned this. I was turning a corner and looking down a huge new open road. I was so close to freeing myself of that baggage hiding in my everyday fears.

First, I had to deal with the rest of the road to Ethiopia. The memories took me again without having to bring them out and dust them off. No, they were fresh, like I had lived them only the day before. Unlike in the past, I didn't shove them down and seek to turn them off. I faced them, allowed them to take me over, take me wherever I needed to go within them. My seat in the plane, the passengers all round me; everything faded and like a movie scene, memories from that dreadful past began.

At first they were fragments, flashes of insanity in a blur that ran all around me. I was crying from somewhere deep, frantic and looking into the brush, wanting to hide. I wanted to escape this clamp around my heart that threatened to take my breath away. The fear amongst us all was a thing you could almost reach out and touch. We were running in a mad sprint away from something we couldn't understand. There was a relief in me we were moving away from the horror of stumbling into that already unthinkable something. This something made me scream inside. It made me want to hide there in the brush and never come out. I was screaming in horror that people might do to us what they had done to those poor people. Now they lay scattered behind me frozen in the mad ending of life. I had to pass through that vision forming again in my mind. No matter how fast I ran, I couldn't outdistance the mind bending idea. These people had had a life, families, children and it had all just ended!

They were back there, right behind me, and I was convinced it was was going to happen to us!

Then flashes of memory began to slow; I was mindlessly running into the bush and my brother Anyon and Deng Ti, were suddenly there, almost frantic, yelling to me in unison:

"*Run Acuach run; run harder!*"

My brothers were still really only children themselves. They were helping Mama keep us together and not get lost or trampled in the stampede. The look in their eyes was one of wild determination as they ran alongside, being the responsible men of our family. They were taking the place of Baba and their elder bothers. It gave me something to focus on, to push down the waves of pure terror I felt. I stopped wanting to hide and instead just wanted to get away from the sound of gunfire and the fighting going on behind us. I wanted to escape death! I wanted our family to get away from this horror.

For me now, *death now had a face*; an ugly monster face I could never forget.

Ever . . .

Suddenly it seemed, just like that, it was night. I was lying in the grass moaning and Mama was there rubbing excruciating cramps out of my legs. I ached everywhere, the pain going deeper than just my body. I could feel the burning scrapes and scratches from just running crazily through anything in front of us. Mama was saying soothing things to me but I couldn't hear her. I had so much I wanted to ask her of the why, why this, why us? I wanted to tell her all my fractured thoughts, but the words would not come. They were stuck in my throat and all that came out was meaningless whimpering. I realized tears were streaming down my face and I couldn't stop them. It was as if my heart were breaking. The fragments and flashes swam through my mind like a whirlpool. They were pulling me down. I was trying hard to make sense of them.

So I could tell Mama what they might mean.

But these things I couldn't begin to understand were happening so fast!

The worst was the smell of death. It was a horrid smell that clung to everything, poisoned the air around me, and made me gag. It wafted through what I called 'the falling down place.' People were so exhausted they just fell down where ever they were when the soldiers got them all to finally stop. They were so exhausted they looked as if they were dead! It was like that nightmare place before and it had the same smell! My mind reeled with horror all over again.

Other children around me were crying and wailing as well, their mothers trying to quiet them. I was startled by the most God awful screaming that came from everywhere at once. It was from me! Mama struggled to hold on to me. I had only one thought, hide! I just broke down. Mama wouldn't let go of me and I collapsed into her firm, comforting arms and cried and cried like the broken thing I was. How long it went on for, I have no idea. I cried until I was drained and there was no more; no more house, no more home, no more safety, no more happy times.

It felt like my life had just ended, at the falling down place, the day of my tenth Birthday.

When I came aware again of this somehow-nowhere-place where we had ended our running, it was much quieter. Most of the collapsed people were asleep. I was still choking back little sobs, but the rivers of tears were drying up. Mama had me blow my nose into some rag and I found myself burning with thirst. I finally found words that would form and asked Mama for a drink of water. Her returning look was one of worry.

She told me, "We have no water here, Acuach Cor. I'll see, what I can do, for my Sarah!"

She left me there and went to talk to a nearby soldier with her can held out in front of her. I watched him pour some water for her out of his canteen. He didn't look too happy to do so. Then there was Mama's smile as she brought it to me. It was such a small amount of stale warm water, but it was all I was likely to get and I drank it down in one gulp. Stale warm water never tasted so sweet, so life giving!

A crazy thirst took me over. All I could think of was water. And now we had no more water? Well every child in Sudan knows without water you die! It was just another kind of way you could suffer a horrible death. I had heard stories told of such things by someone, probably by Grandma around her camp fire in Yalee. I think she told us those old stories to watch us squirm and moan with scary anticipation.

Thinking of her made my tears run again. I saw all of Yalee as another falling down place. Had the soldiers gone there and left those people scattered and rotting in the sun like the others? I asked Mama and I think it shocked her for a short time. Then her words came out all in a rush. She was sure Grandma was all right and would know good places to hide if the Government soldiers came to Yalee. I knew that to be true from all of her stories of the Merle Bahre raids. There were many such places on The Cape. I could picture that happening and it made me feel much better as I rocked there in Mama's lap.

"Now we will pray to The Christ for Grandma and all of Yalee, hey Acuach Cor!", she said, and we did say many prayers till finally exhaustion closed my eyes and I gave way to confused dreams till morning.

I awoke stiff and sore to realize I was the last to wake up and have some breakfast. The family had already formed around Mama portioning out some cold porridge. The hastily formed camp was already a buzz of activity. I slowly winced my way to the ground and accepted my portion of a tasteless chewy gruel. No one had said anything, but just as we were about to begin eating, Chol, who was fussing and mumbling something in his two-year old mostly baby language, said something and we all turned to hear him. Mama asked him what he'd said with a face so serious. What came out was rather shocking. He said clearly, "Them's people", he pointed in the direction we'd run from, "were killed by Siwar Al-Deheb's men!"

We all looked at one another in wonder as Chol lowered his head and said nothing further, staring into his bowl a moment, then continued quietly eating his meal. This surprising reminder from one so young dampened our appetite and we slowly went back to eating. We wondered how Chol could have known what he had said, Siwar Al-Deheb being the then President of Sudan and leader of the Government troops. We finally figured he had overheard village boys playing SPLA war where this slogan was shouted quite a lot. They would shout, "Here comes Siwar Al-Deheb's men, shoot them!", like yelling "rat-tat-tat" noises from imaginary rifles, and would chase those playing the bad guys through the bush.

Meanwhile the prevailing feeling through the camp that morning was becoming more disturbed. Those who had lost children or family the day before when we were running, searched anxiously through the camp for them. One large disturbance happened when our guards wouldn't allow a distraught mother to leave the camp to go searching for her child. She was told some children had died in that attack. I saw the mother fall to the ground and begin to add her wailing to those others in the camp who knew their family or relations had not made it to safety. A man and woman we knew from Kongor came by to talk to Mama, share the sadness and pray with her for those from Kongor who had died.

I wasn't the only one who was in shock from running through the awful nightmare of that dead people place. Even Chol was upset. It was the main topic of conversation for everyone the whole day. Talking about it though didn't help; it made the reality of the danger we faced all the more real. A man came over to us and after a short time I could tell Mama wanted him to leave. He was a man who hung around the soldiers all the time greedy for news. Then he'd go about the camp and gossip his views as if he could be a better leader for us all.

Uncle Arok came by to tell Mama the state of things; something he had done at the start of most of the last three days. The run was stalled for a short time and would spend most of this morning where it was to allow the soldiers who had stayed to fight the Nyagat, time to catch up before we moved on. He also needed to hear their report on how the battle had gone. Uncle already knew he had lost soldiers in the attack. We could see he was very tired. The soldier's movements, coming and going about the camp, were hectic and serious. The Nyagats had taken a real beating and were chased a long way before the Zindia gave up and began their long run back to their Unit. Uncle was concerned those who survived would make their way back to their masters, the Government troops, and report their contact with the Zindia. His final words were that it would be a long, hard run today, as water for everyone was now in short supply.

This other man had shown up shortly afterwards and was being critical about how he felt the Army was protecting us. Mama said very little to him and just listened as he said much the same as Uncle had shared. What he was bringing into the camp in gossip was close to the truth, but what he added was a lack of confidence. He made his personal opinions and fears well known, and when he left, I heard Mama say to herself, "now off, to spread more poison!"

I asked her what she meant. She hadn't seen me sitting there listening so she told me to come and sit with her. Then she gave me a short lesson on the evils of gossip. Yes, it could be a way to pass on information. It could also be a way to pass information that wasn't true. It could also hurt the people who were being gossiped about. She believed we would make it and we needed to believe that. To listen to a man, such as that one, could sap our courage. It could draw us into his beliefs and fears. Worse, it would spread panic and make Uncle's task of getting us to the border all the much harder.

"Do you feel what is in the camp today, Acuach Cor?", Mama asked me.

I was a little surprised, as I thought I was the only one to notice and be thinking about it. I said there was a lot of sorrow from those that had lost friends and family, especially children. After a moment of quietly looking into my eyes, knowingly, Mama said very seriously, "It is much, much more Sarah; it is a building fear. People are losing their faith and being overcome by doubt. That horrible time yesterday has given their fears a face and yes, I feel it too." There was a short pause as Mama looked around the camp, then back to me.

"That man, Acuach Cor, is bringing even more fear and doubt to a people on the very edge. I believe Uncle Arok will do his best and I trust in that. These people don't know him. This man is spreading doubt in Uncle's ability. If the people lose this faith in the Zindia, if the soldiers lose control of a group this size Sarah, it could get very bad for us. Do you understand?" There was a look in her eyes I had never seen before, from Mama...

Very real fear of a kind I had never had before.

The Zindia could actually open fire on us? was the startling thought.

It was not said, but it was there in that look. I understood most of what Mama had talked about, but of course as a 10-year old, a lot escaped me. I could understand a lack of water would create problems. That ache in my throat was already burning its way through my mind and the day had only just begun. I went on my own to a nearby soldier who seemed to be close to us all the time and he gave me a sip from his canteen, a pat on the head and a smile. 'That smile,' I remembered him suddenly from our house in Kongor. He was one of the soldiers there the first morning who stopped me and Abany from going for our travel bundles. I was amazed to see him now again, in my mind's eye, running beside us the whole trip, never far away.

I heard the now familiar three sharp whistles and the soldier turned to me, and said in Dinka, "Go now little one back to your Mama and family." He looked at his watch and added, "we leave, in fifteen minutes." Then he gave me a gentle nudge to send me on my way. Now it would begin again I thought as I watched the soldiers gathered the group before we moved out. This too was becoming a familiar type of order. As we took our place for the run, I looked to see if I was correct and there he was! Again he nodded and smiled at me, as if to say, 'yes you see. I'm right here with you!' I can't tell you how much safer this made me feel.

What Mama had said was true; Uncle would do his best to see we were looked after. I could see that on the other side was the soldier who had given Mama water for me the night before. I was really looking now and recognized there were four soldiers who had been with us from the beginning in Kongor. The unchanging pace began and this huge group of people set off in a different direction and a changing countryside.

It had been hot before, but this place was like an oven as the vegetation grew less and less. Many people running alongside were constantly looking off behind us. I thought maybe they hoped those who had been lost would be seen running to catch up.

No, they worried we were being followed. They were afraid to be in the open exposed to another enemy attack. The feeling was like a dreadful poison, travelling through us all!

By early afternoon everyone was looking as if they wanted to collapse, and I did too. I could feel the lack of moisture, of thirst, taking over my mind. Mama came up beside me and said, "here Acuach Cor, put this under your tongue." Then she passed me a small smooth stone. She was giving them to all us children. I put the stone under my tongue and found it worked! It was easier to make moisture in my extremely dry mouth. Again I was struck about how much my Mama knew. At that age, I figured she must know about just about everything. No matter what I asked her, she had an answer!

Again I could feel the group dynamic changing in the way we all moved together. It was obvious to me we were running out of energy. Even the soldiers were not barking at us to move faster like they did earlier. Many had run through the night to catch up and I felt very sorry for them. It got to the point that even the small stone wasn't helping anymore. The surrounding area didn't help my thirst any as it became more like desert. It only reminded us it was getting drier and drier. The sun beat down on us mercilessly, sapping the strength from my wobbly legs. I started to see double.

This was not good!

'*Water, water, water... please.*' I couldn't get my mind to stop this demand.

Still we ran on. I wondered if it would ever end. There was a short rest break and the soldiers gave the smallest children what they could. Even I got one small capful of water. It wasn't anywhere near what we all needed. We set off again and the soldiers set the run at what was half the pace. Word came back the scouts might have found water. Well, the jolt went through everyone, and wow; they just perked right up and the run quickened its pace back to double time right away. *WATER!*

Then the scouts were ahead yelling too, all excited, "*water water!*"

It was now a stampede. People fell down and the group just ran right over them. Even the soldiers couldn't stop them. We could see in the distance a large body of what we needed the most, but it was full of animals drinking! As the stampede arrived, the animals scattered and let the crazy people have it! Just as soon as the animals ran off, people jumped right in like a wave, laughing and screaming with delight.

We wanted to just join the stampede really badly, but Mama held us back. She was worried about the safety of what was now a muddy swamp. Instead she took us to the edge of the small pond Mama and Achol started to search for cleaner water for us and found water with their hands under the grass to give to us. It was wonderful, clean and cool. After seeing their example we couldn't get water fast enough, so we just did it ourselves. We wanted to get as much of this oh so sweet tasting water as we could. Then we left Mama and Achol to collect the two bottles we had to carry water and joined the crowd jumping into the water. We just went crazy for it. It really felt very good. My skin felt much cooler the moment it touched that glorious small pool of water, now packed with all us water crazy people. We younger children were splashing one another and having some much needed fun. Even the soldiers joined right in.

All too soon, the fun and excitement was over. Whistles blew and soldiers began assembling us again. You could almost feel the resentment. Some said it would be a good place to camp. Other said food was getting scarce; couldn't there be a hunt, hot food and meat for a change? It seemed everyone around us was grumbling. Not far from us was the man who visited in the morning, his voice the loudest of these complaining. I could see he was even drawing sneers and bad looks from the soldiers who were with us again. Mama had proved she was right when she said, 'now off to spread more poison!' Even finding water was not enough for this man; he now was complaining his group was running out of food!

Somehow he implied, it was all the Zindias fault. Somebody must be to blame. I was thinking if it was any one's fault, it was the Government, trying to wipe us off the face of the Earth! We moved out and these thoughts became unimportant; all that mattered was the pace that would carry us to the next place for Uncle Arok to call a stop. I found the difference having water in my body made was that I no longer hurt everywhere. Three days of this pace, was changing my legs too, really strengthening my muscles. I was almost happy with this new feeling. I'd grin a challenge at my brothers and race ahead of them a little. For a few times they took me up on what was an accepted Sarah game, knowing what that look in my eye meant. My sisters didn't bite though and stuck close to Mama.

That worked for awhile till the pain in my legs came back. I knew I'd over done it. Again the ground was harder and my feet were taking a pounding. I was back to 'pick a point, pass a point' again. It was agony; a mindless kind of getting lost within yourself, having no interest in the passing scenery or wildlife. The only interesting thought I had at that point was...

When will it stop?

I had experienced this feeling once before, passed this barrier. I was reaching an almost blissful state of animal grace, a rhythm of my body that matched my breathing. I felt my feet almost float along the land. I was losing myself to an inside something. I was in that headspace and went on like that till Deng Ti caught my arm and said a rest was happening. It took a moment to realize what he was saying and want to stop. When I did, I suddenly heard four whistle sounds. This was a signal I'd not heard before. We were on the edge of a wide grassy plain and the soldiers were all motioning everyone to crouch down into the grass.

It was as if time had stopped. I could feel my heart, racing in my chest. Everyone stopped breathing and it became very quiet. It was then I heard an odd far off kind of droning sound that I did recognize. I turned my head in its direction and far off on the horizon a small dot was moving away from us across the sky...a small plane. I had only just seen it in time before it disappeared over a faraway hill.

I now understood why we had stopped. The whistle came again in rapid blasts. The soldiers were yelling at everyone to get to their feet, "hurry, hurry." Already those in front of the group were sprinting into the open. Soldiers moved in to pick up the smallest children and carry them.

The pace was now double time, almost an all out run. Far across the plain the landscape was changing quickly. I had been so lost in that beautiful running place I hadn't noticed we had been leaving the desert behind. The watering place had been the transition and we were now into open grassland. Across this plain could be seen patches of low brush and trees.

It was this brush our group was sprinting for. I could feel a burning going through me that later in life I understood was adrenaline. Although the grass was above knee height, it was dry from days without rain. This made it coarse and it whipped against my legs as I ran. I hardly felt anything, only later did I discover the burning pain and scratches I suffered when I lay down to sleep. Now there was only one thing to see and that was how far that bush line was away. I wondered what animals we would startle. I imagined them running by in this tall grass. It made me gulp and feel my heart beat even faster. Some people fell down as we raced along, not that I noticed. I knew what that plane represented; government troops!

It was a spotter plane!

We ran right past the edge of the brush and down a slight hill into a natural bowl-like valley with a small strip of forest. It seemed just in time. I was feeling I just had no more in me when again the whistle blew and we all fell to the forest floor. If we hadn't been so supercharged with wild-eyed sweat soaked panic, it would have been a rather beautiful place to discover.

Every day had had a different energy, a different challenge, to overcome. This place was like the African Heart, a small precious oasis in the middle of nowhere. Or at least, if I'd had time to think, that's what I would have thought. We had covered now three quarters of the distance to our goal; suffered the Nyagat attack, the falling down place, water shortage, the small release the water brought...and now, this.

When we'd been attacked by the Nyagat, we were a mindless herd. We had no time to see the army respond to that military threat. What we were about to see, here in the heart, was entirely different. The Zindia were not putting us up for the night, they were getting ready for a fight. Just as soon as we'd stopped, there was a whirlwind of orders and soldiers moved at a dead run, to get into position. Scouts ran out in several directions. Uncle Arok was forming up teams, barking sharp commands and soldiers were checking their weapons. I watched all this in excited, heart pounding interest. Others had that lost wild look in their eyes. I believe they were reliving the falling down place, seeing again all those dead people. They were waiting to die . . . and be discovered in this place!

You could smell the fear, feel the silent scream: Siwar Al-Deheb's soldiers!

Now, I could see the Zindia and their dusty sweat-stained uniforms doing what they did for real; prepare for battle. I could see the teams now up on the rims of this bowl, evenly spaced all round us with weapons held at a ready. The leaders of the teams were talking on the radio with Uncle, sweeping the terrain and the plain we'd just run through with their binoculars. I had to admire them, even if I had no understanding of military stuff. I knew this unit had had very little rest. It had only begun four days before for us. These men had come from a major three-month battle and would continue fighting a war that would just go from one stage, to the next and the next...endlessly.

I realized my brothers, like me, were intently watching this activity progress. We were in a place where it was not yet evening and we were stuck for the rest of the day. We had to maddeningly wait, and wait, for some news of the coming. But what was coming? We didn't know. It let our imagination run wild which was maybe worse. At some point the quiet tension broke and was replaced by crying children and nervous fearful chatter. Had we been spotted, would the soldiers come, could our soldiers hold them off, would we be running soon? So we waited till almost sundown when all went quiet again. We heard the scouts had begun to come back.

Soldiers came through the group and took some people including Mama back to where they held one end of this short valley. Before long they came back to say this would be our camp for the night. The scouts had reported there were no enemy troops in the immediate area. Uncle told everyone not to light campfires and to settle the children as early as possible because we'd be moving out at dawn. He said by late the next day we'd reach the Akobo River. He told us to be brave; the group had done well, to have confidence. We were almost at the border.

Knowing some families had lost their food in the Nyagat attack and that the cattle had been left behind, Mama first fed us and make sure there would be some left in her bin for tomorrow, then took a portion and went off to contribute a share to those that were in need. Abany and I were laughing about something when we suddenly heard a scream. This was followed by the weird barking of a pack of Hyena and it was not that far off! We looked at each other wondering, who been eaten.

I said smartly to my sister, "good thing we are right in the middle of all these people!"

A moment later there came a very loud roar from a lion on the other side of the valley! I don't know why, but we both looked at each other and laughed. We were thinking of Grandma. "Wait till we tell her this story," Abany said with a grin.

We never did find out who screamed or why. Maybe it was the Alek in one of Grandma's stories, being chased by her husband the Lion. We laughed some more and sang the song through together. Some of the other children we had sung songs with came over and begged us to tell them more stories. There were a few more sounds from the animals nearby, but my sister and I made fun of them so the children wouldn't be frightened. We had had enough of being afraid. I wasn't worried by what might be in the jungle anymore. We had bigger things to worry about.

So it was, "Ha ha ha, oh oh, la la la ... so, it's a lion!" *Shrug.* "That's no big deal."

The soldiers woke us before the sun came up. It took no time to form everyone into running order and off we went. We had to cover a lot of ground for our last day. There was still no sign of the Nyagat or the Government troops but there was plenty of talk about them. Tensions and worries about the airplane being spotted were the continuing gossip at every rest stop. The worry seemed to grow with each kilometre passed. It was like a dog worrying a bone. These people would not stop thinking of the possibility. The enemy was coming! It was changing from a fear to a fact that would happen at any moment. Someone said when we got to the border crossing, that would be the place the enemy would attack because they knew that there was nowhere to run and hide. True or not, the rumour went through the group like a house on fire.

The rest of the day was supposed to be at an easier pace after the scouts told Uncle no troops could be seen following us or in ahead of us. The group though, kept pushing the tempo without knowing it, constantly looking behind. Many had that wild eyed lost look, a look of resignation, as they imagined an ending place. A few had already given up hope, especially the ones who had done the most gossiping. People showed what they were made of, what they held in their heart.

Suddenly, and surprisingly, we arrived! We had made the decision on that punishing road to know our souls, to live, to take an opportunity. We had seen reality for what it is. Now we were at the crossroads. Now there was a road that would lead us to the future. As uncertain as it was, it required heart.

Some back there in the heart of Africa, had lost that faith.

The fourth day out from Duk Deng . . .

We slowed our trot and walked until we got to the bank of the Akobo river. Across on the other side was Tiergol, Ethiopia where U.N. people were waiting for us. We had done very well that day and had arrived about 5:00 PM in the afternoon. The soldiers led us, all very excited, to a clearing where we would be crossing the river. We were told the only way to cross it was by boat and the water was infested with crocodiles. Part of the Zindia had arrived in advance of the main group and we passed them on the way in setting up defences to protect the area. We now had to wait for our turn at the crossing. Again a wave of gossip traveled through us as we separated into family groups and got into line.

It was a very big line-up to get into the boats and the boats were very small. They could only carry three or four persons each time. The soldiers at the river crossing organized it so mothers with the smallest children would go first. A lot were scared and chattering about not making it across to the other side, convinced the enemy would attack at any moment. As it was, the crossing would go right into the next day. Those still on this side would have to wait through the night till the morning.

We could hear complaining everywhere. People asked why weren't there bigger boats waiting for them? Why were some people chosen before them? Couldn't the boats go faster? Some tried to push themselves ahead in the line. This made the soldiers angry and they forced them to go back where they had been placed. You could feel the tension building. We worried it could turn from fear to anger and boil over. Both civilians and soldiers were at a very fine line of worn out nerves; the tension could very well snap.

Mama said if that happened things could get very bad for us. The soldiers near the boats tightened their guard and warily eyed the now milling crowd. If the crowd interfered with their job of getting people into the boats, they would simply open fire to gain control. Mama gathered us close to her and I could feel how nervous she was from all of this.

Then I saw the man who had visited Mama. He was no longer screaming about the coming enemy; he just stood at the edge of the crowd, calmly staring at the river. I could see he was looking for the crocodiles he'd been told about. Maybe he'd been told wrongly, he was like that...this man with the contrary views.

"*I'm not waiting to die here!*" he yelled and just like that, he ran into the river and started to swim for it. People were quite stunned by this and for the moment just hung there. He'd made it about half way and some were yelling he was going to make it, cheering him on. Quite a lot of us lost their minds right then. They couldn't wait. They preferred to jump into the water and swim to the other side where they would be safe. It all happened so fast. Pandemonium broke out as a wave of people broke past the soldiers and rushed into the river to follow this man's example.

It was all just too crazy. Many of the people couldn't even swim. This we noticed right away as they began to just float away down river. People on shore were screaming and pointing this out. More screaming was heard and people turned to look up river at a mass of something coming quickly out of the reeds. Now you could see many wakes in the water coming out from where the crocodiles were hiding in the reeds on the far bank. It was these that got to that man first.

The shock of them thrashing in the water with him all a foam and going blood red was too horrifying to describe. Mama tried to keep us from watching this, but it was impossible; everything was happening so fast. It was terrifying this thing going on right in front of us. Some who could swim, and were catching up to this horror, were the next to be attacked. Those who hadn't reached the river had frozen on the bank screaming for the others, "come back, come back. Get out of the water!" Many heard and turned back, but too late. The whole river was turning frothy red. Finally Mama pulled us away from the ugly scene. I heard automatic weapons fire; the soldiers were shooting into the crocodiles giving those coming back to shore a chance to make it.

Just as fast as it began, it was finished.

The enemy troops never did attack; it was a real waste of human lives.

We stayed in the line up for the boats, and finally we got on, and crossed the river.

Chapter 7
Refugee Camp

I was entering a new period of rapid change, both of places and experiences. There was first, the loss of my happy life in Sudan. It was gone and could never be recaptured. The four days I'd just lived through had closed the road to my childhood. It had also forever changed my view of my world and of the depravity humans are capable of. Now I'd be experiencing the realities of the greater world beyond my imagining. I knew, whatever happened I was fortunate to have got out of Sudan's Civil War so quickly and still in one piece.

Events were forcing me to mature, to rearrange the things I had to fear, to become accustomed to what was real and forget what was not. I knew I would have to accept many things I had no control over. Among the first was the world of ideologies, beliefs beyond what we knew of family and tribe. Another was the role of international agencies dictating what would be in store for us; organizations controlling our affairs, telling us what our world would have to contain. Years of manipulation were beginning, right here, at the end of the punishing road out of Sudan.

To start with there was the U.N. A very new idea, this United Nations was for us although in some ways it was similar to Baba's views that peace could be found by uniting the Tribes. It was an idea we would shortly see very different views of, and examples of, in this the U.N.'s refugee camp.

Once we walked into Tiergol, we were received by the waiting U.N. people and the SPLA organization. They fed us and took care of those injured in the river by the crocodile attack. The injured had been loaded into boats right away as there was little that could be done for them medically on the other side.

It wasn't long before we got into another big line up, something we would get sorely accustomed to. This one was for a huge, doubled bladed, white U.N. helicopter that would take us to our final destination, Itang. It was a very big line up. Some people had been waiting days before us and they got their place on the helicopter first. It was brutal watching people in their ignorance, pushing and shoving and doing anything to get on those noisy helicopters with their whirring blades. Each time they thumped their way in to land, we were in the wash of strong winds whipping up dust and dirt into our eyes. The dust storm would be repeated again in their noisy takeoffs.

I have to admit that the noise was rather intimidating. I had, of course, seen helicopters at a distance but never up this close. The first few times they came and went, I had butterflies in my tummy thinking that soon I would be flying through the air in this marvellous modern machine. After

I don't know how many times of watching and experiencing this, it just got to be annoying. We were standing there waiting to be covered again in clouds of dirt and sand getting into our cloths, grinding against our skin. I felt as if I had a bucket of grit coating my teeth. I constantly bugged Mama to give me water to rinse my mouth out because I would hear them coming again, and again, and again!

It all got to be pretty boring, I can tell you!

By then it had become a very long day. I began to feel cramps starting in my legs from standing so long and tried bouncing on the spot to avoid them. The bouncing just reminded me how much my feet hurt. The sand was even grinding in my armpits, making them raw whenever I moved my arms around too much. I was feeling miserable and rather cranky.

Then something happened that gave me the opportunity to do something and feel at least a little better. It was something I could take out my sour mood on. I needed to because the jostling in the line and being pushed around by people every time the stupid helicopters landed was really getting on my nerves.

I'd been pushed ahead of Mama and there were four or five people between us. This one great big fat man showed up beside me. Since I was little for my age, it was easy to be bullied by others. He was thinking he could sneak his way ahead in the line and little Acuach Cor would be an easy target. To Mama it looked as though this guy was going to sit on my head, the way he wriggled his bum into line. So Mama screamed out angrily when she saw this happening "*Acuach! Bite his ass!*"

'*Wow*,' Mama actually letting me bite somebody? This, I was good at. It was how I would sometimes defend myself from my brothers and sisters only to have Mama pound my ass if she caught me! So, I opened my mouth wide and bit him hard, right on the ass. Man, did that guy jump and scream like a woman! He jumped up and down holding onto his bum and loudly complained in disbelief. He yelled to no one in particular, "*she bit my ass!*"

I think that broke a lot of tension, because everyone in the line had a good laugh at this bully's expense. It was really funny and I'm sure I left a great big scar on that mans fat ass. No other thing in all that waiting had felt so good. '*Chomp*' and all the frustration of the past few days had gone right to my sandy, gritty teeth. I had clamped my jaws down into a real pit of angry sufferance. It was an outlet for all I'd seen that day.

But darn it, that man stayed in the long line ahead of us!

Many years went by and I met this person again; he was actually a family member. He remembered the incident and offered to show me the scar I left on his ass. Well, I said to him, "ah, no thank you." He said back, in Dinka, "Acuach Cor, that was one very uncomfortable helicopter ride!"

We hadn't seen Uncle Arok since arriving at the Akobo River. He had gone ahead to report in at SPLA Headquarters and had left the Zindia to his trusted second-in-command. He knew we would be well looked after and that his pledge had been accomplished. Now he had further Military obligations to tend to, leaving us with the information about Baba's preparations for our arrival at the UN camp. We knew Baba had built us a hut there and made all the arrangements for our care. All we had to do was to register with the U.N. to receive food every month.

I'm sure these were the things going through Mama's mind as we flew through the air in that modern noisy helicopter. It had been a long wait to experience it and by then I was really too tired to appreciate this idea of flying very much. I was pretty much numb, staring at the ground down there so far away, not really seeing it through my tears. I was thinking about how wonderful it would be to be with my Baba, who I hadn't seen since he'd gone off to Europe to get treatment for his leg. To me, it felt like years ago. Too much had happened in between to even begin to relate it all to him.

I felt right then I really need to. Soon I would be able to do just that. How I wanted to just crawl into his lap like I was little again, to have him hold me and just bawl. Maybe I could get this horrible knot out of my chest if I could give my shattered heart to his care. Every turn of that helicopter's whopping noise brought a fresh image of total horror to mind. How could I ever get past this day? These last few days, how could I tell Baba about things I couldn't understand and find a way to express how much I missed him? The helicopter was already landing in another strange land, an alien landscape the like of which I'd never seen before. It was rushing into view and out again, into the nasty propeller wash and flying grit I felt I'd never be able to get off my skin.

I would, in so many ways, never be clean again!

The scenes went by in a dazed blur. I was beyond being tired. I found myself sleeping on my feet, leaning against Mama, in yet another long line. We were waiting for our turn to register with the U.N. people. Would all this ever end, these lines of waiting? We were crushed by crowding dire souls, stuck in the stink of unwashed flesh and under it all...

The death smell.

It still clung to me, the face of death. It was still staring at me the endless question I could never answer. Another house of sticks, with a straw hat roof, waited for me to have and hold the nightmares I knew would come. I was heart sick. I hoped seeing Baba would relieve me of that... save me, somehow.

I had mistakenly assumed that Baba would be there waiting for us. Instead there were three SPLA members who'd been Baba's body guards. He'd left them there to look out for us in Itang, and they'd been sent to meet us by Uncle Arok Thon. It was these men who informed us Baba had been called away, was already in Cuba, and would now meet us there.

I have no recollection of the next few days in our new house of sticks. I slept like the dead and Mama didn't wake me. Finding out Baba wouldn't be coming had crushed me. It was as if a part of me died and I became for a time a shadow on the wall. I couldn't talk and didn't want to face anyone. I only wanted to roll over and face the wall. I would not eat. The only thing I would do was force myself to run to the toilet and back. There I would face my shadow on the wall and try not to sleep again, try not to have the screaming dream. This is the one I had fought to forget for so many years, had succeeded in forgetting. Now here I was flying to Africa re-living these horribly painful recollections. I could not be a shadow. I could not disappear. But I could feel, as I had felt then, sorry to have been born. I was absorbed in a something I could not run away from. The dreams... run, run, run, hurry, hurry, hurry! On to the end where Baba wasn't. I cried and cried and cried till Mama could not take it any more and kicked me out the door.

"Acuach Cor, get out and go for a walk. Enough of this feeling sorry for yourself; it is beneath your dignity. If you don't go out and play, I will throttle you with a big stick, and Sarah Gabriel, don't dare come back, until you're hungry!"

Only then did I begin to explore for the next month, my new UN homeland, an unbelievably tortured multi-tribal place out the door of our house of sticks Baba made. Sarah Gabriel rolled out that door and got on with it.

A few days later we registered for school. Now this was an idea I could get excited about. I was overjoyed to be studying again. Not since that faraway time in my poor Bortown, had I been to school. The very idea for a time saved me, carried me away from the ugliness that surrounded Itang. It was difficult because there were a lot of different tribes and there were always fights and name calling. The children didn't know any better, because that was a way of life for centuries. Tribes had always fought one another. In Sudan, we had always lived with our own tribe, the Dinka; whether it was in Bor, Yalee or Kongor.

But here, I had never seen so much hatred. We were taught to respect our elders and be respectful to others. This was an environment I couldn't understand. If we were all working for the same thing, why was there all this bickering and hate?

I found myself being angry with Baba for putting us into this situation. Then I began to see what he had been teaching his family and the anger melted away. I was able to think again. My shadow was still following me, just not swallowing me. I realized I was being selfish. I was making life for my family even more miserable than it was already.

'Well then, if I was going to change that I would have to get happy in the same skin wouldn't I!' I decided.

I made a new deal with myself; I would help out and be happy, maybe even find a friend to play with.

I found her; she lived right next door on the other side of our grass gate! Her name was Andoya. Now I had a friend to walk to school with everyday, to laugh and run around and be silly with, and to pull pranks on Chol when we had to look after my baby brother. I just loved Chol's bubbly laugh; his whole belly would jiggle with it! Andoya was really good at getting him started too. She had a funny sense of humour that always seemed to get us into one kind of a trouble or another.

I knew Mama was happy to see these changes in me and it made me happy to know she was relieved. The fact that Baba wasn't there and was off in Cuba had been hard for her too, even though she tried not to show it. As was her way, she needed to be our pillar of strength, ever mindful of her pride; these sometimes nasty little cubs that were hers to raise, to lift up out of the ignorance around us, an ignorance we fought against every day.

This was the 'playground' and these were the chores we had to contend with. There was standing in these hateful line ups for undrinkable water and struggling to get to the head of the line for the U.N. gruel rations. Then there was fighting against the tribal separations and territories that existed in the camp. And thirdly there was disease. Mama was struggling to create a home for us in the middle of all this. She was trying to keep us away from the many sicknesses that were a constant threat: diarrhoea that plagued us, horrible skin diseases that were everywhere; malaria, diphtheria, a whole list of things that could kill us or make us uncomfortable. There were even itchy worms in unmentionable places. There was an ocean of people in Itang with an ocean of troubles. Life was anything but easy in that cursed refugee camp.

But it did have school for the children.

Really, for me, that was the one saving grace in that confusion. Home and the classroom were the only two safe zones. Many times in walking to and from school, Andoya and I would be harassed by other children from other tribes. They were always trying to get us to fight with them. Neither Andoya nor I knew how to fight and we did our best to ignore them and stay out of their way. I was always taught in our home never fight, that violence never solved problems. Sometimes I wondered if my sister Abany ever caught on to that idea. She was one who knew how to fight and slice you up with words for sure. A few times it had gotten bad and when I told Mama, she told me the same and to ignore their ignorance.

It turned out we were only there in the UN Camp experiencing its problems first hand for a short time. A month after we arrived, Mama moved us to Bilfam where the SPLA military training camp was located. There we found out there was a school program where children could be accepted for study in Cuba. For us it was more than a possibility; Baba had already made arrangements for his children to be accepted into the program! When I was told this, I was really very upset. I liked my school and my teacher in the U.N. Camp. I'd have to leave it and leave my new best friend Andoya. That was a very tearful goodbye, for both of us.

Even worse was the shock that Mama would not be moving to Bilfam with us. She was staying behind in the U.N. camp with Yong and Chol. My family was being split apart! Once again impossible ideas were being forced upon me, beating me down into a shadow. These choices were always stripping away whatever happiness I had struggled to keep. I tried to face the sun, but the clouds would come, cover me with confusion and the falling rain of these truths would turn my little girl dreams to mud. The idea that Mama would not be there with me was like a storm, a flood that could just wash me away. Never had I ever been away from her for long. I couldn't believe this was happening to me.

It was like my first days in the Camp, turning into the shadow on the wall and hiding from reality. I wanted to retreat from all this pain, actions that made no sense to me. It broke me down to a puddle of weak tears and bawling. I tried being angry, ranting and raving, beating down the walls; it didn't work. All it did was make Mama angry. She set to work with a switch to iron that behaviour out! Then she worked on me with her words, her patient ways, explaining that I needed to accept the reality of what was happening. I tried to accept what she was saying, to use my head, to get beyond the emotions of the heart. Yes these things of the heart were good and necessary, but in times like these they sometimes just got in the way of sound judgement. On this idea of leaving her, Mama had her work cut out for her. I had a great big heart getting in the way of all that sound judgement stuff. Acuach Cor could be down right stubborn where matters of the heart were concerned, as long as it didn't result in that switch Mama had in her hand and now was using as a pointer to make her point. I needed to accept this!

Sarah Gabriel would be a big girl and go to Bilfam without her Mama, but she wouldn't like it! .

I will always remember Mama's words then that came to be so much a part of who I am. They came out gentle and strong with some tears of her own. They washed over me and brought me back to the power of the sun.

"Acuach Cor, do you think that this is not hard for me, my Little Tiger? Me, like the Mama Lion and you being my smallest cub. I want with all my heart to protect you the most of all my children!"

She made her clucking sound, gently ran a hand over my cheek and stared with such deep love into my eyes before continuing.

"You must find in yourself courage little one, courage to face these things in life that you must. We want you to have a better future. This is how we are protecting you kitten, to get you to a safe place away from all this. I could not live with myself to see you stuck here in this place, Acuach Cor. In Cuba you will have the opportunity to get the education that you need to have a better life and a better world, better than what is here!"

I could see Mama was about to cry. She pulled me into a hug and I could feel her chest heave, fighting it. She squeezed me hard and sobbed, "do you see Acuach Cor, do you understand what I'm telling you? You have to have courage little one, be strong for Mama!"

I felt like I wanted to cry, just be a little girl. I had tears leaking from my eyes but I fought them with all I had. I was not a baby anymore. I understood Mama was hurting just as much as I was, having to be separated from her children. I hugged Mama back hard and felt a well of strength building in me. It was a strong place I had been finding in me more and more since all of these unbelievable things began in BorTown. Well right then I decided I must promise myself to be brave. I might be small, but I must believe my heart would carry the strength to face the future, for the sake of my family, for Mama's sake.

I must carry this burden with dignity, *a dignity that she had taught me* . . .

Mama wasn't allowed to stay with us at Bilfam but she made sure we were going to be all right before she went back to Itang and her hut in the UN Camp. This was the fist time in my life I'd been separated from Mama and I wasn't very brave. I was frightened. I didn't know if I would ever be the same again. Everyday we had to deal with the sound of gun fire at the base because of soldiers training. It made me want to run and hide and brought back horrible things I didn't want to remember.

Bilfam was all wind and dust. Sand was in everything, even in our food. If it wasn't windy and dusty, it was rain and mud. There were a lot of children with out their families living in the barracks and we had to take care of our selves. The living conditions were atrocious with a lot of flies and other bugs and mosquitoes at night. It was hard in the beginning as we had to cook and clean for a lot of people. It didn't matter if you were young or sick or even if you didn't know how to cook! Regardless, we still had to do our duties.

There had been one memorable bright spot.

Almost immediately on arriving in Bilfam we had a wonderful surprise waiting there for us, two of my brothers! Anyuon, Deng Ti, Abany and I were a family as we wandered around. That had helped to lessen that fear and make it easier to put up with the despicable living arrangements. Bilfam was built as a town to support the military training of the SPLA. The streets were always crowded with soldiers and running screaming children. Most everyone was in uniform; people that weren't stuck out very plainly from everyone else.

One person in Bilfam really stood out, in a big way!

We had been walking down a dusty street not knowing anyone. We'd got to an open field and I heard two things at once. We had stopped to watch a soccer game that was afoot in a field and someone yelled, "*Agor, pass, pass!*" That got our attention. Then Abany squealed, jumping up and down, "*Oh, oh, look, look.*" She was pointing at our Brother Agor. He was not dressed in any baggy uniform and he did not pass the ball. He was frozen there staring at us. Then he abandoned the ball and ran full tilt over to us with the biggest grin I'd ever seen on him.

Our greeting was like an explosion, "*AGOR!*" we all cried at once with astonished joy.

For Agor the soccer game was finished!

When I heard Agor's story of how he came to be there and not in uniform I couldn't help thinking maybe all of Mama's praying worked! How it came together was really rather a miracle. When Baba went to the refugee camp to build our hut in Itang, he found my brother Agor. He told him he had to give up the Army and go back to school. Agor was then very young and Baba was the head of our family. He had to obey his Father whether he liked it or not. Baba always wanted us to have a good education, telling us education is an important part of living. Agor was sent to Bilfam school after helping Baba build our hut and this was where we found him that day. Instead of fighting he was playing a soccer game!

It was good to know more of our family was now in Bilfam and we would all be going to Cuba together. The only thing I found difficult about Bilfam was that although we were all there in school, we didn't get to see much of each other. My brothers were put into a different barracks for boys and the girls were in a separate barracks. The barracks were not so great either, being of simple construction, not round like our huts but rectangular with long walls made of sticks and mud and flat woven grass roofs. They were unbearably hot with all the bugs that lived with us in simple beds made of wood covered in grass and a blanket. That was it.

Sweating and being bitten to death!

I was beginning to feel badly because of the separation after always having my family there to rely on. My sister was in a different work team and I didn't get to see her much either. I was lonely and getting heartsick. Then, in my work team, I was put with (oh joy) Mana who was one year younger than me. It turned out Mana was Nuer. I really liked her right away. Even though we were from tribes that never had seen eye to eye, she didn't care and was a good friend to me.

We were then worked to death, after getting instruction for a week on what our duties would be. Everyone in the place was strict and it was all about the Party Line. We all shared the responsibilities for our comrades. Our responsibility was working our little fingers to the bone, sweating away what little weight we had, carrying firewood everyday and ha ha, ha, cooking. That was a detail we had to learn fast. Bad cooks didn't last long and got thrown into the latrines for serving horrible food. Cleaning latrines was no fun. Thank God we never had to find out what it was like to be dumped into one. We got to cooking good real fast! Only later did we find out the latrine thing was told to us as a joke by our instructor. Nobody complained and ate everything we cooked no matter how bad it was at first. Nobody ever praised it though either.

Man, we were in the Army now! SPLA's littlest soldiers; Salute, salute, salute!

At least that's what it felt like, to be awoken at the first light and have to go looking for firewood for the cook fires and to carry water. At first it was very hard carrying things on my head. I had seen Mama doing it and it looked easy. I thought, *'I will make her very proud of me!'* It took me some time to master the technique and I had many accidents trying it. On the days when it was our duty, Mana and I would cook breakfast before we went off to school. Then we'd attend classes and go back to the kitchen till sundown. Sometimes by the end of the day we'd just fall into bed dead tired and drop right off to sleep, not caring about the bug bites or anything else. There was no time to really play though Mana and I did find time to fool around some. Before work details, orders or studies, they would remind us what we were there for; hard training with very focused, orderly behaviour expected, everyday!

It wasn't as though I never got to see my brothers and sister. After sundown we were given free time to do whatever there was to do in a small town with not much in it aside from the army. There was a central area where people got together for cultural and social activities, singing and traditional dancing, sitting around fires and sharing stories or just visiting to catch up on the local gossip. I'd go there to meet my siblings and spend time with them. I don't think I would have made it if I'd never had contact with them. Instead, I really enjoyed the dancing and spending time with my family. It was truly a blessing.

I also loved going to school although the classes were quite hard for those being considered to go to school in Cuba. I knew we were already accepted to join Baba there because of his position as an Ambassador, but Baba felt we needed to go to the school with the other children to have the same experience as them. He wanted us to be equal and not to be treated as privileged because of his position. Although I didn't like the Bilfam experience much at all, I was determined to do it for Baba, do all the extra hard work, suffer being separated from everything I considered normal and experience the things he felt I should.

Whatever they might be.

One of the things I enjoyed at first was fishing in the lake to feed our barracks of maybe fifty always hungry girls. We would take along a blanket, go into the water to just above our knees where there was always a lot of fish to catch, Mana would hold two corners and I the other two and we'd scoop them into the blanket and dump our catch on the beach. Four or five times like this and we had enough for the day. Well, after a while, it got to be just another chore. Really it wasn't my style to be a fisherwoman, and besides, I found fishing to be rather a smelly thing to be doing. After carrying the catch back to camp on my head, I smelled fishy for days after!

After two and a half months of this, and not once hearing from my Mama, I was homesick and wanted to run away from it all. I discovered some of the other children were secretly talking about exactly the same thing! We got together and did quite the bellyaching; whining and complaining about conditions and talking about missing our families. The group came to the conclusion we should just leave this horrible place and go back to the UN Camp. Maybe we'd have a much better life back there we thought. I spent a lot of time missing my family, even though my siblings were with me because they had their duties too. Most of all I missed Mama. I felt sick and frustrated that there was no way of telling her I didn't want to be there any more. It was the older children who had planned the escape but we'd found out about it and wanted to tag along. We'd had enough of the hard work and horrid living conditions and it seemed like a good idea, even knowing of some of the obvious dangers along the way.

We got stopped right at the front gate after what was a long walk and farther away than we thought. The guard asked, "Where's your pass please."

Pass? What was that? This was how well we'd thought this out. We figured we could just walk out and go home. No way, it was more complicated than that. OK, the older ones said, we'd need a better plan. This front gate and a guard weren't going to stop those determined runaways. Some others thought leaving wasn't such a good idea after all. I was one of those to come to my senses and obey those in authority. We separated ourselves from those sneaking out of Bilfam and went back to accept further tortures, brutal routines and bloody fingers. *Damn dishes, scrubbing floors and stinky fish!*

Our group got back without being missed, but oh man, when the other children were found to be missing, it created a great big stink! After searching everywhere in Bilfam, a large party was sent out into the surrounding countryside looking for them but they were not found. We sat tight and hoped no one would ask us where they might be. Then we'd be in big trouble! The next day, there was another wave of hectic activity and the telegraph was just jumping with gossip. *'One of the runaway boys has been shot!'* At first this was all we heard and we wondered who it might be and how did he get himself shot? We soon found out from official reports how dumb and dangerous it was for them to leave.

None of us had known the Nyagats had been raiding over the border!

A patrol of SPLA soldiers had been sent out to deal with a raid and the runaways had got caught in the middle of the firefight. Manyok Garnade was wounded in the shoulder in the battle. Lucky for them the SPLA soldiers found them and brought them back to Bilfam. It was really a dumb idea. I was so glad I hadn't followed them and gotten into so much trouble. Mama would have just tanned my hide; at least that what I was thinking at the time. *'Whew!'* We others never did get discovered and never said anything to anyone outside our secret little group. We were deathly afraid that the punishment would be extra work details.

It took some time for the news of the runaways to travel on the tribal grapevine for Mama to hear of it. She was very worried thinking her children might have been among those who had left Bilfam and had got into such a dangerous situation.

There were many different theories in the excited gossip as to why the children had run away, with the poor conditions being one. It was exaggerated however out of all proportion with stories of us being starved, beaten or abused. The idea they were just homesick for their loved ones was put aside for juicier and more dramatic rumours to speculate about. The most likely explanation appealed more to Mama's character, but she couldn't help but hear the rest and it made her heart heavy with wondering. Knowing how attached I was to her, Mama thought I just might do this very thing.

Bilfam's poor conditions were much the same as the refugee camp. There was a lot of illness such as diarrhoea, malaria, skin problems, cholera, and hepatitis. It was bad. A lot of people died from these diseases and sometimes no one knew from what. Those who survived these conditions were very lucky. I guess my family and I were no exception. Knowing the conditions, and hearing about the runaways, made Mama very worried for her children. She wished she could take all of us out of there and the U.N. camp but she knew she couldn't.

It was weeks after the actual event that Mama heard of it through local gossip. She had finally received the invitation to go to Cuba to be with Baba. It would take some time for the authorizations and travel arrangements to go through, but she didn't want me to spend any more time in Bilfam while she waited. She decided she would come to Bilfam and visit us, and if conditions were as bad as she'd heard, would take me with her back to Itang. Then we could wait together while she found how Baba was arranging for our trip.

Mama is quite determined once she makes her mind up and somehow she got some extra food for us and set out for Bilfam. She wanted to find out for herself how her children were doing. To say that I was happy to see Mama would be a total understatement; I was beside myself with joy to see her again. I was also a little nervous she might find out about our little ordeal and that I was a part of it. We weren't a picture of health. We all looked pretty skinny for the short time we'd been in Bilfam. I looked very dusty and unkempt without shoes and my hair looked very bad. I looked worse than usual because I had no one there like Mama to fuss over me. Each one of us had to look after ourselves but we had no time to ourselves to really do it.

I told her it was my day for cooking and that I had to go before I got into trouble. I promised I'd come back just as soon as I was done my duties. Mama accepted that, but I could see she was really bothered by what she was seeing. She looked me over and only nodded and said nothing as I ran off to hurry through my work and get back to her. I then skipped the barracks meal, knowing Mama was preparing a meal for us with the food she had brought with her. She had arranged a fairly private place provided for family visits and such things to hold this gathering with her much missed children.

We didn't know it at the time, but sadly it would be the last meal we'd have all together like that for a very long time.

The meal she prepared was very simple but no meal tastes as good as one prepared by Mama's own hand. It was like heaven! For the first part of our gathering there were happy faces all round and all of us felt the same. For the first time since I'd arrived in Bilfam I felt full. Although there wasn't enough for second helpings, I couldn't have eaten another bite anyway, and I actually said that to Mama. Then she asked, "come Acuach Cor, tell me all about your time here?" My response to her request would change the whole face of the gathering and almost break my heart.

I started with what I liked about it most; my time in school and classes. I said it was rather hard at first but I liked my teachers and enjoyed the challenges of putting my mind to work. I wanted to do well, both for my self respect and for my family. For a time we all took turns and I noticed my brothers and sister, like me, were only saying things that wouldn't worry Mama. I figured she knew that too.

I don't remember the specific question she asked me, only the way it was put, and well, that was that. I started to pour it all out; how much I didn't like what I had to do, the cooking, cleaning, looking after the barracks, fishing, carrying water everyday on my head. Mama smiled as I told her I tried to do it just as well as she did and that it took a lot of practice. As I became more animated on how much I hated it there, even Deng Ti tried to give me a look to stop and not needlessly worry Mama.

Well, I was on a roll, pointing out how harsh things were, not really paying attention to how it might be affecting Mama. I started into my biggest fear, that it wasn't a healthy environment. I talked about the white parasite that got under the skin and ate away at the muscle. The only way to remove it was with a needle. We had no idea what type of parasite it was and nobody could tell us or how to treat it. It was said that when the military built Bilfam they brought in sand from the lake and with it came the parasite. They thought that putting sand down would help when the rains came, but when they did there also came a lot of illness. I said I'd seen many people, including children, carried out in sheets having died from this and that to be buried.

I had to stop because Mama just broke right down in front of us crying.

She wailed; she never had thought it would be that bad. "If I had known, I would never have agreed to bring you all to this place!" she said. She covered her face and sobbed. She couldn't stop crying and it was as if she was talking to her self, saying things like, *'why do we have to live like this after all the good life we had in BorTown? I'm so very sad for all my children and wish Baba was here. How I miss him and wish this war had never happened!* It was heart breaking, to see. And it was my fault.

None of us had ever seen Mama lose it this way. She was always the strong one there for our every need. She had been holding it in and hiding from us her increasing worry. Now we saw how this string of events had effected her. It became obvious to us then as she shivered and shook through her torment and river of tears. We were all stunned at first and just gawked at the scene, so unlike our Mother. Finally Mama wrapped me in her arms and sobbed, *"I'm taking you home out of this horrible place Acuach Cor, but how can I leave my other children here? How can I do that?"*

She held me the harder and continued crying, soaking me with her tears. That brought us to our senses and now it was all about Mama! Her children came to her and hugged and kissed her, assuring Mama it would be all right. Agor, Anyon, Deng Ti swore to her they were men now; they could handle Bilfam, to not worry for them. Abany just clung to Mama and cried for all she was worth. I thought it had effected Abany the most and when Mama had settled down she took her for a walk and spoke just to her.

What was done was done and couldn't be changed. It was hard for all of us to say our good-byes there in Bilfam. I was glad to be off and away from the place but more than a little guilty my brothers and sister had to stay behind. If it had been up to Mama, she would have taken all of us home with her right then. Her frustration was in not being able to communicate directly and personally with Baba. He wanted his children to be in Bilfam with the other children so they could go on to be educated in Cuba. She couldn't go against his wishes, no matter how much it hurt her not to do so. Mama never would.

Baba was a very important man in the SPLM/A movement. He was one of the few diplomats with very high morals. He always took his job and responsibilities very seriously, always setting an example for others to follow. He was a man with a big heart, helping others when ever he could. It didn't matter to him if you were very poor, he would help anyone who tried to do his best. He believed we needed to experience the trials the people were suffering to win Independence for Southern Sudan. Living in Bilfam was a trial his children would learn from. Mama could do no less than support her husband, heart and soul, so without his express permission to leave Bilfam, Agor, Anyon, Deng Ti and Abany stayed behind. I left with Mama for Itang.

Once again my life was changing and changing quickly as I was only to stay in Itang one week. Of course I was as happy to see my little brothers again as they were to see me. Also I found my sister Achol Tariff had left army training in Bilfam because she had become very sick and was now back in Itang with Mama as well.

It was about then Mama received word the SPLA had made arrangements for us to stay in Addis Ababa, the capital city of Ethiopia, while waiting for our papers to be processed to go to Cuba. Mama made doubly sure my brothers and my sister in Bilfam were placed on the list too. She wanted to be sure her other children would be following us to Cuba. Her great fear was that somehow mistakes might be made and her children might not arrive to be with the family. It was bad enough leaving them in Bilfam; to think of leaving them on a different continent was just about unthinkable for her.

The officials assure Mama it was so; she need not worry, all the administrative work was in order. Only then did she turn to the packing and preparations to leave yet another temporary house of sticks.

I managed at least some play time with my old friend and neighbour, Andoya. She was really happy to see me again and then sad to find out I would be leaving so soon.

I realized later it was common for us Sudanese refugees to have friends and relations come into our lives again after many years of separation and hardship. So it was with my friend Andoya, as her Father and mine were friends and worked together in the SPLM. At the time we had no idea we would find each other again in Cuba.

I was really happy to say goodbye to the refugee camp and leave the misery of Bilfam behind me. Now I can look back and see how fortunate we were to have gotten out of Sudan at the beginning of a Civil War, but as a little girl I had no perspective to judge, just my own experience. How could I have known the civil war would go on for twenty-two years, cost over a million lives and force many more to flee the country?

Itang would eventually become for a time the largest refugee camp in the world. It would have more than 150,000 people crowded into its small area before it was officially closed in 2008. Many people were born there and knew no other life except basic survival conditions. With no shops, no employment and no resources, they relied entirely on the U.N. for subsistence. We fortunate few got a chance at something better, we just didn't know it yet. This too however, would hold its own hardships and challenges.

All this was still ahead of me.

Soon my childhood and life in Africa would come to an end. I would leave our Motherland for a foreign country half way round the world. I'd be among 600 Sudanese children accepted from Bilfam to be educated in Cuba. I didn't have to qualify to attend this program; it was my father's position in the SPLM that gave me the opportunity to leave my Africa and get an education. Otherwise I wouldn't have had a chance. Me, Sarah Gabriel; I was just one person out of so many; our one family, one family out of all the families that suffered through those war torn years. We children, we earned the distinction, *the Lost Children of Sudan.*

This is what the future, held for me; Acuach Cor of the Dinka Tribe.

Chapter 8
Life in the Mansion

At the end of the week the SPLA proved they indeed had all our travel details worked out; a Land Rover pulled up right in front of our hut. It took no time to load our possessions because Mama had decided to leave a lot behind. She knew the people who lived around us could use the odds and ends she'd collected. We wouldn't need to take much with us beyond our clothes. With the bags packed, we all settled into our seats with a thrill of excitement. Then, our driver took the Land Rover out and away from the UN Camp.

As Itang receded into the distance, I don't believe any of us even turned to look back. In the distance we could see the land rising out of the river valley and the winding, dusty road leading on to majestic cloud capped mountains. Mama, of course, had elected to sit in the front with Achol. I was in the back keeping a firm hand on Yong and Chol. Our driver Omar it turned out was a novel experience too. Soon our bumpy, dusty ride changed as we turned onto a smooth, paved highway. So many experiences that day were new and different. It had been a long while since I'd ridden in a vehicle of any description, but I'd never glided along over roads that had no dust and dirt rising from them. Omar laughed. With a big smile he told me it was called pavement. I could tell Omar was a very good man. All through the trip he was always laughing and smiling and answering the many questions about everything ... from well, everybody; sometimes asking all at once!

For the first part of our trip to the mountains The Land Rover was a chatter box filled with a high level of excitement. We learned that Omar was, of course, an SPLA member, but not only that, he was proud to be the official chauffeur who drove for John Garang, chairman of the SPLM and leader of the army. This gave rise to more thoughts about Baba and just how much influence he had within the party. We enjoyed the stories that Omar shared with us about his job. We, for our part, shared stories of our home in Sudan and life before the war. Not once did we talk of the hardships and horror we had lived through. All in all, it was a happy trip.

Aside from that there were the ordinary travel things, like the boys jumping up and down pointing at passing wildlife. When they weren't doing that they were playing noisy games and fighting, Achol trying hard not to yell at them. Like all kids they always wanted to stop and have a pee, often enough that it really annoyed Mama. At one such stop she decided it was a good place, with a beautiful view, to have a bite to eat. We were now at the edge of the mountain range and would soon be climbing steeply. From where we sat, we could see the highway snake its way up and into the mountains. 'Oh wow,' I thought, "such huge mountains!"

I couldn't help feeling maybe happy times might come back to us. Maybe up past those clouds and over those very high mountains waited a new and better life for our family. As we started into them, the noise level dropped right off and Omar looking much more serious, concentrating hard on his driving.

It was breathtaking. The roads were very windy and terribly narrow. To pass big trucks on this impossible road, we had to move very close to the edge. This was scary! It felt at any moment as if we were going to fall over into the abyss below. Even Mama was frightened through this section, though she tried not to show it. The nice part was looking at the lush green valleys and the exhilarating beauty of the rugged mountains and lakes out our windows. We finally went over the highest pass and began to descend more the same kind of hair raising twisty mountain roads. That again challenged Omar!

Mama visibly relaxed as the highway widened out, became more level and filled with traffic coming and going. I had never before seen so many types of vehicles all in the same place as they zipped by. Then the city of Addis Ababa appeared on the horizon and soon we arrived at our destination. I felt I was in a dream. We were back in civilization again although it was nothing like BorTown and not anything close to what I knew. I had never seen so many large buildings! Everywhere I looked there were amazing things to see. It was all so different from Sudan. The houses had this beautiful grass that covered the ground and was ever so green. Trees lined the streets and flowers were everywhere. So many people were in different clothing. It was so picturesque. I couldn't believe I was going to be living there. The biggest surprise yet was the house we were going to live in.

The house we arrived at was for leading party members when in Addis Ababa on SPLM/A party business. We would stay there as long as we needed to before leaving for Cuba. This huge two story mansion in the Doble Zeid district was like some thing out of a story book. Even to get to the house, you had to push a button at the huge gates that guarded the grounds and they opened all by themselves. Then 'wow,' up a beautiful flower lined drive that led to this unbelievable grandeur. I was totally blown away by the place. It wasn't a house, it was a gigantic Palace and oh so beautiful! There were marvellous gardens everywhere you looked. I couldn't get it into my head that we were really going to live there. My eyes seemed to bug right out of my head and my mouth dropped open. I couldn't take everything in, there was too much to see. I couldn't believe there were actually people in the world who lived like this.

This was definitely, not Itang ... no, no way!

The main floor had a huge entrance lobby where we could meet guests when they came to see us. I thought it was big enough that all of us could live right there. The living room with a marble mantle against one whole wall with vases all along filled with fresh flowers and there seemed to be too many places that you could sit. It had huge tall glass windows and double glass doors that looked out over the gardens that were a riot of colour. The rolling green lawns seemed to have no end.

It was the library that really messed with my mind. It had so many books from floor to ceiling it made Baba's library seem really small. We were not allowed to use any of these rooms. That was all right with me; there were still plenty of places we could go and things we could do with out worrying about being attacked by the Murle Bahre or the Nyagat, or Siwar Al-Deheb's men, or lions, or snakes. Man, I was in heaven, and safe! My heart soared. It was all just too unbelievable. A fantasy.

Holy cow; the formal dining room could seat at least 20 people. It was only used when the SPLM/A came and Mama make a big feast for them. There was another smaller dinning room off the kitchen where the family could eat. It had sliding glass doors that went out onto a furnished patio. We could also eat there and that was my favourite place. We could tumble around on the grass and not worry about breaking anything! The kitchen was also enormous. I thought our kitchen was huge back in Bor but this was out of this world. Everything was right there. I could get a glass of cold water right from the tap! There was so much storage space and it was filled with every kind of food you could imagine. There were things I had never heard of or seen before, or even thought you could eat!

The house came with a live-in maid. Her room was also on the main floor and there were also two rooms for servants. The maid did every thing and wouldn't let Mama do anything. This was good because Mama really needed the rest. She had gone through a lot getting us here. I can tell you mama truly enjoyed having herself a maid. The laundry room was another marvel. I had never seen machines that washed your clothes and then dried them. Yes, this was certainly not Bilfam!

Mama didn't have to carry water to a wash tub or take the laundry out to the river Nile the way we had to do in the dry season. There was no more carrying for her to do. Most Sudanese women are used to carrying everything on their head from firewood, water, provisions and many other things. Here, not even the maid had to carry things.

This was an easy life for sure, the kind worldly people had for themselves.

On the second floor I was given a whole room all to myself. It was one of the seven bedrooms! It had a huge double bed I could get lost in and the mattress was so comfy and, had no lumps! Even the sheets didn't wrinkle as you slept. It was the first time I'd slept in a bed all by myself. It even had curtains made of heavy burgundy velvet that came all the way to the floor. I could close them with a cord that hung on one side and they didn't let the light in with the morning. There were two lamps, one on each side of the bed on two neat small tables. There were dresser drawers that my stuff got lost in and a closet that I would never use. I had more than enough room to make up my endless little girl fantasies and play in.

What was best was we now had bathrooms every where with hot and cold running water and indoor flushing toilets. Nobody ever told me I had to take a bath; I was always the first to take a shower or have a bath. I couldn't get enough of the clean fresh water from a shower or lazing in a tub full of water. That was a luxury not even heard of in Bor. We didn't have to worry if it was raining to go to the toilet or wake up in the middle of the night worrying there might be a Lion to be eaten by or huge long snakes in the hallways. In this new life we had somehow borrowed I felt like a princes in a fairy tale. Like Cinderella I had been found in the country and taken to a palace.

Mama's bathroom was right there in her room. She had the largest room of all of us. It even had a sofa in it where she could read or take tea, and a balcony that you could walk out on to that over looked the gardens and had a great view of the nearby lake. Her bed was bigger than huge. All of us could fit in it with plenty room left over.

At times my brothers and I got on it and bounce around all over it!

Of course this grand house was way too big for only five of us. I had a pang of guilt for my family back in Bilfam, but God willing they would be united with us very soon. I knew they would really enjoy all the food here, especially the abundant fruit. An orchard in the grounds was full of different fruit and vegetables. There were Guava, Mango, Papaya, Lime, Lemon, and many more different types. Outside there was so much we could do. I spent most of the time out there playing with my little brothers, running around in the orchard and eating all the fruit we could get away with.

After three months we were feeling pretty much settled in and I had forgotten it was my birthday. Of course Mama would never let me forget that. I didn't know Baba had sent us new clothes from Cuba and they had a little surprise party for me. It wasn't very large as we didn't have any real friends other than family. So Mama invited Auntie Maid, as we called her, as they were now fast friends and she was considered part of the family. Mama even did house work with her when she got bored, just to help her out.

They were good at pulling it off too. By the time I did remember my birthday was only days away, I remembered a lot! I remembered Mama's promise the day the poor cow got killed that she would have a birthday party for me when we got to Ethiopia. Well now here we were in Ethiopia and Mama hadn't said anything to me. All day I moped around thinking nobody loves me! I never thought Mama would ever lie to me. I spent the whole afternoon walking in the orchard feeling sorry for myself. Then I heard Mama yelling, "*Acuach Cor, come in for dinner. Right now!*" She sounded almost angry.

When I got to the back patio, there they all were. They screamed, "HAPPY BIRTHDAY!" Of course Mama hadn't forgotten me.

Mama had made my favourite dish Anjera along with banana Custard that was so yummy. The biggest surprise was the present beside my plate, all beautifully wrapped in real birthday paper. It didn't last long. I tore it apart to see what it was. It was a wonderful pink dress that fit me just right! It had a cloth belt that tied in the back with a tail. In Sudan you say '*Taly Waraie*' which means in Arabic, '*follow me*'. For the rest of the day, my brothers ran along where ever I went following me. Oh how I loved that dress. I even brought it with me to Canada years later to remind me of Mama's lovely small birthday party in Ethiopia.

There were many dinner parties held for SPLA leaders who came to the mansion for various official reasons. When Mama came down the stairs for the first dinner party, I was totally enchanted. I had never seen her all dressed up before. How beautiful she looked wearing our traditional African dress very elegantly with a wrap of the same material around her head like a crown. It was set off with her gold arrow earrings and necklace. The dress was lemon yellow with black and emerald green and she wore lovely black shoes. Mama looked simply stunning. My sister Achol too was very beautiful. When she dressed up she would really glow! She also wore very elegant African dresses with beautiful curly extensions in her hair. She also put on gold arrow earrings and necklace and looked captivating. Both Mama and Achol looked so beautiful, but it was a very special treat to see my Mother all decked out like a Queen.

I wore one of my best dresses that Mama bought me when we moved to the big house. She also bought me gold arrow earrings, as I had lost mine in grandma's village during the Murle Bahre attack. Yong and Chol wore dress pants and short sleeved shirts and had their hair cut. They looked altogether too cute!

For these dinner affairs Mama had a lot of help from Auntie Maid. They would plan the dinners together and usually come up with something unique or a mixture of Sudanese and Ethiopian foods. We would have Angera, which is an Ethiopian food. It looks like pita bread, but is thinner and little bit sour. We would eat it with one of the meat dishes that had Bervery in it or some of the Sudanese dishes, meats with Okra, or Molokai. All these special dishes always turned out deliciously. My brothers and I were told to sit and eat very quietly when there were adults dining with us. If we didn't, we would be sent off to bed and miss all the funny things the adults talked about. We felt very important to be eating with so many distinguished people and I liked it when they laughed over their adult topics. It reminded me so much of Baba and how he interacted with people at gatherings like this.

When Baba was appointed Ambassador, I was really proud of him. I knew he had gotten a very important job even though I hadn't a clue what it meant. All I knew was that my father was an educated man and an example to his children and his community. I and all my brothers and sisters admired him very much! I loved Baba not for the things he would give us, but for the wisdom that he passed on to his children and exercised in his family. He was a very busy man and wasn't around all that much, but when he was there he made it count. I felt my parents were good examples of a well balanced marriage; they consulted each other in all their decisions.

Because my father wasn't present for these diplomatic affairs, it was up to Mama to represent him with the SPLA leaders and their families. We too were expected to be on our best behaviour and represent the qualities of our family. Mama carried this roll so very well and with a gracious dignity, I felt Mama really was a queen. She fitted right into my fantasy of living in a grand palace representing matters of State.

Life turned out to be very good there in the big house and seven months went by rather quickly. They were happy times and made good memories for me. I didn't know how I felt about the idea of leaving my palace and kingdom behind. I was really just beginning to feel confident that life would work out and that our worst times were over. When we got news the final selection had been made of children who were going to Cuba, everything began to pick up speed again. I had the feeling of moving into the unknown again, of everything up in the air.

We knew one group of 300 had already left for Cuba on a Soviet ship. My brother and sister were in a second group of again about three hundred that would be travelling by plane. I was to travel to Cuba with Mama, Achol, Yong and Chol by plane as well, at a later date.

I was very happy for my siblings and for the other students who had qualified for this program. When they arrived in Addis Ababa, we went to see them at the dorm where they were billeted. Needles to say, it was an emotional reunion. It was awesome to be all together again, even though they weren't the healthiest looking children. Their skin was dry and their feet were all cracked from not having shoes for a long time. It was hard on Mama to see them that way and she cried a lot, but not out of sadness. She was crying for happiness that they were finally out of Bilfam and in relatively good health. A short time later some were released to travel but a few had to stay behind for medical reasons. Well, my brothers and sister were officially off to Cuba! I was disappointed I couldn't be at the airport to see them off, but I knew we'd all be together again soon so it didn't affect me that badly.

We were given our travel papers three weeks later. We would be travelling with the students who had stayed behind for medical reasons. It was exciting; all those last minute preparations. We knew we were going to experience many new things and meet many different people in a culture I knew nothing about. Well that, and the fact I had never been on an airplane before. That was probably what I was most excited about. There were many things for Mama to be all hectic over and at times rather cranky and short with us children. We were forever wanting to know things and bugging her with all kinds of questions. It was sad to say good bye to the big house in Doble Zeid at the same time exiting to be officially off to Cuba and into another new world not knowing what was in store for us. Our imagination was becoming more and more real.

Then at last, it was really time to go to the airport.

Wow!

We flew out of Ethiopia that morning in what I thought was a very long flight, going all the way to the southwest coast of Africa to Luanda, Angola. There we had a lay-over for a week. We were met by a Cuban military officer and taken to a military base where we were to stay. My little brothers and I would not shut up about aeroplanes and everyone got tired of hearing about it, especially Achol! Still, we thought that was the most awesome thing we had ever experienced, zooming through thin air on wings.

I really enjoyed our time at the Military base; these Cubans it seemed to me were a very happy people. They were always in high spirits and, although we didn't speak the language, it gave me an insight into what we were about to experience. Just listening to Spanish being spoken seemed a pleasure. I liked the sound; it was very musical and I looked forward to learning it. I also noted these soldiers lived in an organized and healthy environment compared to what our poor military in Bilfam had to contend with. The soldiers would play with us and take out their guitars and sing and dance with such energy. I felt warmly welcomed to be a guest among them. I was now really looking forward to going to Cuba and learning the language and experiencing the culture of such a gracious people.

We weren't in Angola very long and we didn't get to see too much of it. When we were driven to and from the base, we were able to see some of the sites; enough to know Luanda was a very beautiful place. We didn't get to tour around, but we did have the run of the base and I enjoyed our time there very much. With its clean air and the nice breeze on my face, I enjoyed taking it all in. I didn't want to forget these experiences since everybody was so nice to me. I couldn't understand what they were saying, in that the people of Angola working at the base spoke Portuguese, but it was amazing just listening to them. We left Angola in the early morning and it was on to our next destination; *'Cuba!'*

Yet another phase of my life was about to begin for Sarah.

Chapter 9
Arrival in Cuba, July 1986

We touched down at Jose Martin airport in Havana at 6:00AM in the morning, tired after our long flight but excited to soon be reunited with our Baba. So much had happened to all of us during the separation. On the plane I had many hours to plan what I would tell him. I also thought over what I wouldn't, or even maybe couldn't, say. There were things my young mind had already blocked out. I now had gaps in my memory where I knew things happened that were no longer there. My mind couldn't picture them. It just skipped quickly by to the next chain of events, to this event.

Now, I only thought of Baba.

The anticipation as we crossed to the terminal was so intense, I wanted to break away from everybody and run to see if Baba was really in that building. So many fears were running back and forth across my heart. So many times had my hopes been crushed and for one reason or another. Baba was not where I expected him. We quickly cleared customs as a group and entered the arrivals area where many people were waiting. I felt my heart pounding in my chest and I wiped my sweaty palms against the edges of my skirt. My eyes moved rapidly back and forth through this room full of strangers. Mama, holding her youngest children's hands on each side, was doing the same.

Then suddenly Mama, Achol Yong, Chol and I found Baba there smiling hugely waiting for us. All was well. A small group of students had assembled to greet the ambassador a little way from our family. When I saw Baba step forward with glowing eyes for us instead, my first thought was that I was finally going to live with my Father. He was going to protect and be with us forever! I ran to him for a big hug and was elated to be folded into his arms again and let me tell him how much I loved and missed him. I so wanted him to be there with us, to show him my admiration every day of my life. It reminded me how I missed the time he spent with us in Sudan when he came home to be with his family. There was a lot of time that Baba was away like this on party business, and yet he created so much fun with us. I felt sure, even if it was for a short time, our Baba would try his best to be there for us. It was just in his nature to be a very dutiful Father!

Baba did spend a little time with all of us, then he moved off to greet the waiting students in his role as Ambassador ... *'duty, duty, duty.'*

Darn it!

I was more than a bit jealous when Baba did this. It seemed as if it was more important to him to welcome the students than receive his own Family, even though he had seen us first.

I got over this flood of angry thoughts quickly, this selfishness on my part. I felt proud to be Gabriel Achuoth's daughter! After all, it was his job to welcome them to their new life in Cuba too. Baba looked much bigger than life as we all listened intently to his words of welcome. When all was said and done, it was just good to see Baba again after such a long separation. I was happy knowing that finally I was going to live with both my Parents. It had long been my earnest wish; to see them together as a couple again.

All too soon I found my hopes were to be dashed. I was going to be left without them both! I heard Baba telling Mama my brother Yong and I were going to Isla de la Juventud (the Island of Youth) with all the students from Bilfam he'd just been speaking to. I was utterly heartbroken to hear this from my loving parents. Our Father told Yong and me right there, we were going to live with the other Sudanese children and shortly would be getting on the bus with them. He said it would be good for us to stay with the Bilfam students so we could keep our culture alive and still speak Arabic and Dinka with one another. Baba said very seriously if we stayed in Havana we would go to school with Cuban children and, since we were still very young, it would be easy for us to forget our origins and culture.

I was then praying Mama would convince him to let us stay with them, because I really, really, really, wanted to stay with the family in Havana. I couldn't imagine myself living without my Parents again. I was again greatly let down as Mama agreed with him and they did indeed send us with the Sudanese children to that island.

You could say, *'I was not real happy with this decision!'*

But I was resigned to it and knew that I would have to obey my Father. Ultimately I would have to get used to this separation again. It was so sad; I wanted to live with them both, but we had no choice. They told us we could come home on holidays and that they'd visit us as well. They said we were luckier than the other children because their parents were far away, whereas we had them to love and care about us. That wasn't much of a consolation at the time. It just didn't seem fair!

I tried a different angle to convince Baba to let us come to Havana with them. I thought I'd ask Baba about cooking. "Do I have to cook for a lot of children again?" I said in all seriousness. Then I started babbling; telling Baba that in Bilfam all the children had to live without parents and as a result we had to cook and clean up after ourselves. I said my partner for cooking was Mana who was one year younger than me and that she was from Nuer and we got along very well! I told him I had enough with the past and I didn't wanted to experience that situation again. He laughed, of course, knowing what I was up to and said that everything was going to be just fine. I would never have problems like I had in Bilfam or Itang ever again.

"Acuach Cor," he said, "you're going to love living with the other children . . . *on that Island!*"

No, no way. Nothing was going to convince Baba to change his mind. I sighed and thought, oh well. I gave in.

Baba went on to tell me he was glad I was able to get along with Mana. There were a lot of different tribes in Sudan and we all needed to get along with one another. He promised me things were going to be different in Cuba. I would enjoy the other children's company and make lots of friends.

"Sarah," he said, "study very hard so you can have a brilliant future when you grow up and go back to a new Sudan. Take advantage of this because you are very lucky to have this opportunity!" He reminded us that most other children in Sudan would never have this opportunity. My parents said goodbye and put us on the bus. I tried not to cry, but as the bus pulled away I just couldn't hold it back anymore. Tears ran down my cheeks and all over my new clothes. I couldn't stop feeling abandoned.

Yong was a tough kid and, in a way, always had been. He wouldn't show his emotions. He sat there very quietly and every once in a while would turn and watch me. I wished he would come over and sit with me to give me some comfort over all this, but he didn't. Yong had changed a lot since our Border Run. When he was young he was loud and rather boisterous and fought with everyone. The other kids were scared of him because he carried rocks to throw at people who made him angry. Sometimes he even punched me really hard. At other times he was very good to me and in some other ways he made friends very easily. Now, he was reserved and shy about crowds. Later I considered that possibly he was feeling much the same as I did but he was trying to be the tough guy and not show his emotions. The last thing he wanted to do was to break down like me and cry . . . like a girl; to be weak. That's what that look back had said to me in a glance.

The bus took Yong and me and the other children to a ferry that would take us to the Island of Youth (La Isla de La Juventud). The Island was called that because there were many boarding schools there with children from many different countries.

My sister Abany and my three brothers Agor, Anyon and Deng Ti were already on the Island. Achol was to be going to military school in Havana and our youngest brother Chol stayed with my parents because he was not ready for school.

Lucky him, I figured!

On the bus I tried to picture our new life in Batalla de Kore, Number 12 School, imagining what it would be like. I wasn't all that worried because Baba had assured me everything would be all right. I had a very good picture of everything in my mind from what Baba had told us. Of course it didn't turn out anything like I imagined; it never does. The reality of the years I would spend there would prove this for sure!

When we got to the ferry I was amazed because I'd never seen anything like it. Almost picture post card perfect, it was very elegant and classy and looked like something out of the movies. Inside I was amazed at how big it was; everything looked so clean and white. There were a lot of people on its two levels. I liked the top level best because we could go up and look out over the water.

I was dazzled by it all! I had never been so close to the ocean. It was really clear and blue. You could even see the fish swimming. Most extraordinary were the whales we could see jumping into the air as if to put on a show for us. Man, they were so big, and when they came down on the water they did so with such a huge splash. Even swimming they would leave a long wake behind. It was amazing! The seagulls were flying above us, sweeping in on the people who had food for them. I'd never seen this type of bird before and they followed the boat all the way to the island. They were graceful but very noisy. All of this felt like a dream in my head; a vision that was portrayed before me trance like.

Oh boy did I enjoy the cafeteria; *yum, yum, yum,* and especially the music being played on speakers while we ate. I loved the Latin rhythm even though I couldn't understand the language. It was so musical and full of life. I decided I wanted to learn Spanish very quickly! *To this day, I love Salsa music the most.* Anything to do with Salsa! Like the spicy music and the food I discovered on that ferry...

So yum, yum, *yummy!*

I enjoyed being on that ship so much it didn't matter that it took hours and hours to get us to the island. As I sat and thought over all that had taken place. Then I thought about the people, the music and the language. I would stop awhile to study these Cubans. It was all just so different; they seemed like such happy people. I tried to understand what they were saying by watching their movements. They actually seemed to be talking with their bodies; their hands moved with everything they said. It looked as if they were using sign language, moving their head, hands, arms and shoulders. It was neat to watch. Though I was no closer to understanding what they were communicating with one another, I decided I really liked Cuba from the moment I had arrived.

When we finally arrived on the Island there was a bus waiting for us to take us to our destination; Number 12 Batalla de Korre, the boarding school we were to attend and where we were going to live for many years to come. On the way to the school we passed through Nueva Gerona, the capital of Isla de la Juventud. I was intrigued with everything. To see horses pulling people around in carts was amazing, even oxen pulling carts. In my country we never used our cattle that way. We passed through the town and kept on driving. Now there wasn't much to see anymore, just miles of grapefruit orchards. I wondered how much further we'd have to go.

Soon the bus turned on to a side road that went to our brand new boarding school, standing alone in the middle of nowhere looking very modern. I could see quite a few children walking along the side of the road. When they saw our bus they all started to applaud. I found this surprising and wondered why. Later I learned they had been expecting our arrival. The teachers had told them to make us feel welcome to our new home. Just then the bus driver stopped the bus and said to us in Spanish, "Bienvenido a su nuevo hogar has llegado." (*Welcome to your new home, you have arrived!*)

When I got off the bus, I was amazed to see a lot of familiar faces that I'd lived with in Bilfam. Except now they looked much cleaner, healthier and happier. They were all wearing shoes and smiling beautifully. It filled my heart to see them. It was confirmation of the positive feelings I'd had on our trip to the school. Now seeing these students and how well they looked and how contented they appeared, I realized things were probably not too bad, just as Baba had promised us. At least some of my many fears fell away. I still wondered though how we would get on here without our families to take care of us.

There was a bit of minor confusion right away. Yong and I were the only children who were not wearing uniforms. The other students had got their uniforms at the airport while my brother and I met Baba. Yong and I were not included on the list of students who were going to the island so the students and Sudanese teachers who had come from Bilfam didn't know Yong and I were coming. We were not supposed to be going to school on the island. They understood we were going to stay in Havana with my parents. They didn't even recognize me because I was much cleaner and more nicely dressed than I had been in Bilfam. My brothers and sister were surprised to see us as well. They had thought the same as everyone else had thought. That was one happy reunion I can tell you!

And so my very different education began in this Caribbean country half way round the world away from my homeland. There were 601 Sudanese students attending Number 12 Batalla de Korre. There were 61 girls and the rest were boys; 540 of them. The school was assigned for only Sudanese students. We represented all the many tribes of Sudan. None of them held much love for each other. This would prove to be a very interesting experiment.

At times, *a violent one* . . .

Chapter 10
Reunited in Cuba

I didn't understand the political ideology that fuelled this idea, this idea that had provided this school just for us Sudanese. In a way I still don't. I didn't really find political ideology that interesting. I imagine it was a type of socialist programming. These years of the 1980's were a time when the world was involved in a conflict of ideologies. Leftist or far rightist, mostly I knew nothing about any of it. They had placed us on an Island and created for us an Island unto ourselves; an island of isolation where we would be kept, educated, raised... forgotten.

Here we were; a group of children taken away from unimaginable terrors, the basest kind of living conditions, and flown to a tropical paradise. To us it was an unimaginable modern world, a marvel we had nothing to compare with. For the first two months, to get used to this modern ideological structure, we kind of divided it up and made it into something we were familiar with...tribal Sudan.

Our School was made up of a lot of different Sudanese tribes. The majority were The Nilotic divided up into Dinka, Nuer, Jur (Jo Luo), Shuluk and Anuak. The Murle were of the Nilo-Hamitic C group. In Sudan major conflicts between the Dinka and the Nuer tribes had been going on for many years.

The in-between times, when we weren't involved in learning the program and routines, taught us what life was all about. We were on an island, but being a youth is an island in itself. It's a forming time, spent inside one's self, puzzling over the changes we're undergoing and deciding what we want to become. I was striving to fit in with some group, to be accepted, to hang out, to start friendships. I needed bonds to help deal with these changing foreign ideas.

In Bilfam all of the students had a common enemy; one that all South Sudan must fight or die. Here we had no enemy other than ourselves. In this, my family and its teachings were so unusual it was like I was on another island, surrounded by an ocean of ignorance. Before long the schoolyard started to break down into invisible separate tribal territories. If you were Dinka and you crossed a line you could feel the discomfort of not being welcome in, say a *Nuer* area, or some claimed section of the school itself. Yes, the Cubans used a kind of body language to communicate. So did the Sudanese: the eyes that spit on you, the muscle flexing that said run now or, I'll pound you into the dust! Go; go back to where you belong, you will not find friends in this group. You aren't like us.

That was true; in many ways we *weren't* like them. We had parents here and they didn't. Some held that against us. That my Father was a diplomat created suspicion in others. They looked on us as being somehow privileged. The student gossip carried this reality back to us. It wasn't going to be an easy thing, this making friends, if they thought we were somehow special.

In Sudan most of these tribes don't intermingle. That was one of the major problems at Itang school and at the refugee camp. But in Cuba we all had to learn to live together. Most of the students tried to get along but there were a few who just couldn't let it go. A lot of fights broke out between the tribal groups, mostly between boys. Sometimes even between us girls! Yet the younger children right from the start stuck together, being too young to understand the traditional prejudices between tribes.

Our Number 12 school, had a lot to learn about what unity of purpose could accomplish.

Those first few days it was my family, my brothers and sister, who stuck together. In time, with exposure to the regimentation, and getting past what I could only call the shock of actually having to live up to Baba's decision for my future, to do as he bid me within this new system, I would do my best and make lots of friends!

Meanwhile . . .

The first group that had been sent over before the rest of us had been more indoctrinated in what was expected of them. The idea was that they'd show the rest what the new standards were and how to meet them. We also had Sudanese teachers called Monitors who were there to teach us Arabic and some English so we wouldn't forget our culture. In the two months of holidays, our teachers came up with ideas to keep us busy doing something. They decided to teach us how to be ready for anything, maybe for war, by training us just the way the military was trained in Bilfam.

It was an entirely different setting, yet in many ways just like being in Sudan.

Here it was again like, salute, salute, salute. Yep, we were in the Army now! They would wake us up every day at 5:00 AM and everybody had to be down at the training area, to go through vigorous exercises. They took the training very seriously. It felt like we were getting trained to go and fight. Surprisingly, we got accustomed to the regimentation and it started to actually feel good. We were getting a lot of fresh air and healthy exercise, our bodies and minds benefited, and we started to get familiar with each other and things around the campus.

Our regimentation included keeping our school in a good hygienic condition. We had to organize a system ourselves by groups and take turns cleaning every day. In each Dorm students would select one student to clean up for the day. Girls dorms were divide into three cubicles, so we would have three girls for clean up each day. Our beds were done to military standards and if we failed, we had to do it over again till it was right. After the 5:00 AM boot camp exercises, we'd go back to our dorms and take showers before the clean-up students started their jobs. If, for some reason, one of us was late for a shower, we weren't allowed to shower until the inspection was finished. The students on duty made sure everything was perfect before the inspection took place. In the girl's dorm, we would even pick flowers from around the school to place in our dorms to give a little added colour and make it look nice. There were competitions between the dorms as well. We were given incentives and prizes; everybody wanted to be the winners. There was a lot of competition between dorms and every one tried to do their best.

One of the incentives the best students were given was a chance to go back home to Africa to visit their families with everything paid for by the Cuban government. We would also do academic competitions against other classes, but the best competitions were when we went up against other schools. They were multiple activities to compete in: sports, in the orchard, cutting the grass and collecting grapefruit on the trees. For us students, it was a lot of fun! The Sudanese students won just about every year; we were very good workers. We were so good we won trips to the beach most every weekend and were awarded camping trips.

My favourite retreats with very nice beaches were Arenas Negras and Las llagrumas. The buses would come for us on Friday and most students would go. Those were fine days to earn our rewards.

Every day there was a student assembly before the day started, either to go to classes or out to the orchards. We had to sing two national anthems. First we would sing the Cuban national anthem and then the Sudanese anthem while the national flags were raised by the students. We were organized in the assembly in class groups, lined up by height from shortest to tallest.

After breakfast the students returned to their dorms for inspection. Each student stood beside their bed to sing as the monitors came to inspect the dorm. We students were tidy, organized and took pride in receiving the monitors. If they found someone's bed untidy, they would write their name down and announce them in the assembly, as well as name the best dorm of the day. We also competed against other boarding Schools. We eventually learned that amongst all the schools, Number 12 was considered one of the best organized facilities on the Island. We Sudanese took great pride in that fact. We were very organised, disciplined neat and tidy and yep, yep ... salute, salute, salute. Proud of our national flag we were for sure!

After showering, the students slated to go to morning classes would wear their school uniforms; for the boys, navy blue pants, and kind of cute navy blue skirts for girls. Both genders wore light blue shirts, white socks, black shoes and a red tie. All shirts had to be neatly tucked in. I loved our uniforms. We all looked very nice. They made me feel in a way quite pretty. Our work cloths were cotton pants, long sleeve shirts, a straw hat that looked like a cowboy hat and rubber boots. We took pride in those outfits too as we all started to work carrying machetes.

The whole Island was made up mostly of state owned grapefruit orchards with quite a distance between boarding schools. The students were the labourers who cared for the orchards and picked the fruit. In a way we worked for the state to pay for receiving, or rather earning, our education. We were divided in two shifts, morning and afternoon. While some students went to classes in the morning, the others went to work in the orchard, and in the afternoon the shifts would switch. It was an everyday routine.

This kind of organization wasn't just for our school. All the island schools were run in a similar manner designed to show socialist integration. We were all equal, in our responsibilities and in our rewards. On the Island of Youth there were a lot of boarding Schools. The Cuban government had offered Socialist schooling for some 25,000 children from different areas such as Africa, the Middle East, Asia and South America. Each country had separate schools for their segregated student population.

Everything at the School was organized by the bell. It would ring for just about everything. At the end of the day, it was to take the flags down and us to change into our regular clothes for supper and free personal time. The girls always made sure to look good when going to eat at the cafeteria, because the boys would be doing the same and hitting on them. After eating we'd gather with friends at our favourite hang out spots for the evening. My friends and I would go for walks, gather to sing with the other girls, or maybe play the latest popular games until we had to be back in our dorm with lights out by ten PM. This was mandatory. No fooling around was tolerated by our ever watchful monitors after lights out.

There were a lot of things to do at the school during our free time, especially sports. I enjoyed basketball and volleyball and also played soccer on occasion. At other times, I would go by myself out among the grapefruit and think of how I missed Mama and Baba. It was important for me to have private moments away from everyone in the first few months to help me adjust to my new life.

After about a month at the school we started Spanish classes. We were divided up into different grades. Yong and I were put into grade four. In our classroom there were more girls than boys, most of us being the

108

youngest children. It was difficult for the teacher because the kids cried a lot for their parents and didn't understand the lessons as the teacher only spoke Spanish. The teacher was frustrated because half of the classroom seemed to be crying and those who were paying attention all spoke different dialects. It was a frustrating period for everyone. On my walks alone, I struggled with anxiety.

When I went walking, my shadow followed close behind, pestering me with things I didn't want to remember. I tried to keep my face to the sun and think of the path ahead of me. But, at times I would fail and find myself sitting and crying about my past. I would think of Yalee and worry for Grandma. I'd wonder what might be happening to my friends in Kongor. And what about all the other friends I'd left behind in so many different places? I needed to sort these things out, so I could concentrate on what Baba had told me. I had to do well in all these things; be a good worker in the orchard, learn the language and most importantly, make friends I could share thoughts and feelings with.

It was good to feel the presence of my siblings, but the only one who would really let me hang out with him was Agor. He didn't mind me following him around and seemed to know I needed to spend time with him. He didn't care that I was little or worry that I might embarrass him. My other brothers and sister Abany weren't so generous. They were too busy with the friends they were making to put up with me. I would take these little hurts along to walk with me. I talked to myself and found grapefruit, on the whole, were pretty good listeners!

My shadow was I think a key; at least that's how it felt now that I no longer wanted to jump out of the plane into an empty dark sky.

'Or maybe, a link in a chain,' came another stray thought.

More than a few times I'd thought I should write my life story and all the experiences I'd lived through over the years. Having relived the chain of events over and over, having considered them in different lights and different times and in different places, I had a growing feeling I needed to face an unrecognised centre where it would all fall into place. Yet, always, there were places I couldn't take myself to, events I couldn't drag into the light of day. One was the time I was lost to depression and became a shadow on the wall. Another was Baba not being there in Itang and the effect that had on me.

Somehow, I had rubbed both experiences out of my remembered history.

Pictures and memories of the beginnings of Number 12 school were still swirling through the background of my thoughts, seeking to pull me back. I squirmed in my seat fighting them. There was a nagging something keeping me there in the Grapefruit orchard; a something that needed be recognized. I thought hard on what it might be, right there...

'Walking with my shadow following close behind,' burst its way through my puzzlement. *'Baba?'*

Instantly tears sprang to my eyes and almost angrily I wiped them away. I didn't want to break down and cry; it wasn't needed here. I needed to know what this was. I'd succeeded, and choked back the... well, not fear exactly. It was a sadness that was pulling me down to a mindless wreck and a place I refused to go. Not this time!

Then another thought suddenly arrived. Mama had shown me courage, how I was *'Little Tiger.'* I needed to find that part of me. I needed find something that would help me brave things out. I needed to find my heart; to believe I would . . . *arrive.* I needed to believe I would get to that far off place where it all would make sense. Yes, keep going, Sarah. Get to where you're determined to go. Yet, where was that? What had brought me the courage to plan this trip? What had... got me onto this plane!

'Was I running away from my shadow?'

Was I running from the fear of the dream lion that hunted me, running through my dark places, running from shifting shapes, shapes that became a slithering snake that coiled around my legs? I wake whimpering, *"Mama Mama! I am getting swallowed by a very big snake . . . help, help, help! I am not going to make it to my house any more, I am going to get eaten alive . . . and die!"* Always, just out of view in the shadows, was the house of sticks I could never reach. Could I never get back . . . to . . . home?

These thoughts sent shivers through my body, up and down the backs of my legs. They had the ghostly feel of dreadfully tired legs run almost beyond endurance. I felt a flash; a moment captured when I'd almost give in to the herd bolting in panic, when I'd only wanted ... to hide!

Oh my, I remembered now.

'I left that shadow... in the orchard!'

I tied it all in a bundle and buried it.

It was always Baba who determined my destination, Baba who supplied the ways and means to get there. That was what I needed in life to have and hold. I needed my parents. I needed their guidance and reassurance.

Yet on the bus to Number 12 School, I had felt a profound sense of abandonment! I tried holding onto those short moments with Baba and Mama at the Airport. I remembered Baba stating, *"make a lot of friends. More importantly, Sarah, study a lot and very hard. So that you can have a very brilliant future when you grow up and go back to a new Sudan!"* But then there was blackness, a period of time lost in the shades between, a paranoid period withdrawn into myself.

I still hadn't had time with Baba to share with him the trauma of what we lived through. That day in the orchard, as just an eleven year old girl, I locked them away. There was no resolution for them. I had no means of release. I had no one to explain to me the reasoning things had happened, to answer my questions. They, I held onto! I still had the shocking fear of having experienced them, these shadows that stained my soul. The recurrence of the nightmare, *that face of death*, would wake me in a panic, shivering and sobbing into my pillow. I couldn't start screaming. Mama wouldn't be there to stop me and comfort me and release me into sleep, that day, or the following day after days...

I would live on, without them.

I filled up my time with daily activities and still I was holding this burden. I felt if I let it out, it would destroy me utterly. What's a girl to do? I couldn't deal with them, so I buried them, that day! I realized I was holding myself back from doing as Baba had asked. This funk was blinding me from participating wholly in the school activities. I imagined Mama lending me the courage to do this myself as Mama wasn't there to force me out the door into the present with a loving switch. If I carried this horror around with me, its shades would stop me from developing the mind and intelligence, Baba always lovingly explained to me.

I owned this deep dark thing. It would stalk me forever and a day with no release.

I had no Baba to keep me safe from it. But I had something else. His safety for me was determined by education. Education was the seed that would plant a brilliant future in me. This safety I was always running toward was Baba's idea; Baba's determination of what the future would hold. I was shocked to realize that if I didn't find him in this idea and return to this new Sudan,

I would have no future.

If Baba weren't there this time, I would disappear. If I couldn't hold Mama in my heart, it would shrivel to dust and blow away with the wind. That day in the orchard, shaped my life for many years. It drove me ever forward. It was like learning to multiply in school. If you took those four days of running across the wilds of Sudan and kept multiplying that by four, you would have the number of years that found me, right then . . . *on that plane!* A lifetime of hope had been built on such a few spoken words. They had determined my reality.

They had demanded from me a promise; one I made to myself in the midst of a fit.

It was just like that too, walking along and complaining to all the grapefruit that would listen to my tirade. Duty, duty, duty, running around in the back ground like a broken record; *'it just isn't fair,'* riding along right on the surface and getting deep and deeper into this burn.

"*Well, don't you think so!*" hands on my hips, I Acuach Cor, aged 11, demanded, facing the closest tree. Dinka was just flying out of this really mad little girl, *"how am I supposed to do all this... Why can't I just be happy?"* I was really in high gear now. Here comes the flood, leaky eyes doing their thing all on their own. Suddenly, all the words fell away in frustration. The wind whirled around me, sucking the breath from any thought of courage, pulling me down into the muck. My tears turned my world to water and blurry panic. Even the grapefruit abandoned me.

Look at this weak little chatter box, they said, blubbering silliness, expecting us to listen to such nonsense. "Oh yes poor Sarah," they mocked me, "is this what you need to hear?"

I blubbered and pounded my hands again the mud of my miseries. Man, I wanted to just get up and tear their roots, rip their leaves off and spread them all over that stupid orchard. *"What am I; your slave!"* I screamed into the void. It was so unlike Sarah to say these angry bitter things at anyone. "Yes Mama," I apologized, "out here who cares? Nobody wants to hear me anyway!" Down deep something was rising. I tried to fight it angrily, not wanting to know. I was better than this.

"Why Mama, why!"

A question came out of the depth.

"Why, would you waste your precious breath Sarah?" It was like a voice, but wasn't Mama! It stopped me right in the midst of my fit as I pounded my hands into the dirt so hard it hurt. "What have you to regret Sarah?" *'Being born'* was the first thing that popped into my mind, then *'hurting my hands'* came a close second. "Ah so, you're sorry you were even born?" I realized I needed to stop this. I had to stop feeling this rotten about myself. Hadn't Baba told me to be strong, make friends and study hard for a better future? Was all this self-pity to carry on into my future? Right away I stood up, wiped my tears and smiled. I had buried that stupid shadow with my aching hands. I promised myself this nightmare would never again follow me around. I kept my promises going. I now had a list of them. I knew if I got rid of my following fear I could be happy! What friend would want a grumpy little girl anyway? I promised myself I would be the best friend anybody could ever want to have.

Right then I knew I'd done the right thing. I felt much better right away. I turned and looked up to the sky. "I will do this Baba because I know I can!" I said. I turned my face to the sun with real confidence, left my shadow behind and didn't look back. My future was now my school, my really big house full of children I knew would love to be my friends and family.

I knew that inner voice, I recognized it, it was me. Life could get better. I only needed to try.

My lonely walks talking to the grapefruit dropped right off after that. Even my dreams got better. It was almost as though I was seeing a new light in the world around me after my emotional experience out in the orchard. I realized my isolation since arriving, even in sports, was to avoid dealing with my fears. I hadn't really been seeing all the things going on around me. I was too inwardly involved with the anxiety of being separated from Mama, Baba, Achol, and Chol. I really did miss my little Brother, his sweet laugh and the way he loved to play with me, but I really had to move on.

So there I was, standing in the hallway on the second floor of our dorm more or less hanging out. I was thinking, *'well, time to make friends!'* There were a lot of kids moving past me, doing their thing. It was as if I suddenly noticed, *'hey, there are a lot of choices going on here.'* I began to really look at them, searching for someone my own age. There were a lot of familiar faces from Bilfam and Itang, though not my friends. They could be! I thought I just needed be more open and friendly, to show them I was a good person and fun to hang out with. I thought, 'Man I'm really good at making up new and interesting games. That should be worth a lot to someone,' as I searched the hall for that someone.

A small and very pretty young girl caught my eye. *'Hey,' I thought, 'I know that girl from school in Itang.'* It was Amelo Kerubino. I'd not been introduced to her but I'd heard gossip about her family. People said because her dad had a high position in SPLM/A she was pretentious and always bragging about her Father. I'd never really talked about my dad being ambassador, because I was taught not to brag, but if anyone knew he was they might say the same about me! I hadn't heard her boasting so why should I think she did? If I made her my friend, it would be better to learn about who she was from her!

I didn't want to be influenced by gossip. I had met Mr. Kerubino when I was in Addis Ababa because he, John Garang, William Nyuon and my Uncle Arok Thon, were frequent visitors to Doble Zeit. They would come to see how we were whenever they came to the city. He seemed to be a nice man. I didn't want to believe his daughter thought that she was better than the rest of us.

I realized I'd been staring at her and now Amel was eying me over. I couldn't tell if it was a friendly look she was giving me or not. It made me kind of nervous. As she stared at me I could see she was very self confident. She had good posture and you could see she was educated by the way she handled herself. The way she walked had me thinking she might not be too impressed at me staring at her.

It wasn't hard to see we were about the same age, about ten or eleven. I was still looking at what was one very beautiful small girl with brilliant white teeth and smooth, soft skin. Suddenly her face glowed with the most wonderful smile. She said, "hello, I'm Amelo Kerubino. Would you like to be my friend?" Well I can tell you, I was quite shocked at this wonderful coincidence. She continued by asking me politely what my name was. It took me about a half a heartbeat to happily introduce myself. "I'm Acuach Cor or Sarah Gabriel. I would be honored to be your friend, Amelo!" I just couldn't help myself; I pinched her cheek and gave her a big hug. I could see that that shocked her as her body went all tense.

"Oops", I thought, '*I may have just blown it!* I could feel my face burning with embarrassment. Well, what to do? I was still hugging her. Then precious Amelo relaxed in my embrace and laughed a wonderfully warm laugh and hugged me back. 'Ooo', it felt so good.

Sarah had me a friend! OK, check that one off the list.

Well, both of us figured it was time to find some more. Amelo was truly a giggle to hang out with; just bla, bla, bla, all the time. She was always going on about one thing or another. Her funny stories made me pee myself with laughter (figuratively of course). So we had ourselves an adventure; hunting for other crazy kids like ourselves and I'm like 'OK!' as really it was all Amelo's idea. Mama had been so right about gossip. Amelo was nothing like all the things people made up about her.

Two days into the hunt, and we were in for a real surprise.

Once again I was in that second floor hallway, looking for Amelo, and thinking today might be a good hunting day. There was still time before we had to head to the cafeteria for lunch. I was so focused on my mission I almost missed a most wonderful surprise. There was a small girl in a hurry going the other way down the hall and I got the sudden feeling I recognized her. I turned to look at her at the same time as she was turning to look at me. My mouth fell wide open and... so did hers.

The thought that flashed through my mind was . . . *FISH!*

The recognition almost threw me off my feet. I screamed, my finger pointing at Mana. "You made it, you made it!" I couldn't believe my eyes; Mana had qualified.

"Uh huh Sarah, I really did!" she said, nodding a huge grin and looking so proud.

"Well just look at you," I teased her and pinched her cheeks tenderly. "You're looking wonderful... and Mana, you're so clean!" We both laughed at that one.

"Oh yes, and you Sarah, you're not stinking like fish either!" She'd thrown it right back at me.

Well that was it. We flew into each other's arms and danced around the hall, the kids going by looking at us like we were crazy people. We didn't care. This was Mana, Mana my partner in crime and horrible cooking. My heart just soared to be with her. I grabbed her hard by the elbows. "Hey, come on now, I want you to meet Amelo and we'll all go to lunch together. What do you say?" Of course Mana thought that would be just the greatest and off we skipped down the hall to bigger and better friendships.

When we found Amelo she was already there, excited to introduce a friend she'd brought to meet me, Anot. 'Whoa', what a day! Lunch was tasty, but it was even better for me to have this meeting of the gang happen. We all knew right away this would be a special friendship we would all share, and, through the years, it has been. As time has passed, the four of us have had a special bond; we've become more like sisters than just friends.

They've been my loving family.

The hunt for friends felt finished. For weeks the four of us were enough. We spent almost every available minute in each other's company, in one combination or another as the situations allowed. It was best though when it was all four of us. My days of long faces and moping about on my own, were pretty much done. Yes, there were days when I missed my family and felt blue. My sisters would know and find ways to cheer me up. We did this for each other when it was their turn to have a bad day. Sure, we had times when we would find some reason or another to quarrel amongst ourselves, but it never got bad enough to drive us away from one another for any length of time. We found it easy to forgive one other.

Let me move along now from how we adjusted individually and tell you about the world we, and all the Sudanese children, found ourselves in at School Number 12.

Our dormitories were made up of three groups, young girls, teenagers, and adults. Everyone had their own group of friends, even though we were all from different backgrounds, had different behaviors and our cultures were very different from each other. We were trying to get along. Time worked its magic and things started to get better between the tribes as we began making friends. Abany was now a teenager and made friends with girls her own age. She seemed very happy hanging out with them. Likewise my brothers found new friends and activities. For myself, I was coping with my past better and was no longer so needy of my immediate family.

Our intimate group of four became a kind of cell within a larger group of fourteen; all girls from our dorm and roughly the same age. This would become another circle of friendships that would span the test of time. We planned everything together; sports, walks and studies. Life was improving for me and the other girls as we became more involved with sports and social activities. On the whole, our thoughts were more on school, sports and fun than petty squabbles. I enjoyed sports as they totally engaged me and kept me from thinking too much about missing my parents so terribly.

Almost every weekend, bands would come and play for us. We still couldn't totally understand the lyrics, but it was always great fun, especially for us younger girls. If there were no boys asking us to dance, we didn't care. We were at an age where we would just grab a girlfriend and go dance. Sometimes they gave the students a chance to sing in Dinka, Arabic, Nuer or in any the many dialects. One of the better singers at the school was my brother Agor.

My best friend Amelo and I always wanted to spend time with Agor so he would teach us some of the romantic songs he sang in Arabic. He was good looking, talented and outgoing and everybody loved his music, especially the girls. There were a constant string of them hovering around him all the time. Too bad he was my brother, or I would have been in the line-up for him too! He was also a very good soccer player; the same as my other brothers Anyon and Deng Ti were awesome at basketball. So it went; there were many things to go and get involved with. If we weren't playing sports, we were watching the older students competing. I think my personal favorite was, Five-on-Five basketball, and maybe, still is! Which kind of reminds me of a story . . .

I don't like to be mean or say bad things about people, but that's the way this is going to sound. Why? Mostly because some of the girls in this story (who won't be named, but if they read this book, they'll know who they are) later became really good friends. We all grow up eventually and get beyond being silly and petty.

So it's like that; it's really about growing up and only a bit about basketball or sports.

I think any school anywhere has instances where one group picks on younger or smaller students or maybe just anyone who's a little different. OK, truth be told, for us it was because we were little. Our private group found each other because we all had one thing in common; we were probably the smallest girls in the school!

Outside of our fourteen, there was a group we called 'The Meanies.' At least it started that way. They were bigger than us and some were older. Man, when we saw them headed our way, it was like, "*Oh, oh, look what's coming our way!*" Most of the time, it was a good thing to avoid being where they were, but sometimes that just wasn't possible! It was worse when only Anot, Mana and I were together. They would say things like, "*hey look guys, it's the ugly 111 girls!*"

They called the three of us when we were together 111 as an insult. It meant 'the three sticks,' being that we were bean pole skinny and looked like stick figures. We weren't popular with boys yet for some very obvious reasons. We were rather underdeveloped and they teased us about it. "Ha, ha, you're never going to have boyfriends. *You three! Ha, ha, ha, got nothing to offer.*" Stuff like that. They also tried frightening us, using all kinds of threats about what they could easily do to us weaklings. What they couldn't easily do was catch us! Those Meanies couldn't run for nothing. We were real fast, mostly because we knew if they caught us they'd threatened to, *'break our backs like a twig'* . . . *"snap!"*

Man, that was no fun, that idea! We'd stick our tongues out and yell at them, *"big head Meanies!"* and then run! They never could catch us, but it was better to just avoid them. Name calling and running worked for us 111 Gazelle Girls. The Meanies were really puffed up about themselves. Some were on the school's girl's basketball team. Quite frankly, they weren't very good and lost a lot of games against the other schools. I had the opportunity later of taking the place of some who'd moved on. We got to be a lot better and won more games!

There was a lot of ongoing school competition and Five-on-Five was a big deal. We showed them in time we had some well practised moves and could run circles around them in this deal too. I also gained their respect in Track because the one thing I could always do very well was RUN! I could reach that place in me I discovered in the four day crossing, a place inside that was a long distance float. In that place, racing, *I put pretty much everyone behind me!*

I was first or second, always!

So there it is, just a short story about girls that for a time had it in their heads to be mean to us younger, smaller girls. Most of them got over it and moved on to other things to occupy themselves. They lost interest in us little girls that refused to fight. Besides, you can't hurt someone you can't catch, or in sports, *you couldn't catch up with!*

Even later we would *'whap!'* beat them with words because we could. There are many ways to prove your self valuable; for our group fighting proved nothing.

Chapter 11
Eleven years (very) old

There were other things that proved to be rather more painful. Some times we younger girls would cry because we missed our parents. When I arrived I'd taken my fears and tears out into the orchard alone. I thought I was finished crying, but there came a day that missing my parents caught up to me right in my dorm. I was sitting on the edge my bed trying to sob quietly. I knew I was having a weak moment, but couldn't help the pain of missing them. I didn't realize there was a girl I didn't know very well watching me. She came over and asked me "why are you crying?" I told her I wanted my parents. "How can you be crying", she said rather acidly, "when your parents are here in Cuba!"

She was right; I couldn't be with my parents but they weren't that far away. Once again I wiped my tears and told myself I needed to be brave. I told myself to be strong and have more sympathy for the other girls in my dorm. This was no Big Head Meanie; this girl was serious. Yes her voice had come across strongly, but her posture told me I was actually hurting her. I suddenly realized these children had been through a lot and maybe much worse than me! This comment triggered in me a serious awareness not requiring tears for myself. Instead I felt kindness for her sadness, for whatever her pain was.

I had my fourteen girlfriends and we had shared openly what had happened to us in Sudan and in the Refugee camps, Bilfam and all of that. As a result, talking of those things was easier; I wasn't re-living them, but I'd buried that damning shadow. My problem was I was missing Mama and Baba, not the trauma of the other stuff.

I had seen this girl around and she was usually alone. I didn't know her personal story and hadn't discussed mine.

Now I was struck by how little this rather pretty older girl had spoken to me and then turned and walked away. My tears had dried up. This girl got me to thinking hard. The look in her eyes reminded me of the look I'd seen on so many of the border runners, a look of hopelessness. It told me her experiences had been really hard! Maybe she'd even lost her parents; I had no way of knowing. I knew what it felt like to see friends and family shot and killed in Bor. I knew that face of death, intimately.

Likely, just like that girl . . .

From that day forward, when hurting for my family I never talked about them or cried for them openly. I came to understand what Baba had told us; to be cautious with the other children about his being the Ambassador of Sudan in Cuba or that we had family nearby. He feared they would think we were throwing it in their faces, showing we were privileged children, thinking we were better than them or from a better class than they were. I didn't feel that way at all. I realized because of my dorm mates no one person's pain is greater than another.

It's funny thinking back on all this, I'd never seen Baba in that light before. He held so much wisdom. Being separated from him made me think these deep thoughts. Sometimes they even made my head hurt! I understood later in life what he meant. Baba was so brilliant and my mind was so self-centered. It just went *my, my, my, my, my*, and it was time to go play with my friends. It was time to get off my bed to get on with being just Sarah, a child.

After that experience, I kept most of my feelings to myself out of respect for the others. In some ways I cut myself short. I should have been very proud of Baba for all the things he passed on to his children. Instead, because I wanted to be accepted by others, I vowed to myself not to be seen crying again. It was another something to add onto what was becoming a very long list for an 11-year old.

Maybe too much.

Our school was a long way away from anywhere, but we were provided with transportation to town when we had appointments. The Cuban Government seemed to have everything taken care of. As a result, we started to settle into our studies without much to worry about. Yet, even with all the attention, I still missed my parents. Nothing could change that! Most especially I missed Mama. I continued to have this feeling even though they would come together to the school to visit us or Baba dropped by on his own to visit the students when he had work on the island. At these times when the family was together I would enjoy their company, but it wasn't the same really. I had determined to be very reserved and hold back my emotions. Always in the back of my mind I was thinking about the other students. I didn't want a display of affection to make them feel worse about how they missed their own parents.

Maybe I was taking my list altogether too seriously.

Just the same, I felt that keeping my emotions in check was my duty to my parents. Wasn't this what was being called of me, to grow up, be a big girl, not cry and be silly and weak? All that I knew was that part of me was at war with some other part of me. Some of what I understood I had arrived at for myself. I knew that clearly my homeland Sudan was at war. People were suffering, dying, sacrificing so that a people could have rights and freedoms and not be repressed by Siwar Al-Deheb's regime. I had grown up at Baba's knee, hearing him speak of what the Sudanese Liberation Movement stood for. I understood Agor had fought for those rights with his SPLA brothers-in-arms as he called them that day they came to the house in Kongor. I had experienced the great heroics of

Uncle Arok Thon and The Zindia who got their charge of 200 Sudanese People to safety in Ethiopia. All these great things were much larger than me, than my little world at school. Sometimes I felt so small, like a grain of fine white sand by the lake in Itang.

I imagined there were many more things I had as yet to understand about why we students were in Cuba. As an 11-year old girl, I didn't need to. I needed only to trust that my parents knew what was best for me and for the family. Still, I realized I was part of a greater thing. I could feel it, there was meaning in our role, a duty. Some very basic things were being asked of me. Would my parents have asked if they thought I couldn't do them?

These events had changed us forever. The family I knew was gone. The civil war in Sudan was now shaping us, bringing about some otherness as yet unknown. That much I knew. I could feel the changes in my brothers and sister at school. I was about to see the differences it would make in my parents and my relationship with them. In a way, some part of me deep down inside already felt old. Some deep thing was there waiting for me to discover it. I felt as if it had always been with me, whispering, teasing, a part of my dreams. I could never quite remember.

This gave me a mental reserve the same as in long distance running. I could call on some hidden inner strength to endure, to will my tired knotted legs to keep running. Those buried things I'd seen had made me older than my years, had changed me in ways I couldn't even imagine. The trauma of events would stay frozen inside me. I couldn't emotionally relate to witnessing that which should not have to be faced. I guess it's called arrested development. This little girl, Acuach Cor, would just have to keep moving or die and all the while carrying a fear big enough to last a lifetime. I was a little person but I had to deal with it and move on, so I buried it in the orchard. It was imprisoned there, and in me, until I could find the key to unlock it and let it go.

I didn't like to feel jealous of Mama sharing her time with all the students instead of just me. That was my brain. My heart, the traumatized little girl locked inside, couldn't help it. It was my cross to bear.

When Mama came to the Island visiting and bringing gifts for her children, she would always bring something for the other children as well. My parents, being ever considerate, wanted them to feel there was a parental figure looking out for them too. It would have been impossible to afford individual gifts for everyone, so instead Mama would bring canned goods for the older girls to share as a special treat with the rest of the children. My parents were very good that way. It seemed to me they would do anything they could for the children at the school. When these visits took place, I put into practice my pledge of not showing my emotions too much and not letting my friends see how much I missed my parents. When my parents came by, I would take my friends with me to see them and we all would have fun together, sharing my family time. I was used to that anyway. In Bor our compound was always full of cousins staying with us. This wasn't so much different; it was easy enough to accept this.

Still, it was very difficult not to show how happy I was to see my parents or how wonderful it was to have almost all my family in Cuba. I tried hard not to be selfish, not to feel bitter about having to share my Mama and Baba. But, oh, how I wished I could have thrown myself upon them. How I wished I could have them all to my self and tell them how much I missed and loved them! The role I had assumed made that impossible. It would have been selfish and unfair to my dorm mates. My Parents really enjoyed it when we took our friends to say hi to them and spend some time together. Mama and Baba treated them like their own children. This was easy enough for them to do so naturally.

It was just hard for me!

My brothers, sister and I were united in the idea of not boasting to the other students about our Baba being Ambassador. I remember a lot of children back in Sudan who would have treated other kids badly because their fathers were rich or had a good position in the government. They would act like they were better than the others and that everybody was nothing compared to them. It was just not a part of our family training to think we were better than the other students, or anyone, for that matter. The whole idea of the SPLM was about equality, progress, and creating the opportunity for a better Sudan. Our Father Baba had taught us well about the ideals he had worked hard toward, and we wanted to prove we could follow them.

In all these visits our parents stressed how proud they were of us, in our behaving so maturely, how we were handling our changes at school, how disciplined we were. They praised our efforts at adapting so well. They made it a point to tell us to study hard and take advantage of our good fortune so we would have what was needed for the future of the New Sudan. They emphasized we were exceedingly fortunate to be able to study. They asked us to be grateful to the Cuban Government for providing for so many Sudanese children and taking us out of our war ravaged country. This was a great consideration to our People. Our parents believed it was an honor to represent our country in this manner and it was important for us to view this opportunity this way.

My, my, my, my... oh *my!* It was so much responsibility for our little shoulders.

Our parents were confident we could, would, and why not? We were worthy children and they figured, ready to face up to the challenge. I could see at these times Baba just shined as he looked upon his children with love and pride. It made it all so worthwhile, all these disciplines I was part of. I took those thoughts right into the school and tried all the harder to please our parents and their dreams for us. It was hard to live up to these sometimes impossible expectations, to put up with those who were bound and determined to crawl under your skin and make you miserable. That's why I appreciated the way my parents educated us, allowing us to see things in a different way, making sure we had no real issues with others. I guess that's what made Baba a diplomat. His enlightened advice helped us a lot with all the different students we met, some from very rich families and others who were poor or had no family at all. It helped me understand why some of the students were miserable and not to blame them. I tried always to accept them because I knew they'd get over it and show a different personality the next day.

Time was moving on. Many things had taken place in the two years since we'd arrived in Cuba, things I'd had to become accustomed to. For me, in that beginning, the big thing was being separated from Mama. Yes, I had the experience of Bilfam for those three months. But never until then had I been without her for any extended period of time. By now in 1988, except for summer holidays, it had been more than a year without them. School Number 12 had become more like a second home, my big house, and the students my huge extended family. It's odd, but that's the way it was.

If I could be with Mama at least one of my wishes had come true; she was happy.

Mama had gone through all that we had gone through to be with her soul mate. Baba was oh so busy and I knew they still didn't have a lot of time to spend together. But when they did find moments to share it was obvious how happy they were. Mama would just glow and fuss over him, getting him his favorite tea, cooking the food he liked best. What made me happiest was to watch her tease him! This, more than anything, showed me how happy Mama really was. She had suffered so much; she deserved all her new happiness. When Mama was like this, it spread itself throughout the whole family through her love and the manner she cared for us.

That first summer holiday we spent together was a good example of that

It was in Mama and Baba's first house and the ocean was almost right outside the door. It was a great place to share with friends that the School picked to be with Yong and me. This made for a lot extra children for Mama to care for. Yong had his friend Atem and for me, there was Aluel, plus Achol, Agor, Anyon, Deng Ti and Abany. Wow, plus our cousin Kuir Ton and a student from Havana Samuel Bulen! We were all in that five bedroom house. Amazingly, Mama made it work all summer.

Like the Bor compound, Mama's house was again full of activity. It wasn't a chore for her because Mama had her husband; her life was full again. She was happy to send us all off to the beach because that gave her more time to spend with Baba to herself. Maybe, I thought, that was their plan! Which was great for us. We'd go off with Baba's driver, a Cuban fellow called Alberto, who came with a supplied car from the wonderful Cuban government!

Alberto went everywhere with us, and he was a nice man too, buying us ice cream and treats. I loved the beautiful sandy beach and the ocean so blue. Our days were so full of activity. I really loved it that there was always Salsa playing from somewhere. The beach was way better than swimming at home, because although it was right outside our door, it had a rocky bottom that bruised your feet. Oh man, the sand at that other beach was so wonderful. It was great for building castles for Chol to destroy, or to bury him in. He found a lot of ways to wreck our fun being only five, building channels for the ocean to wash away all our hard, hot work. It was as if Chol was hinting, *"enough! I wanna swim!"*

Mama and Baba's first house really was a nice place until one day toward the end of the summer, the ocean rose up past the doorstep and flooded everything out. It was a real mess and cleaning it up was no fun at all! Shortly after that, it was back to school for Yong and me and our summer guests. Both our friends talked about the visit for quite a while, telling everyone how much they enjoyed their time with our family and how much fun they had. It was a great holiday for us all round.

That year at school, I passed into grade five. My Spanish was coming right along and I thought soon I'd be able to check that off my list. My teacher praised me for how quickly I was learning and that made me feel really proud. I was still trying to translate everything in my mind, figuring it would still be some time before I'd be able to speak this mysterious language fluently. Our teacher, Morayma, had us practicing with our friends all the time, telling us to try to only speak Spanish. Well, that didn't always work, because when we left her class, we'd be right back talking in Arabic, Dinka and Nuer. The headaches we got speaking Spanish, we left in the classroom.

One day as the bell rang and everyone was running for the door, Morayma called to me before I could get away with my friends. "Sarah, do you have a minute please?" I was thinking OK, it will only be a minute. It didn't turn out that way. I went to her and she showed me a book. Right away I could see that it was written in Arabic. "Sarah", she asked, "do you read Arabic?" Well that stopped me right in my tracks. What was I to tell her? I didn't want to admit to my teacher I hadn't been in school for a long time and couldn't read Arabic very well. So I said to her, "oh yes I can read that very well". I was always lying to the teachers for fun, just to see where things would go.

It didn't work too well this time. Morayma opened the book and said, "bueno, (good) Sarah." She flipped the book open to a marked page and placed it right there in front of me. "Could you please read this page for me and tell me what it says?" Because I'm dark, you can't see me blush, but I sure was; my face just burned. What to do, what to do? I was doing some fast fancy thinking to get out of the mess I'd gotten into. I was also thinking if she knew, Mama would be paddling my behind right about now for making stuff up!

There was a picture in the book of a young and sad looking girl. I don't know why but it made me feel as if I were this girl. There was that and the fact I had no idea what was written on the page. I started talking away in Dinka as if I were reading. What came out though wasn't made up it was my life "Acuach Cor is running away from the horrible soldiers, for more than four days. She is running across open plains and is really tired and hungry!" Man, I went on for what seemed like the length of that page. Then I had to stop because if I didn't was going to start bawling right there in front of my teacher. That would really blow my pledge right out of the water about crying in public!

So there I was, all bottled up, staring at the floor. My somewhat baffled teacher became all concerned for me. "What is it Sarah, what's the matter? Are you all right?", she asked. The teachers were used to having to deal softly with traumatized students. "Did something you read make you feel bad?" she asked. Of course I nodded my head and said nothing. She looked so nice and sisterly and asked me softly, "would you like to talk about it?"

I give her a really sad look which is easy if I think too long about those buried things. I just couldn't get any words out and instead got up and walked out. I didn't know what else to do. Well two days later, Morayma approached me in the hall and what she'd said to me was truly a weird coincidence. "Sarah, she said, "I found out what that story was about and I can see why it affected you that way!" Her eyes all compassionate as she continued, "it really was sad what happened to that little girl." Then she patted me on the head and went on her way. For some time after that, it was as if we had this story in common. She was always mentioning some part of a story I knew nothing about. It was too weird, because in time, I almost did get to know the whole story.

'*Whew*', I'd got away with it, *big time!*

That made me add another thing to my list: no more lying and making things up. Fibs can come back to haunt you, or bite you right on the ass. Had I got rid of one real bad shadow only to be followed around by another smaller one? No way!

That wasn't the only translation story during the period.

This one is about Mama and her best friend Conchita. It was an odd relationship they had as Mama didn't speak Spanish very well and had problems picking it up. I think that was how it started between them. Conchita came into her life to help her understand the language and practice by having simple Spanish conversations.

On this day they were struggling along, but having fun with it. I was too, just hanging about listening in. Chol came running to me saying Mama and Conchita were confused about something and he knew what it was and thought it was pretty funny. Mama was convinced she understood what her friend had asked her right away.

It went something like this; "how many Muchachas, (daughters) do you have, Rebecca?" The question was poised to Mama. Well Mama thought about it and replied, "two Conchita, one old and one new!" Conchita's face scrunched up puzzled. "Huh! How can you have one old and one new Muchacha's?" she asked. This made no sense to her whatsoever. By then I was in on it and was giggling under my breath too knowing exactly where the confusion lay. "Well come", said Mama, not understanding her mistake, "I will show you they are both in the garage where I store them!"

By now Conchita is thinking maybe Mama's crazy. Oh how I tried hard not to roll round on the floor laughing. We followed along and Mama opened the garage closet and pulled out two brooms. *"see,"* she said, holding them up one at a time as proof, *"one old, one new!"* OK, Conchita is now blowing a fuse. I'm thinking Mama is going to start getting angry as she's the butt of the joke. *"Muchacha's,"* she holds the brooms out again, forcefully, and a look on her face says *isn't it obvious my friend?*

OK, this had gone on long enough. I stepped forward to explain. "Mama is right, and you are right too, Conchita!" They both turned to me inclined to not let me finish. 'What are you talking about Sarah?' is what they are saying, as if I'm interfering. I giggled, "Well Conchita, in Arabic 'muchachas' means brooms," and I repeat to Mama in Arabic, that 'Muchachas' in Spanish of course means daughters.

"Oh!" they both looked at each other and we all had a good laugh over that bit of confusion between different languages.

They're not really common, these minor coincidences.

By the next summer holidays my Spanish was even better. It just came one day and I began to think in this wonderful language. Even the students were speaking it to one another more and not just in class but at appointments in town and other places. It was truly a treat to know what all these Cuban people were saying all around us all the time. Like Wow, I could really start to understand what's going on in their colourful culture.

I was realizing how much I loved these Cuban people; almost everyone was friendly. Of course, there are grumpy people everywhere. At times it was our teachers giving us grief usually because of personal reasons. It made us look forward and dream of the coming summer vacation and my chance to again experience Havana. Finally I was no longer dreaming about summer vacation, it was here. Baba, who had Ambassadorial duties on the Island, came personally to take us back to Havana with him.

This trip was to be different; it was to be at night. We caught the last ferry back so I thought there wouldn't be much of the ocean to look at. I was disappointed at that but then I found Baba had a private Stateroom. That was again a new experience. It had a TV, food, beds, even its own bathroom! Wow! Yong and I really thought this was fantastic, a private TV. Baba went to sleep and we stayed up all night watching whatever was on. That was a real treat. Now I understood about not sharing the privileges of Baba's posting in Cuba. We were probably the only students at school to have had such things happen to us.

Even after our first summer in la Havana, I was endlessly amazed by the excitement of such a huge city and all it had to offer everyone. In all of my experiences to date, there was nothing to compare to the wonder of so many people of all kinds. One of my favourite parts of all this shuffling between homes was the traveling to and from. It was great to get away from the grapefruit detail and the endless orchard, continuous vegetation that was pretty easy to get tired of day after day. The excitement building towards our actual departure, all the in-between transportation, watching out the windows seeing everything change from mile to mile; it was wonderful. I never tired of the color of the Cuban summer. It was all lush and tropical and green with many different kinds of blossoming flowers; it boggled the mind.

The chance again, even in the dark, to experience the ferry crossing only increased my love of that experience. The growing love of the ocean and its play with the sun, this was a kind of freedom. I felt the wind at the rail and watched the Island fade into the distance. This was the first part of three; the second was the stretch between the Island of Youth and Cuba and the third was the ferry approaching the main island. This was one of the places I learned not everyone appreciated a little girl with an inquisitive nature and endless questions about everything. I loved meeting people, so I had no problem just move along to the next opportunity. There were plenty who were nice and didn't mind all my chatter. They told me what they knew about the ocean, the fish, the birds, or about the ferries themselves. I even talked to the people who worked the ferry. I liked that and thought I might someday like to work on the ferry myself.

We were met on arrival by Alberto our driver in a newer type car he took much pride in. Again I really didn't have much to compare it with even though old cars were another color of Cuba. Years later, in all the places I've been, I would notice this. I didn't know it was government policy, so I thought maybe Cuba being an Island made it hard to get new cars. I was 11 and I didn't know. In Havana the neat old cars were everywhere. Cubans were very good at keeping these old vehicles going and on the road. They were all as different as the people driving them. It seemed a favorite pastime in Havana to just drive around and Alberto enjoyed doing that with us. He loved showing us all the interesting things to discover in his home city.

Havana itself was like that, a mixture of old and new, each area of the city having its own flavor to experience. There was always something going on; dance competitions, swimming, visiting the zoo and a lot more. Alberto knew what would be of interest for us and showed us a lot of the sights and sounds. Baba would come with us when he was free from work and we became the real and whole family I'd always dreamed of. I liked my family and me spending time together without many other people along. That was new too because in our prewar Bor days it was almost impossible to have a whole day alone with Mama and Baba together. They were always surrounded by so many people.

Mama and Baba were in a new house the Government had provided after the flood of the year before. It was in the same area of the city called Playa Nautico and in many ways a much nicer house and quite a bit larger. It had a wonderfully lush surrounding garden and even a gardener who maintained it. Many International diplomats lived in the neighbourhood as it was one of the nicest areas in Havana. The best feature of this new house was its location. There was a beautiful park and playground almost right next door where Mama and I liked to go for walks.

As well, in exploring the neighbourhood, it didn't take long to find and meet new friends for the summer. As I've said, there were diplomats from other countries such as Bulgaria and Russia, who had children some of whom I met and played with in the park. That added even more languages flying around in the mix; it was a good thing we had some Spanish in common. Mostly what we had in common was that they were the same age as Yong, Chol and me and liked to fool around, play and have fun just as much as we did. They would come by and get all, or at least one of us, almost every day for some devilry or other. Mostly we wound up playing harmless games and for the most part stayed out of too much trouble.

Every time I visited my parents in Havana, I would try some scheme to see if they would let me stay with them. For example, I would do everything I could to help them around the house so that, just maybe, they wouldn't send me back to the boarding school. It never worked.

Mama knew me altogether too well. She knew it would be difficult to get me to have to leave; I tried making up all kinds of things to stay longer.

Baba worked at his office a lot. He'd come home in the evenings really beat but no matter what, he'd spend time talking to me about my day and even play with me some. Sometimes Mama had to go to an appointment or shopping for things we needed. She would tell me to cook whatever I liked and take care of my brothers while she was gone. Mama wanted me to be responsible and learn as much as possible while spending time with them in Havana. I would get truly excited when she asked me to cook and take care of everything including the house. Leaving me in charge was a novelty.

What I liked about these visits the most was how normal it was. It was everyday life like I remembered it in Sudan, especially the time I spent with Chol. Taking care of him when Mama was out doing her thing meant I was the big girl in the house because my sisters weren't around. Achol was in Pinar del Rio and didn't come home for the holidays. Abany was on the island in a volleyball tournament. It was all good in my opinion because I wanted to take responsibility and be free to do as I pleased. Having no bossy sisters around helped a lot!

"*Ah ha!*" OK, I feel a sneaky story coming on. You know, like one of me 'acting responsibly.' It was one of those days Mama went out for some reason and left me with the job of cooking the meat for lunch. As arranged the night before, I woke up and made breakfast for my two youngest brothers. Then I took the meat out of the freezer for lunch and started cooking. It all started out well; I cleaned up the house, made the beds and was feeling all grownup as I focused on being responsible for Mama.

"*Hmm,*" but, I also really liked playing with the neighboring kids.

On that particular day our friends from Bulgaria and Russia came and wanted us to play with them. I explained I was much too busy making lunch for Mama. I couldn't play. They were insistent so I gave in, but I said only if we played in the yard by the kitchen so I could keep an eye on my cooking at the same time. Not a problem they said, and we started playing hide and seek. It was a whole lot of fun until Chol went to hide into the house and smelt something burning. He came running out yelling, "*Acuach, Acuach, the house is on fire!*" I immediately ran inside and the kitchen was full of smoke! Thank heaven I didn't see any leaping flames. What a relief. I felt my heart pounding normally in my chest. It wasn't all that bad.

What was bad was the smoke pouring out of the pot I was supposed to have been watching over, not fooling around, playing hide and seek with the neighbouring kids. I immediately got them to run around the house opening windows and doors to let the smoke out while I got the pot to stop smoking on the stove. For the most part, the food still looked OK and I thought we'd got to it just in time. Yong and Chol both chiding me, "Oh, oh," they said, "You're really going to get it from Mama now, Acuach!" I pretty much thought so too, but quickly came up with a not exactly honest idea.

I told everybody I knew what to do. I said it was all too easy, because I was very smart. The only thing I had to do was to take the meat that was not burnt from the pot and put it in a clean pot. I made all the kids promise me they wouldn't tell Mama. I said I would tell her myself. Then I cleaned the burnt pot and with the house all aired out, everything was back to, I hoped, normal.

Well OK, it was back to playing hiding seek again. Not long after, Mama arrived home ready for lunch. I'd had every intention of telling her what happened, but she tasted the food and told me I was a very good cook! Flushed with pride, I decided to keep my mouth shut. Chol was laughing and I could see he was going to tell on me. Quickly I told him I would get him an ice cream if he'd not do so. Chol, knowing if he did he wouldn't get my bribe, kept quiet. I was beginning to figure I just might get away with this small deception.

We sat down to join Mama for lunch and one of the kids who'd been playing with us came into the kitchen and saw what we were eating. I turned around to warn her not to talk, but it was too late. "*Ugh, you guys are eating burnt food?*" she blurted out. Well what choice did I have? I then had to tell Mama what had happened. She didn't even get mad at me; instead she laughed. She told me if I wanted to be responsible, I shouldn't start playing until I was finished my daily duties. "But Acuach Cor," she said, "you still did a good job and lunch was very tasty." She added, more seriously, not to make the same mistake again because I could have burned the house down! From that day on, I was more conscientious and careful with my responsibilities. I thought how horrible it would have been to have burnt down Mama and Baba's home. I didn't want to have to live life with that on my conscience. Yes, shades that would have become another shadow on my soul.

I remember little things, the happenstance of life, done on account of love. They helped me earn the strength to move on with living.

Mama and I were like best friends and could talk about anything and everything. We were always doing things together. Mama taught me many things, like how to embroider sheets, be a better cook, take care of our house and even how to braid hair. I loved learning from her. I appreciated that she was available at that stage in my life and that she shared valuable things between a mother and daughter. I loved to practice braiding Mama's hair. She had no one else to do that detail, so I would do it for her. I practiced a lot with her. One day I braided her hair so perfectly she couldn't believe it. She was so proud of me, that I had learned so quickly. Mama always had nice braids after that. She allowed me do that simple task for her. We both enjoyed yakking a lot and the time we spent in each other's company doing ordinary things.

Mama and I would go for walks after dinner and leave the boys and Baba at home. We would sometimes take long walks to enjoy the cooler evening air. The park was a wonderful place to do this and talk about the future, or just womanly ideas. On one of these occasions, out of the blue, Mama asked me, "Acuach Cor, you see that old couple sitting over there?" Of course I replied that I did. She went on to surprise me with, "soon Baba and I will look like that. In the not too distant future you know. Would you like to see us like that, some day Child?" I didn't even really think of my reply, it just came out. "No Mama, I don't want to see you getting old!" Mama smiled at me thoughtfully and patted me on the knee. "Well you know Sarah, everybody gets old, and if I'm to grow old with your Baba, it will be a true blessing, Acuach Cor." It took me a while to try and picture them all old and wrinkled. But I could always picture them together as they were now, so complete.

I smiled because I wanted to show her why I'd brought along a cassette player. Well, Sarah had a plan. Mama had looked at me questioningly when we'd left the house with it, but didn't ask why. Now was the time to show her. "Mama, I know that you and Baba will always be together and grow old." I laughed and turned on the boom box. I held out my hand to her, starting to dance to the Salsa music. "You'll never be too old to dance, Mama!" I knew that she loved to dance to traditional music, why not Salsa?

You should have seen her face change expression, it was so fast. It almost stopped my dancing around. Mama wasn't looking too pleased with my plan. "*Sarah*", she called to me over the music, "turn it down some." She looked to see if others were watching. "You do this at school?" Her finger was pointing at what I thought were my neat moves. It made me laugh. "Oh yes, everyone is learning to dance like this. Why not you?"

Her look was still hard to read, but I pulled her up by her elbow. "Come on Mama I'll show you how!"

I tell you, it wasn't easy pulling her off that bench. She seem glued to it and shook her head saying 'no no'. "People are watching Sarah!" I just giggled harder, "so come on Mama, dance with me. It's fun." Well, Mama shrugged, then grinned from ear to ear and started dancing. I almost fell down laughing with the moves she was trying hard to copy. She was pretty good too, but doing it with African style moves, so I copied her.

That drew a crowd of passersby, watching a very different Salsa dance style than they'd ever seen before. Mama didn't really see them at first as

131

they studied us. Then they started trying it for themselves and joined our dance circle. Then WOW, Mama noticed them joining and she outright glowed and got right into it, jiggling her body. Man, could Mama jiggle. The dancing went on for about four songs; another color of Cuba. People would join you right in the street and dance. They enjoyed life to the fullest.

Too cool! (an expression I found in Canada, I really liked)

Way to go Mama! I was so impressed that she'd done this. Yet I knew that it wasn't really like her to show off. Mama did it for me. It was at times like this that we were more like just best friends. The music was turned off and we sat back down on the bench. Mama turned the conversation around to me growing up. She was concerned about me dancing with boys like that. That made me laugh. I assure her Salsa music and dance was a national pastime. She understood because she'd seen that for herself. It was just that now her daughter was reaching, you know, that age. Now there were boys and all; it became that kind of mother daughter talk.

It was a heartfelt talk, as old as time.

This would be the last such talk Mama and I would have that summer. There were then only a few more days to pack and get ready to go back to school for another year. As he did when we came, Baba had work on the Island, so we would be returning with him too. All my reasons for staying had been tried and failed. The reality had to be faced. Actually, I was rather looking forward to getting back to my friends. I was missing them and wondering how their summer holidays had been. I realized too how much I loved school and hated that orchard! Oh well, Mama always said we had to face the good and the bad together. It was good that I would continue my education and bad that I would go back to missing Mama and Baba and rapidly growing Chol.

When it was time to go, Chol made a real scene about hugging us and bawling like a baby. *"Don't go Sarah, don't go. Who will I play with?"* he wailed. That made me blow it and I cried too. Yong gave me the stupid weak girls look again. He rolled his eyes and said, *"come on, come on . . . let's go."* But I noticed when he turned away from us, it was with wet eyes. That was just like Yong and his way of dealing with it. He was always the tough guy and all business. I knew that Yong was really looking forward to school and, man, he was good at that game. There was no competition there. It was obvious who the bright bulb in our family was. Even if I was a passable student, I really admired him and was always after him to help me with my school work. He was really good that way and actually enjoyed helping me.

My separation from Mama was never easy. I don't think it was for any of us, or for her, so it was a tearful leaving. As we looked back through the car window, I watched her and Chol waving from the curb until we disappeared from view. It was official now; our visit was finished and we were on the ride to catch the ferry, the ferry that would carry us back to the other life we lived. There would be more schedules and bells to answer to, in school, and in this war going on inside me.

One reason I wished I could stay there in Havana with Mama and Baba was the inter-tribal fighting that still went on. In Sudan at the Bor school I attended, this didn't happen as much because we were all mainly of the same Dinka tribe. Yet that life of easy acceptance was now gone forever.

The fighting between the boys and girls at the boarding school was still hard for me. It made me feel uncomfortable. I felt it prying its way into my world. I didn't like it and I couldn't understand it; it seemed so trivial. I didn't like to fight. It was one thing going through a war and quite another living and fighting with your own countrymen. They were fighting each other for no apparent reason. It was all so confusing. It was easier to get along with the different cultures that lived in my parent's neighbourhood in Havana than it was to live with my own countrymen in school. Was Baba maybe wrong about our culture and keeping it alive? If we couldn't get along with one another, how were we going to keep our culture alive? It became meaningless; another nightmare that kept age old hatred and violence a part of our lives.

I was feeling sorry for myself. All the way to and on the ferry I was thinking through these things. With all that had happened to our family and from the life I knew before in Sudan, I was not used to getting so much attention from my parents. I didn't want that closeness to be broken. It felt good to be around them, especially because there weren't many family members living with us in Havana. But, I had no choice. This year and for many years to come, I would have to return to school. I missed them so much. I couldn't really make my parents understand this because I didn't really understand it myself.

I did have good friends though and I tried to think about them to quiet the inner conflict that affected my life in so many ways. I really did love school and learning and I looked forward to being back with my girlfriends. I had no choice and the orchard work would always be there. It would be nice to be at home with Baba and Mama, to go to school in Havana, this wonderful city I was learning to love. But it just wasn't possible. I had tried to make it happen the way I wished it would and I had failed. I was on my way to what was real. I had to do as I was bidden.

Well, that was all wrapped up into a neat package. I began to feel resigned to my fate and in a funny way, I did feel better. Besides, it wasn't so bad. The summer season was over and another school year was coming. Having two homes was just the way it had to be. I'd had a really great summer holiday, life was moving along and next year... I would be back. I smiled and thought, '*yes, I can live with that!*'

Chapter 12
Torn apart again

I hadn't even been back one day and already those contrary feelings filled me. I realized I felt oddly good about being back to my Big House. The first night back in the dorm I slept like a rock and guess what, I was right back to looking at miles and miles of *grapefruit!* *"Grrr."* Man, I hated to even be reminded that shortly I would be right back to working out there. It was a thing I didn't want to even consider; getting under those short trees, bent over with a machete, red ants crawling all over you, all sweaty after rows and rows of cutting grass. Man, it was a tough detail that orchard!

It was really nice that all my friends were excited to have me back too. The crazy fourteen were back together and complete. It was a real hen fest, yackidy, yak, yak, yak about how our vacations had gone. I held back on at least some of the details, like the stateroom on the ferry. But I told them about my Russian and Bulgarian friends and the fun we had, and they all thought the smoking pot story was pretty funny, not to mention the *Muchachas* thing with Mama and Conchita's confusion over *Brooms* and *Daughters*, the *same and different!* School vacation was pretty good for kids at the boarding school because the government provided a lot of activities. Students got to go on camping trips to different parts of Cuba, some for a few weeks. Those who didn't go camping were taken to the beach just about every day and there were all kinds of sports and festive activities. It sounded as if my friends all had a great summer too, *aside from the orchard.* There was no getting away from that stupid place for them even in summer.

'*Hmm*,' come to think of it, maybe I really was privileged after all!

A few days before school started there was a notice that the first day we wouldn't have classes or orchard detail. *"Yippy!"* I thought. We would instead have an announcement in an assembly in our school's TV room. There was quite a lot of speculation that night; everyone was wondering what it was all about. The next day we would find out, and what it was, created quite a stir. I realized why Baba had brought us back to the Island; he was there in the morning at that meeting. I guess that's what his business here had been about. I could see him right up front with all the staff and teachers.

A teacher opened the meeting and then introduced our Ambassador, Gabriel Achuoth. He announced there had been meetings between the teachers, the board of education and himself. The meetings were to find solutions to the problem that there were a great many students who had little or no education when they came from Sudan. This was true right

135

from the younger members to the oldest students. It had been decided these students could not meet the grades that Number 12 School required to meet university entry level standards. They would be given an opportunity to choose the type of education they wanted from the vocational training being offered. They would go back home with some form of education, even if it was only a six month training course. Others would be sent to Zoroja Pinar del Rio military school. The rest, who were eligible to continue to higher education, would be staying on here at Number 12 Batalla de Korre.

You could feel the confused tension building through the students as another teacher came forward and began announcing names. The students whose names were being announced had to stay to find out about the vocational programs being offered them. You could hear people holding their breath, hoping not to hear their name announced. Finally the list was finished and the rest of us were dismissed and allowed to go outside for the day.

You could feel it; it was like a bomb had been dropped. Almost everyone had friends or family whose name had been called. Agor's and Yong's name had been read out. I was thinking, Yong? He was younger than me. I couldn't see them putting him into a construction program or something like that. What were they thinking? Yong was very smart. If anyone would make it to university, I knew Yong would be the guy. Or the Army? *Salute, salute, salute!* There you go Yong, ten years old, off to war?

What happened inside didn't take long to spread like fire through the students. Everyone was talking about it. It was even stranger for me as it involved Baba and was almost a violent situation.

There were about 200 students who had to go to vocational training. Some of them were very unhappy about taking a short training course and returning to Sudan. They were older and many of them had not been very disciplined when it came to school work. They had gotten into mischief, caused trouble in class and had not listened to the teachers. After the meeting, many of these students were angry over being chosen for these programs. They locked Baba and his co-workers up in the TV room where the meeting had been held and threatened to beat them up. These students were thinking that Baba was the one who had made the selections to sent them back home.

In fact, it wasn't Baba who decided who was to go or not. His job was to inform the students of the decisions that had been made at the Board of Education. It was Baba and his rational way of dealing with people who calmed the situation down. My Father was a good diplomat. He knew just how to talk to them. He explained to the students in a way that made them think about what they were doing. He asked, if he was

136

making these decisions, would he have picked his own sons for vocational training? Again, he said, he was only informing them about the decisions that been taken by the Board of Education. He had nothing to do with the decisions.

I was upset about everything, and confused: Baba being in danger, Yong picked for trade school, Agor leaving for nursing school. My sister Achol was already in Military school. I hadn't seen her very often since we arrived in Cuba, except on holidays and I missed her a lot. At least the Yong situation was being resolved; he was way too young for trade school. It had, in the end, been a mix up. Everything was getting all mixed up again, and it was going to get worse.

What had really upset me was Agor leaving. He'd been able to tell me about how he felt about it. Agor always wanted to serve his country. He didn't want to be in Cuba sitting in a class room while in Sudan so many of his countrymen were dying. He was happy that he had the opportunity to go for training in First Aid. It was training that would be useful to his countrymen and the military he still, in his heart, wanted to serve. Agor told me he never really liked school anyway and had only gone back because Baba had insisted. He was very happy about finishing school in under a year and returning to Sudan, even though he was leaving all his family in Cuba. My parents couldn't make him change his mind and they were worried for him. They wanted him to stay and study in Cuba, to have a better future. It was a future Agor just couldn't see for himself.

That was only the beginning of a season that started badly and just went from bad to worse.

A month passed and all the details of the students leaving for their new duties were worked out. The same was true of our life at school and really, other than that initial upset, things went on as usual for the rest of us. Or so I thought. I was about to find out something that would really blow me out of the water. It would have me make decisions for a lifetime. It would call for a maturity in me I didn't know I had. I was called out of class one day to be told my parents were there to see me and Yong. Of course I was excited to hear this, but something inside me was apprehensive. I had a feeling something bad was going to come of this surprise visit.

It would turn out to be another of those revelations that would turn my world upside down. Just when I thought everything was finally working out grandly. *'Blam!* I was informed that Baba and Mama were going back to Sudan!

They had taken us aside in the Principle's office for a private meeting. I knew something was up because Mama and Baba's expressions were all gloom and doom. I tried to ready myself, knowing whatever was coming, it wasn't going to be good. I knew it because all the family was present in that room, even Agor! That tipped me right off.

Baba said he was leaving his post as Ambassador. He was being called back to Sudan to do work for the war effort. He added that he was going to write a book about the history of the Sudanese People's Liberation Movement and needed to be back in Africa to do it. He was going to address the whole school with his announcement and had wanted to tell his family first. The announcement just hung there for a moment like a vacuum; none of us believed what we were hearing.

It was Mama who broke the silence. She asked us to remember we came to Cuba to study hard, to be educated for a better future, and that in the future we could do something for the new Sudan and for them too. To me, it sounded empty. I could see Mama was collapsing inside, holding in her tears, trying to be strong for us. She was supporting her husband in whatever the coming trials represented for the family. There was no room for discussion about this announcement. The political decision was already settled and their travel plans were set. They would be leaving in two months.

That was that and off to the school announcement they went. They left us there in shock with tears falling to the ground. It was so crushing and for me I felt as if the walls were moving in on me, as if there was no air. It was the house of sticks all over again. How could we have a home without Mama and Baba? My dreams were falling apart, unravelling into confusion. I was only just beginning to feel stable, thinking two homes were a good thing, having holidays with Mama and Baba in Havana. Now here they were to tell us this was no longer true.

I didn't know whether to be angry or run off the edge of the world screaming.

Again I went through a short period of lost time.

The buried bones of my travel bundle had somehow risen from the grave to bite me on the you know where! After Baba finished his public address to the school, they came back to say goodbye and take their leave of us. I don't recall the exact reaction of Yong and me, other than we had not taken this revelation of their leaving very well at all. We were truly freaking out!, that much I remember.

The very idea they were going to leave us behind was just not acceptable. I remember in a tantrum, saying things like, "it's just not fair, it's just not fair, Mama. Can't we go with you?" I don't even remember Mama's response. I just remember huge sobbing and plenty of tears. Baba took her out of the room for a time, to talk soothingly to us before they had to leave to catch the ferry to Havana.

From that point on, the rest of the evening was totally lost to me.

The nightmare lions came to my dorm, *stalking me*.

I awoke again to those screams I had to suppress, to lie there shaking with a taste of real fear. For a couple of days, it was like wandering around in a fog. Even the teachers were treating me oddly. They knew the news of my parents leaving had been a real shock for me. There seemed no real pressure from them for me to do anything. It was as if they gave me a couple of days break. All I could think of was that in two months time Baba and Mama would be gone from me. *'It's not fair, it's not fair!'* was playing over and over in my mind. My nights were spent trying to not go to sleep and dream. Even when I got to sleep I rolled around and couldn't get comfortable. My mind just would not shut up. It was a jumble of invading confusion, a continuous background mumbling.

My friends tried to do their part and help. They tried to talk to me. I couldn't reply. I took it out into the grapefruit jungle but I couldn't find the place where I had buried my troubled bundle. Everywhere in that orchard was the same, row on row. Well, oh well. There was a lot of ground out there to accept my sorrows and so I picked any old spot to fall down into my well of tears. It always seemed to be close to the same spot although I could have imagined it. This time the trees were bigger, and gave more fruit.

There was no resolve, no adding to a list. I felt only sorrow, saw only the bleak grey that takes over the sky just before it rains. Only a needle of positive thought poking me. All my friends here lived without their parents. Now I did too. I needed to be there with them, wondering if this grey would ever leave. Could I just accept the Big House was my home? *Maybe.*

Through the rushing trials of emotionally charged events, another Sarah was beginning to emerge. I had passed two birthdays by then in the Big House even though they never had birthday celebrations. I was now thirteen and the rhythm of school life had it own reality. The seasons changed regardless, the years moved on. I was moving whether I liked it or not into my future.

I left the orchard with the realization of something else that must be faced.

Yet how, was the question.

I was no longer a little girl. I still had little girl hopes and dreams certainly, but did they still apply? Not really. Next summer I would not be going back to Havana. All the things I had expected to take place were no longer real. For a week, I watched, observing, the school and its life. I could see my friends and most of the students really seemed happy. They were adjusting to life here without their parents and some had no family at all. I at least had Anyuon, Deg Ti, Abany and Yong. Even on most weekends, I still got to be with Agor.

I thought about going back to Sudan and weighing the idea. It was as if the little girl in me could accept nothing but going with my parents wherever that might lead. It didn't matter! Then the old bones creep up on me and I had another set of fears to go through. Could I really see myself going back to my country in a Civil War and so much horror? Could I go to school there? Would I even be able to stay with my parents when we got there? Maybe I'd have to go to another Bilfam, or even back to the UN camp! That did not sit well with me, not at all. No way!

I decided I did not want to go back to Sudan or anywhere in Africa. Cuba would be a good place for me to grow up. I loved the people and their way of life. And well . . . there was Salsa to consider. Nope, I couldn't fly away from this music, the dancing fun we had almost every weekend and even dance competitions.

It wasn't Baba's fault the SPLM was sending him back to do other work. It stood to reason if he had to go back, then Mama would have to go with him. I had seen how much it hurt Mama to have to face that reality. As a teenager now, I had to face these realities not throw a fit like a little girl. That I had to control my own life was yet another kind of fear. Did I have the ability to make my own independent decisions? This was a very difficult question to ask myself, one that crept its way into my consciousness for most of a month.

I started getting used to the idea of staying in Cuba without my parents. I was even rather excited for the future. Deep inside though, I was sad, insecure and anxious. I convinced myself to be brave and not burden my parents. I felt one day I was going to finish studying and I'd be somebody really important with my education. I'd be responsible and confident. I would help them in the future, just like they'd been helping us.

It was like the sport I had learned that I really liked; basketball. My thoughts were like dribbling the ball at a full tilt back and forth across the court. When the opponent ran at you, you'd let it bounce and back you'd run to keep it going. Of course, in the end someone had to win. All games had rules and I was even good at making them up. It was just that in this game, I had to figure out how anyone would win. I decided to serve up my hand to get control of the ball, all confident. It was a powerful stoke of determination. That game began.

Once again Yong and I were told our parents were back to see us, all serious and concerned. Oh man, did they steal the ball! They had my shadow diving to reach the ball with a plummeting crash, missing the return entirely. There we sat, all wide eyed, our hearts hammering in our chest. I was busting at the seams to tell them of my brave determination to accept my fate, to relieve their burden with self sacrifice.

Baba had on his most serious commanding father face of final say, and his fast ball curve dribbled right by. "We are here my children," he said with dramatic sigh, "to tell you we have changed our minds!" His eyes looked haggard reflecting compassion and hard consideration. Father got right to the rebound. "Mama and I have decided, after careful consideration . . ." Baba took his stance carefully and then let go a three pointer. *"Acuach Cor, you and Yong will be coming back to Africa with us!"* Mama, his second on the team, nobly nodded her head, knowing the ball was all in their court. Baba passed off the ball to Mama as Yong and I swung our heads to look at each other, like... 'what?' Yong's eyes were as wide eyed as mine. I saw his top lip quivering. Though I had no idea of his thoughts, I saw in his eyes he didn't want to go back. He was pleading me, *'Acuach take the ball, take the ball... pleeeease!'*

I turn back to butt in and steal the play, but Mama dodged that with a now-listen look. "I'm so worried for you Acuach Cor." I could see Mama was trying hard to show how important this was for her. *"You're too skinny; you don't eat enough!* You're such a picky eater and they tell me you still don't eat properly." I could see Mama couldn't imagine me living there without her supervision. She really wanted to take us with her. I was thinking it wasn't a very strong play, this statement. Still, I listened to see where it would lead. *'I have to go back to Africa, cause I'm skinny?'* The food at the U.N. Camp was just horrible and Bilfam was even worse! Man, there I'd be real a skeleton. *Dead.*

End Game.

Yong looked like the game was already lost and nodding. *'Yep, Sarah's skinny. Score one point for Mama.'* I felt a burn; *skinny people make great basketball players.*

OK, enough fooling around.

It was actually a very serious day and I've been trying to cover a hard moment with a little funny play by-play. In reality, these moments with my parents were to influence the rest of my life and create seemingly endless heartaches.

It was true; I was really a picky eater, especially, when it came to pork, and in Cuba pork was a common food item. I always thought pigs were very dirty looking animals. I couldn't imagine myself eating them. Yet this meeting was forcing me to think about it. I had convinced myself that Yong and I needed to stay there in school. That meant eating pork. Mama, who knew me so well, had actually brought that up as an argument although not exactly as I have presented it.

Now there was more of Mama and Baba giving their reasoning for us to go back with them. The more they talked, the more the courage built in me to be strong and present my decision. When the opening came, I took it. Yong really did look like he was thinking 'go Sarah go!' He nodded his head vigorously when I made my points for Mama and Baba to consider. I swore up and down I would eat better and even try pork; anything to convince Mama I was grown up enough to handle staying in Cuba.

I talked fast at first so they wouldn't cut me off and they did try. Baba gave me a look that said, *'now that's enough Sarah, you're going to Africa!* I just kept right on going with all my reasoning. I wanted to make this decision for myself. It was then when I put it that way, Baba began to listen and nodded his head to the rationally presented points I made.

My winning argument went like this. "Baba," I said. I had my hands on my hips and I put it to him as seriously as I could. "You told us to study hard here and we could make a difference. If we go back to Africa, *we won't be able to study!"* Baba switched teams.

Two points for Sarah.

That was pretty much the turning point because Baba started talking to Mama about my good points. Yong and I knew then we'd scored and won the game. *High Five!*

They were very happy to hear me talking like that and it looked as though they were relieved. They must have known taking us back to an uncertain way of life was not really viable. They knew it really was best for us to be in Cuba. We would be safe and would be getting an education and that was something they couldn't guarantee would be available for us in Africa.

Mama felt better. She knew I would always look out for Yong. Yong and I were in the same classes and when we went to Havana, I was always the one to look out for him because we were close in age. This was basically the last conversation. I promised that all of us would do our best, and I would look out for Yong.

The only thing that Yong did say, in response to that, was *"I can look after myself, Mama!"*

As good as my word, the next time it was on the menu, I tried pork. Right away I thought I would choke on it. I found it was tasty, and probably good for me, but I still didn't like the look of it and the smell turned my stomach. After a month of trying, as I promised Mama, I found I was eating pork and enjoying it! I was convinced now it was good for me and I wouldn't be skinny forever. Maybe all this time, I was only missing pork meat. Well that didn't turn out to be the case and I'm still skinny, like a stick. I was also eating and finishing everything else on my plate. I don't know how, but Mama found out I was eating much better. I was thinking maybe she had spies everywhere. Was someone checking up on me and telling her about my activities at school and especially with food?

They were becoming convinced their children were going to be all right and were mature enough to handle things at school and living on in

Cuba. I think it was important for them to know this before they returned to Sudan. And return they did. We had one final visit with them and Chol before they left. Mama took me aside and told me that she'd agreed to let me stay because she trusted me. She said I was a big girl now and I could take care of myself. I was so proud for her to tell me this, but at the same time devastated, knowing soon they would be gone. She gave me that final oh so warm loving hug and a kiss goodbye. There was a lot of that for everyone. It went on for some time because no one was in a big hurry to have it end. Before they left, they promised us they would write and keep in touch. It was almost impossible to say good bye, so we didn't.

It ended with Baba saying, "don't worry, we will all be together again someday!"

If Baba said it... it must be true.

All this brought my school work into focus. I realized the whole wide world would be out there waiting for me. I was going to study hard and make my parents proud of me. One day all this would be over and, as Baba had said, *'We will all be together again someday!'* As to the *'not to worry'* part, how could I do anything else but worry for them? I held on to the promise of their corresponding with us back and forth, not knowing it wouldn't be that way at all. No, not ever.

I was more concerned about the kind of life that lay in store for them back in Africa. I kept my fingers crossed for them and made myself stay busy, continuing with my Spanish and engaging in activities with my friends or the many music activities going on at the school. I loved sports. I was getting better in Basketball and really counted my blessings. I had my brothers and sister there for me when I needed them. This was my life now.

Two months after Baba, Mama and Chol left, Achol went back to Africa after finishing her military training. About the same time, Agor graduated and it was time for him and the other students to return to Sudan. We never got to say goodbye to Achol so we told Agor with some seriousness to write and let us know what was happening in Sudan and how Baba, Mama and Chol were getting by. It was hard because we'd expected them to write to us right away on their arrival. I was worried something bad had happened to them. I imagined plane crashes and all manner of horrible things that could have happened. Again came that, *'it just isn't fair'* stupidity.

I thought if I wished hard enough, their letters would somehow start coming.

It was tough for me to let go of Agor because he was my favorite brother and we'd always got along famously. He would never mind when I tagged along with him. Now my Agor was gone too. I was upset and I started having strange premonitions I was never to see him again. It seemed each time one of us was separated from the family, we were somehow separated from the rest of the world. My world at least. As it was, fate would leave the five us at Number 12 School for the best part of the next four years. Then the thinning down of our family in Cuba would continue till we all left that life behind. Well, that was coming. More hardships and trials were on their way. In the many changing seasons, we tried to keep a family life, such as it was, close to our heart.

Chapter 13
At School

Eight months passed and we still had no news from Agor or my sister Achol for that matter. I thought at least I'd have news from Agor. He'd assured me he would search out where Baba and Mama had settled with Chol and send news when he found them. In my mind I figured it would be at the U.N. Camp where Baba had built the house of sticks for Mama. I also imagined they were at the mansion in Addis Ababa. That had an equal chance of being true because the SPLA headquarters was in the Ethiopian capital.

Auntie Mary Apiu, some months before, told us she'd seen them in Addis Ababa as she was leaving to come to Cuba. She said, in a short meeting, my parents had asked her to look out for us. At that point at least, Auntie's news had eliminated the fear that their plane had crashed into the ocean.

My constant hope was that they weren't suffering in that terrible UN Camp.

It was with the idea of discovering the facts that I made my first attempt to contact the SPLM in Havana. Pagan Amum had taken Baba's position as Ambassador and I thought if anyone knew, it would be that man. I had already tired the staff at school, bugging them about letters and telephone calls. I took the issue to Anyuon. I felt he was now the responsible Baba replacement as our eldest family member. All of us were very concerned. We met often to wonder what had happened and find ways to get some information about our parents. At school we'd been given calling cards for long distance and Anyuon had to pick a time in town to make the call. Even this created an anxious waiting period.

I remember waiting with excitement for him to come back with what I hoped was glorious news, only to be sorely disappointed. It was one of many such times, torn between hope and disappointment. My brother too was frustrated because he couldn't even get through to Pagan Amum. No one at the SPLM office knew anything that would help us to locate our parents. All we could do was just wait and hope that any day now we would get some letters. They never came.

Any day now turned into years of frustration. All we had were each other and life within the boundaries of Number 12 School.

Another uncelebrated birthday came and went. I had periods of deep depression over this heartache. Then I tried to pull it together and remember my dedications, my list and my periodic visits to bellyache to the grapefruit. I hoped talking to the trees might make me feel better.

Their only advise was to forget about it, move on and let time tell me what was what.

My friends were helpful as well. I would get going with them and it helped me forget I was so unhappy. They had the same problem. They too were always waiting for news from home.

We were all in the same sinking boat.

One day there came a notice John Garang was to visit the school. It had all the students talking and hoping he was going to bring letters and personal news from home. It didn't happen. John Garang had visited the school in 1986 when Baba was Ambassador with a message of support for the students and a description of the aims and purposes of the SPLM. He emphasized how important we were to the future of our country. He stated very clearly, "in the future, when you become professionals, keep your culture and ahead of everything, respect your family!" He went on to explain the objectives of the war and why the Civil War had started. He said the movement was fighting for the opportunity of each and every South Sudanese to have an education, social development and especially, proper health care. He also thought 'the separation of the state and religion' was very important for some reason. John Garang ended with his hope for a long peace and the distribution of wealth and prosperity for all Sudan.

We were really in awe of the man. *This*, was *John Garang!* The man who started everything for us all! It was all good. I understood at least some of what he'd shared with us. During John Garang's second visit, the one I'm telling you about now in 1989, we were taken to Tarara International Camp in Havana. This was a bit of a surprise, as we thought he was coming to our school. His objective this time was to fortify the SPLM in its relation with Cuba and the socialist world. It was an address to the country of Cuba and we students were only there to act as a colourful background.

Really, I couldn't even tell you what the speech was about. It was all political and business concerns that were way beyond my understanding. After that visit, he was off to Nicaragua to meet President Daniel Ortega. He was hustled off the stage by bodyguards and that was that. Off to the buses and back to the school we went. There had been no opportunity to meet him. All the students were disappointed as there were a lot of unanswered questions, mostly concerning home. They were questions, that in the end, nobody had answers for.

We were all of us in a kind of information limbo. All we had were the standard explanations of why we were taken to Cuba: *study, become professionals, go home!* So what else was there? We could only concentrate on what we knew. No one was going to help us connect with home. Africa was the past. We were on an Island, both physically and emotionally, and

146

had to rely on ourselves. Number 12 School became home; the oldest students became our parents. These searches had done something to us all. It was never really stated, or even talked over, but a major change had overtaken us all.

After that visit, all the tribal conflicts at our school came to an end.

The students become one family. Sure families have fights and disagreements; it just was no longer about turf. I watched the change take place and was never so amazed. I wondered many times how it came about. Eventually I realized it was because there was no contact with our homeland, no detailed news about the state of the civil war even. We were isolated. We had no real contact with the outside world.

We didn't even know who the Beatles were!

Every year we had a lot of activities on the Island of Youth, especially sports competition between schools such as volleyball, basketball, soccer and handball. My school was famous for basketball. Why? We had a lot of really tall guys and they were all good athletes. Sudan is known to have some of the tallest people anywhere in the world. I guess you could say that gave us an advantage over short people! It created quite a rivalry between the schools. As our guys were pretty poor losers, they'd get into fights after the games. Some of the schools were afraid of our boys. I thought they wouldn't let them win because of this. Me, I just thought fighting on principle was stupid. Ya, well; stupid boys will be boys.

We were no longer stupid girls. They were chasing us all the time, trying to gain our attention. Hey, do the math! There were a lot of boys and very few girls to start off with. The number got even smaller because some had gone for six month nurses courses and the like. Well, OK our virginity was protected in one way. The rule at the school: *you get pregnant, you go home!* The school just had no facilities to take care of babies and that rule had been well explained right from the beginning. Of course some girls didn't listen, so that further decreased the girl population.

I did have boyfriends, but I always was aware of what Mama told me in our womanly talks, things I've followed throughout my life really. Mama said there would come one special man, like her Baba. So in my relationships, I was pretty serious and, like my food, picky about choosing. Sometimes I was without boyfriends for long periods at a time. No big deal; I was in no hurry and most of these guys were like the word says, 'boy' friends. The first one I had was really only a boy and my friend. We would hang out, talk, and maybe hold hands and go for walks after supper.

I studied hard too and, you know what, it never did any good! I still had to bug Yong to help me pass tests. I guess in some areas I was kind of lazy and sports were more important. I would leave studying for tests to the very last minute, then scream. "YONG!" and be up half the night

147

cramming with a pretending-to-be-angry Yong. Boy, do I love my brother. He was always bailing me out and never complained.

The rest of my family (other than me) were really very smart and did well in school with their grades. By then the teachers could see Yong was rather special, always at the top of his class. For him, education was very serious; it was competition for Yong. He was the best chess player at school and involved in anything that would challenge his mind. Yong was also really tall and placed in a junior team in basketball. Though he never went on to join the senior school team, he was always with his friends on the court after school playing Five-on-Five.

Sudanese are really competitive people and sports are a major part of life. Tribal people had to have a lot of endurance, like me. We are runners. Soccer in Sudan is the National pastime and it was in that my brother Anyuon shone. He was a man who could do it all. I was so proud to watch him play. He had an advantage being left handed and so was very unpredictable. This was especially true in the beginning when the other schools didn't know this. Our Number 12 school had a secret weapon; *Elijah Gabriel.*

I mention this now because in the family we always used our tribal names. We also had and were baptized with Christian names and the teachers only knew of us this way.

Ok, now an explanation.

I just realized I haven't mentioned this in the book till right now! So let's just get this out of the way and carry on, alright? You know of course I'm Sarah. If you haven't guessed by now, my tribal name is: *Acuach Cor.* My oldest sister *Achol* had no Christian name. Later in life I would find out she was a cousin who had come to live with us and was adopted. My other sister *Abany* is known as *Marta.* Now the boys. *Anyoun* you know already is *Elijah.* My oldest brother, who I haven't really mentioned a lot because he never left Sudan, *Deng Did* is named *Fredrick. Deng Ti* is called *Michael,* and *Yong,* who likes to be called just *Yong,* is *Emanuel.* Confused yet? I am, just a little.

Sorry, I didn't put this list in alphabetical order, "*ha, ha, ha.*" Actually, *oops!* I forgot *Chol* known as *Job* because, he left with *Mama* and *Baba.* OK, no more fooling around.

I have a bunch more I could tell you about my brothers and sisters, but they will enter and re-enter further along in my unfolding story. The following two years from 1989 to 1991 were the good years. This period was the pinnacle of our stay at Number 12 school. In my life it was like a pause, like holding my breath. Time seemed to flow by in schedules, ringing bells, moving from sports events to much awaited holidays away from work.

It was the program of our world.

The program is what I lost myself in, filling my time, concentrating on all the great things we were involved in. It was a time of transition, the leaving behind of childhood, the putting aside those things buried, and the almost ghost like memories, unclear and rarely thought of past traumas. I considered only what was right in front of me. With no choice, I just had to grin and bare it.

That damn orchard!

The time in the orchard was blocked out the most. I would just go out there and go on automatic pilot. After so many years of this shifting every weekday between school and work, there was no thought involved in that orchard. I knew every inch of the job. At times it could be fun, when we knew no one was watching, to have grapefruit wars between the short stocky trees. Well, that was pretty much the only one amusement you can have with grapefruit! Other than that, it was a mindless, never ending slog. At least half the time spent on Island of Youth, was in the orchard.

I hated that mandatory detail with a passion!

I don't think there was a student on that Island who didn't. No matter the country or culture we came from, we all had that one thing in common. I bet no matter where they are in the world now, none of them buy grapefruit. I know I don't! I see them at the supermarket and for a few seconds get depressed. I feel like starting grapefruit wars with the other shoppers buying them. Why even import such ugly sour fruit!

Soon in the sinking ship that was Cuba, we would be eating a lot of grapefruit every day. Only that was still to come. Right then we ate really well. We had three meals a day plus two snacks every day. It was taught that nutrition was an important part of life, to keep up your strength for sports... *feed the mind, is to feed the body!*

It was a fluke of nature I thought that picking time came right before the end of school. Then for two months the orchard, miraculously, didn't need us. "*Yippy!*" I'll bet if there were a kingdom, or a song, based on Freedom and Joy...

It for sure, contains no grapefruit.

Festival de la Toronja (grapefruit). Yep, you might have guessed. Every year this ugly fruit got its own festival. Even though we hated that fruit, that festival was a big deal on the Island of Youth. People came from all over Cuba to participate. We understood it totally; it was a celebration for the end of the harvest. The picking was finished for another season. "*Yep, yep, yep, yippy!*" that's how we felt. We thanked the gods of all things that are wonderful. The grinding torture was put away for a while. The rewards and the bounty were as promised. The noble grapefruit was to be delivered to the worthy subjects of its subjected toil.

The Festival de la Toronja.

Here was our kingdom of song, for the Island of Youth, our joy and freedom. And...it was all about, *Grapefruit!* It was our ball & chain, our prison duty, our toil to pay for no crimes that we could think of, only maybe the branding of 'Student!' Well, that's not entirely fair. The students weren't the only people who worked the orchards. Grapefruit was the major crop of the island and it took many hands to pick them clean. The harvest was very much a local social occasion with whole families out there doing their part to share the work. Socialism. This was very much like Cuba. I was learning about the blending of cultures, Spanish and Socialism, the mixture of the old and the new.

The celebration, the fiesta as old as time, was where at the very center, I held a secret. I felt as if it were known there was a chance everything would just disappear and be no more. I considered this long and hard because that was the year I put away a thing that was almost impossible to give up. I had carried this thing around within me since I was I think about five. I kept it a secret because it sometimes got me into trouble. For me it was a sparkling jewel, a piece of a crown. It was a place where I could disappear and, even at times be invisible! For as long as I could remember, the one thing I was really good at, but which wasn't considered valuable, was an overactive imagination.

The one person in the whole world that I had ever shared it with was my Baba.

I had even taken that jewel and, in the middle of the orchard, after a grand display of dark thoughts and angry tears, placed it in my travel bundle and buried it along with all the Shades of Shadow I couldn't deal with. It was the only one thing in the bundle that shone and held the Light of promise. This jewel held all I had ever wished for, held all my hopes and dreams that all and everything that could be imagined to be right and true. It contained all the fantastic places a child could entertain herself with, and well, the one thing Acuach Cor was really good at.

Making things up.

What gave me the will to continue the story was when I was little. It was a bedtime story, a fairytale I carried on into my play. I imagined it with my dolls, kept it mostly to myself and looked for it in our few children's picture books. I listened hard for it in grandma's stories and Dinka legends. So it was, that I had held onto this untold story. It was a story Baba fueled with one simple statement, "Acuach Cor," he once said, "the imagination is a wonderful thing." It must have been a sleepy time story and began with... "Can you imagine" and, that was it. He made up a small story for me about a wonderful kingdom.

At the end of the story a King came home from a long journey. It was cause for celebration and all the people of the kingdom of course lived happily ever after. It was a pretty common sort of fairytale, one I added

150

magic to, creating fanciful wonders and riches the king and his family would, of course, have. In my story Baba was the unrecognized King and the chain of this fantasy meant Mama was the Queen and their children, princes and princesses. I tried to talk the younger children and my friends into adventures in this kingdom, to run around in our castle in Bor, and play out this fantasy.

At times, and through the various stages of my life, and in running to Baba, the staging of my fantasy became almost too real. It almost made it dangerous to believe in my fairytale. Remember the SPLM mansion in Addis Ababa when Mama would get all dressed up to entertain guests, when she would walk down those stairs and enter just like a Queen? Think of Baba off in Cuba, the journeying King, and us living in this unimaginable splendor. I'd never experienced anything like it before, except in my fantasy. My huge bedroom was the ultimate place to make my fairytale so visually extravagant. I would make tents in the desert out of bed sheets and blankets and smuggle in tea service to serve and entertain visiting royalty. On it went, those wonder places. Of kingdoms and palace gardens, such was the fertile soil for a little girl's imagination in the midst of adult realities that were far beyond my comprehension.

This was a place where I could make it disappear.

Those images were still fresh when I came to the Big House situated in the middle of that forest of grapefruit. It didn't help any that Wow... here was a castle and all these children are waving at the bus. I snuck in the thought with a suppressed giggle, 'the princess has returned!' Such delicious thoughts these were in the beginning. Gradually they began to turn to smoke and ash. Childish daydreams; they began to fade and be unimportant as I accepted the growing reality.

Sarah Gabriel, the ordinary girl from Bor. I was only one of many displaced Dinka who must find a place within this adopted ideology to force down fantasy. In a way, I did so by just transferring it. I found I was good at writing. I had a very big note book were I would draw and make up stories. One of my favourites was about a little girl (me) walking a very long way with a dog and cat towards a village far away and a home in a house of sticks where her monkey lived in the trees. I'd seen others have pets and wished I could have one for myself as I'd had in Bor. It was one more thing to add to a wish list that couldn't become a reality at Number 12 School.

The festival of 1989, when I was fourteen, was that turning point. Yes, I was really happy the orchard work was finished for the year. I hadn't been to the Festival de la Toronja in 1987 and 1988 because I'd been in Havana for the holidays. So this wonderful event was known to me, but I'd never attended. My friends were really excited about it and couldn't wait for it to come. Many times they talked about it coming as we toiled in the orchard. They told me how colourful and exciting it all was.

It gave me something to look forward to instead of worrying over my parents and what to think or do about them. I was mostly worried for Agor. I didn't know why, it was just the way I felt. I couldn't shake this shiver I had whenever I thought too long and hard about my brother. I would lie in bed and pray for him, pray that he was safe and not involved in the war. I knew he was and that made it worse. I hoped since he was a medic maybe that would keep him safe, not being a soldier in the forefront of all the action. Sneaky thoughts came to me sometimes and I would fight them. If Baba was the King and could look after everything, he'd always have a way of getting to what was needed. Why hadn't he found some way to reach us? It was what I needed. Why hadn't I heard from them and where were they? Were they even alive?

My worst fear; that they were dead.

The beginning of the festival brought my fairytale back. With all the preparations and decorations in place, it was so like some magic Kingdom. Maybe the King was coming home, itched the small inner voice of unreasonable and unrealistic hope. There I was on this street the town had blocked off for the celebration. It was all getting started and I saw people going by in costume. Man, I wished I could have been one of them. Their costumes were so beautiful, especially the women. Wow, way too sexy to be real. They had tall plumes of feathers on their heads, sparkly bikini tops, and long sweeping cloaks. Each and every one was different. The men wore gleaming white bulbous sleeved shirts and tight white pants, more than that I don't remember. I was too busy drooling over the women and their wonderful gear. Later in the evening it was their dancing together that really set me off. I studied their moves and my friends and I for a long time afterward, tried to duplicate them.

It started with a parade that was more like a street party and everyone could just join in, so we did. There was food and drink all up and down the street, and cheap too! For the boys of the school it was a real novelty. There were big trucks called Pipas... 'full of beer.' The next day there were a lot of hung over boys wondering around feeling sorry for their fat heads. 'Hah', I thought, serves you right. I had seen quite a few making fools of themselves, trying to bug me to dance. No way! The stupid boys were drunk and even stupider. A few of the girls were stupid right along with them, falling down on the dance floor.

Then Amel dragged me off by my elbow all excited. *"Come on Sarah, come on . . . it's time!"* For what I couldn't imagine, but I let her drag me away from the dance floor. We followed a lot of people going somewhere. I have to admit, I was pretty pleased with this whole deal. *All supplied by, Grapefruit?* Great, I could relate to that and wondered if maybe this would be a big grapefruit fight. That'd be the caper! What it turned out to be was really spectacular. I can say, using an English youth expression, '*it blew my mind!*'

Like the the Beatles, I'd never before seen a display of fireworks. That was new.

What it brought about in me, was something very old, a fantasy I hadn't thought of in a very long time. This was like the people celebrating the homecoming of the King! The sparkles of flame shooting into the air were captivating. The 'oh's' and 'ah's' of the surrounding crowd carried my mind right away. 'Oh Baba, where are you', came the unbidden thought. I wished both he and Mama could be there to experience this with me. I knew Chol had never seen anything like this. I could see him right here beside me squealing with delight. "*Look Sarah... look, look!*" It was a good thing everyone was looking up to the sky because my eyes filled with tears.

Right then I remembered my childhood fairytale and it was like this was welcoming the King Home. I imagined for a moment that's what it was. There I was with my tiara and jewels all shining. There was one brilliant display, a really big one that lit up the whole sky. I made a wish that Baba and Mama, wherever they were, were safe and that everything was alright for them. That explosion hung there in the sky for a long time, like it was happening in slow motion. The thoughts of our kingdom felt so real. Then the falling sparkles fell from the sky and sputtered out. It made me realize the tale was for a child. This made me feel angry.

Something inside me was telling me I had to give it up. Why? Why should I give this up? Well maybe so it didn't seem so crazy arguing with myself. As the fireworks finished and people began to move away, I stood there staring off into the darkening sky. I thought I mustn't cry and be childish, mustn't cling to silliness about a fantasy Kingdom. I needed to put it away if it was always affecting me this way. So I did. In my mind's eye I took off my crown and Acuach Cor took out its jewel to hide away in her heart. While Sarah turned and followed my group of friends back to the dance floor, this idea came. 'Move on Sarah. Build a life, be real with yourself.' The festival was only the beginning of that year and there were many more things planned. I left behind an old dream for a new life...

I had a new dream, a new Sudan, and somewhere down that road a brilliant future. It was a new fantasy.

That was the point and purpose of being on the island of Youth; to feed our minds.

Our fantastic teachers were passionate about us learning Spanish. Knowing we needed to really explore the culture, they made it fun to learn, made it into a thing to look forward to. Those two summer holidays of the between years hold some of the best memories of my life. On

153

school holidays they would take us to different provinces to spend about a month getting to know the country. This is what the teachers had prepared us for.

We would mix with the culture of Cuba.

I was fourteen and the one thing I thought of at the time was experiencing the moment. I loved moving from one thing to the next that had nothing to do with grapefruit! Boy, this I found exciting. Anything that didn't involve that stupid place was great with me. Most every weekend we would go camping. The best part of that was the food. They would give us a lot of canned meats, cookies, candies and much more. I don't know why I couldn't get fat because I was eating a ton. I seemed to always have my tummy grumbling for feeding. I was enjoying being at the school, having fun with my friends.

The idea of camping in Cuba is very different than, say, in Canada. For instance, there was no taking a tent, or cooking on camp fires. These camps were like a little village. You rented small cabins and there was one place for everyone to cook. Each school brought their own cook. There were all kinds of games and activities and I even learned how to ride and love horses. That was the thing I remembered the most, and still miss.

What I liked best were the dances. Oh boy! *Salsa!* There were dance competitions at outdoor dance floors with judges watching. At the end of certain songs, they would pick the best partners. I won my fair share. I knew I was a pretty good dancer, but Amel was awesome and even better. All the boys wanted to dance with her nonstop. We girls had a blast there and music was a big part of our reality. In many ways, it was how we learned to improve on our writing in Spanish. I was fascinated by romantic songs and when I learned Spanish, my friend Mana and I would translate Arabic songs into Spanish. Later on, as we started to listen to Spanish music, we began writing out the lyrics of the Latin stars we liked the best.

All well and good, but the 90's were about to unfold. World events in that period meant freedom for millions, but the end of decadence for us. It was just like the way my life had been going. There would be periods of time where there was a sense of security. I would let down my guard and, even though there were things that weren't perfect, like not knowing where that missing part of family was, life seemed to be really good, and productive, but never predictable.

Then whoosh, in would come a wave and fill that leaky boat, and I'd need to bail like crazy to keep things afloat. The transition to those events was away out there in the ocean building that wave. It came with the new decade, fueled by age old world problems, many of which we didn't understand. We certainly didn't understand the ways this would affect our well being. The world's stage was about to force us to face conditions beyond our control. It would show us how fast a tsunami can raise the oceans surge.

It would change everything.

Chapter 14
The Collapse of Communism

By the coming of 1990, the topics and tensions in my schooling had created in me a kind of maturity. There was an energy in the air, a type of charge that was electrifying, the idea that we were entering a new decade. The 80's and all the things that occurred in that decade were part of my childhood and were historical events. These were the parts of my life connected with Africa: our fleeing Sudan, the horror I'd witnessed that would colour the rest of my life, the insecurity of shifting realities that had taken us from one temporary home to another, Baba's efforts to get us out of Africa and into the safety of the SPLM educational program in Cuba.

It included settling into what was, for us, a very intensive program; learning a new language, and more. We had to adapt to the culture we Sudanese students found ourselves immersed in. We had to deal with the complications involved in our training and simply growing up into some level of maturity. All of this had happened to me in the course of seven years since our family fled Bor. You could say all of the things that had happened to me were, in a manner, an education. Life had in the 80's taught me some pretty hard lessons.

So much of my childhood had been a series of traumas that had shattered the foundation of normal development. They had created situations that were literally incomprehensible. To deal with this gamut of emotional frustrations, there had been periods of growth and clarity, relationships that brought about better times and even found joy. Fortunately I had the kind of resilience only children can exhibit. I had to change with the changing seasons, had to play the hand life dealt me, exist in the world as it was. Now Cuba was shaping my life. My inner world of childish fantasy, this imaginary Kingdom where I'd held a special view of my family, was now folded in on itself and put aside. Two years had passed since Festival de la Toronja had so altered my reality. I'd attended another in 1989 that held just as much attraction and fun as the first. School work and the seasons of the dreaded grapefruit orchard, would for years to come remain a constant reality.

Even as the decade changed, the routines of everyday life seemed the same as before. Most of 1990 continued to be part of the good life of being in Cuba, other than the fact we still had no news from Africa about Baba, Mama, Chol, Agor or Achol. Life moved on and we attended to our disciplines with a dedication that kept us motivated. It was the bond between me and my siblings that, in a way, separated us from the other students. We at least had part of our family and its constant interaction. It was a true blessing for us. We gathered together often to talk over the things that were serious and meaningful to our family integrity.

It was at the age of 15 as I passed into grade six, that I felt I was becoming more mature. All of us had gone through all these changes together. We were all gaining strengths as we got older. None of us were children anymore and our conversations reflected that. Through our education we were learning more about the world around us, about history, about current events, in the school as well as in Cuba and the greater world at large. We could see how the culture of Cuba was changing us, and all the students, as we absorbed more of it.

Each of us had opinions about, well, everything. There were always current topics and gossip going on in and around school life. Some of these I found interesting, and some I stayed out of, depending on the subject matter and just what it involved. As the year progressed, you could feel the building of the wave that would eventually overtake us. Sometimes, the hint came from the teachers. They'd be all a buzz with the latest news of what was taking place in their country and how it affected them.

This would filter down and ultimately affect us. Life at Number 12 school would change radically with world events that were coming to a head. It began with rumors, muttering about in the background, things heard second hand and guessed at. We wondered what they might mean. Having my older brothers helped me because they were where I gathered my information. If I didn't understand something, I would go to them and ask what they thought about the news we were hearing on radio. In addition we got some news concerning Sudan and the state of the Civil War. This was brought to the school and shared with the students by our current Ambassador. The information gave us a better understanding of why our efforts to contact people in Sudan and the surrounding countries was nearly impossible.

By 1991, the civil War in Sudan had entered its eighth year. The country was living through a major drought. its economy, never really that stable, was in shambles. The ongoing cost of the war was eating into the vitals of a starving people. There was a spreading famine. There were divisions within the SPLA itself. It had developed into different factions and splinter groups. This led to more confusion as to the movement's aims and purpose. There had also been major shifts in which foreign powers were backing each side in the north/south war.

Through 1990-91 the Sudanese government supported Saddam Hussein in the Gulf War and this changed American attitudes toward our country. The Clinton administration prohibited American investment in Sudan and supplied money to neighboring countries to repel Sudanese incursions. The US also began to isolate Sudan and began referring to it as

158

a rouge state as the north began shifting allegiance towards the Soviets. This caused a shift in US support in Southern Sudan and it started to become more sympathetic to the SPLA. These were the type of topics we discussed in informal forums held periodically with our Ambassador. Or at least this was what I thought was being put forward as I listened to the students trying to understand what was happening in our homeland so far away.

Mostly it was of more interest to the older students. We younger ones went on our merry way and carried on with our school activities, sports and fun times like the ongoing school dances. While the greater world built its power plays, like moves on a chess board, I felt all the talk really didn't affect us that much. I was never more wrong. That summer of 1991 saw a coup attempt against the government of Mikhail Gorbachev in the Soviet Union. It became known as The August Coup. Gorbachev tried to reform the state with his policies of Perestroika and Glasnost, based on economic and political restructuring and openness. These reforms and principles were not well received in some areas of Russian politics.

The abortive August Coup was like a rock thrown into the pond and the ripples became a growing wave. Before Gorbachev had a chance to really implement his policies, the Soviet Union collapsed and was formally dissolved, to be reassembled as the Russian Federation.

It is a very big pond and the ripple effect changed many things irrevocably in the world as we live in today. It is the nature of history that no one person, no country and no nation, is exempt from them. These multi-dimensional ripples have a name; they are 'Cause and Effect.' They're always linked, but the effect part isn't always immediately apparent. There I was, enjoying what seemed to be a relatively good life and smooth sailing in a wonderful boat. (Cuba) I was feeling talk about all the political and economic stuff wouldn't really affect me that much. I realized my wonderful boat had some leaks but it looked really sturdy and well maintained on the surface. Then I heard 'slosh, slosh' sounds coming from below decks.

Oh man, we're in the middle of the ocean... somebody call the coastguard!

You have to consider where we students were from and the lifestyle we'd had in Africa before we came to this beautiful country, Cuba. To us this place was a paradise by comparison. The country seemed to have it all; the best of all worlds. We were innocent. We had no other countries to compare it with. Already the ripples were beginning to have an effect on Cuba. Then the economic reality of Russia's wave arrived upon her shores. It would cause major changes that would alter our awareness. They would, in a very short period of time, lead to changing scenarios and economic hardships, not only for us Sudanese students, but the whole country struggling to keep the boat afloat.

After the death of the Soviet Union, Cuba entered an era of economic hardship that became known as 'the Special Period in Time of Peace.' The immediate impact was the loss of nearly all the petroleum imports from the USSR. Before this, Cuba had been re-exporting any Soviet petroleum products it didn't use to other nations for economic profit. This had been Cuba's second largest export. The effects were felt almost immediately as other areas of Soviet support was withdrawn from Cuba. The country's transportation, industrial and agriculture sectors that used petroleum products became paralyzed. Government cutbacks began to take effect in almost all segments of the economy. These conditions were to last for most of the 1990's. Of course these cutbacks directly affected the Island of Youth. Us!

I wondered about starting Chapter 13 right about now. Should I, like in high rise elevators, just go straight from Chapter 12 to 14 and pretend there wasn't a thirteenth floor? In Cuba, when anyone mentioned numero trece (number 13), they would say in Spanish, "tocate." It's silly; it means *'touch yourself.'* Who knows why? Is it a Spanish thing? All this Soviet withdraw was certainly bad luck for Cuba. Then as the wave grew, bad luck for its people and in the end, bad luck for Number 12 School! Man, I hope there's some spell that will protect us from having a Chapter 13!

"TOCATE!"

For us the good years had flown right by. Now, at the end of 1991, we could see how this all would affect us directly. The most obvious effect was the quality of food in the cafeteria. The first things to go were the snacks and treats. There were fewer buses and their schedules were cut in half. Our time spent in town became less and less frequent. There were even rumors we might all be sent back to Sudan and the funding for our education stopped altogether. If the government were considering closing immigrant schools on The Island of youth, that would include Number 12 School.

This came to an end when Fidel Castro made an address to the governing body. He said Cuba would not send the immigrant students back to their countries, and to paraphrase his statement, "We will share what we have; where one can eat, everyone can eat!" Castro went on to say, "Whoever can't handle the situation will have to decide whether to leave or stay with us here in Cuba through our difficult times. We will share the little we have with our African brothers and Sisters! We have made a commitment to educate our nation's friends and we will not break that promise, no matter what!"

Some of the countries that had Students in Cuba started sending money to their students, but other countries couldn't help their students financially as they were more poverty stricken than Cuba. Like us! There would certainly be no supporting funds coming from Sudan.

By this time we had been through three Ambassadors, including Baba. The last, like Baba, had been called back to Sudan for some reason we were rather unclear on. As the shifting of foreign power backing of the SPLA changed, the SPLM offices in Havana became vacant. Then we got lucky and Jok Mach Nai from my home town Bor was appointed our forth Ambassador. Like Baba, he was an educated man and had been in Cuba representing the SPLM since 1987. He took a lot more interest in the students than those he'd followed. Like Baba he became a father figure to us all. He did his best to get news from Sudan and helped students try and connect with their families. In the beginning he was very party connected, but less and less SPLM contact became apparent, and eventually all contact with Cuba was severed. Jok Mach Nai stayed at his post even though he received no pay from the SPLM. In this, he was just like Baba; extremely dedicated to the same original principles John Garang created and stood for.

I truly admired this man who was, in reality, my Uncle. He had married my Auntie Mary Apiu, who was really my mother's cousin (confused yet? It's a Dinka deal), who had seen Baba and Mama in Addis Ababa. They had promised them to look out for us. Because of things ending up as they had and, as luck would have it, this promise came to fruition. They looked out for all the students equally, just like Baba and Mama had. It was a blessing for us to have this happen, to have this family inspire us as things went from bad to worse. With time, as I became close to their children, from '91 to '92, they did just that.

The decline in the quality of care at the school was very rapid, although the educational aspects remained the same and sports and entertainment activities went on as they had. Through the spring of '92, the food situation at the school became really bad and there was very little meat. If there was any, it was so tough and stringy it was almost impossible to recognize what it was. The main course we had almost every day was rice; rice, rice and more rice. The staff at the school told us they'd had budget cutbacks and it was going to affect our food supplies. Rice in Cuba is a major dish and that's what we got. So it was rice with beans, rice with eggs, rice stew with water and that barely recognized meat; then no meat, no beans, no eggs.

Yes, it was just, rice, rice and more rice. And, for desert... rice pudding!

You do by now understand how much we hated orchard work. Well, before picking season we started looking forward to ripening grapefruit. This horrible fruit started looking pretty good to us. It seemed more like food! I hate to say this, but we started looking forward to getting out into the orchard. It is a hard thing to always be hungry, to never feel like you have enough in your tummy. It begins to eat away at your mind and makes it hard to concentrate on anything else.

Just as soon as the grapefruit was edible, we ate rice at school and grapefruit at work. Even then, we couldn't eat too many or it would have become noticeable at harvest. We didn't want whoever ran the orchards to go out there and see all their trees empty. So we did a pretty good job of thinning through them all so it wouldn't be noticed. It couldn't be helped. There they were, inches away, teasing you: "eat me, eat me!" Then you'd fall for the temptation and gobble a few, even take some back to school for snacks later.

It got to the point where school work started to suffer and grade averages dropped for all the students. It was easy to understand in hindsight how important nutrition is to learning. You know what they say; 'to feed the body, is to feed the mind.' With hunger, the mind can't really focus properly.

Despite this, in talking between family members, we always remembered our homeland and the conditions our people suffered in the famine. Yes we were hungry and Cuba was beginning to suffer economically, but in Sudan there were people dying of starvation. We students were aware of these things due to Ambassador Jok Mach and his visits to the school. He made sure to remind us of the trials our country faced and reiterated why we needed to study and do well in our chosen fields so we could to go back to Sudan when the war was over and help. This wasn't just theoretical; some of the older students would be finishing their three years of college soon, like my brother Deng Ti studying Agriculture and Anyuon construction.

I had no idea what I might study toward. I racked my brain trying to think how to help my country through my main interest, sports. There was a suggestion that in other countries there were physical education teachers and I thought, 'now there's a good idea!' The one thing I did know was that I didn't want anything to do with medicine. No way! I decided to leave these ideas for the future because I had a ways to go yet to reach graduation. Besides, I was deathly afraid of seeing blood. I'd seen enough of that to last me a lifetime. Maybe I should study something to do with food. I thought a lot about that idea all the time. My poor tortured tummy was always bugging me, "Feed me, feed me!" I was shedding weight and I couldn't afford to lose any more. I was trying at sixteen not to be self conscious and I was already stick skinny and small.

Soon there was other news for us as a family to worry over. Abany told us that she'd had a check up and it was confirmed; she was pregnant. Now, as the school rules required, Abany would be sent back to Africa. It was another rock thrown into the pond, generating ripples of 'cause and effect' to consider. There are some things you can prepare for and others that just happen and have to be contended with. I was beginning to see the end of things. Abany like my brothers, after completing grade nine,

162

had qualified to leave Number 12 School and go into a three-year college vocational program. They would decide where life would take them from there when their education was finished. Deng Ti and Anyuon would finish their courses in one year. Abany was finishing grade nine and now, being pregnant, decided to continue on to college and take a veterinary course she'd be unable to finish before she had her baby. Life after that would have to take care of itself.

Yong and I had qualified for academic programs that would carry on to university. We'd have to stay in Cuba longer to finish our education which meant we had to deal with the reality that our family was again going to be separated. There were so many things we just couldn't prepare for. We understood we were there to get an education and to go back to Sudan after the war, but we had no idea how long that war would go on for. It had been going on for almost 10 years and there was little hope it would stop any time soon.

These were the pressures we had to contend with; not knowing what would come from our journeying to foreign lands. Our only hope was that someday what we were doing would better our homeland. In the meantime, we still had to face the reality of the conditions caused by Cuba's economic problems.

With the petroleum shortages, the government cut back more and more on the bus schedules. It became hard for us to plan when you could go to appointments in town because you never knew when you could get back to school. To further complicate our lives, if you missed meals none was saved for you and you'd just go hungry. It was about four kilometer walk just to get to the bus stop. If you didn't get there on time, you might spend hours waiting for the next bus. Sometimes the bus would just keep right on going because it was full and not pick you up. The bus going to town was one thing, getting back was something else. There were lots of people waiting in lineups to get on the bus. As it got worse, there were fights to get on. At one point a Sudanese student died when the bus was so full they couldn't close the door and he fell out.

A problem then developed between our school and the Namibia Boarding School further up the road. The bus stopped right in front of their school. On one of the trips from town, a Sudanese boy got in a big fight with a Namibian student to get onto a crowded bus. That was enough to start a major issue between the Namibian students and the Sudanese students. There was now a small war going on between schools. The Namibians would wait at their bus stop for the last bus and to see if there were any Sudanese students to attack and nobody would do anything about it. It got worse and worse till we stopped taking the bus. The alternative bus went the long way around and there were fewer of

163

them and we had to walk a long ways to get to the bus stop. It was very frustrating.

Finally it got right out of control. Some of our students got together and were all pumped up with an idea to end it. They got together with a plan to take the fight right to their school. A full scale attack was planned on the Namibia Boarding School. The plan was to have a group of students take the last bus from town, get out at the Namibia school and start a fight. At the same time, another large group would leave our school to walk there and meet the other students as they got off the bus.

What actually took place was that a student in our school who had been at that planning meeting thought it wasn't a good idea and reported it to one of our teachers. The plan was already about to take place; the information had come too late. So the teacher phoned the police and told them what was happening. The police stopped the boys in Gerona from getting on the bus and they were arrested and held in town. Meanwhile back at the Namibia school, the fight began and our boys were badly out numbered. It was a brutal fight and a young Sudanese student named Deng Achieck was killed in the battle. They were losing and had to retreat, leaving their fallen brother where he fell. On their way back to the school, they saw a young student walking along the road. Thinking he was Namibian, they pursued the young man and killed him. It turned out to be a double tragedy because the young man wasn't Namibia but Angolan and just in the wrong place at the wrong time.

It was so sad and stupid that this dispute turned into such a tragedy. No police had shown up to stop it from taking place because they thought arresting the boys in town would solve the problem. It didn't. After an investigation some arrests were made and some of the instigators from both sides went to jail. As well, after this incident, police were posted at our school for a long time until everything calmed down. Actually, it was a relief having them around. At least we were able to continue our studies in a more relaxed atmosphere. Before that, everyone was always keyed up wondering if there would be more violence. A short time later the Sudanese student association with our Ambassador went to the Angola school and apologized for their loss. They then went to the Namibian students to resolve their conflicts. Again there was peace between the schools involved. We were never going to get along, but at least it was much better.

This event had affected me a lot. I didn't understand how things could get so bad so quickly. We had come from a country that was full of conflict and hate; why had it started with another African country? It was as if the whole world was going crazy. I carried this cloud around for some time, wishing things could be better, different.

Then something hit me that turned everything upside down.

Anyuon and I had gone to town to follow up on a lead that had come through that had something to do with Agor. Anyoun had a number to call in Ethiopia and we were all excited to find out what the information was about. After many failed attempts, maybe we'd finally find out where our family was in Africa and how things were working out for them. When we arrived in town, the feeling I'd had about Agor came back. I was kind of afraid when Anyoun actually got through to someone because he was listening very intently. I could see by the look on his face, whatever the news was about Agor, it wasn't good. I got dizzy and my knees went weak.

Even as Anyoun hung up the phone, I knew Agor had got himself killed over there in that stupid war and I started to cry. My world was shattered; I couldn't believe I would never see my brother again. Now he'd been taken away from me. I don't even remember the ride on the bus back to the school. I was numb with the shock of it.

All of us were grief stricken when we got together and shared the few details Anyoun was given in this short telephone message. We learned Agor had given his life for what he'd believed in and had been killed in action in Ethiopia. It was the worst news I'd ever received and caused the darkest day of my life. How can words even begin to describe those feelings? I can't and won't go there.

Today as I wrote this, those feelings came again, altogether too real. I had to take a break and have time away from this page. Many times in the sharing of my life and times, and the memories of so many varied experiences, I've had to force myself to move through them. I've had to force my mind to go into corners of myself that I don't want to re-live and know. That I must go to, to tell my story. Like this day, for my beloved Agor.

I had to remember the shattering, the breaking apart and the grinding pain of this loss for my family. The kingdoms collide and we peasants must pay the price. In shedding the cloak of mortality, children sacrifice for ideals such as freedom. These souls are now gone from us and are no longer oppressed. It is we who are left behind to suffer the void they leave us with. It is we with the empty place that can never again be filled. For these thoughts I cried, and cried, an endless stream. Agor's sweet face was burnt into the forefront of my vision. It took a very long time before I was able to accept the reality of never seeing him again, never be able to listen to his beautiful voice as he sang his stories and songs that were so heartfelt. No, I was wrong, as I've seen Agor again today. With tears that cannot be held, he will live forever within my heart. Today again I dedicate this story, to my brother Agor Joseph Gabriel. His family lives on with his memory, honouring his beliefs and his ultimate sacrifice. Agor gave his world to the ideal of a better world. He took a stand against oppression, to protect his family, for a cause.

I loved my brother with all that a heart has to give. I prayed for his safety. I hoped he would return to us. It was not enough; reality claimed Agor and broke my heart.

A few months later we were told we'd be transferred to another school. This was a big shock for me. It was like having to leave behind another home. When they told us the name of the school, it was fitting, Number 13 Carlos Balino School.

Oh man, with all that had happened, 'TOCATE.' (Bad Luck... touch yourself)

It's alright, because it would all just get worse and had nothing to do with luck.

Only cause and effect, ripples in the pond; the end of innocence.

Chapter 15
Diversity and Conflict

Again we packed up our things and said goodbye to a familiar place. I'd lived at Number 12 Big House for the best part of six years and it was my home. I had many good memories of my time there, this last segment maybe not so good. But still, it was hard to leave, hard to wrap up another part of my world and move on to the unknown. Amazingly, for all the time spent there, I was all packed up and moved in one day, '*poof*,' off to other experiences in troubled times.

Actually it wasn't so bad. Number 13 (tocate) was a good school and not much different than what we had left behind. It was in good repair and for that first year, we were the only students to occupy it. Then the government brought in students from Guinea Bissau two years later to share it with us. That was different because we'd only really had contact with Sudanese. Now we had to learn to share with another culture. I found these students to be, on the whole, good people, happy and fun to hang out with. What made it unique was we were in the same leaky boat; they were from a very poor country too.

All of our teachers were the same so classes were not that much different, other than we were with new students from a different culture. They learned Spanish like us, but spoke Portuguese among themselves. That's where I learned 'chee chee,' meant 'I have to pee pee!' Many things in Portuguese are the same as in Spanish, so really it wasn't hard to understand what was going on with them. It was rather one sided, because they had no idea what we were talking about in all the different languages they heard from our side of the school. It was easy to tease them because they didn't know what the jokes were about, although we were never mean in doing this.

The fourteen girls I had started out with were still a mainstay and still hanging out together, although the dynamics changed quite a lot as we grew older. It was like a flow of coming together in ever changing smaller groups. Much of the sharing now was about current boyfriends and the young girl soap opera of everyday life. Mixed in with the shortages we suffered through, there were still things to look forward to. In many ways being mixed in with students from Guinea Bissau made events and activities more interesting. At first there was a general separation that stood out and in sports it was us against them. Then over time as friendships formed, the teams got mixed together. It was at weekend dances we could see that they were as music crazy as we were and really good dancers.

I believe it was a positive experience, that time of our lives. We learned that different cultures had a lot in common, that no matter what country you came from, the same things were important in the quality of life. When tolerance was practiced, it was easy enough to accept differences, even admire them. For me it was exciting to learn about their country, their culture and to see how proud they were of where they were from. Just like us they shared in the suffering of the shortages; there was a bonding in that as well. The economic realities that Cuba was going through affected everyone. It wasn't just the students who were going without, our teachers and staff were going through the same thing with us.

In those years, between '92 and '93, many things took place with my family. My older brothers and sister were in college and I didn't get to see them often. Even with Yong being in the same school, I'd see him in classes and all that, but he had his friends and activities that were different from mine. So there was a kind of separation that we lived with as a part of our everyday reality. The biggest event to take place was Abany having her baby girl; she named her Dunia (meaning world). I was really proud that Abany choose this name because I had suggested it. It was from one of my favorite Arabic songs by Mohammed Wardy. I was also very excited by the idea I was now an Auntie.

Abany was not allowed to keep her baby with her in the dorms. Instead there was a government daycare program on the Island. It wasn't uncommon for college students to have this very thing happen and there were quite a few Sudanese babies in that daycare. Whenever I could, I would meet Abany there and spend time with my beautiful niece. She was so bubbly and happy, and real chubby! Dunia was a very healthy baby and well looked after in the daycare. Abany, I could tell, was going to be a very good mother she so fussed after her Dunia and cuddled her up. There was a real change going on between me and Abany as well. Knowing Abany would be leaving was part of it. I had never really hung out with her. She had different friends with her being older, but at least I still knew she was around if I needed her. When baby Dunia was born, it was like a tie and a new bond of family was created I can't really explain. We grew closer and more affectionate with one another.

I rarely saw my brothers unless there was a family meeting called for trying to locate our parents. Sometimes I would see them at special events. For example we would come together every May 16 to commemorate the first day of the Civil War in Sudan. I had seen them as well at events like the Festival of Toronja, but this was all coming to an end. Deng Ti and Anyoun graduated and were about to move to a transition house in la Havana. I was dealing with the knowledge that in some short few months, when all their travel arrangements were completed, our family would again be separated. We were baffled because the SPLM/A didn't seem to want them back; at least it appeared that way to us. There was no communication with Sudan, so it was unclear what or where the students were going back to.

As the days progressed, I became more anxious. Would they be sent back into the war, or a refugee camp. I was very concerned for Abany and Dunia; the situation in refugee camps was not good at all for babies; or for anyone for that matter. We learned there were no longer Sudanese in Itang as the political situation in Ethiopia had changed. President Mengistu Mariam fled Ethiopia in 1991 after a long, drawn out rebellion and the new government was not as sympathetic to the SPLA. The Sudanese refugees went instead to refugee camps in Kenya and Uganda, so we had no idea what the students going back would face. It all seemed so pointless, to have all this education and experience. How would it be used? Maybe the countries around Sudan might find some use for them, give them jobs until the war in Sudan was over.

It didn't turn out that way.

In the end it was the Cuban Government who organized the students return and decided to fly them to Uganda. I'm very proud of how Cuba lived up to its obligations to us Sudanese. Even in the midst of their own problems, they still did everything they could for us. They took the responsibility for our welfare when even our country seemed to abandon us. There were many students who had no interest in studying and a lot who were trouble makers who made it difficult for those who really did want to study. The Cuban government decided to take these back to Africa, plus all the young women who had babies. So it was that Abany was included in this flight back to Africa. Anyoun was a different story, as he was supposed to be on that plane as well.

My brother thought there was plenty of time. He had a girlfriend in a different province, so he decided to spend the time waiting with her. Then he got a phone call from the Ambassador, "Anyoun, you missed the plane!" Oops! Well it turned out to be a good thing he did miss that plane. Things didn't go well for the returning students. Anyoun, and several other graduating students were now in a kind of limbo. When the Cuban Government learned of the difficulties experienced by the students they had sent back, they refused to send any more back to those conditions. They held open the opportunity for these students to further their education and lucky Anyoun went on to study Agriculture in University of Ciego de Avilla. Deng Ti, Abany and Dunia, as well as Dunia's father, flew away out of my life. There were only lucky Anyuon, Yong and me left in Cuba.

At least we did get to go to Havana and see them off. I tried hard not to show how hard it was and not cry. I didn't want to make it any harder for them. It was weird because we were all trying to do the same thing. It was hard to do. Then we didn't care and let our feelings show anyway, although we still tried not to leak tears. That didn't work all that well either. There were a lot of promises to seek out our family and send letters. You know, we never did get letters from Africa, not one. Life I guess just got in the way and everyone had their problems. Whatever the reasons, it just never happened. For us in Cuba, we would have sent letters but we never had a place or an address to send them. Maybe it was destiny at work on that deal, who knows.

I'm going to shift now a little away from 'my story' to share what happened to Deng Ti, Abany and her daughter Dunia on their return to Africa. I decided to add it here, as it happened in the same timeframe as when I was at the Number 13 (tocate) school. Of course, I didn't learn their story 'till many years later in research for this book. It includes a little from my sister Abany, but it's mostly from my brother Deng Ti and what he told me by long distance on the telephone. I will try my best to tell this story, keeping in mind that it's second hand. I hope to deliver all the information I was given, correctly, with maybe, just a dash of humour.

Midway through 1993, the plane carrying all the students from Cuba landed at Kampala, Uganda. After all their documents were checked, they found no one was there to meet them, no one had any plans for their return, no one had even expected their arrival! They had all this education and preparation, they had come to back to Africa to help and nobody seemed to care. Cuba had done its part, even flew them home. Now they had this rude awakening. It left them lost and frustrated and not a little scared. They were wide eyed, innocent; what now? They must have wondered what to do, standing lost and a little alienated in the middle of an unfamiliar airport.

Who did show up were representatives from the U.N. They took them to the Salvation Army where they spent the night. The next day they were taken to Enbarara Refugee Camp. Finally they were told the SPLA had arrived and to only be surprised as they loaded the girls and babies into the back of a truck and, drove away. Off Abany and her daughter Dunia went with the SPLA people, separating them from Dunia's father. He had no choice but to stay with Deng Ti and the other puzzled young graduates. The girls were taken to a Sudanese camp, to wait for family members to pick them up. Of course, no one would be there to claim poor Abany and Dunia.

Deng Ti and all the other students were left wondering. Maybe there was another truck coming. None came. They stood out for quite a long while, not knowing what to do.   At this point they had a bit of an insight.

When they heard the news of what was happening in Sudan they knew there was no way they wanted to return. A consensus grew that maybe immigrating to other countries that were accepting refugees, like the United States, Canada or Australia, would be a better idea. A U.N. Sudanese agent told them that he would get copies of their Cuban documents so they could apply to leave the African continent. What they didn't know was that the Sudanese agent, who they thought worked with the U.N., had lied to them; they were not going to get their documents back. When they went looking for the man, he was nowhere to be found. He probably didn't even work for the U.N. People in those days, did a lot of this kind of thing, taking advantage of people who knew no better. They learned they had to watch out for desperate schemers, doing whatever for needed money.

At least this was how they were admonished to do when the incident was reported.

For Abany and Dunia it was the beginning of five years of living in refugee camps. The mothers and children were first taken to what was the main Sudanese Camp in Uganda. Even if the situation had been poor in Cuba, the Babies were healthy and were well fed. In the refugee camp everything was scarce and filthy and babies and young children could get deathly ill. It was really very hard for Abany in those years, being entirely separated from her family. Deng Ti was on a path that never did connect to wherever she ended up as he was shifted between different refugee camps. One thing that was known was that, for a time, Dunia's father had found her but couldn't look after them. They were separated again for many years before being reunited in the United States.

Deng Ti wondered many times where anybody was to be found in this sea of humanity. He struggled with the designation of displaced refugee and all the confused hardships we had to face being one. This all went back to decisions that required immediate attentions the moment the homecoming graduates step off the plane. With all their acquired education and qualifications, it didn't seem to mean very much. It's hard to imagine being dropped off in a strange country with promises that blew away like smoke and again go through another kind of culture shock. Yet the some two hundred students Deg Ti was with all stuck together through what must have been a sense of total failure. To make matters even worse, they couldn't legally travel in Uganda and could only stay in refugee camps where the U.N. placed them. They had asked to go to Kampala to find out more information, but you couldn't go to cities in Uganda unless you had a travel visa, and that was very difficult to acquire.

With no choice, they were placed in the Rwandan Refugee camp, Nyakinvara. Like most Refugee camps it was in very poor condition, but Deng Ti and his graduates stuck it out. The refugees there wondered who they were. The people couldn't understand why these good looking young men in their nice clothes were in the camp with them. They looked like educated rich kids. For the graduates, they also had no idea what they were doing in that refugee camp and why they weren't taken to the Sudanese camp. It was a good thing they'd made a strong entrance and impressed these people, because within a short period of time, conditions at the camp caught up to them. No matter how fast you can run, there's no out-running bacteria.

It then just runs right out of you!

They all got diarrhea, really bad and not really funny. It can kill you! As you get weaker, your immune system goes to Hell. Then the other diseases floating around those camps can get a grip on you, and off to Hell you go! Or Heaven, depending on how good you've been. I tell you when your suffering this thing you do believe you're in Hell. You get delirium, hard sweats, bad dreams and have no energy to make it to a toilet. It's also Hell for the people looking after you. These boys really lucked out as the Rwandan people were their saving grace. A group of women took pity on them and would take the milk they were getting for their children and give it to these young men who were looking like pathetically sick little boys. They also cooked for them while they were recovering.

They were told by many they didn't belong in that camp. They were educated and could probably get jobs in the city. That was true, but it wasn't possible. It didn't take long after recovering that Deng Ti knew he had to get out of there. To hear the stories of how long some of these people had been in refugee camps, the horror stories of what was happening all over Africa; it was like the world had gone crazy. Deng Ti's years away from these problems in Cuba had been so different.

The UN people wouldn't let them leave the camp as they had no travel documents. They took it on themselves to plan a way out. The first step was to pretend they were going to stay so they wouldn't be checked on. Then they would try to get to Kampala or Kenya. They came to the conclusion they shouldn't all leave at the same time, because they weren't sure what to expect on the way. They figured if the first ones who left didn't return, it would mean everything went well. It seemed to be a logical idea and everyone agreed to the plan.

Deng Ti was in the second group. They waited those few days and after the first ones had obviously not been caught and brought back, they knew it had worked. They sold all they'd received from the U.N., like blankets, sheets and even some of their food. With the money collected, Deng Ti's group of grads crept away in the dead of the night, knowing they were in for a very long walk ahead of them, with lions in the bush and in their minds. Man, this was for sure not Cuba! It was lost in the deep dark of African night. It took them several days to arrive in Kampala and they were relieved to be reunited with the first group who they found almost right away.

It didn't take long for their escape plan to go astray. They hadn't considered how badly they stuck out and the chatter in Spanish between them gave them away. The authorities stopped them and asked to see travel papers, the ones of course they didn't possess. The police were going to put them in jail, which scared them badly. Because of their unique story, about being Cuban Graduates, the police called the UN people to figure it out. They were asked by the U.N. to choose whether to go back to the camp for UN assistance, or go to the Jail. They were all very adamant that they would not go back to that camp, no way!

So off to jail they went, for what turned out be only one day.

'Whew', how do you spell relief?

They had visions of being locked up forever in a foreign prison work camp for this horrible no-document crime. It didn't turn out to be that bad. If they promised to go to the U.N. offices the next day and after, leave the city, they would be let out. Deng Ti could tell, because of their Cuba Graduate story, the Police were treating them differently. At first they didn't believe them. Then it was like, 'who could make up a story like that?' After this even the authorities were suggesting alternatives for what they might do. So it was their suggestion to go directly to the main U.N. offices and who to talk to, and how to get there. Yes, a very helpful policeman, one who got a good meal out of that deal!

The next day they followed the directions and located the U.N. offices. After a short wait they received an interview. There were quite a few options presented to them, one being that they could choose to go back to Sudan. Because of the education they'd received they could be useful to the government in power. Deng Ti thought that might not be a good idea. Because they'd been taken to Cuba by the SPLA, they would be looked on by their own people as traitors. But, because of their dire situation, some of the grads decided to accept the offer. After all, the SPLA had abandoned them, that was the way they looked at the idea.

This group of grads was sent to the Sudanese embassy in Kampala. The Sudanese Ambassador was more than happy to receive them and promised they would have a better life in Sudan, being educated and all. It was like scoring a three pointer hoop shot for the Sudanese government against the SPLA team. News came from Sudan about the grad students who return home for the betterment of Sudan. The government played up that propaganda win big time! The SPLA people found out and were very surprised they had missed the ball on that play. It was a free shot in the government's favour against the SPLA's poor plan and the penalty was to lose their students to the opposite team. Although it was nothing close to being the game winner, it did hurt them.

By then the original number that had left Cuba had divided and gone many different ways. Deng Ti's group was no different. They felt none of the proposed U.N. alternatives were acceptable. It was a tricky decision, but they decided to stay and see what they could do in Kampala. Of course they hoped not to run into the nice policemen that had let them off so easily. It wouldn't happen like that the second time. This time they knew when out in public to speak Arabic or Dinka, and believe it or not, that wasn't an easy thing to do as Spanish was by then the first language for the Cuban Students.

They separated into smaller groups looking for the Sudanese community. Through this Deng Ti heard of a familiar family name. He and three others went in search of the home of Yar Poles. It really seemed he was their last hope. Yar Poles did help them out for as long as she was able, then took them to a group of her Church members who, in turn, helped them out for a while. Through these contacts they were introduced to an SPLA group that offered to take them to Keyikeyi so they could go to study English. Then they would come right back to study more at the University in Kampala.

At this point the grads trusted no one. They listened and nodded their heads, 'oh yes, good idea.' These avenues always seemed to come back around to having something to do with refugee camps. They figured it was more just dribble play. By then they were catching up on this African game play. They came up with what they felt would be a better plan. 'Go direct to the hoop!' and beat them, at their own game!

It went something like this; they told the SPLA people, "OK gift us the money and we will take a bus and we will go to Keyikeyi." Then they went to the U.N. and told them, "we've decided to return to Keyikeyi refugee camp, but we need money to do so!" It worked, and they went instead to a refugee camp of their own choosing. At Uyabe they could be processed and maybe sent to different countries that where taking in refugees. It was a slim hope, but at least a hope. They were rather surprised when they got there to meet up with the rest of the grads. It was a "funny, meeting you here" kind of deal. They laughed at the fact they'd all had the same idea in different places.

For a while the little side play felt like a triumph. What little money they had pooled went rather quickly as they waited to see if they would be accepted in the processing agenda. This turned into a trial of survival in the worst conditions they had yet faced. They received food from the U.N., such as oil, corn, sugar, and salt, but for them to have better food, they had to take the corn and process it to flour. But to do that they had to sell all their other food so they could pay someone to turn the corn to flour. It was a vicious circle and only ended up in them being hungry and sick again. They developed illnesses like anaemia and some had severe eyes problems and couldn't see very well. Their situation became so bad Deng Ti and some of his buddies gave up waiting to die and went back to Kampala to Yar Pole's house for few days. They, by that time, wanted to go to Nairobi, but it was very difficult because they had no passports to cross the border.

Yes, this coming back to Africa was a great idea. Not really. By now Deng Ti had but one game plan; get the Hell out of this nightmare! Deng Ti`s gang decided to leave Kampala and try for something better. They got lucky and meet a Ugandan bus driver who swore he could get them across the border into Kenya and on to Nairobi. That was if they had the money to pay him to do so. They pooled all they had and the driver frowned for a heart pounding moment. It looked as though he wouldn't accept it. Then relief; he would take all that they had. It became a very hard trip to make because they'd not eaten for sometime before they got on the bus. Along the way people would buy food for themselves and the grads would just hold on to their hunger and try not to stare at the people enjoying their food.

Deng Ti figured the money they'd given the driver was a bribe to get them across the border. Whatever it was it worked, and they pulled into Nairobi late at night when everything was closed. Going out to the U.N. offices for help then was out of the question, so they decided to go to a police station. Some of them were pretty leery about that idea, since they'd just crossed the border illegally. It turned out to be a good plan and they let them sleep in the cells over night. They knew it was OK because they left the cell doors open as they had explained their whole Cuba story for them. Hey, it had worked once before in Kampala, why not here? Well, much the same, they told them how to find the U.N. offices and they got a good breakfast to boot.

Next day in the morning they went to the U.N. office. For the U.N. to accept them they had to fill documents which took most of that day. They had no idea how long they'd have to wait for the U.N. to accept them. Again that night they went back to the Police station and were warmly received. The police were interested in them telling stories about their life as students in Cuba. It seemed they were pretty impressed and it went on into a long night of sharing. It was good to see the police in Nairobi were good people and not anything like some of the stories they'd heard. They really seemed to like Deng Ti's gang of border jumpers.

The following morning they checked in at the U.N. to see how the processing was coming along and were told it would be some time yet. In deciding what to do for the day, they remembered that Sister Victoria, who they'd met in Uganda, had given them an address she frequented in

175

Nairobi. So they went to one of the churches and asked for the address and luckily, it was the same place. They asked for Sister Victoria and were told she was in Nairobi, but not in at the present. They had also been given an address for a Sudanese community office. They were trying every available avenue of assistance so that might be a good place to try next. It did seem to be a very good lead because when they walked in Deng Ti right away recognized our Baba's best friend Ayang Alag. We considered him to be like an Uncle to us. Deng Ti introduced himself and Uncle Ayang told him he was busy and suggested he would meet him later at the Church. Deng Ti went to the Church but Uncle never showed up.

It turned into a good thing because Sister Victoria was back and she was oh so happy to see them. That wonderful Nun took those grads right away to be introduced to the Sudanese community in Nairobi. Maybe they would find other family members who might be of assistance. The community did help them out by finding families or someplace where they could spend the night. They took Deng Ti and two others to Uncle's house, where they didn't get a very good reception.

Uncle was dismayed when he saw them. He said life wasn't easy in Nairobi. His house, where his large family lived, was very small and he already had a house full of relatives. He didn't have any room to accommodate them. He took Deng Ti to my Cousin Akima Majok Deng's house. She was very happy to see Deng Ti and Akima welcomed my brother staying at her place. The other grads were sleeping in other places around the Sudanese community. Akima graciously offered Deng Ti to invite the others to stay and eat with them anytime. Akima was very supportive of all the Grads and happy to lend her assistance.

It became apparent that they weren't going to get much help from the U.N. offices in Nairobi. Deng Ti and what was left of the grads, many of whom had chosen their paths and had melted away into this nowhere land of day to day struggle to survive, made plans to keep on following their dream of leaving Africa. They journeyed onto Hipho, which was another refugee camp between Kenya and Somalia, but found only more of the same; another crowded refugee camp and with no documents. Thank god for cousin Akima who sent what money she could to Deng Ti to help out. Without this kindness, starving to death seemed a very real possibility. No matter what plan was tried, their situation always only got worse.

It had been two years now of this running from game plans of maybes to disaster.

Just when it all seemed utterly hopeless and Deng Ti felt he would be mired in this trap forever, there was a seeming miracle. Once again a family held in high regard was located and in that very camp. It was Uncle Arok Thon's family, the Commander of the Zindia who had got us out of Sudan. Deng Ti was saddened to learn his hero of ten years previous had died in a plane crash and his wife was now a widow. She, for reasons of her own, took Deng Ti and my cousin Kuir Manyank in and adopted them like sons. Deng Ti's major struggles were finished. He had found family and a home. In time that family applied for refugee status in the United States and was accepted. Uncle Arok's wife signed the papers to include her sons, Deng Thon and our cousin Kuir Thon.

Off to America they went, with their miracle, of no plan. All of which proves no plan is a good plan. When plans go bad, follow your dreams. Deng Ti found his when he stopped looking.

Chapter 16
Days of Hunger and Frustration

I was in complete ignorance of all this at School Number 13 (*Tocate*) because Deng Ti and Abany didn't write and let me know what was going on. I had no idea what happens to family when they go to Africa. It was as if they had fallen off the edge of the Earth. I was getting pretty angry with them and all their promises. Why couldn't they just take the time to pick up a pen? It couldn't be that hard could it? Well, if they were in a refugee camp, I knew it could be really hard, that life for them. The life I was having was difficult but nothing compared to that idea. I tried to keep this in mind whenever that angry cloud came around. I didn't want to feel that way about my missing family. For all I knew, they might all be dead!

God, what a horrible thought that was. It was a really sneaky thought too, wiggling its way into my nightmares of 'maybe's' and 'could be's' of what had swallowed my family so thoroughly. I was beginning to think coming to Number 13 school (tocate) was jinxing all of Africa and affecting every one over there. Maybe the whole stupid world was going crazy. I was convinced it had totally jinxed mine.

'God, you have no idea,' went my seldom said prayer.

Things were going horribly wrong in the school. Sudanese people are quite superstitious and I was beginning to wonder myself. It was possible, wasn't it? The state of affairs in Cuba was becoming even worse, the situation at school was pathetic, I was pathetic. I can imagine you, the reader, are getting sick and tired hearing about it.

'*Wah, wah, wah,*' poor hard done by Sarah! It felt just like that at times.

It was true; conditions during this period were intolerable. There were no more fun weekends, no more camp outs or visits to other parts of the Island. It seemed hopeless having to get used to these dramatic changes. We had absolutely nothing. Even essential things, such as shampoo, hand soap, toilet paper, laundry soap; everything was getting cut back. We weren't getting new clothes or underwear, sanitary napkins, deodorant, or shoes. More things were being rationed all the time. Actually, we were becoming desperate. Amel received a bag full of clothes from her parents in Ethiopia and she let me borrow some when I went to Town. I was at a point where all my clothes were no good at all. Most of them were worn out to rags. My friends and I liked to look good when we went out so we cut up some of our uniforms and made them into miniskirts. Well, 'you do what you must, as conditions demand,' Mama used to say.

There was no work available for anybody and especially for us. Even if you wanted to try to make extra money, no one would hire immigrant students. We were totally dependent on the government for everything.

We received an allowance of five pesos a month which was equal to twenty-five American cents. The bus was twenty-five cents Cuban, a sandwich was about one peso and a juice twenty-five. Local prices like this, and our allowance had to last a month? "Yah, right!" it was never enough...

All right, here comes the really hard part!

With no money for extras, it was especially hard for us girls. There are some topics that maybe shouldn't get mentioned when it came to womanly concerns. I'll brave it out as I think it's important to understand the entirety of these effects when it came around to our periods.

If you're a man and blushing, you can skip this part, OK?

'Oh how I hated this time of the month.' I think all of us girls really dreaded when their time came around. I would cut up my bath towel into five or six little pieces so I could use them as a pad. It was an unsanitary situation, but necessary. Each time I used one piece I made sure to wash it right away and hang it up to dry. Being that we were using them as sanitary napkins, we girls would hide them to dry and since there wasn't enough circulating air in those secret places, the pads would sometimes still be damp and not nice to think of. This resulted in unmentionable rashes because the pads were hard as we couldn't wash them properly without soap. Remember, soap . . . *was a luxury item.* Man, total girly frustration! To even write this horror almost makes me cry for the embarrassment of it all!

For those who didn't skip this paragraph, "how's it going guys, relating so far?"

Well, there was no other alternative, other than to keep the makeshift napkins on for a long time, even till their color and odor were bad and long past needing to be thrown out. I had no choice, so I cut up the rest of my towel, leaving only a small bit to dry myself with. As time went by there was no towel left and I had to live without that luxury too. To add insult to injury, there was the water situation.

Why I have no idea, but the water just stopped running. Maybe it had something to do with the electricity going out every Thursday at 7:30PM, I don't know.

From this time on, none of the schools on the Island had running water. They opened a hole in the floor to a cistern that held gray water. We had to use a rope and a bucket to get water and each girl had only one bucket of water to wash with... napkins and all. And no towel! 'What, you say, why not just run round naked and dry off? No way! I'd hang around in the washroom and when I thought I was dry enough, get dressed! It was, at times, a pretty chilly way of doing things, especially when the weather was bad.

We found out the hard way it was bad, this thing called gray water. We were warned not to drink it. There was a water truck that came by once or twice a week that supplied our drinking water. They told us to keep bottles of water on hand for those days in between and fill them up from the big bottles that came on the truck. This wasn't always possible, and being thirsty, we'd drink the grey water anyway. This turned out to be a very bad idea. Kids started getting sick from that cistern water beneath the floor. It probably would have been all right if the water had been boiled first. We never thought of that, and besides, they would never have let us into the kitchens to do this anyway.

Some, if not all of those effects, were pretty humiliating. The staff would just shake their heads and say, "well we told you not to drink the gray water!" Having to go to the doctors and tell them some of these complications was difficult. The suffering however was bad enough that it was impossible not to go for help. The itching was maddening. It was easy to see who was suffering from these problems as sitting still was impossible. The itchy scratching; I won't even go there. I tell you when the medical help kicked in, you were truly grateful and relieved that there were doctors on earth.

Nobody laughed at anyone suffering these complications.

I had been through hell and back. I was very polite and nice to everyone and continued to be a chatter box with my family and friends. As for the other students, I was known as the quiet one. Shortly after the worms and stuff, I was pretty short on patience. I was thinking all these headaches just had to stop. I couldn't take it anymore. One more thing and I was going to just, snap! It was as if I were going through the motions and just waiting for something that would set me off. Then I had a day where that's just what happened.

All students had their daily duties at this cursed school. One first thing in the morning after breakfast was to make sure the hallways were cleaned and to pick up the garbage around the grounds. That day I was my usual happy self outside after doing the hallways. It was my turn to pick up the garbage around the school with a classmate. It was grapefruit season and there were rotten, half eaten grapefruit everywhere. It was disgusting. Students were just throwing them out the windows! We had got about half way through this chore and noticed the Guinean girls were being disrespectful, throwing grapefruit out the windows and laughing at us. We asked them to stop but that only made them laugh all the harder.

I felt a burn beginning; this just wasn't funny.

I'm not one to take this kind of insult lying down. 'SNAP! Before I knew it, I was running up the stairs garbage bag and all. Running to their dorm, I burst into the room and told them rather nicely it wasn't nice what they were doing. I asked who was doing this. They only snickered and said some rude things in return. Well that was that. I'd had enough. There were all these horrible things we had to contend with and now them being ignorant; I totally lost it. Since I still had the garbage bag full of rotten grapefruit and other unmentionable trash, I shook it out and started throwing it all over their dorm. It splashed and thumped on everything, onto their beds even. Nasty garbage was just flying everywhere.

For a moment they were all wide eyed; not believing what they were seeing. I didn't care. It was like 'bring it on you bitches.' I was ready to fight. I was tired of being little Miss Nicety Nice. I don't think I've ever been that mad at anyone, ever. I think I was a little crazy there for a moment. There was yelling and screaming going on as now these girls were fighting mad too. Well, the Sudanese girls had seen me running down the hall with my garbage bag. Now they heard all this screaming and swearing. Some of them really liked to fight, *'oh boy, the rumble's on!'* Although that was obvious, they were surprised it was little goody, goody Sarah who'd started it.

There I was in the middle of the dorm, garbage all over everything, surrounded by some very angry Guinea Girls who wanted to rip my head off. The Sudanese girls burst into the room and I came to my senses. 'Oops,' Oh man, what had I got going here? I had never been in trouble like this before and I definitely didn't like to fight. If there was ever a problem, I never asked any of my family to help or to step up for me. As a result, I felt really bad being the cause of this upheaval, but good that my girlfriends were ready to rumble for little me. Really, it was a good thing it never got that far.

It turned out a teacher had watched it all go down. He'd been standing outside with my brother Yong who'd pointed the action out to him. Mr. Domingo, who was our PE instructor, burst through all these screeching banshees going for their claws, and broke it up. He'd seen the girls who had instigated it and they all got into trouble.

It was funny, because after that all those girls just got friendlier.

"Hey," went the whispers, "don't mess with crazy Sarah!"

That incident, thank God, was the last for that cursed school. It wasn't long after that we were told we would all be moved to another school. More students at our school had graduated and moved on to college or university. There weren't enough students to make the school cost effective. After students vacated these schools, they would never be used for schools again. They were going to be turned into apartments, or hostels, and some even became resort hotels. The times had changed and the Island of Youth with them. It is now mostly an island of resorts and tourism.

Like us, everything was changing and moving on to something else.

I had to admire the Cuban spirit. Even though these were desperate times, their love of music and dancing kept them smiling. You could still hear it everywhere you went, music and laughter. I loved it too. It was the only way we kept ourselves going. I could completely submerge myself in the music and forget my hunger pains for a little while. Every weekend at the school they put music on for everyone to enjoy. Then, all too soon, the fun would end and it was back to the orchards and eating grapefruit in season. Sometimes when it wasn't in season and we couldn't wait for them to ripen, we were so famished we'd take salt out into the orchard with us to cover the sour pucker.

So in our new Big House, everything stayed much the same.

The activities and the cutbacks, the horrible food, school work and all that went along with... grapefruit. There was always the never ending orchard work. The only difference now were the cultures we shared these things with. We were quite the Multicultural school now! In many ways I'm thankful I had this experience. It taught me a lot about Unity and Tolerance. I learned that our world's population is in a way balanced. We are so different in many ways and at the same time, much the same. If I'd stayed in Africa, I would never have learned this. It changed me in ways I could never describe. I'm different because of my experiences in the world. It was a blessing to have had the opportunity to experience this cross section of humanity.

Number 47 school was now made up of seven different nationalities: we Sudanese of course, and the Guinea Bissau students who'd come with us from Number 13 (tocate) bad luck school, as well as students from Cabo Verde, Angola, Ghana, Congo and Mozambique. You should have heard the chatter going on in that school! There were different languages flying all over the place. It was this blending I found to be quite beautiful in its way, this kind of diversity. I was thankful we all had Spanish in common or it would have been impossible to understand anything going back and forth. Even so, at times it was just like that; incomprehensible bla, bla, bla in whatever dialect.

In some areas things were awkward because not all these students were in as bad a way as we Sudanese and Guinea Bissau students were. Most of them were getting funds from their home countries and had begun the practice of cooking their own meals in their dorms. For us it was very hard to be hungry around the smell of cooking food we could only dream of. We'd go out and be anywhere else, to not have to be exposed to that torture. Mostly we just walked around because we didn't have the energy needed to play basketball or other sports.

That was the biggest drawback, never having enough food. I loved sports but I found I didn't have the energy to perform up to my true potential. It was the same with school work. I just couldn't concentrate properly and grew tired easily. I had never been sick in Cuba up till then, but I started to feel unwell. I think it was mostly from eating too many grapefruit to kill my hunger. I began to have fairly severe stomach problems and, to this day, have to carefully monitor what I eat. I do eat mostly very healthy food now (when I can pass McDonald's) which is covered later in the book. Imagine. A section on how to lose weight! Believe it or not, there came a point when I ate too many Big Macs and not too skinny was Sarah. I hated my overhanging Big Mac problem.

The water supply became a serious health situation for the students and this more than anything, was affecting our general state of health. The bathrooms became very unsanitary. There was no extra water to flush the toilets and keep them clean. It got creepy because the students used them anyway and, well, *'the smell was overpowering.'* I'm not holding back on any of the details. You could see worms growing in them toilets. This was so much so we even found them wriggling around on the bathroom floors. It got so bad we had to close them washrooms and go outdoors in the bushes. Then there was the problem of having to go in the dead of the night. The long run for the bushes was common. There was no toilet paper; we had to make do with anything we could find, including, our school note books. I don't know what happened to my work book with pictures and my precious stories... butt, you can imagine.

It was a bum deal. But let's not go there, alright!

It was disgusting, thank the Lord Jesus the staff finally took things in hand and forced a crew of students to undertake a cleanup. Bucket after bucket, wearing clothes pegs on their noses . . . uh, just kidding. It was a very stinky and gross detail I'm sure, but it did get done. They cleaned the toilets and the bathrooms were kept closed until the water supply got better. Which it never did while I was at the school! The water situation affected more than just the bathrooms, the dorms began to get really stinky as well (especially the boy's half). The cause was our smelly rotten socks and dirty underwear. We tried to keep them clean, but it was not easy without water. There wasn't enough water to wash the bedding either and our beds got infested with bed bugs. That was the worst; waking in the morning bitten to pieces by those nasty critters. You could just not get rid of them. There were times we had to do our laundry at a lake about 3km away. If we didn't return on time for lunch, we'd get absolutely nothing to eat. Again, we had no laundry soap. We still wanted to keep our clothes clean, and if some of us had a little bit of their laundry soap left, they would share it with the others. Most of the time we didn't have any. The laundry soap that the government gave us was supposed to last one month but it didn't. It wasn't just our school either. All the boarding schools on the Island of Youth were suffering the same. We only had to suffer that badly for one year at that school, then a whole moving ordeal came around once more.

Now we were in Number 61 School, our last Big House. After changing schools, Yong was elected our Student Body representative. We got an offer from the Angolan representative for the school. They were very lucky and had their own private small bus. They said if any of us needed to go to town, if there was extra room we were welcome to ride along. Some of our students took them up on this kind offer. We continued to be teased by the better off students about the state of our clothes and things. We had to wear floppy runners with their soles almost falling off, but we did our best to keep our clothes clean. By then they were mostly rags. It's hard to keep our pride under those circumstances.

On the bus there were some of the Angolan students who didn't like us riding with them. They started bad mouthing us about our shabby clothes. When the Sudanese students got off the bus, they were embarrassed and felt it was wrong to be treated that way. Yong advised us Sudanese students not to go on to the bus at all and the problem was resolved, saving our pride. It was good advice on Yong's part and the manner in which he put it to us at a general meeting made me feel proud of him. The way he handled himself, and the manner of his presentation, reminded me of Baba.

One day another opportunity came that seemed pretty heartening in our search for information about our family in Africa. It came when we had almost given up trying. No matter who we got hold of in Africa, they knew nothing. The short time we could get on long distance remained the biggest drawback. Even Jok Mach was baffled by our lack of success getting information. It was especially hard on us as others did get messages at times, and letters. We wondered all the more. If they could get through, why not us, especially with all the connections we thought Baba held in the SPLA? They could tell us nothing of where he was.

Wouldn't you know, the break came because of that unlucky #13 tocate school. Two years before we'd had an interview with a U.N, official, Mr. Aragon, at that school. Our Ambassador and the Cuban Board of Education had contacted him concerning our situation. The aid program he worked for, ACNUR, was strictly for assisting refugees. He needed to verify we were refugees in Itang before he could go any further. The U.N. took the search to Africa and it turned into a lot of work on their part. Two years later, now, OK? We eventually got our assistance, and it really was a big help.

"*Praise Jesus...our prayers are answered,*" is what Mama would've said (I'm not that religious, but it fits). A day late and a dollar short, would have been closer to the truth. Another way of saying the same thing:"*nunca es tarde cuando la dicha es buena!*"

You don't know how happy a person can be to have something as simple as soap, and WOW . . . toothpaste! I finally had a towel. There were a number of things that are necessities or, as I've told you, life can be miserable. When Mr. Aragon came with the news and our first delivery of goods, we had an opportunity to talk to him about the search for our family in Africa. ACNUR found a record of us attending the program in Itang, but hadn't found any direct family. He promised to look into it further. The only response we got personally was a letter from someone who claimed to be our Uncle. We'd never heard of him. In the letter he talked about how difficult his life was in the Refugee Camp and made no mention of our family. We were very disappointed, knowing this person only was thinking of himself. He may have been related, I don't know. He was certainly wrong thinking we had the good life here in Cuba.

We never did hear directly from Mr. Aragon again.

It was a very good feeling going around in the school because no one was laughing at us anymore. Before we received help, the other students would laugh at us, because of our old ragged clothes and shoes. We waited with dignity, without complaining or asking them for help. After we got our first help, life was much easier. We all put together some stuff such as soap and shampoo to give to our Cuban teachers because they needed the help as much as we did. It was very emotional to know finally I would have deodorant, soap, shampoo, shoes, underwear and clothes especially. All the girls were so thankful to once again have the ultimate luxury, sanitary napkins!

It didn't take us long either to figure out more ways the care packages could help us. We never had enough money to shop in stores, so we took the greater percentage of our extras and traded them for necessities that would make life worth getting up in the morning. There were, by that time, only fifteen of us Sudanese youth left in the boarding school program. It was a real process when the delivery guy came in his truck with boxes for our next run of the good stuff. The loot came out, it was all divided up equally and then the almost fun part kicked in. Sarah the trader put together her list, dividing up the care package with what was needed and what could go. Not just me, all of us would put extras together to pass out among our teachers.

The Cubans by then were not only our teachers, but mentors and more like family. Some had been with us right from the beginning and were closer to us than other, newer teachers. We respected and cared for them. They were suffering these hardships too. We knew some even had large families to feed on very little wages. We felt it was a way of giving back to them for what they were doing for us and the amount of dedication it took to really like us. I imagine that wasn't easy at times.

Each of us had our connections where to go trading, filling out personal lists of needed monthly food stuffs like beans, sugar, oil, salt, onions, garlic and the most treasured... eggs! Sometimes this was followed by a whole chicken to make special evenings for family and friends. It was these planned events that gave us students our pride back. Finally we had something to offer and give to one another. It was great to show off what we'd traded for. "Hey, look at my new shoes," that cost me half my laundry soap. It seems a rather silly thing, but as our lives improved with this assistance and things like our clothing got better, we actually received more respect from the other students. Yong and his speech had proven to be right; we remained what we were... Sudanese! It didn't really matter what the others thought of us; it was what we thought of ourselves. It mattered, the manner in which we survived our trials, with dignity.

By the summer of that last year before graduation, our world had improved a great deal. Our grades had improved and my sports had got a lot better, now that we were getting better nutrition. I was a little sad the fantastic four were no longer together at the school as they had always been a year ahead of me. They were now away at university and I missed Amel and Mana a lot. I recognized by then how much had changed in our world. It was just me and Anot Elijah left to carry on being teenagers from the original fourteen girlfriends. That left a tight group of five of my sisters to create our social life together. As summer and graduation grew closer, I saw many of those changes weren't good.

The students had got into some bad habits to entertain themselves. There was a lot more drinking taking place and for many of the teenagers, partying became the most important factor in their social life. To fit in was to party, drink alcohol and be wild. Not me. I thought that wasn't a good focus, wasn't my idea of fun. I watched as many of my friends lost interest in school and sports, dropping away from what we were doing there in Cuba. I was studying hard and had no time for fooling around. There were many traps in that idea. It was the way so many of the girls had got into problems, like getting pregnant. For them, the social aspect of life took over and was more important than the future. I could never lose that thread. My family had got me there to create a future, whatever it was to be. I first had to prove to myself I could graduate.

After all the things I'd lived through, I wasn't about to forget why and how I'd got to Cuba. I noticed that almost no one talked much anymore about how they got here; only the stupid gossip about life at school. I knew the social life was not what was important. Somehow it always came back to Baba. I knew from him, getting this education was the important thing and what I needed to focus on. People need fun for sure, but what is fun? For me sports first and a very close second, music and dancing. Besides that, I stayed focused on my family and its goals for the future.

187

Being so close to the finish line was spooky and made me nervous. I came up with what I was going to go to university to study; money! After all, that's what we needed the most and what we didn't have. That's what made life livable... *money!* Somebody has to manage that money, so hey, accounting made perfect sense. I put that on my list of promises I would never let go of and got right onto recruiting Yong to help me study. When he had time, he did help... *a lot!*

It felt like a race now, a long distance race of huge proportions. The start line was in Bor, fourteen years previous. I'd just had my birthday in April, passing my twenty-third year of life. It was kind of old to be finishing high school, but all these years of running had got me this far. I had a dream and I wouldn't stop running till it came true. Some day all these trials would be behind me and my family, all together. We wouldn't have a house of sticks. No, we'd have a big beautiful house in a family compound like we had in Bor! I imagined that my education and university training in Cuba would make this dream real. Somehow down deep I felt this was really Baba's dream for us. I tried not to think of my parents or my missing family too much. I had to focus on my studies and win this race, to cross the finish line.

The future was out there beyond this goal somewhere, in adult responsibilities. I had again passed another marker. It rather surprised me this adult idea. It was kind of spooky in a different way. It was life out there in the wide, wide world beyond the life I knew in Africa and boarding school in Cuba. It was out there that I had to prove myself, do what was needed with my education. I had to put together all the things in my world I was missing. This idea scared me to pieces. So much of my hopes and dreams relied on graduating, getting to the real deal... university.

Chapter 17
Graduation and University

From what I was to see in other countries like Canada, graduation is celebrated and is really a big deal. It wasn't like that in Cuba. There were no big parties and prom dresses. I didn't know about those things anyway, so it was no big deal. You passed tests that said, OK... now what? You could go out with this education as it was and get a slightly better than average job or maybe go straight onto college without any further testing, then get an even better job. They were jobs we Sudanese couldn't get in Cuba anyway. It wasn't what we were there for. When we were done, we couldn't even live in Cuba.

That was a big issue to have to wrap your head around. The Civil War was still dragging on in Sudan and we couldn't go back there. It seemed to me the only alternative was to go on with our educational opportunities. If we had the capacity, we could continue on to University and hope that the War would at some point end. At this point, we still had no idea if we would go back to a New Sudan or the regime that held sway. If that were so, would we want to go back, stifle our beliefs and lend our resources to a regime we believed kept Southern Sudan in ignorance and poverty?

There was another alternative; that was to apply to a country that was accepting Sudanese refugees. Many had already chosen that route and succeeded. There was a group that went to Canada right after our graduation. I'd been asked if I wanted to be a part of that group, but I turned down the opportunity and continued towards my goal of going to University to study accounting. I thought it would be a useful asset for the future of our family in this ideal of a new Sudan. I could work for the family businesses and manage our resources. I kept this at the forefront of my mind and that's what motivated my studies.

I knew writing the University entrance exams would be the real challenge for me. We had to study for the high school exams to get a grade average to qualify to take the extended University exams, which followed right after graduation! So the entrance exams had to be studied for at the same time. Thank God for Yong, as it was his intelligence and capacity working alongside me, and his seriousness that carried the day. I made the grade point average to take the university extension, and of course Yong scored very well as he was going for medical training to become a doctor.

The days just before that series of tests were very stressful. Since I was going into accounting, I had to do well in Math skills. I knew I was good

189

in Math, but I fretted over whether I'd be good enough. The other hurdle would be in passing the Spanish University qualification for reading and writing comprehension. I had been in Cuba for a number of years, I spoke the language fluently and I'd written in Spanish all through school with passing grades. But . . . would I be good enough? It was a constant anxiety. Yong thought so and kept telling me not to worry. How could I not worry over such a thing as that, so much was riding on getting into University? If I didn't, then all the pressures of just where to go from Cuba would be front and center. I'd seen my fair share of what was necessary to apply for refugee status and immigration papers, and the waiting involved, to worry about that too.

After all that, the exams seemed easy for me. I studied very hard for the first time ever and Yong had been right. He told me one way to study is to help others study who were having difficulties. That worked really well and after the exams we waited impatiently for the results, I felt confident about my work but still nervous. Yong's scoring was right there at the top. Mine? When I saw them, I jumped up and down with real joy. I'd made the grade and then some. Yong had been pretty confident that I'd pass as well. He promised if I did, he would buy me a bottle of wine. I told him not to because I don't drink. He was really happy for me and told me he already had. "Acuach Cor, I went ahead and got you that bottle of wine anyway. I knew you'd make it!"

It was one of the best days of my life. It was my dream come true. This determined that I'd qualified for the university. It was the toughest exam ever in all my days of school. Now my dreams would be set in motion and become real. I'd promised Yong when I passed the exam I was going to really party and it was like, 'well why not, this is my day and I'm going to get totally smashed!'

Everyone was really in a party mood because it was the end of our boarding school days. Before the evening dance, all the student girls, about 40 of us, went into town first for pizza and ice cream. We walked around just enjoying this day out to say goodbye to our Island of Youth. Many of the towns people were sad to see us go. Over the years we had built a lot of friendships there. In some ways we were sad too, just not on that particular day. It was purely celebration and excitement because we were going on to a different and hopefully better life. For us girls, we were saying goodbye to each other as well, as many were off to different cities and schools. This day was the last we would all be together. For me this was rather sad as well. I knew my life beyond this event was going to be entirely different. All that day I went through many emotional feelings with a kind of anxious excitement over it all. It was impossible to keep track of how I felt. Forty girls can generate a lot of energy and it made for a very memorable day for us all; that last outing together. Mostly we could

190

hardly wait to back to school and dance our buns off. We wanted to party and leave Number 61 School behind, forever!

I'd only had an occasional drink. Right up until the day of our celebration dance, I had never been drunk. I thought one bottle of wine wouldn't hurt. I was having a lot of fun and the music and dancing were great. Maybe one bottle of wine shared with a group of friends wouldn't have been. When I popped the cork and drank that first deep swallow... I thought, 'Mmm, tastes just like a fizzy soda!' I didn't share that bottle with anyone and more or less chugged it right down like pop. Well hey, it didn't take long before . . . *'Yahoo! Just watch Sarah dance now!* I was spinning out on that dance floor like a top. Then 'Wow,' the whole dance floor was spinning around when I stopped. That was interesting. It was a good thing I'd only had that one bottle of wine. At that point I could have gone right on to have more. I didn't. I was tipsy but not out of control and enjoyed my one rebellious night out.

I think almost the best part (after which I don't remember much at all till morning and a horrible feeling I learned later was a hangover) was when a large group of us went for a walk down the road singing songs and waving our hands in the air. I think everyone there was smashed. I remember Yong was there and really having a good time. Then, Blank.

The celebrations were finished and the moving on was taking place. Everyone was busy making plans and packing everything up. I couldn't believe it was all finished. I counted up all the years and the many changes I'd gone through in these boarding schools. I remembered all the way back to my day walking around the house in Bor, having to face leaving my home and the only place I knew. They were now totally different circumstances of course, but oddly it felt much the same way. My days with the Big Houses were done. They held the same security, because of the different experiences and times of growing up in them, they too had become a kind of home.

I even went out into the orchard and laughed. "I'm not going to miss you at all grapefruit, but thanks for listening anyway!" I stood there for a moment wondering if the trees were sad to see us go after all the care we'd given them. 'Naw, I doubt it', I thought. Then I walked away and never looked back at that place of blood, sweat and tears! I could have sworn I heard one large sad sob. I think it was my travel bundle saying, "what, you're leaving me here?" I yelled back, "You bet!" I went back to my packing and left it there. I wanted to leave all that heart ache right where I buried it.

There was to be one final happenstance on the Island of Youth, that would color our leaving Nueva Gerona and not in a good way. My girlfriend Nyanuer William and I had planned a trip to the Big Island and Havana. The ferry left very early in the morning and due to the bus

191

schedule the two of us couldn't catch that first ferry. We had a friend in Nueva Gerona, the place I've been referring to as 'town,' and made arrangements to come to town the day before and spend the night.

That evening I didn't sleep well. I had a bad dream about being attacked by someone in the elevator. The next morning, I told Nyanuer about my dream and how badly it had affected me. "We'd better take the stairs then, hey Sarah", she said, smiling at me and it made me feel better. Off we went after saying our goodbyes to the people of the house, in somewhat of a hurry to meet the ferry.

Nyanuer and I were both carrying a travel bag over one shoulder and a purse over the other. As we were leaving the building, I saw a man standing on a balcony in the building across the street. When he saw us, he immediately hurried into that apartment. I don't know why but I felt a shiver run through me, as if my dream had somehow been a warning. I turned to Nyanuer to tell her we should hurry and she looked at me strangely. I looked back and saw that man and another were coming out of their building and he was pointing at us. They were tough looking rather large guys and not very well dressed. Right away I knew we were in trouble, as they came walking fast toward us.

Nyanuer saw the look on my face and noted them as well. "Don't look back and don't show we're scared, Sarah," she said nervously, as it was obvious they were following us. It wasn't light out as it was still very early and we weren't in the best part of town. I looked back one more time and they'd disappeared around a corner. We knew they were still back there and didn't know what to do but keep walking fast. In less than a minute they reappeared, this time with their faces covered with black masks. I felt really scared. Their wearing masks wasn't a good sign at all!

Then we just ran. It was stupid really because in our panic we ran in different directions. The two men split up to chase us as well. I was freaking out knowing that I'd lost Nyanuer, but there was no time to think about that. I was close to a building and could see lights on in some of the apartments. I ran up next to the building and just as he had got right into my face, did what I was best at. *I screamed bloody blue murder!* In a different situation I would have actually laughed to see coal black eyes go round in panic, looking around to see if anyone was about to watch his attack on poor little Acuach Cor. Mister Mugger made his mind up fast, as I wouldn't stop this wailing scream at around three-hundred decibels three inches from his nose. My bad dream decided to run away. *'Whew, I'd got lucky!'*

Well that got the neighbourhood out of bed and into the street in a hurry to discover where this God awful noise was coming from. I was shaking really badly and trying not to pee myself and still screaming. I had trouble stuttering out the real problem. *"My friend, my friend Nyanuer"*, I

192

kept crying over and over. Finally I calmed down enough to ask the crowd to call the police; my friend was in trouble.

A few of the men who had come out of their homes, went running off to look for her. I was relieved to see how worried they all were and astonished at how fast the police showed up. There had been some other violent robberies in the neighbourhood and they were very concerned for Nyanuer's safety as well. It wasn't a very long wait before a police car show up with Nyanuer. I was never so happy to see her, until I saw her face. They had caught up with her and Nyanuer had been beaten. Her eyes were all swelling shut and blood was everywhere. I found out later she was beaten badly because she wouldn't let go of her purse. She had fought back and had pulled one of their masks down. Her attackers heard the approaching police car and ran away. I was informed later that day they'd been caught and a couple of days later we had to go to the police station and identify those local criminals.

Right then I was rather annoyed, because the police were taking Nyanuer to the hospital and wouldn't let me go with her. I raised quite a stink and I think the policeman was getting rather put off with me too, screaming in his face like I was. It didn't help. I wasn't allowed to go with my poor hurting friend.

Now what?

That was the end of our trip to Havana. This stupidity had wrecked our plans. I had no choice but to head back to the school and walked back through town all afraid, waiting for those masked men to jump out of the bushes, or from behind cars, or out of dark doorways. Despite my fears, I made it to the bus stop without getting molested. To add to the already maddening frustration, I then had to wait forever to catch a bus that never seemed it would ever show up! As it turned out, Nyanuer looked worse than she actually was and, after being treated at the hospital, the police got her back to the school before I finally arrived many hours later. The staff, all worried, told me they'd chewed out the policemen for not taking me with them after such a horrendous attack and just leaving me at the scene of the crime.

Nyanuer was shaken up, but she was one tough girlfriend. She laughed about it later and, all excited, told us of how she'd whammed the guy in the head till his eyes spun with the purse he was trying to steal. It was good she could laugh about it. I knew at the time just how scary it had been for us. It was good as well those robbers had been caught and that we'd pointed them out to get them off the street and into jail. As we moved on with our lives, this added a spooky story to what we were leaving behind. These were happenings we needed to get beyond and into a world awaiting our arrival.

When it was actually time to leave, it was doubly hard as Yong and I were going to different Universities and worse, even in different provinces. Youg was going to Camaguey to study Medicine and I to Matanzas to study accounting. It started off right away on the wrong foot. Yong and my identification, important documents and high school diplomas, were packed into my luggage. Between changing buses, ferries and what have you, when we arrived my luck ran out. I searched and searched; my luggage was missing.

What now?

I had only the clothes on my back and Yong was really frustrated that all of our papers were gone. It seemed as if he wanted to be angry with me but couldn't, as how could this happenstance be my fault? He knew it as well as I did. There we sat in Havana wondering what to do about this huge inconvenience. We especially needed our school documents to present to the University when we arrived. Not to mention the fear of not having identification to even prove who we were. Again, thank God for Yong. "I'll phone Jok Mach Sarah," he said, "he will know what to do!" Off he went to find a phone and sort this mess out.

Yong got back just in time before his bus was to leave. He explained I would need to phone Jok when I arrived at Matanzas. Jok would phone ahead as Ambassador to have them expect me. He'd explain to the administration the problems we had. Yong smiled, looking relieved. "It will be OK Acuach Cor," he said. "I don't have time to tell you everything, but Jok Mach is taking care of things, you'll see!" I think Yong could see I was on the verge of freaking out and was breaking into tears. He gave me another of those looks, like 'come on Acuach Cor, don't or I won't be able to deal with this.' Then he said, "I have to go Sarah, my bus is leaving. Just give us a hug, and let's be strong, OK?" I tried and was just shivering with dread. Never had I been away from Yong. Never had I felt so separate, and so exposed.

It was a horrible two hours spent on that bus worrying about what would happen when I arrived in this strange City of my future, a future where I couldn't even prove who I was and couldn't even change out of the clothes I'd spent many hours traveling in. I was unsure of everything! I spent most of the trip trying not to totally freak out. I felt self conscious; sure everyone on that bus was staring at me. Nyakoba had been watching this difficulty and broke through my nasty thoughts. She told me not to worry. "I'll be with you when you go through all this Sarah and I'll lend you some clothes till we figure something out!" Well it was exactly what I needed from my sister and hey, very reassuring.

It did work out rather smoothly too. We were taken to the University and Jok Mach had done his part; I was accepted at registration. This included where we would be living. It was small but acceptable accommodation, not that I had a choice in the matter. I phoned Jok Mach just as soon as I got settled in. His manner was so calming and direct. He put me at ease right away with all the information on how he was fixing the problem. Within a short period of time the school board sent photo copies of my graduation information and diplomas. I also gradually got all my personal identification from University sources.

The best part was talking with Sarah Jok on the phone. "Oh my god Sarah," she said with real passion, "you have no clothes?" "Nope" said I, "all gone!" I was really surprised by her next revelation, "Guess what, we are immigrating to Canada, Sarah! I can't possibly take all my stuff with me. I'll sort through it and send you some nice clothes, alright." Again, it was exactly what I needed to hear. We talked for a while and it came down to those dreaded tears for both of us two Sister Sarah's. I was going to miss the Mach Family dreadfully. I had spent so much time with them through the years. My Auntie Mary Apiu was so like Mama. She had taken me under her wing as if I were her own. I thought back to the only information I had of my family. Baba and Mama had met them on their way to Cuba from Ethiopia. The Mach family had promised them to watch out for us. They did, and then some. This family was a constant for us; always there when we needed them the most. They had become my family.

I was sad that they were leaving Cuba, but at the same time, happy for them. I'd heard a lot of good things about Canada being a great and wonderful country! I'd often thought, of all the places there were to immigrate to, I would choose Canada first. Maybe if the war in Sudan went on forever, as it seemed to be doing, when I finished University I would set up my Big House there. In a very few months after I got some wonderful clothes from Sister Sarah, the Mach family immigrated to Edmonton, Alberta along with another group of Sudanese students.

Our original numbers were steadily dwindling to a very few.

There it was; all the Number 13 bad luck (tocate) had got itself rearranged. Sarah Gabriel was in the home stretch. I was working my dream and even though I was alone, I was working for the family name. We would own the Big House and Compound some day or I'd die trying. For the first time in my whole life I was totally on my own without family or relatives close. I have to say, this idea scared me a lot, for a while anyway.

I got set up in our apartment complex with shared rooms, and bathrooms, and not an inch of privacy! By then I was used to that anyway, between sharing one room with brothers and a sister in tiny stick houses and years of life in boarding school dorms. I had one boon and a memory to cherish; my huge bedroom in the mansion where a one-time princess had the bliss of luxury all to herself... a dream world of six months!

There was no time to miss family. So much of my new life was engaging and different than I was used to. I had Nykoba my roommate and surrogate sister to fill that place and later, I found Martha William. As things went on there were a lot of developing friendships and interesting things to do together. In that whole University, there were only four Sudanese Students attending. Two of those were a girl and a guy who were already there. They were only in our group for a few short months before they immigrated to Canada. That left Nykoba and me. Nobody at that University knew anything about us being Sudanese refugees. We were just students and what a blending it was... a blending of cultures, period.

I was really wide eyed and innocent for quite awhile. We are talking real culture shock here; nobody treated us any differently. It was absolutely liberating this University lifestyle with too many differences from boarding school to count. No one monitoring us, we could go anywhere we wanted. The one point that was somewhat the same ... I was always hungry. The food there was worse, if you could believe than at school. One time I found a worm in my rice and stopped eating rice at the university cafeteria altogether.

This left me to eat almost nothing, just like everyone else who had no money.

At university we received at least a bit more money. On the Island of Youth all we had for the month was five pesos. Here I received from the government sixty Cuban pesos, equal to three American dollars. This allowed me to buy a bit more food for myself as the university food was disgusting and almost inedible. I was getting used to that too. Everyone we knew was always complaining of the food and the poor state of the Cuban economy.

I didn't care anymore. It was all old news and I was dealing with it anyway. Why complain, it doesn't help matters any. That's just Sarah; the future will be what it is.

If we strive to make it better.

When this type conversation came up, I changed the topic. It wasn't like me to settle for all the doom and gloom; there were better things to talk about, like all the great looking guys on campus. It was a smorgasbord of choices. They were from any number of countries and backgrounds, and all of them were hitting on me too. Let's not go there, enough said. Hey! It was a unique experience at first, but after a while I found it kind of annoying. I was there to get educated not run around chasing relationships. For a lot of people it seemed, that's all they were interested in, all the time, non-stop. It just wasn't me.

I was interested in my courses and found that yep, I was pretty good at math, maybe business too. I dreamed quite a lot about how all this would apply to our family fortunes. We'd be all rich and powerful us Gabriels. I could see us taking over Sudan, having swimming pools, beautiful houses and maybe, a Land Rover, or three!

I have to admit I had some pretty big dreams, and a pretty dreamy boyfriend or two. Well Five, if you're counting. (Just kidding) I really didn't have time for that and only had the one boyfriend. He was pretty nice. We were in the same course, but he was older and almost finished, with really high marks. I hooked up with him only because he could help me study; poor fool! (just kidding) It did help though. He turned out to be a really good boyfriend who never pressured me, or argued. He was a kind and generous person really. My boy friend of no name (I have my reasons) was really very intellectual, and it was fun to go out to cafes with him and meet people.

The thing I enjoyed about University life the best? No damn grapefruit.

We had our own world, free of that slavery, right in the middle of a City with no buses to get anywhere for any great distance. You could walk, ride a bike and there were so many interesting places to discover. It was a whole new life. It opened to me parts of Cuba I had never experienced before. It was deeper and had oh so much more color for the senses. "Oh man, la musica muy bonito!" [the music was awesome] There were all night dance clubs or we could just walk to a public square and there would be local community dances and get-togethers with a ghetto blaster. One of the reasons for keeping this no name boyfriend was that he could really dance and loved music as much as I did. He knew a lot about music and where to discover it happening in the city. It was here that I saw truly live performances of Salsa. At school we thought our bands were awesome. Here I realized how wrong that was. These performers were excellent and seriously professional; the quality of their Salsa music stood right out.

My love for this music and culture just grew and grew. There was a point I wished I could just stay in Cuba. I still love Cuba and respect the country immensely for all the things it did for us displaced Sudanese Students. Cuba has an amazing culture really and is very diverse ethnically. It had a little of every race on earth there with very little separation, and it seemed to me, everyone was treated equally. Many times later in life, I've thought Cuba a good example for the rest of the world. We should all get along and share the world's resources. I imagine there is corruption there, as there is everywhere in the world. That's not a cause for cynicism; change it.

Or die trying, like my Brothers and Sisters were doing in Sudan.

So we could have our share ... a few paved roads, a school system, maybe drinking water, and jobs. These are things everyone needs to have, along with freedom and security. Everybody really just wants a chance to get ahead and to be safe. This is what makes them human. No one wants to be like an animal; running for days on end from the slaughter.

I was still trying hard not to think too much about that.

From what I learned about Cuba in school, the current Government was trying to do things differently; not that I think too long and hard about politics and the ideas that seem to be wrecking our world. It seemed to me people were looking in the wrong places for solutions. I think we have to seek those solutions in ourselves first. One by one we can make a difference. I learned we need to be educated and the manner and quality of education makes a difference. Everyone in the world requires a basic education and the opportunity to better themselves. A few of us from Sudan were granted this opportunity; too small a percentage to make a real difference. I realize this now, like that saying, it was a little late and too long in the coming.

I loved Cuba, and for a great part of my life, in a very odd way, it was my home.

Although nothing can replace one's origins, I was fluent in the culture. It was a blessing in the long run that we Sudanese were segregated initially. Baba had been right. Had I been educated in Havana, I would have lost my culture, just melted into the Cuban landscape. It was like that in University. I realized I was assimilating this Latin culture. Spanish was now my primary language. I hardly spoke Arabic at all anymore, although I'll always speak my tribal Dinka. I had left Africa at a very early and impressionable age. Most of the memories of my homeland had faded, other than some good childhood glimpses before the war claimed our future.

I was enjoying my University education and did well as the first year went by. I had all my plans laid out and thought the next four years would go smoothly if they were anything like the first. My social life, I admit, was making my Cuban experience all the more interesting. Yet something was missing. I missed the camaraderie of the Sudanese students and the trials we'd endured together. I missed the feeling that we had a purpose being there. Now there was only Nyakoba and me at University. Anyuon and Yong did communicate with me at times by phone, but those contacts were few and far between. In some of the conversations our missing parents would come up. Yong told me, in one of the calls, some of the Students who had gone to Canada, with the help of the Sudanese community there, had easily found their families in Sudan.

This lit a fire in me that could not be put out.

For a month this idea ran through my every waking moment. I had, in the past, mostly ignored thinking about places like English Canada. With a Cuban university education, and learning the language, it would mean starting all over again. At the time this was an option I wasn't willing to consider. On the other hand, it didn't seem the war in Sudan would stop anytime soon, so if I couldn't go back to my country, what use was all this education? I'd flip flop on that idea and then hear Baba's voice burning through my consciousness; "*Sarah, take advantage of this opportunity, get an education and come back home... to a New Sudan!*" I had dedicated my life to the ideal of pleasing my parents, meeting this ideal that had been really forced on me. Our lives had been shaped by the trauma of needing to go where happenstance guided us. This safe haven of opportunity was a gift I was obligated to my father for. I had to suffer through any and all trials in order to attain Baba's desire for us. I needed to be a part of the greater order, to fit in to our Big House, even suffer grapefruit and survive the ruining of my health.

Then I arrived at an idea, '*is life only about survival?*'

For me, it wasn't just about physical suffering and effort. My true suffering wasn't about the hardships of life in Cuba. This I could do. I would suffer any and all of it, for the betterment of my family. No, the real suffering was mental. It was the years of torture wondering where Baba and Mama were, and my little Chol. I was twenty-four and I couldn't even picture what Chol looked like now. I wanted with all my heart to get an education for my family, spend the next four years on my own, study hard and be this dream, but my need to find my family was greater!

My interest in University, in only one day of combined reasoning and revealed logic, fell away to ashes. I just couldn't see myself staying in University for another four years. No way! Working toward a degree that might not help me? This made no sense. What consumed my mind was that I could spend those four years in Canada concentrating on finding Baba and Mama. This gnawing hole in my heart had been part of me during my time at the Big Houses. I was full of dread over my parents. All the students were suffering this, not knowing of what was taking place with their families in Sudan. It was heartbreaking when my brothers and sisters would get news that broke them down, learning the Civil War had claimed their hopes and dreams. It had already done so for us when we got word about losing Agor that way; how hard that was to accept. There was a part of me that was beginning to believe that had happened to Baba, Mama and Chol. Why couldn't we find them? Why was there never any news, even from trusted sources, that would help us locate our family? Were they dead? This caused me many nights of absolute terror and out-of-control tears. I came to the realization that no matter the outcome of this, I needed to know! I couldn't live this way, with the trials and suffering, not knowing why I had to continue this path of the ideal. I had talked Baba and Mama into letting me stay in Cuba. It had been my decision. I was thirteen then and had made an independent choice. I was an adult now and it was the same. I had to face the reality of conditions. If

I stayed in Cuba and all the economic realities here, it would be four more years of being short of everything and hungry, not just for food, but for information. This living hunger for my parents was so powerful, it could not be denied. At that juncture, I knew...

I would apply to go to Canada.

The very next day I talked to the only person I trusted, Nyakoba. I told her about my decision and she surprised me; she had been thinking exactly the same. "Sarah, we will go together!" The plan was on, and off to Havana and Mr. Aragon's ACNUR offices, we did go. We asked questions and they were very helpful. We even ran into other Sudanese students there doing exactly the same thing! I found Amel and Anot were there as well. Although Nyakoba wasn't a member of the original Fantastic Four, she'd do. It was a really neat way to kick this all off, having a short time with us crazy four of fourteen girls, back together again. We were all excited at the possibility of starting a new life together in Canada. It was like a dream really. This trip had planted a seed of hope; to find my family and go for a better life. Deep in my heart I knew I'd made the right decision. Nyakoba and I went directly back to University and quit.

My boyfriend wasn't too happy. I gave him a hug and tried to make him feel better. I told him I'd miss him, that I'd write him every day and never did. I think I did write a few times and then gave up because he never wrote back. I called my brothers and told them about my plans. With Yong, it was like a moment of dead air, then "WHAT!" Anyuon seemed happier for me, but worried that I was going to Canada all on my own with no family. That was really precious for me; hearing that from him, more words than I'd ever heard him say to me all at one time before. I teased him back saying, "Just how will you get by here without me, Anyuon?" He laughed.

It wasn't quite finished yet; we had to go to an orientation program with Embassy workers at a school in Havana. All the Sudanese students were there and it was like old home week as we learned some things about Canada we needed to know. There were the differences in law and the two languages. What I found really interesting was the weather. I'd heard from others who had immigrated how they froze to death up there. The Embassy people said, yep that's true; you had to watch out for polar bears and Icebergs too. Which actually was true; there are parts of Canada like that! Just not where we'd be going! They did tell us we would have to deal with lots of snow.

Well I couldn't wait for that idea. I remembered when I was little; Baba had gone on a trip to Russia. He told us amazing stories about this white stuff falling out of the clouds. We couldn't picture that at all and asked, 'what is this white stuff snow?' What does it feel like? He laughed and said, "It feels like ice cubes that are light and disappear when they melt quickly!" Until that day 'till I first saw this phenomena myself, I thought snowflakes were square.

Well, the day came when I was about to find out, and not just for me, as there were about a hundred of us leaving on the same plane. Imagine, a whole plane all to ourselves! Anyuon and Yong had come as well to see me off on this new adventure. That's what it was like for me. I don't think I have been that excited about anything ever. I was sad in only one way, to be hugging my brothers and leaving them behind. I wished they could be coming with me. They assured me that it wasn't what they needed to do. They felt they had to finish what they'd started, in Cuba.

They only wanted the best for me and thought going to Canada was the best decision. Though not really saying it in so many words, they were placing their hopes in me. They too wanted, more than anything, to learn where our parents were. They were leaving this family responsibility in my hands. Yes, it was the most important thing to us as family. We said our goodbye's and I climbed the stairs to the plane. I had decided on my Future.

I was off on my family mission and a new chapter of my life.

Chapter 18
CANADA

I again felt like a refugee on that flight north of the equator. Here we were once more, this small group of African people, now no longer children, flying thousands of miles away from the life we knew into uncertain circumstances.

On the last trip like this one, I was a little girl traveling from my homeland with Mama and her children. We were so excited we were going to be reunited with Baba and start a new life in a foreign land, Cuba. Then I remembered that life, the long suffering I'd experienced because of Baba's arrangement for his family. My mind was filled with scenes from those passing years. I traveled through an airspace of quiet sad, almost frightened recollection.

I knew that sneaky travel bundle had somehow gotten out of the orchard and made its way into my luggage. There it was again, reminding me of the events that formed Sarah Gabriel's world. Acuach Cor, a Dinka child of tribal Africa, was in this marvelous modern jet, miles up in the air. I felt as if my ancestors were watching this event through my current experience. My parents were missing from me, I was missing from them. I wasn't lost, only displaced, from the soil of my heritage and the wonder of it all. There was a tightness in my chest that had nothing to do with cabin pressure.

It was a mystery our family could experience such things, even this flight; Acuach Cor's leap into the unknown. I not only had to contend with the pressure in my chest but butterflies of excitement in my tummy. The little girl was there again with me; this entity I had wrapped so carefully in my travel bundle and buried under layers of grief and confusion. The butterflies were from the feeling I was flying to find the answer to those mysteries. If I could find them, this mythical bundle of childish wishes, I could find myself. Acuach wanted out, she needed to again be a part of this experience. She was Africa. I needed her. She was my courage . . . the reason that I had taken this chance.

To my surprise it was only a three-hour trip on our Air Canada flight from Havana to Toronto. Toronto; even the names of places in Canada sounded different and were hard to pronounce. It was one of my major worries, the idea of having to learn English. I fretted a little over this as the plane banked and the announcements came on with bells and lighted panels I couldn't read. They flashed out, '*put on your seat belt*.' I couldn't understand the announcement, but I put on my seat belt because everyone around me was. We were landing! The scene outside my window stopped all thoughts about language differences. The city of Toronto was unfolding beneath me. It was huge. I could see all these tall buildings and freeways going everywhere and it all so tiny, like really busy tiny ants. '*Like, Wow ... Canadian people!*'

I was really anxious and excited. The girl sitting next to me looked over my shoulder too, chattering away about goodness knows what. All too soon the plane touched down and all that disembarking stuff took place. I didn't know what to expect, but walking through a tunnel into the terminal wasn't one of them. We didn't even have to go outside! All the people seemed to be in a great hurry and some, with very serious looks on their faces, were really determined to get to where they were going. This was totally opposite from where I'd come from. Cubans are really quite laid back in just about everything they do. Yes, it would all be very different in Canada.

Everything was so well lit. I'd never seen so many lights. The airport was modern. Even though I didn't really know what that meant, I was beginning to get the idea. It looked so bright and sparking clean. I had seen many people walking all over everywhere; how could the floors be kept so clean? I was to learn Canada, as a country, is a clean place, well looked after mostly. Later on I saw parts of cities that were old and not as well maintained, as poverty exists everywhere by different degrees and standards. But not that airport! It was so exciting to be in Canada, we were speechless, taking it all in.

I think we moved along too slowly. People were constantly bumping into us and giving us dirty looks. I was beginning to wonder, if maybe Canadians weren't all that friendly. Immigration Officers were waiting for us and they accompanied us to their offices in the airport. They talked to us very authoritatively. We had no idea what they were trying to explain to us. We all wore our big smiles and nodded our heads, so I guess they thought we understood them. You'd have thought they would have brought a Spanish translator with them to deal with confused immigrants from Cuba.

By then we were thinking these were very nice Canadians as they passed out jackets, ear muffs, winter boots, gloves and whatnot. All we knew how to say in English was, "thank you, thank you!" for these very thoughtful, welcoming gifts.

When we left Cuba, it was wonderfully tropically warm so we only had summer clothes on and in our bags everything we had was light summer wear with not one jacket or sweater between the lot of us. With all the orientation we'd just gone through, we'd not understood this winter wear would be needed . . . *for that day!* We could see it was a beautiful sunny day in Toronto by looking out the windows. There was no snow on the ground, so we stuffed all these nice thoughtful gifts in our baggage and carried on to wherever it was they were leading us. Our larger group was being split up and some of us were going to other destinations in Canada. Our group of about fifteen would be staying overnight in Toronto, before going off to wherever we were going.

I was the only one who would be going to Ottawa. I was really happy it wasn't winter yet as we understood the snowy winters here were extremely cold. I had no idea what cold was, and never experienced anything like what awaited, right outside that door! You would have thought we would have caught on by then, seeing all these people pass us coming in, wearing all their cozy winter gear. As we passed them on our way out the door, we wondered at the looks we were getting. We even giggled amongst ourselves on the way to our waiting mini bus. That lasted for about half a heartbeat! It was like running into an invisible wall; the rudest alien shock of my life.

We are talking about instant Arctic cold, shivering, and goose bumps.

You never heard such screaming from one group of black people. In our all too thin Cuban summer clothing, we fell over ourselves in a stampede to get back inside those doors and precious warm safety. Now we understood what the immigration officers were trying to tell us. Man, was it cold out there! Looks could really be deceiving; sunny and cold at the same time. How could you explain that? Well, in one word . . . Canada! I started looking for Polar Bears, everywhere! (just kidding)

We ran back inside, ripped opened our bags and put on those lovely winter clothes. We had thought they looked ungainly and quite ugly really. They were all the same lame green color and goofy style. 'Yep, yep, we're in the army now,' is what it felt like. My friends and I made fun of each other, saying finally we were in Canada and from that moment on we'd be living like chickens in the refrigerator.

By then we were receiving a lot of attention from others at the airport. Some of them were laughing. When we noticed this, we didn't know whether to be offended or what. My boots and jacket were very big for me; I was actually swimming in them like I was wearing Mama's clothes. I guess we were pretty entertaining and it was good to see people laughing. You could see it in their faces; they weren't being mean, they were laughing with us. It was comical how we were obviously not from Canada and were reacting to the cold babbling away in Spanish.

I had to admit the winter clothes were awful, but gloriously warm!

Who cares if you look funny? I certainly didn't. Not at that time anyway. Today? I wouldn't be caught dead looking like that. No way! What I did understand from this was that winter was no joke. It was going to take some getting used to. I was still cold when we boarded the mini bus. I think it was because of the very thought of it, all frosty out there, was making me shiver. Even though I was on a heated bus, all zippered up and secure, in toasty winter wear, I knew...

I'd have to soon leave that bus.

On the short trip to the hotel, we all gawked out the windows in awe at the passing scene. The buildings were so tall and had amazingly beautiful glass walls that shone with the sunlight like mirrors. There were so many passing cars. They looked totally new, like they were from outer space, and none of them was blowing black smoke. The roads were beautifully paved and had no potholes. But there were way too many stop lights everywhere! Again I noticed everyone was in such a hurry; busy, busy, busy! Canada was a busy place.

It looked like everyone here was rich, and Wow, the hotel we came to! I couldn't believe we'd be put up in such a place. In Cuba, it would have been a simple dorm kind of deal. This was nothing like that. I was thinking only rich people could stay there; the carpets must have cost a fortune. There was so much splendor and everything matched. I had never seen such different lights hanging from the ceiling with crystals like tear drops. In reality, it was a fairly average Canadian hotel.

It's not like Cuba didn't have beautiful hotels, it does. But they were different and if you weren't rich, you didn't get in them. So for us, it was like a big privilege. One of the hotel workers told us to follow him and this tight knit group followed along, not about to get lost in this seemingly huge posh Hotel!

When we got to the room, all of us walked right in. To our shock, our guide was shaking his head. He tried getting his message across to us by holding up two fingers. Even then we didn't quite understand his meaning. Boy, this room was too big for only two people. Where were the others going to go? And which two? I guess we looked quite funny to him, because he was laughing pretty hard at our antics.

It all eventually did get sorted out and, 'oh boy' were we happy with that place! I bet I spent three hours in the shower with all that hot water that just kept on coming! I had to stop this wonder because of Anot pounding angrily on the door for her turn, three or four times. Each time I yelled out, "I'll be right out, I'm almost done!"

It was heaven.

I was really going to like this Canada.

There were just so many excesses to enjoy, like those wonderfully comfortable beds where we could just lie there and watch TV. When we first turned on the TV and changed channels, I jumped from shock. I couldn't believe it and in my excitement fell back on the bed laughing. "Hey Anot ... look at all these channels!" There were lots of them! In Cuba we only had two and couldn't watch many things. Most of the time Fidel Castro would be giving long speeches on both of them. My friend and I ran to see my cousin Rosa and our friend Josefina in their rooms. They were doing exactly the same thing, changing channels. We were all excited and stayed up late watching TV, even though we couldn't understand everything since it was in English. We didn't care; we watched movies and then we talked, and talked. It was such a fun evening spent in decadent splendor.

Mostly, what I recall was TV and having fun all evening with Anot. We knew soon we wouldn't see each other as she was off to London and no, not England; London Ontario. I knew I would miss all my fabulous four sisters terribly. You know, we did have dinner somewhere that evening, but for the life of me, I can't remember where. I do recall the next morning's breakfast perfectly for obvious reasons. An Immigration officer came to pick us up for the breakfast and it was gigantic. I couldn't believe the amount of food so early in the morning. My plate was full to overflowing with eggs, sausage and pancakes, and even toast on a side plate. Then a fruit juice on top of all that! It was a lot of food, compared to what I was used to (little to none). I couldn't finish even half of that yummy meal. Neither could my friends; we were just not used to so much food and so many choices.

Our amazing meal finished, and after the bus trip back to the airport, it was time to say goodbye to my group. It was quite a difficult moment for me. These girls—Anot, Josefina and my cousin Rosa—had been with me right from the beginning. We all were pretty happy, a little anxious about where we were going, and elated to have the opportunity to become Canadian Citizens in this land of plenty. We knew it was one of the best countries on earth and we hoped there'd be lots of good paying jobs for us all; at least after we learned English! It was a tight time table we had for the day and all too soon off they went to their different Canadian destinations.

There was now only me and I was taken to more . . . 'orientation.' I saw a lot of moving lips but had no idea what even some of the sign language meant. I did my best to listen hard and still didn't understand a word. Well, maybe I did one or two. The whole extent of my English was 'hello, goodbye, thank you' and the most important, a questioning look followed, by... 'washrooms?' I was being sent to Ottawa, Ontario, as had my friend Amel. She'd gone there three days earlier and I was really excited knowing she was expecting me. This much I did know. The immigration people had made me a cardboard sign with my name on it. They worked hard to get me to understand someone would be waiting there at arrivals in the terminal with the same sign.

There it was, and I was off on another step of my adventure. All I could think of was that I was that much closer to my goal; finding Mama, Baba and the rest of my siblings. My heart soared thinking of these things, picturing in my mind they were all healthy and happy. Not dead; God what a brutal thought. It was possible. I had to at least try to face that possibility, what it would be like to receive that dreadful news. It was much better to quickly skip over these feelings and see them safe and in a nice home somewhere.

The flight to Ottawa took no time at all. It was like the plane went up, and then just started right back down. Even though the trip was quick, I realized Canada was a huge Country. I'd seen maps in Cuba when they told us where we might end up. There were Islands in the Province of British Colombia almost as big as all of Cuba.

Or, so they said.

I disembarked and went off to claim my luggage. This took no time at all and there I stood outside the appointed arrival gate, waiting. And waiting and waiting. Surely this sign the same as mine would be there shortly. Soon I was the only person standing at the arrival gate, holding that sign in front of me like some shield. 'It's me Sarah Gabriel, I'm here. The sign says so!' Then I began to feel rather put off. 'Where the Hell was this Immigration person with a matching sign?' Maybe I was in the wrong part of the airport. I started marching around the airport from one end to the other and everywhere in between. I was the only one in that whole airport with such a silly sign.

I had spent much more than an hour doing that and it was getting me nowhere. I had to do something. I was getting more and more anxious. I couldn't ask anyone for directions, couldn't read the signs. Who could I ask out of all these people behind their counters? I did know what Hertz rent a car looked like, so I ignored those desks. I wandered around hoping to hear someone speaking Spanish; not one!

Finally I just picked a lady who looked nice and was smiling all the time at everyone. I waited until no one was at her desk and moved in to try and make her understand my problem. I pointed at the sign, at me, and used every word of English I thought might apply to my situation. This woman was really good at smiling, but that was about it. She nodded a lot and said 'Yes, you Sarah' and pointed at her badge, 'me, Brenda!' I was about to throw my sign in the air and freak out. This was getting to be more than I could handle. I just walked away from smiley Brenda. It wasn't her fault; she simply couldn't understand Spanish.

I went back to see if there was anyone with a sign waiting back at my arrival gate. Part of me imagined some government worker was there wondering where I was. No such luck. I stood there for another hour, tried walking hopefully through the airport, and tried one more desk clerk who, again, didn't understand what I needed. Finally back at arrivals I found a bench to sit down and felt totally dejected. All manner of thoughts were rushing through my mind. Maybe the people here hadn't got the message. Maybe no one would ever show up. Then what would I do? I had no money to eat even. I was beginning to think about that and my grumbling stomach. It had been a long time since my beautiful breakfast. I thought about Amel, somewhere in this city I'd never been in before. I had no phone numbers to contact her. I had no phone numbers for anyone. Imagine trying to phone somewhere where nobody speaks your language.

I was lost.

That feeling just kept on building. People walked by and the noises all around me seemed to be closing in on me. I felt like I was in a horror movie. I felt this horrible feeling that no one could help me. I started to cry and it wouldn't stop. All the anxiety of all this confusion caught up to me. There had been so many changes so fast. I began feeling maybe I had made a mistake coming here. I knew if Yong were here, he would know what to do. He always did. It was all I could think of, sobbing away, my family; where are they? How could I find them if I were lost? Then the heartbreak came. I could see Mama's face right before me. I started to outright, wail. "I want my Mama! Where are you? Acuach Cor is so lost!"

Then it was as if Mama was looking at me and all serious; not acting at all like I expected. "Acuach Cor," she was saying, "look at you there crying like a little baby?" She tisk, tisk'd and wagged her finger at me, "You get up from there, right now!" I could hear her voice so clearly. "How is this nonsense helping you, feeling all sorry for yourself?" That stopped all the fussing and I wiped my tears away. How would Mama expect me to handle this?

'With dignity', came right away and 'courage.'

It was my own decision to come to Canada. If I wanted to survive in this country and find out about my family in Africa, crying was not going to help. I felt a sharp headache coming on, and thought, 'What am I doing to myself?' I knew right then, I could rely on no one but me. These immigration people could only do so much. Right now I had to do something for myself and get out of this stupid predicament.

I had to do whatever was necessary to find my family. This was my mission; crying wasn't going to solve anything. I had to find someone and make them understand immigration was supposed to meet me, and they hadn't for hours and hours. I opened my bag and checked through all the papers and documents I'd received in Toronto. I laid them out on the bench and tried to decide which might be useful. I picked who I thought was the most likely person to help, the one I talked to first. I marched right up there and plopped my papers onto her counter and let them speak for themselves. It surprised me how fast this nice smiling woman Brenda recognized my dilemma.

I used every word I could think of and pointed at my documents. "*That me, me Immigration, me no house, Cuba me come.*" With my totally broken English, I decided not to give up and repeated again, "*that me, me*

Immigration, me no house, Cuba me.' Finally she said something, still looking puzzled. I had no clue what it was, although it sounded like she was asking who would be picking me up. I told her again, *"me no family, me Canada Immigration. Come for me Sarah Gabriel."* Then she said, "Oh! You're waiting for somebody from Immigration to pick you up! "YES, yes!" I nodded like crazy, hoping I understood what she was telling me. It looked as though she finally had and directly made the phone call and actually got through right away.

Finally after so many hours waiting in despair, they sent somebody to pick me up. I was feeling totally exhausted by then. When the guy started explaining the reason why there was nobody waiting for me at the airport, at least that's what I thought he might be talking about, I didn't care anymore! All that mattered was that I was no longer lost. Those endless hours of suffering and loneliness were over and done with. The Immigration guy kept talking to me but I didn't know what he was saying. It sounded as if he was enjoying himself, because he laughed all the way back in the mini bus. I could tell from the expression in his eyes, he was trying to cheer me up. All I could do was to laugh back, like it was funny. Yah, right, a lot of laughs! I said something back in Spanish, so he wouldn't feel as if he was talking to himself.

What I was thinking was that I was about to see my dear friend Amel waiting for me at Reception House. I could hardly wait to tell her about all this horror! We arrived and Amel was there excited to see me. I ran to her for a big hug. I couldn't help it and started to cry all over again, my frustrating time at the airport still with me. Amel didn't know that and pulled back, looking at me oddly. Then, so like Amel, she gave me a big smile and said, "What? You miss me already Acuach Cor? It's only been three days since we left Havana!" It was true; that made it sound silly. I nodded and hugged her tightly again.

"I got lost, Amel!" I sniveled. I didn't want to let her go.

She got away from me somehow. "What? No way. Well, come on, tell me all about getting lost Sarah." That was all the go ahead I needed and it all poured out; how no one was there when I arrived in Ottawa and how many hours I stood there with that stupid sign. I didn't even get to use that useless cardboard. Amel thought it was funny, that part, and the way I was describing it. I didn't think it was too funny at the time, but Amel was making me laugh and I felt better. I wiped away my tears and smiled and told my sister, "here I am with you again, Amel. There's no need for me to cry anymore, eh."

She smoothed down my hair and gave me another hug. "Ha, only Acuach Cor could get lost on her second day in Canada!" Then her laugh came again and she started jumping up and down, all excited. "Come on, I'll show you around. You have to see this place Sarah, it's great and, guess what?" Of course I asked her what. "They put us in the same room; you'll be in with me Sister". It made sense as there were only the two of us Sudanese in Ottawa and the room at Reception House had been per-arranged for us. Now Amel was in her element and thoughts of the airport experience evaporated.

Like a couple of teenagers, we burned up the stairs and ran down the hall to what would be our room for the coming month. Amel right away flew through the air and flopped onto one of two Queen sized beds. "This one's all mine," she giggled and rolled around. "Plenty of room here, hey Sarah," she said with a grin. "Not like those skinny bunks we had to put up with in the dorms." That was true enough. They were just big enough to fit into and if you rolled over you fell out of bed. The mattresses were like in the ones in Sudan, filled with cotton. As they got old they got lumpy. It really was a beautiful room, big and bright, with large windows that looked out over a back yard, with a view of big city buildings in the background. We spent a few minutes putting my stuff in drawers, what little I had. Then it was off to experience the rest of this big, beautiful house.

It was the first such house I'd been in, and Wow, everything in Canada was just so different; like everyone in the house. There were people from all over the world staying there, and none of them spoke Spanish. They were to hear a lot of it that day. Amel took me right to the kitchen first and told me to eat whatever I wanted. That was something unexpected and completely new to me. Eat anything, and at anytime I wanted! "Wow!" That was definitely doable, given how little we'd had in Cuba and even less in the refugee camps or Bilfam. We never had an excess of food, never. Well, maybe once, long ago, at the mansion in Ethiopia.

This idea was still astonishing to me. I could go to the kitchen and grab anything to eat without permission? Since I was hungry after such a long wait at the airport, I thought, I'm going to eat everything I see in this kitchen. They had every kind of food I could think of: bread, butter, rice, meat, vegetables, juices, tea, coffee; so much food. It was everything I could have imagined and hoped for. Unfortunately, I needed time for my system to get used to all this rich food, again, something I'd never experienced before.

While Amel and I were talking and laughing, the girls who worked at Reception House seemed to be having a lot of fun just watching us. They were enjoying our talking and laughing as much as we were, although they didn't understand a thing we were saying to each other. My guess was we looked like a couple of children playing and having fun with our Canada experience. The kitchen experience with the food probably made them figure we'd been starved half to death. What they couldn't know was; we were.

Our grand tour ended in a very nice sitting room in front of the TV and flipping through channels blindingly fast. Again the staff must have thought we were nuts, spending all of two seconds watching anything. We pointed at things we thought were weird and laughed our socks off. There were other people around and the TV was for everyone. We finally got the message; we hadn't been able to find anything in Spanish anyway. Of course we had no idea yet about satellite TV and such. If they'd had it, I'm sure we would have found some Spanish programming.

The rest of the day was nearly perfect. I'd finally calmed down and enjoyed taking ever thing in. I spent some time organizing my goals. I was in Canada and I had a plan to learn English quickly so I could do whatever it took to find my parents. This would be the greatest hurdle, speaking the language so I could find work, save money and go back to Sudan if I found them. I was in a hurry to make all this happen. It had been ten years since I'd had any contact with my parents. It was too long. I'd given up most of my previous goals to accomplish a thing so necessary it was painful. Canada was my hope. Cuba had been frustrating because during all the time I'd been there, I'd had so many financial difficulties; it had made a family search there impossible.

That night I couldn't sleep, thinking about all the things I had to find out. I tried hard to imagine them without having much luck. I worried about this new culture, and then there was this idea of a very cold winter on the way. I'd felt the cold the day before and it wasn't even really winter yet. God, what would that be like? I'd turn into a living ice cube I thought. 'Well if the people here can live with it, I guess now I'll have to too!' I figured. I didn't think that would be my major concern; it would be getting the money I needed. This in itself was a whole chain of needs I would have to face. Tomorrow wasn't soon enough for me.

The next day though was, again, a more relaxing time with Amel.

We went for a walk around the neighbourhood. There was no time like the present to get used to being out in that cold fresh air. Our walks expanded into taking the bus downtown, which wasn't that far away. In truth, we hadn't adjusted to the weather yet and walked too far in all that cold fresh air. Somehow we got directions on how to catch the bus and get back to Reception House. The idea of getting lost in that huge city didn't appeal to me at all. So it was, that Amel and I discovered... Malls. Oh, what a joy that was. Holy cow, so much stuff could be had here in Canada, if you had money. We didn't, but it didn't stop us from looking and dreaming about the money we could make here. Then we could have all this stuff!

Boy, then look out. I had several hundred outfits already picked out!

Amel is so much fun to do stuff with; she's goofy really. She could talk me into doing just about anything. "Come on Sarah, let's go into this store," she said on one of our first days out wandering. We were about to open the door and, BAM; we jumped back in shock. *It opened for us!* People passing by were staring as we went in and out I don't know how many times laughing, pointing at this totally new Canadian marvel. Downtown was like that; there was just so much to see. It was nothing at all like anywhere we had been. After that experience, we kept a look out for different kinds of doors. You'd be surprised how many we found too.

The one I liked the best was like a merry-go-round ride, you know, those tube like deals that spin (revolving doors). We saw it from a ways off. We were so juvenile; two more or less adult women running down the street to ride around in a door or maybe find a good elevator in a really tall building. I think we even stood outside with our necks stretched, counting the floors. Well, it was the neatest thing we'd ever seen. We'd grab that bar and walk the door around. So there we were, round and round we'd go, laughing our guts out, trying to figure the timing to get out of the thing. Finally we'd dive out. The people in the building were really enjoying our exuberance. Obviously we weren't from their country, judging from our matching winter outfits that were way too big on us.

We were standing in the lobby after another go round, laughing and having a ball. A woman in the lobby started pointing at us and wagging her finger angrily. I think she thought we were laughing at her, but we hadn't even seen her until then. We didn't know what to think. It just made us look at each other and laugh all the harder as we heard her yelling about calling 911. We knew about that from the orientation, this number got you the Police, Fire and Ambulance. We figured she needed the funny farm people, the way she was ranting, raving and blowing a fuse. About what? We had no idea.

We responded to her with a string of Spanish and questions about her calling 911. Her eyes got all puzzled at what we were trying to say and she walked away. That's how we passed some of our free time together.

There were English classes at Reception House we had to attend. I guess it did help some. I still wondered why they never brought in anyone who could speak Spanish. I would have thought we'd have learned faster that way. As it was, we spent most of our time struggling to understand every word they said. It reminded me of how difficult our first days in Cuba were; this was much the same. In this way my month at Reception House flew right by.

Both Amel and I make friends easily. So we made a lot of friends at Reception House and had a lot of fun being there. During the same period, we also met a Sudanese guy that came from Egypt. Through him we met other Sudanese Nationals living in Ottawa. They came to visit us and on several occasions took us to their homes to serve us Sudanese food and hear our stories about living in Cuba. It was nice to spend time with people from my homeland, speak my language freely, and enjoy food I hadn't had in many years. It was very exciting to see the Sudanese and their large community. It only made my desire to return to Africa at some point all that much stronger. Many of these new friends from Sudan, until then, had known nothing about us 'Lost Children of Sudan.'

It was heartening to be understood, to feel their concern for us and find they were supportive about finding out lost loved ones. We could see how being away from our culture for so long had changed us. We found our own countrymen in a way strange, their habits now not really our own. We were different and they were forthright in telling us so!

In a way, at some level, we were Cuban... Latino. We were a mixture of ideals.

I was hoping to stay and live in Ottawa with my friend Amel, but unfortunately that wasn't possible. I told Amel I had decided to move to London, Ontario and try to get a job as an accountant with a Canadian couple I had met briefly in Cuba. They had given me their number and had told me to get in touch with them when I got to Canada. I had been in touch with Anot in London. We talked about my moving there as there was no work in Ottawa. Anot was still living in the reception house there, so we thought it would be a good idea to find a place together. Amel was very sad about my departure, but we both knew our dream was to find a job, work hard and help our families in Africa. For some of them, we represented their only hope for a better life.

Chapter 19
Mission Priorities

It was November 1998 and I was on my way to another city. Even with the frustration of not speaking or understanding English, it didn't matter. I had my plans and they seemed to be pushing me to move, at what sometimes seemed a hectic pace. Things had been changing fast since my decision to quit Cuba and give up a lifetime of dedication to getting educated. I imagine it was like that for all us students who immigrated to other countries. Amel, for example, had already moved to a house with one of our friends, Julia Amon from Cuba. We all had to quickly decide where we needed to be. My goal was based on getting that offered accounting job in London. I figured, with any luck, it would all unfold from there.

It wasn't much, but it was all I had.

This time I didn't fly, I took the bus instead. To make sure I wouldn't go through the same experience I had when I arrived in Ottawa, we arranged that Anot was to meet me at the bus station. I also made sure I had her phone number handy. This time, I wouldn't need some silly sign to announce myself. I felt much more prepared and thought I had all my bases pretty well covered. Still, even on the bus, I checked through all my information to reassure myself. The last thing I wanted was to feel lost and abandoned again.

I did have a unique experience changing Buses in Toronto. For the whole trip there of about five hours, I talked to no one. I'd got off the bus with my bag and went to the first guy I saw. Without thinking, in Spanish, I asked him where I could find the bus to London, Ontario. To my happiness and surprise, this man answered me in Spanish. Before he could even finish telling me about the bus, I lost it and embraced this stranger in an excited hug. "You speak Spanish!"

I almost yelled this, right in his ear. As I was doing this, it suddenly felt really awkward. In Cuba, people just hug you back. This young man went really stiff, and I went 'Oops.' I stepped away and he was looking at me like I was from outer-space. What could I say? I blurted out, "I'm sorry, I forgot I'm in Canada!" Now he was looking at me like for sure I was from different planet! "Como?" (what) he said, looking puzzled. I took a deep breath, gathered my courage and explained to him that I'd been told people in Canada were very reserved. He said again, "What?" looking like he didn't believe me. "Never mind," I said, feeling my attempt to communicate was a lost cause. I thanked him and started walking away.

Well his face changed quite radically and he yelled "Welcome to Canada!" He asked me to wait, in Spanish. Even if it had been a weird encounter, it was good to hear. "I'm not reserved," he said. "I like friendly people." That threw me a little. Then he added, "can I carry your bag to your gate for you?" That threw me a lot. What could I say but, "OK." This now friendly fellow Spanish speaking man who worked for Greyhound kept me company while I was waiting. It was the first time in Canada I'd carried on a whole conversation with a total stranger in Spanish. It at least proved to me this was possible and made my trip feel less lonely.

For a change, things were working out as planned and I was in for a bit of a treat. As soon as I got off the bus, I spotted Anot's huge smile and my heart swelled that she look so excited to see me. Then I noticed Anot wasn't alone. There was a whole group of familiar smiling faces. They were four other guys (I'm sorry I don't remember who) I'd known when we were all students together in Cuba. It was a neat way to be greeted and I felt, 'this was more like it.' Canada was getting less and less strange by the day. I would have a gang to hang out with.

Not that I really got to do a lot of that for a while. You don't know the meaning of hectic. Anot is a go-getter kind of girlfriend and we had a lot to accomplish in a short period of time. First we had to find an apartment. There was a lot of help being offered to us, but time was short. Anot's month at the reception house was done at the same time as mine. She had a lot of things organized with Immigration before I even got there. We had no clue really and some of this house hunting activity was confusing. Fortunately, Immigration workers took right over and the day after I arrived, they found us a wonderful apartment. And guess what, not one of them spoke Spanish. That was the most confusing part; them struggling, us struggling and nobody understanding anything! It was silly really.

I should write them a letter. Now I've spoken English for eleven years. I figure interpreters would make things a lot easier on immigrants.

It is really quite remarkable what Immigration Canada does do for people like me who come to Canada with refugee status. We got all our immigration papers in Canada the moment we arrived. We also got our social insurance cards and health care documents. Immigration also helped us translate our school records from Cuba into English. It was incredible to me the amount of help we received from the Canadian government. As we were growing up in Cuba, we thought they had a very beautiful and wealthy country till the Russians left. We thought the whole world was going through the same struggles as Cuba. It wasn't until we were older and got a bit of news from the outside world that we started to see there were other alternatives. We had no idea other countries lived in such abundance. Coming to Canada was a real eye opener. We were much like children, coming out of the wild.

Renting was expensive in London. Anot and I had a beautiful place with two bedrooms in a decent neighbourhood for $900.00 a month. We thought that was a huge amount of money and wondered how much it was going to cost living in Canada. I never in my life had even paid rent before, or bought groceries. It was like an impossible dream come true to be living in a home with only two people after 12 long years of living in boarding schools sharing everything with other girls. For the second time in my life I actually had a really expensive room all to myself.

My objective, once I got to London, was to locate my family in Africa, but I hadn't a clue how or where to start looking. It was always on my mind, but there were things that had to get done first. I had to get settled into my apartment, had to experience this new life living in a land of plenty of everything. I wanted to do it all; go to movies as I'd seen an actual movie theater. I wanted to go shopping and buy my own groceries. There were so many things I'd never experienced or done before.

I now had the opportunity and Sarah Gabriel was going to become a Canadian!

'Oh ya,' and have a lot of that great stuff!

We needed a lot of stuff too, to fill our empty apartment. My first thought when I saw all that open space; how are we ever going to own enough things to fill it all up? Again Immigration solved the problem; they bought us everything we needed within a week. For me, it was like every day was Christmas. Every day more stuff just kept showing up. Both Anot and I couldn't believe this could be possible. We really then believed Canada must be the richest country on Earth! When I said they supplied everything, I mean absolutely everything. I later found out all these things done for immigrants would have to be paid back to the government. At the time, with the language barrier, much of that wasn't clear. Still, it was then a wide eyed experience as our apartment filled with all the necessities we would need to live our Canadian experience. To even have an apartment was a Canadian experience.

For the next while I spent my time getting used to everything and making my lists. I was trying to organize what I would do with all the time available, besides cooking, laundry and everyday details that needed to be looked after. Meanwhile, the weather outside just kept getting colder so we didn't go out all that often. Instead we watched quite a lot of TV. I thought if I watch a lot of that, I would learn English faster. It didn't work very well.

Immigration had made it clear this was the first thing to work hard on. Right away they organized English courses for us twice a week. The teachers didn't speak Spanish either. I was learning words like, cat, dog, door and ones I knew already like bathroom, water and it seemed boring. I would need to learn much faster if I was going to find my parents and

217

fulfill my goals. London seemed a nice enough city. We would go to English classes then Anot and I would go exploring and see more stuff we couldn't buy. We spent most of any extra money we had on food. The second week there, I had my first experience with a supermarket. Never in my life had I seen such a variety of yummy things all in one place. We had a tight budget, so all those yummy things stayed right where we saw them. Still, we bought a lot of meat, rice, beans; you would have thought we were still back in Cuba. I saw one display and I almost ran the other way . . . *grapefruit!*

It wasn't long before we started to meet the Sudanese community through the older students that had arrived in London before us. They came over to see our new apartment and welcome us. We had a nice dinner and visit. We shared stories about our trials in getting to Canada. It seemed they were doing pretty well with language and they helped me learn phrases I wanted to know, like "do you have a job for me please?" This led to another idea; asking about language. I hoped it would help me get a job in one month's time.

There were a lot of Sudanese National community gatherings. At these get-togethers we would share a pot luck dinner and visit. These dinners brought the feeling of tribal community from Sudan to Canada. For us students, it was an education, having been away from our own culture for so long and immersed in Latino culture. It made for a totally unique experience. At the first one we were invited to, I was a little shy. These people weren't at all; they wanted to know all about us. They especially wanted to know how we students had ended up in Cuba. The questioning started right away. It was for me a culture shock as I had to shift from Spanish because everyone there was talking in Dinka or Arabic.

My Arabic wasn't too bad, but it took a little while to keep up with the jibber, jabber going on at these events. It was hard to concentrate with children running around screaming and laughing and the constant movement of friends visiting and catching up on family news. My friends and I sat together at the party and enjoyed our culture; it was very beautiful. In Cuba we had activities where we demonstrated our culture, but it wasn't as original, or spontaneous, as the way the Sudanese community gathered here in Canada, I enjoyed it a lot. Everybody was so nice, even if some Sudanese teenagers called me aunty. It was weird; I didn't much like it. Did they think we were old? But no, they were doing it to show respect. Everything the community was doing was so different from what we were used to in Cuba. I realized we had become, to some degree, our own unique culture, one they were having trouble relating to and thought a little strange.

The women of Sudan are really quite reserved and dress accordingly, while we liked fashion in a Latino way. Showing your belly button was no

218

big deal to us, but it raised these women's eyebrows a lot. Well, combine that with short skirts and the like, and it was a recipe for gossip. You could see it in their actions, pointing to us and whispering among themselves. The women sat separate from the men, but we would head right over to the guys we knew from Cuba and hang out with them. I guess in their eyes this made us bad girls.

Oh well...

We didn't let that bother us because we didn't know what all the whispering was about. Sudanese people love music and dancing too and these gatherings were for entertainment as well. Mostly they were in halls the community chipped in together to rent for these occasions. So when the music started, we would grab the guys and off we'd go onto the dance floor to party. At times we would bring Salsa, you know, add some spice. The younger generation of Sudanese brought their music too and introduced us to a whole new deal; rap. Well, when we got out there, did we swing! You should have seen those eyebrows go up and wide-eyed disbelief. The kids loved it and asked us to show them our moves. Those ladies, however, now believed we were a bad influence on the whole community; these bad Girls shaking their bodies around. It wasn't hard to tell why they got upset, their husbands and the men there thought our dancing was real entertaining.

I don't mean that in a bad way. They would ask us about our dancing and we had only one explanation; Cuba! The community couldn't get enough about that topic. There we would be with a table full of interested men talking and the women staring daggers at us. I found out they were interested too, but we were afraid of those looks and a little worried sitting with them. In time, the women got over it and realized, by talking to us and making friends, we were nothing like what they were thinking. We didn't want their men.

After a couple of these gatherings, things began to change. They would ask us to bring our music and Salsa got played a whole lot more. Some of the women got up and started to copy our dance moves, laughing and enjoying themselves. They even grabbed their husbands and pulled them onto the dance floor. The music seemed to bring even more energy to an already enjoyable event. Salsa can do that you know! I was thinking I was really going to enjoy living here in London with these kinds of gatherings. It was like having a little of home right there in Canada. As I mingled more, I made friends and, to my excitement, during the introductions, some there said they knew the Gabriel Achuoth name.

My family!

My anxiety level immediately went way up. One of the first of these contacts turned into a story that raised the hair on the back of my neck. A lot of these new friends were refugees from U.N. camps. One man knew of my family and had seen them. He knew other friends who knew them as well. This really captured my interest. My mission seemed to be closer to being real. Then he told me the sighting was just before an attack on the camp. His story was really very graphic and reminded me of scenes of my own traumas. He told of people running and automatic rifles mowing friends and family down, explosions bursting all around them. I almost had to ask him to stop, but I couldn't. I had to learn more about my family, so I forced myself to listen. I hadn't really thought about these things since burying my bundle.

Although this excited me greatly, that the man had actually seen my family, it also deepened my fear something bad had happened to them at the refugee camp. That evening after the gathering, this feeling grew. I tried to talk to Anot about it, but just couldn't. I retreated to my room and fretted over my feelings. The story had triggered visions from my childhood; graphic images of people running from certain death.

Exploding bombs, the sound of automatic rifles and fear in people's eyes as they ran, chased through my mind. It was so like Bor so long ago, yet right there and so real. I tried to sleep and prayed the scenes would go away. But no, they had started at Bor and just kept going, pouring out of my memory. Somehow, I knew it was my bundle. It had got out of the orchard and into my luggage to remind me of what I'd tried to leave behind.

Off across Africa I ran those four days over again.

At some point, I had drifted off to sleep and found myself in a deep dream. I heard screams and felt the panic amid smoke and explosions as shadows moved around me. I saw flashes of faces run past. I did what I needed to do . . . run with them to get away from the bloody horror behind us. I saw over my shoulder those I knew dying at the hands of the Nyagat. The scenes were happening at a frightening speed. I stumbled over a bloated corpse. My heartbeat is trying to burst through my chest; I can almost run no more. I want to give up and know I can't as lions are eating the dead. I'm screaming for Mama. "Mama, Mama where are you?" I search for her through the dead all around me. 'Am I the only one alive?' I ask myself. It seems there are only long dead corpses.

I am stopped by true horror, the severed head there in front of me. White worms are crawling from eyes that look right through me. I had slipped through unmentionable slime to lie there with this nightmare, face to face. The lips of this monster form the words: "Run, Acuach Cor. You will not find her here!"

I'm up again and running. I look behind to see if more are getting away from the falling down place. Out of the smoke comes a lion, his coat all matted with rusted blood. His eyes glow only for me. Now I know I must try and out run this lion. Is that even possible? It's like running in sand. Agor is there in front of me. It looked as though he is going to run past me and fight the Lion. "No Agor no," I scream, "run!" He can't hear me and only points for me to run 'that way.' I follow his direction right into Grandma's village. Small lions are pacing circles around Yalee as though waiting for me. I can hear Agor fighting the Lion, trying to slow him down while I'm beating on doors of the houses of sticks screaming for help. No one comes out to help me; they are only peering out their doors as if to say... "go away!"

I am frantic and looking for Grandma's hut; they all look the same. I run back into the village gathering place and there's Chol sitting in the dust crying and watching the circling lions in wide eyed fear. He looks up to see me running to him and he smiles and asks "Acuach?" There is no time for hugs, the lion is right behind. I grab his hand and run for the closest hut; it is Grandma's. She is at the small door, waving me in. "Hurry, hurry," she seems to be saying. Chol and I crawl through the short archway to safety.

We are shocked. As we enter we find Grandma isn't there. I run through the interior, as does Chol, looking for any kind of weapon. Little Chol looks so determined and brave. He laughs and looks at me, "it will be alright Sarah, wait and see!" He passes me Grandma's big cast iron frying pan. I am a little put off with him as he giggles stupidly and sits down in middle of the room to watch the action. Doesn't he realize how serious this is? I hear the lion circling Grandma's hut sniffing. Then he lets out a thunderous roar that shakes the very Earth. He's found me. I can sense him crouch down. He is going to crawl right in the door after us. I look to Chol like, 'you ready?' Chol only smiles.

That makes me angry. OK, it's up to me to bash this monster on the head and be done with it. It seems all the little lions are all excited and making a racket out there like some celebration. What, all happy? I'm about to die and they've come to share in this skinny meal. 'Well, we'll see about that,' I thought as I swing the frying pan around, testing its weight. I get myself in a fighter's stance in front of the door. "*Bring it on, Lion*," I yell in the silence.

This is it, the creature is through and I'm in mid-swing with everything I have. Then the mighty lion looks right up at me and Baba says... "Acuach Cor?" It's too late, I'm about to kill my Baba! "BABA," I scream in absolute horror. The weight of my deadly swing throws me right out of bed onto the floor...

I jumped up looking around and 'Whew,' shook my head. It was only a dream. In a moment there was a soft knock at my door and Anot was on the other side asking worriedly, "you alright in there, Acuach?" I was still groggy from sleep and replied, "Baba's a lion, Anot!" She opened the door and peered in at me. "What?" she exclaimed. I told her my dream as we sat on the bed together.

Anot thought it was a good dream. She surprised me with the comment, "you know Sarah, it reminds me of that song we all used to sing together!" I thought about it, and it did in a way seem to be like the traditional children's story. Many parts of the dream stayed with me over the next few days, especially the severed head telling me I wouldn't find Mama there. Well, where exactly would I find her, you old head? I began to feel better and thought maybe they all weren't dead. Was that what this dream was trying to tell me? I wondered about Agor and cried several times thinking about the loss of my brother. I remembered how he was always there looking after me. I went over that part over and over. And was the Lion Baba? I couldn't help but remember the pain I'd gone through to reach Ethiopia, and how I needed to tell Baba about these horrible happenings, and that he wasn't there. For the first time I realized I'd never got to talk to him about those days of fear and how hard that had been. I just ached to tell him.

This was a need in me that was planted so deep; my Baba needed to know how we needed him so. He needed to know when he was gone from us it was like a hole in me that could not be filled by anything else. Somehow this dream held more for me than I realized. I struggled hard to remember all of it. Even as I tried to, other dreams followed that were even more vague and strange. Old spirits were trying to reach through to me. They were trying to teach me a dance I should know, hearing the beating of drums and the singing of our songs.

These dreams faded as the days wore on and classes, homemaking and living in London took their place. Anot and I went shopping with the little funds we had and bought Christmas presents for our small group of friends... and then, Wow! We were on our way up the block walking home from the bus stop. It gets dark really early during winter in Canada and dusk arrives at about 4:30 PM. It was odd because the very air seemed to be charged with an energy of some kind. I even asked Anot, "do you feel that?" She just look at me puzzled. It happened...

It came slowly at first and we almost didn't notice as we kept walking. "I know what you mean now, Sarah," Anot squealed with excitement. She pointed into the shinning streetlight. Now it was my turn to feel puzzled. I was going to ask her 'what?' Then I saw a fluttering falling through the dark into the light. We both jumped up and down and yelled with childish glee... "snow!" And, by God, 'It wasn't square.' We ran home with our parcels and made our way quickly back outside. Again, Wow! The flakes were just huge and were covering the ground so fast. This was true magic! Then, Bam! For the first time in my life I'd been hit in the face by a snowball. Anot had started a war, but I'd finish it.

We stayed out till we were soaked and frozen solid. It was so beautiful as the snow covered more of just everything. The cars parked along the street turned to mounds of white and sparkled magically, like glittering tiny diamonds. Man, how could people drive through this stuff? Many times in our snow fight we'd slipped and fallen on our backsides. We discovered snow was very slippery. We would also find out that snow could turn to ice. That stuff was dangerous! So was the cold. We were finding you could only stay out wet for so long in a snow storm.

It was a whiteout they called it, and it didn't stop for several days. This showed us something about Canadian winters. People grumbled about it all the time, but when it was snowing, they loved it. You could see the joy on their rosy faces and puffs of breath when they talked to you. This changed when they had to go shovel the stuff, or when a passing snow plow buried their car. Then they'd be swearing away as they shovelled them out.

I had been deathly afraid of the idea of winter, but as I experienced it, I thought it wasn't too bad. I had endless fun playing in snow, catching snowflakes on my tongue and a Canadian friend showed me how to lie in the snow, move your arms and legs back and forth, and make... snow angels.

Of course I also learned winter could be plain miserable.

I'd been having some down days, getting myself up and dressed, catching the bus, and walking with Anot through slushy cold mush to another appointment with frustration. I just couldn't learn English fast enough. No matter how hard I tried, I was making what felt like little or no progress. Actually I was making a little progress and some of my friends who had been in Canada longer were helping me. Still, I knew so little and it was horrible not understanding everything going on around me. It made me fear I wouldn't be able to get a job anytime soon.

Mostly things, though, were alright. I was happy with the connections I was making with the Sudanese community. These cultural events seemed to be happening all the time, organized by different people. It was great to see them unfold. In a way it brought back some of my happy childhood in Bor.

As a little girl, and being a Sudanese child, the rule was to be seen and not heard. Nor was I allowed to get in Mama's way when she was organizing similar types of social gatherings. 'Help, or go play,' she would say. If I wanted to help, she would teach me. If I wanted to just fool around, I got chased outside to play. These social engagements were not events to play around at. We were kept on our toes and expected to act in a certain manner, and always with respect. Otherwise we'd get spanked...

By anybody at those gatherings. We towed the line, or lookout!

Well, what I saw now was how these women were representing their sub-tribes in what was a traditional competition, to out-do the last gathering. I was also familiar with gossip and would listen. I wondered at what I heard without knowing why. The neat part was going to see how the next gathering would be presented, even the choice of music and when it was played mattered. "Did everyone have a better time this time than last?" was a typical question that would come out in the subsequent gossip. It was funny because now they all wanted us to bring salsa. The music was really catching on and got to take up more and more dance time. They would ask us to bring more salsa fun to entertain. We were getting to be minor stars just doing what came naturally.

That month there was a potluck every week and getting larger all the time. I was meeting many people who knew my family. At one, an Elder man was introduced, who I found out was an Uncle. Not that he was Baba's brother, but he was from Baba's tribal region Congor, were everyone is related in one way or another. Sometimes to call someone an uncle, is a mark of respect to an Elder not of your generation. This was a well respected Elder in the Sudanese community because he knew my family. The community knew many of us were seeking our lost relations. It was an interesting topic for them to talk about and word of my search was getting around.

I talked with this Elder. He seemed a nice man and appeared interested in talking to me. When I introduced myself and said my name, his eyes lit up. He said, "Oh yes Sarah, I'm your uncle and I know your family very well!" My jaw almost hit the floor and my heart started flipping around in my chest like a fish in a blanket. Oh my, did I pester that poor old man. For some while, he couldn't get one word in edgewise. I beat him up with a barrage of questions that just did not stop. Finally, he had to ask me to slow down, I was plain wearing him out. He did want to tell me what he knew, I just wasn't letting him. Years of pent up frustrations were fuelling me; I needed to know all . . . *and, right now!*

When he got me to calm down, he began to answer my questions. Not far into this, he dropped a bit of information that had me stopping him right there in his tracks. "And Sarah, your dad he's married to a very beautiful young lady!" Baba was married to another woman? My God! My mind just went wild. My imagination was throwing things at me. Had Mama been killed? I had visions of my dream: the severed head, the falling down people lying everywhere, being chewed by little lions. My heart wasn't just flipping around, it was about to explode and leave pieces of me all over that hall. "WHAT!" I screamed. The poor old guy almost fell out of his chair. "What do you mean? How about my mother? What came out was almost angry. I always imagined my parents were going to be together forever. "Where is Mama? Is she dead? Is she alright? Where can I find her?" I blurted straight out, demanding an answer.

It took him a moment to compose himself. "Uh no little one, I do not know of where your Mother might be," he said, "But no, she is not dead." He looked sadly at me and continued. "I am in touch with the family and from what I know, they are all fine." He patted me fatherly on the hand, "I will when I go home and look for your Baba's phone number, where he can now be reached. Don't you worry."

Now it was my turn to run around like a mad thing looking for a pen and paper to give him our home phone number.

Chapter 20
Touching Miracles, Wishes Come True

The entertainment in the hall was just about to begin, the music was starting and I'd given my phone number to the Elder. I was trying to get into the dancing mood and enjoy the rest of the evening, and couldn't. No way! It was like being covered in fire ants; I couldn't sit still. I left early. I didn't even tell Anot I was leaving, not wanting to spoil her evening, as I knew she'd volunteer to leave with me. She hadn't heard what I'd just gone through. On the way to my rendezvous with destiny, I bought two phone cards and caught the bus home, chewing my nails all the way for the first and last time ever.

I needed to be alone with this revelation. The idea of Baba with a new wife was burning a hole in my heart. There were so many things I didn't know and I was so close to the answers. In a very short while I would have the phone number to fill years of torment. To say I was excited would be an understatement. I had to fight with myself not to call Cuba right away. But no; I would wait for when I had confirmation this was actually real. I had wicked thoughts about this old man never calling me back... and just what I'd do to him if he didn't. It was an endless evening sitting right next to the phone. I was hoping because he was old, he would go home early. I hoped he would realize what I needed to know was more important than some social gathering.

You would think with all these things going on, what happened next would be impossible. I was sitting in the kitchen at the mansion in Ethiopia watching Mama bake bread when the phone rang. Mama, turned to me. "Answer the phone Acuach Cor!" Of course I woke up with a start, asleep with the phone beside me ringing off the hook. It was the Elder with the long needed number to my world of Africa. Just as soon as I hung up, I found myself dialing that long number. It rang and rang and rang...

No one picked up after minutes of trying.

I thought maybe I'd dialled wrong, and tried again. On the third try, it dawned on me, "Oh ya, there's the time difference." It would have been very early in the morning there. I felt instantly foolish, either no one was home or they were ignoring the ringing and very angry with whomever might be calling at that ungodly hour.

My mind was just flip flopping through too many things, real and imagined.

I knew I'd have to wait for the next day, but I figured going to sleep would be well neigh impossible. I had to try anyway, although part of me was thinking that I didn't want to go there and have some silly nightmare.

227

I got into my pyjamas, crawled into bed all ready to roll around with my thoughts and, fell right off to sleep. 'Poof,' I opened my sleepy eyes... and, it was morning.

I lay there for about two seconds before my chest filled with sunshine... BABA! 'Bam,' I was out of bed and running for the phone in my jammies, my fingers flying over the numbers I somehow memorized, despite all the other stupid numbers calling cards come with. I crossed my fingers, praying to all the powers that be for someone to answer. The international call went through and it rang three times before someone picked it up. I recognized this person instantly; it was Baba's voice that came through. I was laughing and crying at the same time. I shrieked, *"Baba, Baba... is that you? I can't believe I'm talking to you!"* Dead air... he didn't recognize my voice. It had been so long since we'd talked, and of course in Cuba I'd just been a little girl. Obviously, I was the only daughter who was not in Africa, so in a moment he pretty much figured it out.

"Acuach Cor? My daughter? Is that you?" I could hear his voice quivering almost nervously, before bursting finally with joy. "Oh my daughter . . . we have missed you so much!" he said with almost a sob. My turn; I was thinking 'yes Baba . . . me, your lost child.'

Tears stopped my voice. I had to force myself to talk. "Baba, you're married again? *And, where is Mama?"* More dead air. I could feel my face going all hot. Answers, answers, answers... I needed them from my Baba. I waited him out, holding my breath.

Baba laughed? He was still very funny, loving and caring sounding, but a little bit slower in the way he came across explaining life to me. I had been away from my culture a long time, there was something I'd forgotten or didn't want to understand. It was common in Sudan to have more than one wife. There were quite a few questions flying back and forth before I arrived at a better understanding of Baba's point of view.

At one point I asked him forthrightly, "Baba, do you still love Mama? What happened? Why are you not together anymore?" Again he cut me off with his short deep laugh of assurance. It once again calmed me down.

"Of course I love your Mama Acuach, she is the Mother of my children and I am very lucky. She is a very nice woman too and keeps very good care of me!" He laughed again and told me without skipping a beat, "My second wife is about your age." I was just blown away by this information and asked him to pass the phone to Mama. Baba then told me she wasn't there with him in Nairobi. He said Mama and my brothers, sisters, sister in-law and his new wife were living at the refugee camp. He said he didn't live in Nairobi either. He explained that he went there occasionally to an Uncle's house so he could write his book. At the refugee camp he said the conditions weren't good for writing. Staying in Nairobi there were fewer distractions, there weren't so many people around and he had a computer and electricity. I asked him, "When can I talk to Mama?" "I don't know," he replied, "because there are no phones at the refugee camp Acuach. The only way you could talk to her, would be if she came to Nairobi." He said that would be very difficult because they had no money for the bus.

I was beginning to understand the hardships they were living under. Baba felt bad that he couldn't do anything to bring Mama to Nairobi to speak with me. And I felt bad to hear they were in such a bad way. Baba had always done well financially. He had a good position in the past and lots of money. I wondered why things were very different for him now, after all he was a very respected and educated man. Baba had questions as well. He wanted to know about Anyuon and Yong and how and where they were. He was happy to hear they were continuing their education. He asked about how it was for us during those missing years in Cuba.

It was surprising how much Baba knew. He knew Cuba had fallen on hard times and this has caused him to worry for his children. This was how we eventually got around to how for so many years we couldn't find each other. It wasn't as though Baba and the family in Africa hadn't tried; it was as though they were always one step behind us. What with them having to change refugee camps and us changing schools, addresses changed, mail didn't get through and it all stayed out there in the unknown for all concerned. All too soon my ninety minutes of calling card reached its maximum. I was tempted to use the other card and call right back.

As it turned out, that wasn't possible; Baba had things to do. He was quite upset and felt bad that I wasn't able to talk to Mama. I told him I'd work it out somehow and get money for Mama to take the bus to Nairobi. We spent the last of our minutes arranging times and how to keep in touch. I was worried all over again that I might lose them. When Baba heard this, he again laughed. "I will never lose you again, Acuach Cor . . . never! You will see, from here on our family will prosper. We are together now and there is strength in that my daughter."

As it was with Baba, he had a way about him that made anything appear possible. It was hard to end that call and hang up. An hour and a half isn't enough time after ten years of separation and no contact whatsoever. The emotions I went through were so mixed. I went to my room and cried, both happy and sad for quite a while. I would think over Baba's words and my heart would soar, see my Mama's face and just bawl for loneliness. I missed her so much I couldn't breathe. It was to form a driver for me. My mission got all the more focused... bus to Nairobi, talk to Mama! It consumed me.

I was the family accountant fully trained and armed with my one year University. I really needed to sharpen my pencil. This extra money had to come from somewhere. I spent hours at the kitchen table with a spreadsheet of daunting numbers. I tried shaving off tiny pieces of my woefully limited income. Although we always had just enough, it was just barely. Where would these pennies come from? Mama would say from Heaven, "Don't worry Acuach Cor; good things come to people who are deserving and live life rightly." I would hear her say these little bits of wisdom in my head all the time. In a way, Mama was never not with me, correcting me. I needed that, all the time.

There were ways. I found pennies and put them away. I'd put the leftover change from groceries right into the Mama fund. Going somewhere I'd walk and not take the bus. Bus fare went into the Mama fund. Three or four months of penny pinching and a couple of phone cards were bought out of the Mama fund. Even Anot contributed pennies. She would laugh, "Here Sarah, I cleaned out my purse." Ka-ching, into the Mama bucket it would go. I made an immigrant friend at the corner grocery, a very nice Korean Lady who had a Dinka name, Kim. It was about all I could understand, yet somehow we seemed to be able to communicate and not talk. This was where I was buying phone cards. I would come in and she would roll her eyes as I'd dump a pile of change on the counter to pay for that latest phone card.

Kim knew this was important and about family. Besides, she could always use more change for their store. The Kuoy family always seemed happy to see Anot and me come into the store. Kim told me it was very important to learn English and gave me some new words to learn. Usually these were about counting money, which I got really good at in English. The rest of it wasn't going very well at all.

It was growing more confirmed for me the family would someday all come together again in one place. I'd got hold of Anyuon and Yong and gave them the news of finding and getting a phone number for Baba. They were astounded it had taken place so quickly. "It's a miracle," is what Yong told me. It was the most emotion I think I ever heard from him. I could hear him struggle to not get choked up and show it. I could picture him even as he was saying these things, eyes all moist. I knew he now would study even harder, toward his goals. Anyoun wasn't easy to reach but I eventually got through. He already knew from Yong much of the news I had to share. Yet it was obvious how excited he was and he too was talking about his feelings and stuff more than was usual. For me, that was a miracle as all we usually talked about was sports. I felt a side of Anyuon I had never realized before and it created a greater bond between us.

A lot of the past pains were beginning to fade. All the past trials were worth it to know the family could be reunited. Maybe we have to suffer to appreciate the good stuff when it comes around. For a few months I had not one nightmare; I was too busy, I had no time for that deal. I had only one mission, fill Mama's bucket! I too was continually amazed at how it had happened. Years and years of nothing, then it was like the universe opened the door and granted us a thing that was so huge for us. It was a thing we were beginning to think wasn't possible, yet it all just fell right into place. It required a change of course, rearranging goals, and accepting another road to a dream of the future. All seemed to be arranged, just for us Gabriel's.

What I needed to arrange was somehow to get Mama's bucket full of real money.

I knew when Baba would be coming and going from uncle's House in Nairobi. I kept calling until I could speak with him again and learn more of what was happening to the family in the Refugee camp. Then I'd pass this news on to Yong and he'd pass it to Anyuon. I was a link in the chain of that Universe; my family's current world.

We were getting up to date on everything. It was a miracle. Can you imagine the distance of time and place that needed to be accomplished to have any degree of family relations? There were different time zones; everyone was in a different cycle of day, day for me, night for them. It created some small misunderstandings in the swapping of stories, and still does! Yet this is the life and times of an Inter-Nation family.

A family where the telephone is King.

This is how those next four months passed. It seemed so rapid, all these changes taking place. Christmas, a thing our culture holds little connection to, had come and gone. Snow and Christmas, I found, went together hand in hand. Christmas (Navidad in Spanish) in Cuba was like that for us Sudanese students as well. Now in Canada it was again entirely different. I liked the little colored light-bulbs Canadians dressed up their houses with the best. Now the snow was beginning to melt and everything was a mess. I learned that snow could get to look kind of ugly.

During this period I ran into Victor at one of the Sudanese gatherings. He was then living in Windsor, Ontario. I knew Victor from Number 13 (Tocate) school, think you can guess it didn't turn out that well between Victor and me. Nothing in Canada seemed to work out for Victor and he went back to Sudan and became really wealthy. That added another long distance relationship to my life. Victor phoned me every day or traveled from Windsor on the bus to see me. He was always complaining about how he couldn't find a job there no matter how hard he tried.

Finally Mama's bucket paid dividends; my investment matured and I turned all those pennies in at the bank to be turned into a Western Union money order. I got a hold of Baba, who it seemed like magic had just arrived in Nairobi that day. The plans were laid, the money sent, Mama's bus trip organized. I was told this was really a big deal for Mama, to travel, and for a time get out of that refugee camp. She was said to be beside herself with excitement. She was going to actually speak with her Acuach Cor! Me.

The time between for me stretched out over a large part of the universe and crawled along like a snail across that space. By God, I was going to talk to Mama! A gazillion things ran through my mind. I would gush all over her. I bought three phone cards from the Mama fund. I was going to be fully prepared for this event.

In many ways, my conversation with Mama was even more intense than with my Father. It's hard to describe or explain, so I won't. It's a mother/daughter deal. Why? Because, to this day, I can't remember the first five minutes of our blubbering conversation. That was the most important part of that connection. When the extremely emotional stuff passed, we got down to the more serious news about, well . . . everybody; on both sides of our world and on separate continents. I can tell you three phone cards were not enough.

A lot of what Mama told me broke my heart to hear. I thought I'd had it bad, but I had no idea. That part of Africa was a mess. Of course Mama had a wholly different view than Baba. The Civil War meant something entirely different to women and children. The most difficult part of that phone conversation was talking about Agor. Only a Mother can understand the pain of losing a child to ideals they don't understand. In Sudan anyway, all of that is the man's business.

Period.

Not saying that women don't have opinions about all that... they do.

The women are just not included in the decision making and the ideas behind it; they only make the extreme sacrifices. So goes my thinking on that one, and, I confess, I may be wrong. War just confuses me and makes me angry. The civil war had just gone on too long, wasting so many lives, and she was still concerned for her eldest son. My brother Deng Did had been wounded, she knew that much. He was still out in the field somewhere. It was hard for Mama, not knowing how bad his condition was.

Our conversation had begun with love and tears and moved its way through us going to school in Cuba and how that went. Mama even laughed some. When I got to grapefruit, she cried some, especially about my burying my travel bundle. I told her how much I missed her and the times when I just ached to not have her there. I wanted her to hold me and soak her with my weak tears. I wanted her to be proud of me, to understand how I got tough and decided to be strong like her. I told her about making my own decisions based on what was best for me and asking, '*how would Mama handle this?*' I said I knew now how to deal with everything life could hold for me if I did things right. She really cried when she heard me state the truth. "Mama I learned so many things from you!" There was a short space there when she just couldn't talk.

We moved on and she told me about life in the Refugee Camps; how they'd lost us and how frustrating that was for her. She was always bugging Baba and the children to try harder; "find my babies!" I asked her about the attack told to me by the elder at the potluck a month previously. "We weren't there, Acuach Cor." I thought yet another uncle telling me nonsense; then Mama continued. "By the grace of God we'd just got out of that camp. We ran just as it began and missed the worst of it Sarah!" She said with all the changing Camps, and the hardship of each one, it became harder and harder to just live from day to day. There were many things for her to manage, too many I thought.

There were too many families living in those dreadful round stick houses. It broke her heart as the war just seemed to go on forever. The children born in those camps would know no other better life. She told me with great strength, she was glad we were in Cuba and didn't have to live that way. Many times it was this thought that kept her going, even when she had no news of us. Our life must be better than the life she was experiencing with no future. She dreamed we were all fat and happy. She was a little upset to hear how hungry we'd been there, yet for years now they had lived on U.N. gruel they had to line up for every day.

I remembered how that could be, but of course it had been worse. She told me there was never enough. Many times she'd had to go hungry so the children could eat. That was so like Mama, to ignore herself and look after everyone else. The family in the camp included my brother his wife and two children, Chol now a teenager, Baba... and my new stepmother? I thought Mama would sound all angry at that idea, but she wasn't. She was happy to have the help, and besides--this really blew my mind--"it was my idea, Acuach Cor! I found her for Baba myself."

Yep, I had been out of the country way too long. The idea was just so alien to me, how could I handle it? If Mama had arranged this, I guess I could accept this woman into my life as family and move on. I didn't have a choice; no one would be on my side to hate this person I didn't even know. I might even like her when I got there and met this new mother. Still, I was having problems relating to that, so I gave up and said nothing.

I then had a real shock; Mama's health wasn't good.

At first Mama didn't want me to worry about her health, but after many questions, she told me she had picked up some type of eye infection and had had it for many years. She worried about not being able to see her children in the future she dreamed of. All those years she'd been thinking with these eye problems, how would she see us as adults? We would be so different from her memories. She thought maybe she was going blind as others in the camps had done for one reason or another. It was not uncommon as there were few doctors and little medicine to deal with all the diseases that circulated.

It was this that stood out in my mind. I had always pledged that when I got older I would look after Mama, give back to her for all the things she had done for us. Now was that time. Mama needed me! I was in a country that could do that. Just how and how fast, was another deal all together. My Mother needed medical assistance, now! I knew I couldn't bring her to Canada, so I would bring Canada to her.

In whatever way, I could.

I, Acuach Cor, would find the way.

I would get an accountant job. Mama had gone back to the Refugee camp. I wanted to help with her eye problems, but more than that, I wanted to get my family out of there. Then they wouldn't be suffering those kinds of problems in the first place. I was going to need a lot of money! It seemed like such a huge task, so beyond my capabilities at the time, an impossible goal.

After that call, I went through a phase. I thought about all the difficulties my family had lived through, all the things my parents had, in the midst of tragedy, just kept going and accomplished. I could do no less, I was a Gabriel! Maybe the universe had opened these roads of opportunity for just this reason. It had got me to Canada at a time when Mama needed me the most. It was odd that way; like it had been at school when my life was all mapped out. My plans were all in place, then my interest in that idea simply fell away and Canada took its place.

Finding my family was the most important thing. I knew I needed to do that more than anything, even getting an education. To have it all fall into place so quickly after years of frustration was really a marvel. Now I'd actually spoke to Mama. I'd heard her voice, listened to the frustrations she'd had with no contact with us children in Cuba. Some of my questions were beginning to get answered, but I had a whole lot more questions, believe me. It wasn't enough to hear them on the phone; I wanted to get right on a plane and go see them, to be able to feel them, hug and love them up, especially Mama.

I could see down that road. It seemed to stretch on forever and was very far from where I was now. Now, what was Sarah Gabriel going to do about it? A few days of just living the everyday, doing laundry, making dinners, brushing my teeth went by. Always, in the back of my mind I was making up things that might work. Robbing banks was out of the question. My mind giggled at such stupid thoughts like this that would just show up while doing laundry. Three days later, I thought it might be the only way.

I called my friends who had offered me a job when I was in Cuba. They had told me to contact them when I got to Canada and I had. They had been busy and I was settling in and they promised to get together soon. That had been three months ago.

Carla had called a couple of times just to talk to someone in Spanish. She too was lonely for Cuba and we had a lot to share about the Latino life and music. She always had music playing in the background when she phoned me. I had even invited them to come to one of our Sudanese events. She said she and John would like that.

I thought this would be a good excuse to call as there was a gathering the coming weekend. I figured I couldn't very well call them up and right out of the blue ask for a job; this idea needed to be introduced a little. If they came to a gathering it might help. And it did! To my surprise, Carla said on the phone she'd been thinking of me all week. And, yes, she and John would love to come to a cultural gathering. She even said her husband was really into that sort of thing. I'd told her there would be music and dancing. Carla really got interested at that point. "I haven't been dancing in a long time Sarah. Will there be Latin music there?" I assured her there would be.

It all went over well and they had a really good time. I could see Carla was enjoying our group and the Spanish banter was flying. Also, I was quite surprised John was doing very well and speaking a lot more Spanish then when I'd first met them. They were a very good dance team too. They spent most of the evening on the dance floor; it didn't matter what kind of music was being played. I couldn't have had a better plan because, as the evening was coming to a finish, they said they wanted to have me over to their home for supper. John raved about how Carla was an excellent cook.

Carla was an awesome cook, at making Chinese food!

It was a wonderful dinner. I appreciated the change from my pared down budget of beans and rice. The penny pinching was doing wonders for my figure. The first thing Carla said was, "Sarah you're too skinny, sit down and eat!" John talked through dinner about his business and how well it was doing, in Spanish. He was practicing and I could see how proud Carla was of him. Her English was getting better too. I didn't know what they were laughing about. It sounded pretty good anyway.

I thought, 'bingo . . . perfect'. Their business was going good and I thought again the universe was helping me out. I didn't say a thing about my plan through dinner, waiting for the perfect time. We got together in the living room for a glass of wine I didn't like and took forever to drink while I tried to smile. Then it came as John again mentioned his business.

"We are so busy," he said. "It looks as though I might need to hire more help!"

Well hey, I pop right in there and mention the offer they made in Cuba.

John didn't say anything for some moments, just stared at me and smiled. Carla looked surprised, "Oh that's right John, we did too," she said, looking like she thought it a good idea. My hopes were rising; this could be very good. Think of that, so short a time in Canada and already an accountant. John looked to me, *oh, oh*, with compassion. "I could use the help Sarah", and began in Spanish, looking flustered. Then he carried on with Carla in English, needing a translator. This was the kind of nervous waiting I was used to.

It seemed as though Carla was trying hard to convince her husband to hire me. I crossed my fingers. John wasn't buying it, I could tell. I wasn't going to have a job and I patiently waiting for the translation to find out why. Carla said they would give me a job, but "Sarah, you need to have better English skills and quite a lot more training in Accounting!" Well, I knew all that was true, I was just hoping for a miracle.

They were very supportive. Carla knew from our phone friendship about my connecting with my family and wished she could be of more help. It just wasn't possible right at that time. They offered to hire me in six months at what would amount to an apprenticeship, an entry level position that would help pay for further education. They would sponsor my career and living in London. I had to think hard on that one.

It seemed a very rational way of getting a professional life in Canada.

I spent days mulling over schemes, but didn't come up with many. Damn English anyway. There was no quick way around that problem. Then along came a lightning bolt and the universe pointed the way, via Victor. He called from Windsor four days after dinner with Carla and John and said he was on his way to the bus. I could hear he was excited about something. I asked what was up and he said, "just wait till I get there, Sarah!"

I did too. I thought through some of the stuff we'd been going through. 'Oh my God' I thought, 'he's going to ask to marry me." *No way!* I thought of a lot of reasons I could give him to tell him... *'no way!* I practiced a compassionate look in the mirror. "Victor" . . . but all I could come up with was; "no way!" There was just nothing else that described what I thought of that idea, of marrying Victor.

Sure enough, he had that glow about him. I took him into the dining room and sat him down at the table. I felt confident and fully armed. All I had to do was just say what I felt. "I'm sorry Victor... but, no way. I like you but I'm not ready for marriage, unless you have a lot of cows." (Just kidding) I'll get to that idea, just why it's no way, in a moment. Not this girl. I don't live in Sudan anymore and don't want a husband. Especially with more than one wife!

Victor was going to learn this, right at that table . . . right now.

Chapter 21
Brooks, Alberta

I had wasted a lot of emotional energy for nothing. I almost tore a strip off poor Victor for my silly premonition that turned out be nothing like what Victor was excited about. He started to pour it out so quickly I had to slow him down to discover what it was he was trying to tell me. My head was still full of marriage stupidity and my rejection of my boyfriend and about how I wasn't ready to be tied down. I had a mission and nothing was going to get in the way of what I'd found . . . *my Family*.

Victor knew all about that, understood very well what I felt and had suffered the same as I had. It turned out this was what he was trying to tell me. He opened a newspaper and pointed to an ad in the help wanted section. "Look Acuach, friends phoned me and told me of this place." I was a little impatient, because I couldn't read the gibberish he was showing me. Then he said, "this place will hire anybody Sarah. You don't even have to speak English." Well, *holy cow* that grabbed my attention! Angels were running all over the place; 'this is it, this is it, this is it!' They trumpeted and my day turned rapidly into a dream come true. "There are some of us students already working there. They've got work killing cattle." Well that picture stopped me right there. Killing poor cows? It wasn't really something I could see myself doing. Did they give you a rifle?

I actually asked him that. He smiled hugely, "I don't know Sarah, maybe?"

We both chewed on that one a while. We talked about it with his limited English skills and figured out it was called a Meat Packing plant. Well, you have to understand our Sudanese attachment to cows, like the story of my brothers and the ugly bull. Cattle are almost a sacred thing for us. To have a poor cow shot right behind us for nothing when we were attacked by Nyagat's with rifles was an outrage. But, sure, we kill cows too for food. So this just might be a doable thing for us in this place called Brooks, Alberta. Where was this place?

We found out; it was further away than Cuba.

I could get a job and not speak English? It didn't take long to say goodbye to a professional accounting life in London.

Sarah was in gear, plans quickly established, travel arrangements made, economic realities considered and Victor and I were on a plane, on our way to kill cows. We hoped it wasn't in a field with rifles. Once more I had to leave dear friends to their lives and move elsewhere. Anot was horrified; she couldn't see me killing cows for a living. I was way too small. How could I carry them off the field?

None of us had a clue on day one about any of all that. It was pretty funny really. It created a lot of silly stories and laughter. In the end I took half my Government check and paid Anot my half of that month's rent. I bid her a tearful goodbye at yet another airport and boarded our flight to Calgary, Alberta.

We were off to Cowboy country.

When we arrived, we stayed with Sudanese students who were already living in Calgary, all part of the plan. Calgary was a very nice city to arrive at in the spring of 1999. Thank God all the snow was finally out of my life for a short while. It was warm and cheery. Birds were chirping and everything. We weren't there long before one of our new friends, who had a car, suggested a drive. We all piled in and went for an exploration of Alberta. These guys had already been to Brooks so it was interesting to see all the sights they pointed out along the way. As we got further away from the city, I began to admire this wide open country. With so many farms and agriculture, and cows, Canada is a marvel. It's so beautiful. The riches here to some people from third world countries are unimaginable.

It seemed everyone here was rich.

It was a nice drive of about two hours till we reached the Brooks sign. We got out of the car and looked down on this small city. It was a beautiful warm spring day but we were assaulted by the most God awful stench. That sign, should have read. 'Welcome to Stinkville.' It was from the Lakeside Packers slaughter house that we were there to get a job with. Strangely enough, you do get used to the smell, it just takes a while.

We got back in the car in a hurry to get away from the stink and drove into town. Till then, I'd only ever been in very large cities. Brooks Alberta was tiny in comparison. There was almost no one on the street, or in cars for that matter. We got out and walked around. Usually people in Canada almost always stared at a group of black people. Not here. We went for a walk around town thinking maybe we'd have dinner somewhere. Not one person we went by paid any attention to us. We found out later that Brooks is very multicultural and people working there come from all over the planet.

We even stopped and asked a person, more or less, "where is everybody?" He was nice and friendly and explained most people in town worked at Lakeside Packers, and they were all at work at that time of day. Brooks relies on Lakeside for most of that town's employment. We had a nice meal and tried to find friends who were all at work at that hour. We kicked around awhile and finally got hold of the friends who we'd arranged from London to stay with. They were the ones who had said, "Yes, come to Brooks Sarah and you will get a job!" Our friends from Calgary dropped us off and we got all prepared to go kill cows for a living. Of course by then our other friends had straightened out all that silliness.

In Sudanese culture everyone extends a helping hand, especially us Students from Cuba. When I applied for a job at the plant, my plan was to find a place on my own later. My friends there were more than happy to have us stay with them. My new roommates helped me to apply for the job at Lakeside. My first worry was I needed to write a resume. I'd never had a resume before and I really didn't know what it was. I had never worked at a paying job before in my entire life! I had, till then, only been a brilliant student.

That's not true; I did work before for twelve years with stupid grapefruit and wasn't paid a dime to do it! But it was nothing compared to Lakeside's idea of work. I was afraid I might not get this job because I didn't have any experience, but the worst thought on my mind was being very skinny. I thought it might be a major reason for not getting the job. I looked as though if someone touched me, I'd fall and break my bones. With the help of my friends, we made up a resume saying I was a very hard working young girl. They made up a not so small fib that I'd worked in a green house in London, Ontario. It didn't matter to me; I hadn't a clue what a greenhouse was! I had done lots of work in Cuba, we made it all up. I knew I could do the job if I got hired. I knew myself well enough. To make all the lies (I was horrified to put in there) in the resume look real, I try hard to convince myself. If they hired me and saw me work my butt off like I knew I could, I could prove myself. It was fun making up that resume and it looked pretty convincing.

One of the guys took me to Lakeside for the interview as my translator. The smell was over powering. It smelled like something I'd experienced before. I almost panicked right there as visions of dead bloated bodies ran through my head. I told myself to be strong and deal with it. Mama needed her eyes!

I was freaking out, thinking they would spot my lies right away. Too many fears were flying around my anxiety. The little devils were telling me, "you'll never get this job, you're too skinny!" At the same time angels were singing, "no worries, no worries, no worries!" I wondered which side would win out.

I wanted the angels to win out, even if I never went back to church.

We went in and when I saw this plant's interior, it took my breath away. Lakeside Packers is a very big and busy place. It has 2,500 workers from different cultures divided into three areas: Kill floor, Cooler, and Processing. At the door there was a security guard who received people. They asked me for my name and it was explained to them I was there for an interview. They looked it up and then they gave me a visitor's tag and told us where to go. They let the other guys come in with me because they knew their way around and my friend explained he was my interpreter.

The guard nodded knowingly and away we went. I wondered what all the talking was about?

Like most of my experience in Canada so far, I was just following along, wondering.

When we entered the building everybody was staring at me, so I asked my friend "is there something wrong with me?" I smoothed out my clothes, thinking I must be dressed wrongly for an interview. Having never been to one, how would I know? He laughed and said, "Well I don't know, maybe because you are so very skinny Acuach. Maybe you should eat a little more beef, lots around here." Then he continued on laughing at my angry look. I was very nervous about my interview and got seriously scared about how much blood I was seeing on the workers' clothes and on their skin. I'd already seen a lot of gory detail in the first four minutes. But I thought to myself, that this was what I needed. So I will do this and try not to throw up. Although I wished I could pick a different job so I didn't have to see blood and gore everywhere.

I entered the interview room with my friend, but he had broken English too, so the interviewer called in a Spanish guy who worked there to translate. Otherwise it was going to be a lot of sign language. I felt better because it was going to be easier to say my lies in Spanish. The interview went well and I spit out all those convincing lies, really impressing them. Inside my head I was remembering when Mama used to tell me it was not good to lie, but another part of me was saying, "this is all for you Mama!" Those angels were really working hard for Sarah Gabriel.

After all, it was a big moment for me. I was leaving behind student Sarah and taking on the real world of adult responsibilities. I imagined all the money I'd be sending to Mama as I lied my ass off. It made it easier for me. During the interview, they asked me to pick where would I like to work, and say why. I thought, 'how the Hell should I know?' So I said "the kill floor please," because I couldn't imagine myself working in a cooler like a frozen chicken. I thought I might want a rifle and said so. The Spanish guy was laughing and then he translated in English and they all started to laugh. They didn't understand I was making a joke. They just didn't know Sarah. I poke fun at stuff all the time, and even if they don't understand it, I think it's funny. This time, they thought so too. The interview went *a lot easier* for me.

Knowing at that point, I had a job.

I was sent to a nurse for a physical exam as all potential employees have to do before they're hired. I was thinking this time I had no reason to lie because I was in great shape, physically skinny but really fit. Sarah Gabriel is one awesome athlete and basketball pounder, and good at shooting hoops! I felt very confident when the nurse started testing me.

Part of the examination involved moving around and I confidently followed her instructions, knowing I didn't have to speak any English. It was very funny, each time I repeated the movements she would say "Very good!" I had a big smile on my face and respond smiling "yo, say senorita!" Then she moved me to the next exercise. I had to flex a machine that showed how much power I had. Again I passed the test with flying colours. The next exercise was to bend my thumbs and that seemed to go well. Then she asked if I had ever broken thumbs before? I didn't understand what she was talking about so she called the translator back to ask the question again in Spanish. I told him my thumbs were OK, and just very flexible. My thumbs and fingers, if I hold them straight out and push them back, make a sort of backwards 'U.' The nurse had to write it down and that worried me a little. Then she gave my file to human resources and for the first time smiled.

At the Human Resources office when I handed the file over, they told me they would call me if I'd been hired. Thank you very much. I thanked them very much and off I went home, full of hope. I wanted that job badly and I didn't want to wait too long before finding out if I'd got it. Three days later they phoned me and told me I would start the next day for two weeks on-the-job training. In a class room, Sarah was back to being a student again. I was so happy that for first time in my life I had a real job with pay and not just grapefruit and stomach problems for twelve years hard work. Even before starting work at Lakeside, I was already planning to send most of my money to my family in Africa.

My first day of training was in the classroom with a lot of new people. I was the only one who couldn't understand English. We started watching a movie about how things work in the meat industry. We also had to learn about safety for workers in the work place. The instructor explained some things to the class after the movie, and again I didn't understand a word of it. This was getting to be really frustrating. I could see that not being able to speak the language was going to interfere with my job. This worried me quite a bit. I saw that there would be a lot to know to work there.

After a week of training it was time for action. When they told me where I was to work--I had asked so nicely-- they put me out on the Killing Floor. It was an area that was my worst fear and blood was everywhere. Oops! How was I to know? It was bad.

They put us out in the plant at the stations we'd be working at and introduced me to Cory, our zone supervisor wearing a green hard hat. There were different coloured hats to recognize who was what. I was very proud of my hard hat being yellow, which was for all the meat cutters. Besides, yellow is such a sunny happy color, just like sunny tropical Cuba.

241

Well, that's what it reminded me of, and it kept me happy wearing the stupid heavy thing that was always giving me a pain in the neck.

We all had to wear hair nets, white pants, white tops, and black boots. Also we had to have safety equipment such as ear plugs, eye protector glasses, and mesh gloves to name a few. That first day entering the real deal, with Cory who I really got to like, I felt truly self-conscious. All this stuff I had to wear was definitely not high fashion! I felt like I was a Star Trek alien, bug eye glasses and all, walking in these huge clunky boots that made my legs just ache.

I had a really cool gunfighter belt for my knives though. If they weren't going to give me a rifle, at least I was armed and dangerous. After Cory gave me that neat belt, with knives and a steel sharpener, they started teaching us how to hold and sharpen our knives. They advised us not to hold knives in our hands if we were not using them. Knives should always be stored in the hip belt when not in use. It wasn't easy to learn how to sharpen my Knives. I found it a very big challenge. The worst thing was, I couldn't follow the rule, *Keep the Knives in the hip belt!* I was very stubborn and just liked the feel of them in my hands and was always catching hell.

When we arrived on the actual killing floor, all the employees were gawking at me pass, which didn't help my nervousness any. Cory was explaining things I should know but I wasn't paying attention. I was focused more on how many carcasses were passing by, scared they would fall on me.

The line speed was ridiculously fast and I was freaking out about crossing onto the other side. My supervisor said to me loud over all the noise, "Don't be scared. If you just keep moving, you'll be OK." I'm watching hard as his lips moved, knowing he was telling me... run. I waited a frozen second gaining courage before attempting to cross over to the other side. I ran very fast and some of the employees laughed. I entertained them with my scary face, while in my head I was thinking, "Oops, this is going to be a big, challenging job." But I thought to myself, "No matter what, I will make it." I was one hundred percent sure about making it, but as I was looking at the guys working, it seemed very hard and fast. They sharpened their knives without even looking and trimmed the meat very quickly too.

After the tour of zone number 3 it was the end of the work day for me and I was given a personal locker. I was told to be back the next morning at 7:00 AM sharp. That was going to be my start time, Monday to Friday, ending at 4:00 PM because I asked them if I could work the "A" shift. Because I'm a morning person, I'd asked so nicely I got my way. That meant I didn't have to work afternoons or the graveyard clean up shift.

I went back to the house with aching legs, really very excited about my new job. The next morning, I woke up actually too early for my first day of work. I didn't have a car, so I wanted to be ready so I wouldn't hold up the guys who were giving me ride. I didn't need to bring lunch to work because, when we were at the training session, they gave me some sort of credit card they usually give to new people. The credit card was to be used if I or any other new employee needed to buy lunch. The company then withdrew the money from our pay checks. I figured I would need it until I got paid, not having any money as my London funds were all used up. It was a pretty good deal after being there only a week.

I picked up my work uniform and went off to my locker and changed. By 7:00 AM sharp I was on the killing floor dressed to kill, knives at hand. My supervisor was waiting for me and introduced me to my trainer. You'd think I'd had enough of incomprehensible instructions. She spoke no Spanish. How was I to learn from this person telling me things at a hundred miles an hour? I guessed they hadn't told her I knew no English. She didn't seem to notice as I tried in Spanish to slow her down... "Hello, I'm not understanding you!"

All I could understand was hair and other things I prefer not to mention. (bovine poopy, ca, ca) In my head, I wondered what the heck this job had to do with all the things she was mentioning. It was all spaghetti to me anyways, her forcefully pointing to things I should be cutting. It was complicated this kind of sign language. All I wished for after an hour of this was to have someone who could explain it to me in Spanish.

I could see the people working with me on the line were laughing at me because of the look I had on my screwed up face of disgust. I think she finally guessed the Hell I was living through and got Jose, the Spanish guy from the day before, to help me understand what I had to do. I thought it should have started that way. Like the Immigration people in Ontario, it was just like that. I had wasted most of the morning learning nothing. This English was going to kill me, slowly. It was bad.

I did everything she showed me wrong. Tina, who's name I learned in the lunch room, was pretty nice. I have to hand it to her; she was very patient with me, and with Jose explaining the job, my understanding got better as the day went on. I was getting to the point of knowing what I was doing; all I needed was more practice. When my first day of work was done, I went home bone tired and my brain hurting. There was just so much going on in there. Big chunks of cow were whizzing by, people running from one to the next. It was noisy too, even if muffled by the earphones. I was trying to hear Jose--he was a fast talker too--my hands moving too slow and feeling clumsy. It was going to take some time to be as good as the others. I watched to see how they were doing it... fast.

Everything was fast and bloody, then just really bloody fast. It was daunting. But I would show them. I'd be just as fast or maybe even better; if they didn't fire me first! Tina did say through Jose, I did alright for a first day. That was heartening. I went to bed early that night and slept like the dead. I was just burnt right out.

There were some things about my first day on the Killing Floor that bugged me, one was just that name. It was just so not like me in my sunny hat. My clothes were covered in blood and I couldn't really stand the smell of the place. It was disgusting. Words could never express just how bad it was. I didn't think I could last another minute, let alone the whole day. The evening seemed to drag on and for some reason I felt very sad. Possibly the main one being it was not the kind of job I would have wanted had it not been for the situation that I was in. But when I thought of my family, back in Africa, I knew it was better to have this job than having nothing at all. There was more to it than just that. There was my reaction to killing and what it was associated with, blood. For some time it was hard to just not throw up. It was only the thought of what this job would mean to my family. The money was the factor that had brought me to Brooks.

I would do this, I had to. I would get over the smell and the pain I knew was coming from working that long standing and running to the next carcass. I saw how hard these people worked, and my legs ached after just one day. I spent an hour just massaging my feet so I could feel them. Damn, I just hurt everywhere. "Never mind Sarah, it will work out. I'll do what I have to, even if it kills me!" Then I staggered off to bed and a dreamless sleep.

The alarm was like an angry bee. I wanted to throw it out the window. I didn't want to get out of bed, thinking it was going to be really painful. It wasn't. I was surprised and heartened. I had made it; I could do this and ran for the shower. Being late and getting fired was a real concern. It was like that for awhile till I figured out there was no way they fired anyone. You have to really mess up, cut your arm off or something like that. After a week, Cory took me aside. I was freaking out, "on no, I'm done!"

It was lunch break and I figured it was the horrible news. I even thought he was wearing a nice face just so I would take it better. It wasn't like that at all. Cory sat me down and told me how well I was catching on, but, "Sarah, you have to put your knives in your belt when not using them. You're freaking people out!" He said it laughing and I laughed too after Jose explained it with a big grin. He nodded like, 'that's true,' indicating he thought so too. I went back to work on cloud nine. I was doing what I said I would; proving to the boss I could do the job. Small skinny Sarah could slash with the best of them. About an hour into the afternoon, something to the side of the line caught my eye. I whirled around to see what it was... Everybody ducked and jumped back, cringing. Oops. Then most of them started to laugh. I guessed these were the ones who had talked to Cory, trying to pull my chain a little to prove their point.

In twelve years working with a machete in the grapefruit orchard, I never had a belt or sheath to put it in. It took me some time to get used to the belt deal, but I never had an accident slashing anyone. Thank God. At first no one wanted to work the line beside me because of that. Later I had no problem and people wanted to work with me all the time because I was very fast and never held up the line. The supers didn't like it when they had to slow down the chain. You had your piece of the carcass and it had to come off at your station. The piece work for me was trimming the carcass at more or less the first part of the line. I had the idea in the first week and by payday I was beginning to gain confidence and speed. I was being accepted by the other workers.

I was hanging out at lunch time with Jose and not just because he could speak to me in Spanish. I was studying his conversation in English with his friends. I'd listen to him without interrupting and save up words to ask him what they meant. He caught on and didn't mind smiling when I started using those words. He'd laugh when I used them all stupid and wrong. A lot of things in English came out backwards, like, "Where's my keys car?"

The first pay day was unbelievable. I got my pay stub as it was a direct deposit and all our hours were noted on a statement. I looked at the amount and my jaw hit the floor. "I'm rich!" I had never had that amount of money to myself, not ever. I got almost twice of what I'd been getting in my Government check. To me, at the time, seven hundred and eighty dollars every two weeks was a lot of money. Consider that in Cuba for eleven years I'd received five Pesos (25 cents) a month; then later in University, sixty Pesos per year. That's three dollars American. Well, all things being relative they say.

I was to learn that a lot of that money doesn't go very far.

It was a lesson I learned that day. I may have not completed my accounting program, but I have a head for figures. I knew how to really sharpen that pencil and make those funds go a long way. I had my roomies all paid up, groceries for the month, all the things a girl must have and toothpaste even. The thing I loved most about Canada... toothpaste, and it was always available! It's silly the things one values as everything in countries like Canada is always available. They're available even when you have no money, as I was to learn when I faced the hazards of credit cards. Finally the magic left-over figure arrived.

I phoned Baba. We talked again with two phone cards. I didn't tell him right away about the money, because he wanted more news about the family. He didn't know where I was or that I even had a job. When I told him to expect this said amount of money by wire transfer, I could feel it, he was shocked. At first he was worried for me. "How are you doing this Sarah? You don't get that much from the Government do you?" I told him I had a job killing cows. Baba knew a slaughter house was a wickedly hard job. He told me I was too small, go back to school.

I said no to that. I said the family right now was more important and that some day, when things got better, I would go back. The first thing I told him was to talk to Mama and tell her about the money. More would come to look after her eyes. "Are you sure Sarah? You must look after yourself there first," he said. I explained how I had worked it all out and teased him about being the family accountant and money manager. "I took my education very seriously, Baba! I learned what my priorities should be from you. Family first." There was a change in his attitude then. I could feel he was grateful and proud of me. I felt brave to stand up to him too. Little Sarah always could, and did. It was a blessing now to be connected.

In another week and three days was my twenty-fourth birthday: April 27, 1999, again with no celebration. I couldn't afford it. I was happy anyway. Work was getting better and I was up to about a hundred words of important English. "Move up the Line," shop talk. In my case it was "Move line up!" and everyone would tease me.

It was Friday and I was off work and had gone for a run. The best way to get past sore muscles is to push them further. To keep up with the line, I kept up with my athletic training. Any sports jock knows this. It was military drill like in Bilfam; up at dawn and jumping jacks, yep, yep, in the army now, salute, salute, salute. It's all about discipline. If you don't push yourself, you don't arrive alive.

So there I sat, in the time I could steal from my roomies, in my favourite chair, a LazyBoy recliner that had seen better days. The TV was on but I wasn't paying any attention to it. This is what I was thinking about, Basketball. Man, I missed the gym and shooting hoops. I shocked myself, thinking how long it had been since I'd done stuff like that. I'd been so involved in pushing ahead; I'd had no time to myself. I was always moving from one goal to the next. As I lay there, I realized, my life was a series of events.

I thought of all the things that had effected this forced movement.

To have only been in Canada a short while and have all these things take place eight months after making my decision in Cuba to move away from the only life I knew, it was amazing. Those hopes and dreams were still not that far behind me. This road I had come across before in times like this; collecting myself, determining where I was and why. It's a serious place and one that doesn't come around often, but it makes us who we are. I am deep down and always will be, Acuach Cor, a Dinka child of Africa. These were phases of myself, my story . . . a life. I had left that to become Sarah Gabriel, a teenage Latino Salsa Girl, a student, one of the lost children of Sudan. What was I now? I was an adult in Canada with very adult responsibilities. It felt good. It filled some part of me that was necessary.

Life is forced movement; there is no going back to the past. It is gone and can't be brought back, but it does come around in feelings thoughts and memories. It came around for me in the Lazy Boy. It took me to a place of familiar comfort that is me. I fell asleep with the thought, "Grandma, Grandma, tell us a story; you know the one."

This thought took me to a dream that wasn't scary. I think it was about Grandma telling me where she was now; a long plain of tall waving grass that moved with the wind and made sounds like chimes and little bells. Each strand was decorated with flickering sun flashes in rainbow colours. Somehow, lions got into the picture, fat and lazy and golden in the sun. She was a lioness and her cubs were all snuggled up to her listening to the whispering of ancient stories she told.

It was so beautiful I wanted so to stay there with Grandma as she licked me clean. It was time and the story finished. She had to go off with the hunt. She was not old but golden and beautiful. She looked back over her shoulder once and smiled.

The phone was ringing.

Chapter 22
Family Matters

I must have been sleeping there for quite some time. It was dark outside and I got to the phone before anyone else. The room was a'chatter with visiting friends, typical for a Friday evening. Rivers run deep. I picked up the phone and punched talk with butterflies floating in my chest. Thoughts of Grandma were still with me. I could almost see her face before me in the struggle to wake up, punch talk and stop the ringing. Though fading it was like her whisper was singing through.

The Dinka language is so sweet, caring and full of love. "Mama?"

I couldn't hold back after hearing her say, "Spring Girl, how is my little one? How are you Acuach Cor?" I couldn't answer and just broke down in a river of tears. Mama too was crying with no words to express the connection flowing over the lines from so far away. It was like there was a current of electricity that filled the room. The background chatter in the room stopped. Everyone was looking at me. No words needed to be said to them either as I heard someone say, "its Sarah's mother." They felt the river too and they all stopped, waiting to listen to this event for Sarah. Finally we both touched the African Earth, a grounding that required talking. Mama blew it; she started to sing to me the baby songs she used to sing when I was little. Man, I was going to pass out; Grandma sang us that song too.

So much for words. Another round of water came to the surface and flooded the living room as I ran with the phone to my room. I was feeling too exposed in front of all my friends. It was too much. I couldn't face breaking down and bawling in front of them.

This was a private family matter.

The real meal deal was that I had to get it together and be able to talk about the things that were current. Mama was phoning from Africa and we didn't have a lot of time to discuss my plan. It was a plan I'd thought over for days. It consumed me. I asked her about her eyes and the doctors and how that was going. Mama said she was extending her stay in Nairobi to continue treatments. She said her eyesight was already getting better.

That was a big relief for me. We had talked the first time about conditions in the refugee camp and they were much the same, although I was getting a better idea of how it was affecting the family. Of course I knew how bad it was because I'd experienced at least some of it myself. Mama sounded sad and much older as she talked of how caring for the children was wearing her down. She was worried she couldn't care for them and keep up with their needs. She spoke of having to care for them always being sick with one thing or another.

I'm back on the plane. God, my eyes are just gritty! All I could think was having a shower as hot as I could possibly stand it. I was dreaming how good my bed at home felt. I was sliding back the covers after that shower, with that oh so clean Bounce fresh drier sheet smell. It was lulling me to slumber with not a thought in my pretty little head. Not like here, with a tortured mind, that would not shut up! I thought through the annoyance of the stupid air conditioning blowing against my neck. '*God, how long have I been awake now?*' It was true; I'd been awake basically through three airports and two continents and I was on my way to a third. And that continent was the second largest in the world, *my Africa*. So, not counting a three hour pass-out snooze that was filled with *nightmares*, I'd spent the whole trip wrestling with these totally unacceptable memories. I mean, what the bloody hell? Would this nightmare flight *never end!*

Well, it was almost done. One more hour and we would arrive in Nairobi.

At dawn. *Yip, yip . . . yippee! Thank God!*

I also had to give thanks to my life saver stewardess, *Wanda*. Since my mad screaming episode, she was there every twenty minutes checking on me. She begged me to sleep. "Jet-lag can just kill you, you know Sarah," she said, bringing me pillows, drinks and trying to chat and make me feel, what . . . human? I couldn't hear her half the time. I was lost, who knew where, with memories zipping through my mind at a gazillion miles an hour.

I imagine this was why Wanda was so worried about me.

Sarah Gabriel, the Zombie. Was I going to go over the edge and start eating passenger's brains? That was mixed with an outer-space kinda deal! I was mumbling and moaning, "*I need sleep, I want my bed, I need my Mommy!*" Seriously, it was getting ugly.

Then, I was gripped again. It was never going to end.

How I hated being broke. Payday to payday, without end! Cow after cow, running through my nightmares, mooing, '*Please . . . don't kill me!*' over and over. I had to get off the Killing Floor. God was going to strike me dead for being the Cow Killer I was, with my cool gunslinger knives, and deadly belt! I was a necessary killer, one the little girl Acuach Cor *would just hate.* To her, every animal on earth was precious. Well, except Snakes. Maybe Hyenas, as well. OK, the list could go on and on, and Acuach did love eating cow! OK, we won't go there.

'*There just is not enough time.*'

My editor laid down the law today. "Twenty-four chapters, Sarah. A hundred and twenty thousand words."

OK, so here I go. I'm in Brooks, money is more than tight, but as the family accountant, I had it all figured out. I was now supporting my family in Nairobi in a two bedroom apartment.

Really, it was now just routine. The alarm got me up every morning to face my commitment to my plan. Then I'd work through the hours necessary to fulfill my obligations to the Gabriel name. I had accomplished what I had set out to. I had no time to think about the past. It, in a way, did not exist. The only thing that mattered were the details set out on my kitchen table, a very sharp pencil and hope. I could afford to feed my skinny self. I had gone to Cory and begged for overtime hours. I'd do absolutely anything! My English was improving and Cory got me all the overtime I could handle. Why, because that was my goal, to be the best and fastest cutter on that floor. It was paying dividends. The nagging accountant was pleased.

My body though was dying.

Some days it was hard to get out of bed after sixteen hour days, three times a week at time-and-a-half. My life was a meat grinding run to the next carcass on the line. This is why Cory was my guy. I was a Hot Rod and management was beginning to notice. The crew around me matched my pace and that line never slowed down. I wouldn't let it! Not with a family to feed. I would run to the post office with the money order in hand, budget all looking immaculate, the books all screaming.

I need more hours . . .

It seemed there just weren't enough hours in the plant to contain the drive and pace I'd set for myself. I didn't hang out. I didn't go to bars. I didn't party. I worked until I couldn't anymore and fell into bed exhausted. Every minute of every day was for my family...

I received phone calls constantly. More and more relatives needed this and that. Sometimes I wondered how these family cousins had gotten my phone number. I was obsessed. All I'd been through was to improve myself, to get back to the New Sudan.

They needed me, needed my job, my dedication. I had to get my family out of the horrors of the war I, thank God, never lived through! I couldn't even relate to it; Mama, all those years, living in *a house of sticks!*

That thought never left me. I imagined Mama breaking her body every day, striving to make a life of nothing. This, Sarah Gabriel could not live with, and now I wouldn't have to. Mama was so happy. I could hear it in her voice all the time. The one thing I blew extra money on were phone cards. I was building as close a relationship as I could afford to have with Mama on the other end of my life line to Africa. This was my saving grace.

I could do it. *Mama* was going to get her mansion.

I was my family's lifeline.

I wanted to buy a brand new car for everyone in Africa. I thought I was rich.

Victor was getting to me. He wouldn't take me out dancing on those few nights I wanted to break the routine and have some fun. He never wanted to go anywhere. Sometimes on Fridays or Saturdays, we would visit friends, who did sort of party Cuban style! We would dance up a storm in the living room, or anywhere, at the drop of a hat. Now that I could live with, whenever my body wasn't falling down tired. In a way, we became the stars of our growing Sudanese community. We were among the first in a wave of Sudanese nationals who began to arrive in Brooks. The word was out and more countrymen were arriving all the time. Unfortunately, they also brought with them Sudan's tribal trials.

There were more social engagements, larger parties and gatherings, and more gossip. I tried to stay away from it, to not get involved with what was being said in the community, to not talk about others. But that didn't stop them from getting on my case about my private life with Victor. He was from the 'wrong' sub-tribe for my kind in the opinion of those who were from Africa.

The Cuban crew even started to get into all these complications all over again.

Had we learned nothing? Our education was for a Global Ideal, not the segregation and conflict that had fueled our stupidity and wars for centuries. Some wouldn't let it go. There were fist fights over political differences. Who wants to go to a party where drunken Africans are in the yard swearing and beating each other stupid because a tribal taboo was imagined, the wrong man, or woman chosen? These things, I still didn't understand.

By midway through that first year, I'd had it with all the superstitious African hoobie joobies and all the mombo jombo that goes with. In a lot of ways my countrymen were total strangers. They couldn't understand me either when I wouldn't wear the right clothes, back down from their stupid arguments, or when I tried to explain the world I'd grown up in of many cultures and nationalities. They'd never even heard of them. They didn't like a woman with a back bone. They just wanted one who would lie on her back. I watched them treat their women like garbage every day. I had them visit understanding Sarah all punched out and bruised. They were accepting a life of slavery, as was expected culturally!

Finally, Victor and I reached a bridge we could not cross. There just wasn't a future for use together and we both knew it. Not that we were tired of one another. I was Victor's roommate. I loved him yes, in a brotherly kind of way. He thought we would just settle down with good cattle killing jobs, get married, have kids and watch TV. As I said earlier,

Victor went back to Sudan and became very successful. In the end I was very happy he had moved on. It was good for both us.

I moved out and made a deal with my sister Martha Elijah. We had been in school together from the beginning. It was the perfect solution as we spent a lot of time together anyway and got along famously. She was my cousin Deng's girl friend. We found a great apartment, of course within my budget. We went shopping and bought some new furniture and things to decorate and take pride in our new home. There soon came a celebration Martha knew nothing about, even though we had all kinds of plans for the social life we could now have. I was being sneaky, as some other bigger plans were not working.

Then I got a really new creative idea. It was called the Halloween of 1999! It was my first experience of the Canadian night of scary stuff. In Cuba they have a similar idea 'Dia de la Murte' (day of the dead) that I did know about. Man, that just got my imagination rolling and Acuach Cor came out to play. I decided, because everyone worked twenty-four seven, the community could use a break. Gee and golly, maybe even invite non-Sudanese! I would show them what international tolerance could accomplish. Anyway, I tried and the community . . . freaked out and locked their doors and went into hiding! I couldn't figure this out. Sudanese are always looking for a reason to impress everyone with the next greatest gathering sponsored. What was the difference?

In the mansion in Ethiopia, I just loved playing dress up. I understood you could go door to door and get candy! My kinda deal. Free stuff! Well I looked at some of the costume ideas and told my friends Mana and Nyanakuek to go get Halloween costumes. I said we could have a lot of fun dressing up and looking different. We could celebrate just like they celebrated here in Canada. I told them I was going to buy myself a costume even if they weren't going to dress up. At least they came with me to the store, to keep me company and see if I was going to really follow through with my crazy plan. I looked around the local stores and there were a lot of different costumes. I was totally amazed by them, they were so beautifully wicked and flashy. I picked the most scary, ugly and horrible one I could find with a devil's mask and all! My friends thought I was going to pick the sexiest of outfits. That was their idea of dress up.

Well so much for their participation. There was no way they'd be caught dead looking like that. *No way!* I was going for the 'Dia de la Murte' look. I thought let's go for a Cuban kinda mixture here. My costume even came with a plastic machete . . . *perfect!*

I would kill them all and bury them in the grapefruit Zombie orchard.

The Sudanese community didn't know the meaning of Halloween. They assumed in Canada it was a devil holiday. Most of them had no clue about the meaning of this crazy foreign deal. I decided to take advantage of the situation and have fun with it by scaring them to death. I was thinking it would be really funny.

It wasn't.

I took my costume to Mana's house and they sort of agreed to my plan. They wouldn't dress up, but Mana would go along with me for support. Nyanakuek... no way! We even tried to tease her into it. 'Un uh,' she was having nothing to do with Devil Day. I didn't want anyone else to discover my plan, not even my roommate Martha Elijah. I wanted it to be a surprise. My friends and I were hanging out at my place, five of us girls. OK, *'yuk yuk,'* it was time for me to put on the Acuach Cor show.

Me and Bilfam Mana, my tiny partner in crime, man we were pumped! We started telling our first really scary stories, about the bad stuff that happens to people, ghosts and ghouls we were only guessing at. All these wide eyed girls were just ah-shivering at our Devil Day of the living Dead. We said it would strike in about an hour, and people . . . would begin to disappear.

They fell for it but we didn't know that!

I lied, telling my other two friends I needed Mana's help and that we would be right back. We left the two Marthas in the apartment and went to another building and I put on my horror costume so I could do what I was good at, *scaring people to death!* It was really scary too. The pull over rubber devil mask was blood red and black with a mouth full of fangs, and of course, horns on its head. There was a really cool long black cape. I wore a puffy sleeved white shirt and black pants. I topped it off with gloves that had long claw-like nails. I almost enjoyed the dress up part the most.

Mana agreed to hide. Well, because she looked just like Mana and that just wouldn't work, would it? I went to my first victim's door and when I knocked on the door—there were a lot of Sudanese living in the apartment—one of them shouted "It's open! Come in!" But my plan needed someone to open the door for me. I ignored them and kept on knocking harder. Finally one guy had had enough and decided to open the door for me. When he saw me he was in shock. I could tell he was scared, his eyes went all buggy. He didn't turn red or anything, because he was black.

Man, I could tell that he was about to really pee his pants.

I wanted them to think that I was a real devil so I didn't help him out. The poor guy was stuttering and didn't know what to do, whether to run or faint. After an awkward moment of staring, he just turned and walked slowly into the living room looking over his shoulder with his same wide-eyed boogie man look. I could hear the guys asking him who was at the door. He told them I can't talk right now. He said go and see with your own eyes. The guys asked, "What is it? Is it something really bad or what?" They were making fun of him, telling him he was breathing like someone who'd seen a devil in the jungle. Then they laughed at him. He told them that that was exactly what he had seen! THE DEVIL and, *he's right at the door!*

Mana was on the ground laughing, she couldn't hold it in, but she was still hiding. Right away one of the guys came and then ran back and said his roommate was right. They were saying, "It's a bad day!" Maybe that Canadian devil guy was about to kill them. My friend and I couldn't help it any more; we started to laugh really hard. It was ridiculously entertaining. Not for the tough guys though, who felt embarrassed when they found out it was little skinny Sarah rolling around on the floor in hysterics after I'd ripped off my mask. *Surprise!* And this was the toughest black guy in Brooks!

We went to a couple different places and even got some candy from a nice Cuban guy. The Canadians were all laughing at our tough guy scary story. We saved the best for last. It was the right time for people *to begin to disappear!* The girls were there waiting for us to come back and we were already a little late from getting candy. That was the coolest; tiny little 'Oh Henry' chocolate bars. My fav, *yep. yep.* Well, as they say, the show must go on, and we did much the same when we got back to Martha's and my apartment. I knocked really hard on the door and waited. we could hear the two Martha's moving around but not coming to the door. *'Bam, bam, bam.'* Mana giggled as she knocked again pretty hard and, as planned, I covered the peep hole with a gloved hand.

"*Who is there?*" came through the door sounding suspicious. Neither of us said a peep and struggled not to laugh and blow it. "*I can't see who's out there,*" one of the Martha's whispered to the other. *'Bam, bam, bam, bam'*, went the door and we hear a squeaky little scream and they jump back away from the door and yelled in Arabic. "If we can't see you, we're not answering the door!" 'Bam, bam, bam, bam, goes Mana and shortly Martha tells Martha, "open it anyway, because it could be someone who doesn't understand our language." Martha *open the door*. Martha sees THE DEVIL standing there waving the machete. She freezes in a half a heartbeat. Then she's in a rush to shut that there door in a real hurry, her eyes all popping out of her head.

Well that isn't going to happen and I jump to and shove against the door to keep it open. Both big strong Marthas are too much for me. I didn't want to say too much and I say to Mana quickly, "help." She is all dastardly grins and jumps to. I get my Devil mask around the door and I'm waving the machete around. WOW, you should have heard them screaming then. Mana and I had to jump back away from the door or get squished in the process, as they slammed it shut. *'Clack'* went the deadbolt. "Go away or we are calling 911," was screamed in broken

English. I had the machete swishing around under the door and Mana is going, "*Ooooo, Ooooo, Ooooo*" making ghost noises. I'm laughing evilly, swishing my killer weapon under the door, *'Mua, ha ha ha, Mua ha ha ha!*" We thought we'd hear more freaking out and screaming and would have to run fast before the police arrived. Surprisingly, that's not what took place.

"Martha, Open the door," said Martha and Martha replied, "What, no way!" "I think it's Sarah" the first Martha said with conviction. "No way, I'm not opening this door. Go call 911 before we are murdered!" Well that was it. When we heard that, Mana cracked first. For the second time in one night we were rolling around in a carpeted hallway laughing our asses off.

The door swung open, Martha was there with her hands on her hips still arguing with Martha. "I told you it was Sarah," she said. The more they argued about it, the funnier it got. Then Martha says to Martha angrily, "So what, call the police anyway!" and they started laughing. Martha said to Mana and me, "you guys really did scare us!"

I'd laughed so hard, I peed myself for the second time in my life.

It was a very special day for us, it was so much fun. Maybe they wouldn't agree, but I loved Halloween. Yeah! After that year, I couldn't scare anybody else because a lot of my friends knew what had happened on Halloween 1999. Brooks is a small town and it soon got into the local gossip. That first Black guy from Africa never did live that one down. He got teased about it for quite a long time, until . . .

He beat somebody up over it.

Pretty much everything for the rest of that year and into the next went back to the routine of just life. Christmas was again not celebrated much because I was short of funds. I was sending the majority of my money to my family in Kenya. It was nice though and was celebrated in our Sudanese community. Then the New Year was a big deal because of the new millennium and passing into the year 2000.

Back to work I went. There was no more childish fun like my Halloween scaring friends to death. I was an adult now with grown-up responsibilities I took very seriously. One thing that contributed to that feeling was that I'd bought a car. I'd learned how to drive the year before and passed my Alberta drivers test with flying colours. With help I had memorized the driver's manual because I still couldn't read English. I bought a used Chevy for eight thousand dollars. I'd scrimped and saved till my fingers bled to do just that extra.

In 2000, I made up my mind I was going to get a brand new car. I went to the bank, got a loan, traded in my Chevy and bought a really zippy totally awesome (I thought) Toyota Echo. I loved that car and am still driving it. It has given me ten years of trouble free driving. I was pretty excited and phoned Mama to tell her my news. I just got more phone calls from relatives convinced now Sarah must be rich!

That was about the time I discovered Credit Cards, Oops.

With access to even more money, I was actually fairly careful with the idea, knowing I couldn't go hog wild and buy everything I ever wanted. I was getting into a much better lifestyle, but I had lost some part of Sarah. I would work, work, work and had no time for anything else. I didn't go running. I had promised myself that I would go to a gym and play basketball; I never did. I suppose running all day at work was exercise enough.

The biggest change after I bought the Toyota, was that I met Ronny, a white guy from Nova Scotia. I met him of course at work; where else would I? I went from work to home, and occasionally shopping; the ordinary things. I was in a bit of a rut and not really enjoying life much. Ronny changed that. He was good for me and a man who knew what fun and activity was all about. We would go visiting, go out for dinners, go dancing; he was good at all those things. Ronny told me there were a lot of Black people in Nova Scotia, but I was like no black person he'd ever met.

Ronny was always asking me stuff about Africa. At first I told him about being a little girl there, that I really didn't know much about Africa and that I was raised in Cuba. Well he just wanted to know more about Cuba. Ronny was interesting in that way; he liked different cultures. So alright, I took him to a Sudanese gathering.

When we walked in holding hands, every head in the place turned and stared. I could just hear the gossip mill crank up to full speed. "Sarah's with a white now! What and no tribe? How do we treat this man? It was weird but really not for very long, which surprised me. It was all Ronny. He was a really good person and made friends easily. Although a quiet type person, the Sudanese liked him because he was always asking questions about Africa. That, and he didn't get involved with anyone other than me.

I did take some flack about going with a white guy. I didn't listen and really didn't care. I liked the way Ronny treated me. He loved me and there were no tribal complications. I wanted to be free and clear of all that. I wanted to mix with everybody and not just have the Sudanese community as my only social contact. Ronnie introduced me to his world, Canada. I was going to be Canadian and a world citizen in my heart.

There was one part of my education I didn't need to go to school to learn. It was life experience. I was different from my tribe, my countrymen, even my race. In Cuba I grew to love all cultures. I found people endlessly fascinating. I developed a thirst to know more and more about the world I was a part of; it was a part of the journey I was on.

This idea would lead me to so much in life. I believe that it got me to Brooks.

Ronny and I were always together and went everywhere together. Then we were really together as we got an apartment and lived together. All the Sudanese community thought that was not a good idea at all. I told them to lead their own lives and moved on with building my reality.

Ronny and I stayed together for eight years.

The most important breaks for me in Brooks were blowing money on phone cards and then looking forward to the next set of calls networking with all the parts of my family. There were so many, each of the children held different gaps between us. There were worlds of experience, with many years between, where we knew nothing about each other's lives. The first and hardest aspect of those calls was to speak of Agor. There was a curiosity in me about what happened and where, but really I didn't want to know or face the facts. Each family member was dealing with it in their own way as well. Some would not go there at all and I had to change the subject.

Each call was so different, from playful and laughing to sadness and tears. It was what I needed to be me. It was like Brooks was at the end of the earth and only a stopover place for somewhere else. These telephone calls were rearranging our family as well. You could feel the difference, the relief that life was heading toward some normal course. I was getting information all the time about how their lives were improving. Things for them weren't perfect, but they were better. It was normal now to get out of bed and not worry about a bomb falling out of the blue and destroying your life. We had suffered so much and a part of me knew those times were at an end. These were the kinds of conversations we shared.

I made it a point to get to each of my remaining brothers and sisters, now that I had found and helped my missing Mama and Baba. I needed to know how their normal everyday was working out. I was a snoopy. I dug for information if they didn't give it up fast enough. For Chol, it was like pulling teeth. He was a teenager now and I was still treating him like the little boy from my memories. Sometimes he didn't like that. If I got overly mushy and emotional, he didn't know how to handle it. He'd say stuff like, "I have to go Sarah, the guys have a soccer game going and I'm expected, OK?" and pass off the phone to the next person on the planned agenda.

I organized it that way, finding out what everyone was up to and when they'd be home for these calls. It was like going home for a visit. There was one call that in its way was the best. Everyone I'd planned to talk to was there and I'd finished and Deg Did just dropped by. He wasn't expected and was supposed to be off somewhere with his unit fighting. It was a short conversation as Deng Did never was one with a lot to say.

What Deng Did did say was that he'd been shot in the center of his left hand and had lost a lot of dexterity. For me it was a horrible moment as I imagined him holding up his hand to stop a bullet. Deng told snoopy Sarah it didn't happen that way but didn't say how it did. Then he passed the phone to Mama. I always ended my calls by saying good bye to home through Mama.

Then there were the calls to Cuba. This was an entirely different world and not in Dinka, without all the background chatter and laughter of Mama's home. It depended on just where these conversations were taking place. Mostly they were in offices, or friends' houses, and were quiet and sensible as Yong or Anyuon discussed family matters in serious Spanish. I was always interested in the education I had walked away from to carry out my plan to financially support the family. The family is what most interested them; how people were doing. They were still not getting any contact directly from Africa as I was, so I was the go between, passing information back and forth. The family also gave me questions to ask them. It was confusing sometimes.

So there it was; this switching between separate universes, my normal everyday preparation for work and looking after personal affairs thousands of miles away. This juggling act made me wonder what next as I struggled to gain a better understanding of Canadian life, especially learning all the nuances of this stupid language frustrated me so. Ronny helped a lot in that department, helping me structure my English better so I wouldn't say things silly and backwards. I still do at times and people smile and try to correct me. Then I would switch gears and think on Cuba and all the feelings I held in myself from that world. I still thought of, and missed, schooling. I'd always loved the idea of learning more and teachers who befriended me. Then I would think of engaging with the primal center of Africa and all those childhood memories that surfaced with them. I would talk to my brothers and sisters of the world we remembered and had to leave behind; our childhood in Bor.

That still left the other wild card, America. My brother Deng Ti was continuing his education there under his assumed name with the Arok Thon family. So add yet another world to my associated tribal family. It always somehow boiled back down to that... we are Dinka. It frames all that we are. Africa would never leave us. Deng Ti was getting a lot of recognition for his basketball, being recruited to play for a university team and ending up in Iowa. He was also continuing with his goal of being a diplomat. He is probably, other than Baba, our family's best talker. Well, all the brothers are good talkers. Deng Ti just has a way about him that is very engaging. He was also the closest to where I lived. There came a time in my Brooks experience where Deg Ti came for a short visit. I was so happy! Then, as things must, he went back to his world and left me to contend with all of my designs for home improvement.

I dreamt a lot watching that TV show, about how I would someday build Mama her mansion and the wonderful things I would add to our world together. In one call, I wanted to connect with my sisters and it just worked out that way. It began with Achol who was married now and had a beautiful daughter. That was the point when I started to ask everyone to send pictures so I could see my nieces and nephews. They are all so beautiful it breaks my heart. She was happy with her marriage, and well. Her husband treated her well. There wasn't a whole lot more than that about her personal life, so I asked what she was doing with the SPLA. She was still serving in the army as she had been trained to do in Cuba. We talked about her view on life in the refugee camp and how hard that was for her. Then she finished by gushing all over me with praise for getting them to Nairobi. That was hard for me, as I didn't want to be singled out. It humbled me. I was only doing what was right.

One sister down, one to go. I still had a gazillion questions in me to ask about Abany, my competitive sister who makes great tea, because I let her, who I had to fight hard to get to do anything with me, who I gained so much respect for but could never tell her so. I wanted her to open up to me and share her innermost thoughts. I wanted to become closer and care for each another. I wanted to really know what was going on with her. I knew if other family were around, I wouldn't get the real meal deal. I told her outright, "Abany, take the phone into the bedroom. Let's sister talk!"

I heard Abany ask Mama, "Mama, Sarah asked me to talk in the bedroom, she wants to talk sister talk. Would that be alright?" I heard Mama say softly, "Good idea!"

With that I knew Mama knew what was what.

It started off a little slowly with me pushing some. I could feel her holding back. This was the only time that I could have this kind of talk with her because she was only visiting. She was actually living with her new husband and large family in the refugee camp in Kenya. I could hear from her voice cracking that she was not happy with her world. I knew Abany was close to tears. 'Okay big sister," I said, "spit it out. Tell me!"

That was all it took and it spilled out like a river.

Abany wasn't happy with her arranged marriage. She could never say anything about it because it had been a tribal affair arranged by the family. There was no way this could be discussed in front of everyone in the kitchen. Mama had said what she had softly, because women have no say when it comes to trading women for cows. They have to suffer these facts of life gladly because the family is looking after their best interest. Their feelings have nothing to do with it. Mama knew in her heart what her daughter was living with and needed to talk to somebody. Since I was in Canada, there was no threat of me bringing it out in the open accidentally. She came right out and told me she was not in love with this man. She was his third wife and he was insistent about her giving him what the contract called for... children. This is the expectation, you are a cow! A chattel.

The real problem was that Abany was still in love with her daughter's father and high school sweetheart. That love had never faded for her. The love of her life lived in America. She made the mistake of telling me she wanted to run away from it all.

I told her, "good idea, Abany!" At first her response was all, "no, no, no, I couldn't do that!" "Well why not?" I asked, all logic. "And shame the family Sarah?" I told her straight what this tribal idea of family honour had done was to shame her. Dead air.

"Sarah, don't tell a single soul, alright?" Of course I agreed. "I've already planned out how," she said. I laughed; she was already ahead of me. "It's in the works." Abany told me whispering and conspiratorially and, wow, it was a really good plan. Her sweetheart had gotten hold of her and the plan was being kept hush, hush. Not even our parents knew. The paperwork was already forged and departure was just days away. Her daughter Dunia would go to America first.

This is how it all went down.

Dunia got out first. She arrived and I talked to her in South Dakota. It was so nice to hear her cute little voice all excited to talk to her auntie. Anyway, Abany had it all arranged to leave the country one month later under an assumed name. That was sneaky and I admired that part. She went to Nairobi and stayed at Achol's house, still afraid someone would find her out. She was worried her husband would come and get her before she could get on the plane. At the same time she felt horrible that she was doing such a disgraceful thing to her tribe. She knew if Baba heard about it, he too would take her back. Even Mama could never know because she'd just take the news straight to Baba. It was a very hard time for Abany. It was unbelievably stressful to go against cultural expectations she didn't believe in any more after Cuba. I got a phone call; it was Abany calling from South Dakota.

"Sarah," she shouted, "I escaped. I made it. I'm a free Woman!"

Chapter 23
Moving On

The one constant in the universe is change. It's sometimes said the more things change, the more they stay the same. I know that's just a saying but it sure felt that way to me. After three years in Brooks, Alberta this very small town was like that. The one constant in my life was contending with a relentless routine in which I felt I had no choice. My years in Cuba at school were just that way. Every day was the same, whether in class or out in the orchard, with its mind numbing repetitions. The seasons changed, the grapefruit ripened and the harvesting took place, but it was all the same, same, same, even as the years moved on.

The work on the Killing Floor was also a constant daily run. It was hard on the body to keep the pace required to meet the day's quota. Always I was looking forward to the weekend and needed rest. Community events came and went with the seasons. The extreme winters of Alberta were no longer unfamiliar or in any way shape or form a novelty. When the end of winter came it was a release. I no longer had to rush to get out of the freezing depths of Hell, to get to the welcoming warmth of the plant. I was happy to put away clothes I needed to survive this extreme weather. I had a whole list of things to contend with and a few things on the calendar to look forward to. What was always ahead of me on the road was my obligation. I was finding adult life can be somewhat daunting in this respect. As the dreams you wished for become the reality, in many ways it's nothing like you imagined. Things just evolve into what they are and we contend with that. I think my education in Cuba taught me to face reality head on. We were taught discipline and perseverance by the restrictions forced upon us by world events we had no control over.

Canada wasn't like that. Many of those thoughts faded into the background. There were no shortages; material things were always available. Or at least they were if you had the money, or willing to take on debt in order to have them.

Thanks to movies from the West, people back home thought everyone who lives here has lots of money to spare. Sometimes I would send them money and other times I would have absolutely nothing to send. They would always wait for two more weeks so I could send them money when I got paid. I still haven't figured out how they knew I got paid every second week. It was very tough making so much money and not be able to enjoy it. But because of the situation in Africa, I was totally OK helping and didn't complain about it. It wasn't easy, but it was necessary!

Shortly after my sister Abany arrived in the States, my brother Anyuon came from Cuba after completing his university degree in agriculture. He came to Calgary and then moved to Edmonton to learn English. I was happy that one by one my family had started to come to North America, but when I tried to bring my parents, they absolutely refused. Baba's desire was to finish his book and Mama didn't want to leave his side. They said they were too old to adapt to the long cold winters. I tried to convince them by telling them I would make sure they stayed comfortable and warm. I kept trying, but I couldn't convince them. I realized they would never leave Africa. Their roots were there. All that they believed in was to work toward the New Sudan. For Baba his book was all of him, and all of him belonged to Sudan.

Anyuon finished his English classes in Edmonton and one year later he too moved to Brooks for work. He said he had done the right thing finishing his studies in Cuba, but for the moment, he wanted to put his degree aside and start cutting meat at Lakeside Packers. He wasn't happy about not using his degree, but he was OK with his decision because the family situation was demanding. He wanted to help back home too. A few months after he came to Canada, my younger brother Yong, phoned Anyuon and told him his ex-girlfriend from Cuba was pregnant; he was going to be a Baba. The news took him by surprise. He was happy about having a son, but he realized he'd have to start working even harder at Lakeside Packers so he could provide for his new family too. Yes, family matters.

The pressure on me of sending money to Africa started getting better because I now shared the job with my brothers and sister. We were all sending money to our family in Africa. It was great having help from my siblings. I even started to cut back my overtime. My back had started to get sore from cutting meat for two years without missing many days from work. Plus there was the overtime I had to do to keep paying my own bills. By the summer of 2001 my body finally just couldn't take it. I'd been doing the same job, day after day, and my back was getting worse and worse. Finally, I couldn't do it any more and had to report it in 2002.

Lakeside was not happy with my report. They wanted me to only see the company Doctor. I knew he wouldn't do too much about this; just send me back to work without even some days off. The doctor had given me some medication and it made me dizzy at work. I thought this might be dangerous. I asked about it and it made the doctor angry, so I went and got a second opinion from Dr. Kits, my family Doctor. It was his opinion that if I didn't stop then, I would seriously injure myself and have back problems for the rest of my life. He wrote a note to Lakeside Packers recommending they put me on light duty in the plant.

I took the note to the main office and they didn't like that either. They gave me a week off. My doctor hadn't recommended that and I didn't know what to do. I went back to work anyway and was in pain every day. I could hardly get out of bed. Three days after I'd refused the time off, I got a layoff notice. That was that, end of Lakeside packers.

I was already on Workers Compensation and was receiving money every two weeks covering a percentage of my wages when going for physiotherapy. Yet when I was laid off I had to apply for Unemployment benefits because it didn't cover my injury. For six months I hung around getting bored, looking for some easier work. My back was feeling a lot better and I felt I could at least do some kind of light duty work. There just was nothing in Brooks, other than that stupid plant. I hung out mostly with Rosa Mach and her son Daniel who I just loved to death. There were odd times when friends needed babysitters and I filled in, but there was no money doing that. I only did it because I love children. Ronnie was still working hard, so our home wasn't suffering.

Of course I had to cut right back on the money I sent to Africa. It didn't hurt them too much because all of us were sending funds. I found out that Unemployment would help if you wanted to go back to school. I began looking into that idea, but I didn't like what was available at the local College. I had it in mind to continue on with accounting and go back to London. It always, no matter who I talked to, came back to that dreaded English. Even after four years in Canada, my English sucked. Even Anyuon spoke English better now than I did! Then I thought of Anyuon and his learning English in Edmonton. I realized school was the only way. By now I hated Brooks anyway.

Sarah Gabriel could take this place no more, not another day!

The day I made the decision Ronny came home from work. He walked in the door and I said, "Ronny, I'm moving to Edmonton!" My hands were on my hips and I looked all determined. That was that. *Period.* I was prepared to leave it all behind, including Ronny. I think he saw that in my eyes. He hadn't even put down his lunch box when he responded, "you're not happy here Sarah?" He looked like a lost little boy. I said, "No!" He thought a moment and then it was like he made a decision. "Even if your unemployment ran out Sarah, I would support you." Well I didn't even consider that. "No Ronny, nobody but Sarah supports Sarah!" My hands were back on the hips.

Now he looked even more sheepish and blurted out, "Well, can I come?"

It was what I wanted to hear and I gave him a big yippy hug. Ronny smiled after the smooching, still hanging on to his lunch kit. He was getting covered by Sarah kisses and laughed, "I guess that's it, eh? We're moving on, Sarah, together!" I was really surprised how fast Ronny made up his mind right there at the door. Within a week we left Stinkyville behind and didn't look back. I was happy to say goodbye to bad business.

Of course for me it was one whole week of goodbyes. I had made a lot of friends there. Cory was really upset about how the plant had handled my case. A lot of the people on the line were sad to see me go and said they missed me at work. Every place I had been was like that. I will always think of these people and how they hold a place in my heart. Many of them still phone and we talk, catching up on what's what in Stinkyville. When the gossip is really stinky, I just nod and say, "Oh, is that so?"

Well by now, you know me, I had a plan. I was thinking of staying with the Jok Mach family, at least for a while, but because cohabiting is frowned on by Sudanese, we would have to live separately. We both decided that was no good. Ronny had friends in Edmonton who we could stay with and after a month we found our own place. For me it was a real treat to go and visit the Mach family. They were all excited to see me. it was as close as I could get to being with real family.

The two Sarah's were back together, comparing clothes. We would always swap clothes and wear each other's stuff.

She almost cried when I hugged her and thanked her for the clothes she left me in Cuba when I so needed them. I also got to hang out with Monica, and Achol the youngest, was excited about helping me with my English. I was surprised how grown up she had become. She wasn't a little girl any more, but a teenager who really wanted to bring me up to speed on music too. It was she who explained to me who the Beatles were. The Mach family was a good place for me during this period. I loved spending time with them because they treated me as one of their own.

Ronny had no trouble finding work and was employed right away. I went looking for work everywhere and gave out resumes. It was a very short resume because I didn't feel good about making things up. Most of the jobs that got back to me were like McDonalds at eight dollars an hour and I turned them down. After Brooks and making fair wages, I could see my work was worth more than that amount of money. Part of the problem was my broken English and that still haunted me.

After three months in Edmonton, I was getting pretty bored at being unemployed and watching soap operas. I wasn't even learning English because they were Spanish programs. I think they're better than the originals like Days of our Lives, racier and more romance. Of course I had been in touch with the Sudanese community there. They called us Cubans and we called them Gauchos. The community really opened my eyes to the different problems facing immigrants in Canada. They made me feel Cuban again with an outsider's perspective as they really treated us differently. I again had my negative thoughts about bringing tribal life with them. I didn't enjoy the social parties as much as I had in the past. There were quite often fights which at times became fairly violent with weapons even. For the most part though we had fun and I laughed because once more we got Salsa going which became a popular dance thing.

Then things changed for me. The universe had plans I guess for where I needed to go. I broke down and decided to finally apply for English at the College. I did the testing hoping to get into the English as a Second Language (ESL) program and Unemployment insurance would have paid for it. It turned out to be a more advanced program than I was ready for. I took the Link test and passed. It was back to learning cat, dog, door and, of course, where's the bathroom. It was horrible and so boring I could scream. Many of the people were Chinese, or Russian, or whatever and the racket during breaks sounded like the whole world in one room.

There was one job in Edmonton I wanted. I had applied for a position at North West Foods which was a meat processing plant for beef and bison. I was hoping for that job as the wages there were equal to what I'd been making in Brooks. I was running out of Employment Insurance and began phoning them three times a week. They had thought I couldn't do the job and maybe didn't believe my resume because, when I'd had my interview, I had put down my job experience at Lakeside but told them not to contact them. I figured they'd just get hold of Human Resources and the computer would tell them I'd been laid off due to a back injury. I didn't want this place to know I had a prior back problem.

Probably the lady in personnel was getting sick of hearing from me and decided to interview me again. Dan was the plant manager who interviewed me the first time too. He still looked pretty skeptical. Even as I walked in the door I could see it in his eyes: Too small. Knowing it was a meat cutting job I wanted, I went right at it to convince him otherwise. I wasn't about to let this job pass me the second time around. By the end of the interview he still wasn't convinced, but it was obvious I understood what went on there. In the time I worked there, I liked Dan. He was a good person. He decided he would give me a chance and started me off in the meat packing section. The day my Employment Insurance ran out NorthWest phoned and gave me the job. Man, life just has a way of just working out for me.

It was good to be employed again with a reason to get up in the morning. I really do need to stay busy. The English deal got dropped. There were too many new people starting and the whole cat and dog deal began all over again and I quit. Later I came back and passed the test that let me move up to ESL. Back to College I went for night courses three times a week. Combine that with work and I was very happy with my world.

Mind you, I was still not satisfied with my position. When I started in the Packaging section there were three of us working the area. Within a short period of time as I got used to it and picked up speed, only two of us needed to work the station. Some days I worked it all by myself and I found the work fairly simple. At first here were young guys carrying the big meat trays over from trimming to our line. Then, for whatever reason, they quit doing that and I had to do that job too.

It was here that trouble started between me and the supervisor. I don't like to complain but I'm not afraid to tell bosses what I need, or how to maybe make the job I'm on go better. Well, he'd come across all nice and then never do anything about the things I suggested. Either that or he'd talk to other workers and they wouldn't do what he asked of them. Many times I wondered how he got that position. I could see people on the floor standing around doing nothing but talk while the line slowed down. Mostly his job appeared to be standing there talking about hunting, or whatever. About the time I was getting to really hate the guy, he came and asked if I knew anybody who could work as well as I did. My opinion of him got a little better. I said ya, I did, my cousin Monica Mach.

When Monica came on the line, well we just flew but still the meat bucket task was too much for us. Our stated job worked just fine, but the supervisor knew we were doing the bucket job, that it wasn't part of our job description, and still he did nothing about it. We even had other employees yelling at us from a different department to hurry up and do their job. It was pretty frustrating. I wanted to tell Dan about it but felt I shouldn't. I didn't want to get this jerk into trouble. I knew Dan didn't like some of what was going on out on the floor, but the situation seemed to be getting stupider. I would have fired that guy!

The universe decided to help me out and get me out of that guy's department. One day the main trimmer was off on holidays and they didn't have anyone one to cover his position. I overheard this and knew they didn't want to look for a new person. I walked over to their Supervisor and said, "I can do that job!" He just stared at me like, *'ya right.'* So I stepped right up to the plate feeling that *'oh ya, I'm Sarah Gabriel,'* hands on hips, I'll show you. "Listen you give me the knives and I'll show you in an hour what I can do!" I'm sure he was thinking, *'Big Head!'* a Sudanese way of saying a bad word. I was tired of people thinking I couldn't do the work. I'd show them a thing or two.

He was a big bruiser too. He grinned and gave me the knives. He was waiting for me to fall on my face in about two seconds flat. "OK girly girl, show us what ya got!" It was all snickers with his buddies. They were thinking this was going to get silly. They even slowed down the chain some, thinking I'd need the help. Within five minutes he was looking pretty serious and turned the chain back up to speed. In fifteen minutes he walked away. He came back in an hour as it was break-time anyway. "Well, you did good," he said. "You surprised me. I'll talk to your Supervisor, and you can fill in till Henry comes back."

Henry came back and I was kept meat cutting. On Henry's first day back he looked at me like, 'what's this, a girl and real skinny?' Within a couple of minutes, he was smiling and nodding his head to me like, 'you go girl.' Henry, he was alright, and I did show him a thing or two. As our chain got turned up a notch, everybody else started to complain. At least Dan was happy. Every time he went by me he just grinned or said, "good job Sarah!"

Changing departments was an improvement, but the general situation really wasn't any better. There was a lot of harassment going on through the whole plant. It seemed that no matter what was tried, there was a feeling of general discontent. In many ways, it just wasn't a good place to work. I was kind of upset because Monica found her job too hard on her back. They still hadn't changed the meat bucket problem. The jerk supervisor was always giving her a bad time till one day she just got tired of him and quit.

I really was not happy with that place. Monica had family and didn't need the money as badly as I did. I was still sending money to Africa so I just put up with all the stupidness going on around me. Meanwhile Ronny and I were getting along well as usual. We had a good life going on there in Edmonton, so I felt it was worth it. College was going well and I was beginning to notice an improvement in the way I spoke English. I found I was now thinking in English. It was like one day it just kicked in and I stopped trying to translate everything in my head. It made talking to people in the community that much easier. I would go to the store and actually understand what the clerks were telling me. Ronny too noticed the difference school was making.

I really liked going to school. At times I wished I was just a student again and not killing myself over cows. One can only take looking at dead cows day in and day out for so long. I was having some weird change going on inside me at that time as well. In Sudan the women there have mostly big bubble butts. The men really like all that jiggly flesh. They're attracted to big gals for some reason, probably something to do with the ability to have lots of babies. Women in our community had been telling me since before I could remember I was too thin. I wondered if maybe it made me ugly and unattractive. So alright, I decided I needed to put on a few pounds. A lady told me if you want to gain weight fast, eat a lot of McDonald's burgers.

Right, like I needed more cow?

Strangely I did, and darn, I got to love those burgers and fries for my thighs. It was working and I started to pack on the pounds and put away the burgers like they were going out of style. Ronny didn't mind and we liked going out and not having to cook. I think he also liked my butt better too. Then I found the down side; half the things in my closest I loved so well didn't fit me anymore. I felt sluggish, and no matter how many burgers I put away, I would never gain the jigglies anyway. I just wasn't built that way. Where I was gaining weight was in the waistline; I was getting to look like I had a beer belly.

Ever since coming to Canada, I hadn't done any exercising or sports. I hated the way my body was looking; it just wasn't Sarah. I decided I didn't care what people thought, I needed to feel better about me inside. I didn't feel good. I wanted my clothes back. I didn't want to accept having to move up to fat girl sizes!

So like always, I made a plan. I went to talk Monica into it as I wanted to start going to a gym but didn't want to go alone. Monica didn't take much convincing. She thought it was a great idea. We started to go for walks that turned into runs on a regular basis. Still I wasn't losing any weight and couldn't understand why. One day I asked my trainer why I couldn't lose weight and she asked about my diet. "I'm not on a diet," I told her. She told me that wasn't what she meant. "No Sarah," she said, "just tell me about your eating habits." That's when it came out about my addiction to McDonald's. I was still eating there all the time and hadn't thought to cut back. "Oh." That was like a no brainer and it was no problem for me anyway. Ronny and I were back to more rice and beans.

I got results almost right away. I was feeling better about myself, like I was on the track I wanted to run on. I started to get out and run more often, just because. It was a good way of blowing off steam as well. When I got out running it was like the world fell away and I forgot about things that bugged me for a while. The women in our community started to notice I was letting go of my weight and frowned. I just ignored them. I was beginning to think I'd learned a valuable lesson; I needed to not be judged or to be judgmental of others. We are all different and want to feel good about ourselves. It's not good to shape yourself to the way others want you to be. It's better to discover who you really are and what things make you happy.

Externally I still had problems. I didn't like my work and it was really beginning to bother me in a big way. I was being myself there and working hard and they liked that. What they didn't like was me being straightforward and using my mind. I tried to always seek ways of making the job better, better ways of doing things. But when I talked to anyone about it, they would get annoyed with me. I learned to just stay quiet and do my job the way they wanted it done. It was easier that way.

I'd been in Edmonton a year by then. I was at work one day and noticed there was smoke coming out of the ceiling. Other employees were looking up as well and in different places. It was like we all figured it out at the same time as the fire alarm went off. People were running around screaming, "fire, fire, we all have to get out!" Well of course we all ran out of the building and fire trucks showed up and we watched our jobs burn down. At first I was like, *'oh no.'* Then strangely, I felt relieved.

I had a friend Lillian who had worked in the office who knew people who had a meat packing plant in Falkland, British Colombia. Lillian had actually talked to her friend Dennis there. He was interested and asked if we knew of any more people we could bring with us. He wanted us to start like yesterday. I had other friends too who could go with me if asked. I had pretty much made up my mind as soon as Lillian told me Dennis was paying fourteen dollars an hour. That was good enough for me, I was moving to BC. Moving on. I went and told Ronny. Again it was like, "What?" "Yep Ronny I'm going to somewhere warmer. I've heard this Okanagan Valley is beautiful and I'm going to find out!" It was about two seconds later Ronny said with a shrug, "I guess were moving on then."

Chapter 24
Paradise Found

So far my Canadian experience was big cities and cowboy country. Yes, I'd worked hard and found my family. I had now owned a couple of cars even. I'd done some exploring in Alberta and Ronnie liked to go for drives in the countryside too. I'll say this; Alberta is wide open kind of country. Well we packed up the car and all my furniture went into cousin Monica's basement to come back for someday. It was fun as we set off in a caravan of three cars. My student brother James had taken all of two seconds to say, "oh yes I'm in. BC you say? It's beautiful there Sarah. You're going to love it." So there was Ronny and me, James, and Ronny's friend Dan Tuck and his old pickup truck.

The four of us were off on a new adventure, to beautiful British Colombia.

We took a different route than I'd ever travelled before that made it really interesting. Well if you find farm fields interesting and cows, lots and lots of cows. I ignored them, not wanting to think of just where it was they were going. Anyway, it was good to leave Edmonton behind for a while; travelling was a treat and had a holiday feel. It was the open road and me driving Echo into the unknowns. My car was a really happy ruby red baby beetling off down the highway, purring putt, putt, right along. The countryside began to change; a lot more trees were filling up the pasture land. I got the feeling the wilderness was coming as the highway began to rise and I could see huge mountains off in the distance. I could see they must be really high mountains too, because it was the summer of 2004 and really hot out. The windows were rolled down, the wind blowing through my hair and keeping the sweat from getting into my eyes. Now you could feel the air cooling and smell pine tree forest going by and, oh man, those mountains still had snow caps on the very tops.

I had of course heard about them. Now I was being introduced first hand to one of the wonders of the world; the Rocky Mountain range. We weren't even in them yet and already their grandeur was breathtaking. Ronny was getting a kick out of my pointing at everything. "Would you look at that Ronny, oh Wow look, an eagle!" Ronnie talked about his mountains in Nova Scotia and all the wildlife we were going to see, and we did, when I wasn't worrying first about the endlessly twisting highway as we climbed up into the sky. I hoped we wouldn't fall off the edge into oblivion. I was really white knuckling it there for a while, gripping the steering wheel and driving oh so careful. Then James began to beep, beep like, '*hey! Wait for me!*'

James was even going slower than I was.

Dan in his truck was way ahead and that's what stopped me from being freaked out. I wanted to catch that there old truck. I wanted to show Dan the Echo could keep up with the best of them and not get outdone by some truck. Traveling like that in tandem was great fun on that stretch of highway, it seemed to climb forever. At the top there was a rest stop and I followed Dan right in. We got out and waited for James, for quite a while it seemed. Dan looked at me and grinned, "Hey, you kept right up with me Sarah." He stretched hard and looked at the spectacular panorama spread out before us. There was a deep valley down there and a chain of mountain lakes sparkling in the sun all emerald green. I was taking all this in with a memory tickling away in my subconscious. Dan broke into my thoughts. "Beautiful huh, bet you've never seen anything like that before!" His saying this brought that memory right to the surface.

I looked right at Dan. "Actually I have. This is very much like a place I drove through as a child in Africa." His face changed expression; that had caught his interest. I carried on with my heart swelling in my chest. "It was driving through Gambela National Park in Ethiopia on the way to Addis Ababa when I was eleven Dan." I pointed to the surroundings. "It was very much just like this but with worse really narrow roads!" We were seeing the winding number one highway so sculpted in comparison.

Dan seemed to appreciate a whole new me. He wanted to show me something. It was a sign. I still didn't read too well, but it didn't matter as Ronnie was reading it to me. The sign told us we had reached the summit of Highwood Pass and that we were at an elevation of 7310 ft above sea level. Well that had been interesting and now we knew we were way up there in God's country very close to the heavens. Ronnie and I walked to the lookout holding hands to take it all in, this royally grand panorama.

I was fighting back tears a little as my trip with Mama and the family through the Ethiopian mountains was running away with my emotions. It was too beautiful up there and like Ethiopia, a Polaroid moment. It was like you know your heart will hold on to it forever. It was like taking a picture, and years later, something will touch it and your heart will bring that memory back to you. It felt like it right there, right then, at that moment. 'Click!'

As things go, moments such as that are left behind. Scenery changes and life moves on. During another stop, and after pointing at deer off the highway, I saw a beautiful red fox with her pointy little nose and two pups running after their mama. There was a lot of wild life in Jasper National Park to see, bears and even a great big moose standing knee deep in Moose Lake! All too soon we were on the other side and winding down through the pass and into B.C. In the six years I'd been in Canada, I'd never seen so many different kinds of scenery. In British Colombia there are five distinct climactic zones, from West Coast rain forest to Semi-Desert and everything in between.

You are driving along out of the mountains and the trees tell you something is different. We had been on the road for some time and soon it would be getting dark. We were somewhere south of Prince George and Ronnie was pointing all excited as Dan's break lights came on. He was pulling off the highway. I was wondering, as all I'd seen were a bunch of cows. I thought, 'so what?' Then I saw these were big and furry with huge shoulders and realized they were Bison. It was a Buffalo ranch and they were right there beside the highway munching grass, ignoring us! Well that was cool, but I was the one that got back in the car first. I wanted to move on and get to this Falkland place.

It was like holidays over boys, we are on our way to work. "Let's Go!"

I wanted to get there and was getting really tired as it was. We didn't make it in one go. At one point we had to stop, pull over and sleep till the morning sun heated up the vehicles and made it impossible to sleep any longer. As it turned out, we were only three hours out of Falkland. There is like one Hotel on the main street of this tiny village and that one main road is the highway going through. Blink and you'll miss the town. We followed our directions and found our way to Medallion Meats, which turned out be on the left hand side of the highway and not hard to find on a Sunday morning ten minutes out of Falkland.

Medallion turned out to be a pretty interesting place to work. The pace was much slower than we'd been used to. It was like being able to do the job with your eyes closed. The plant was really a lot smaller then Lakeside with maybe twenty people working there. It didn't take long to get to know everyone and we were a good crew. For the first month the four of us lived in a travel trailer, what a horror that was. You couldn't turn around to brush your teeth. You'd walk out the door in the morning and the goats and Lama were saying hi and wanting you to feed them. We all got to be pals and they liked to play with me. The goat even used to let me ride around on her laughing, a bah, bah, rodeo. We even got to go to the real live Falkland Rodeo this tiny town is famous for.

The work was easy, the pay scale what we were looking for, but we needed to get out of that stupid trailer. Priority number one on my to-do list, find a place to live and anywhere but Falkland! Not that Falkland was a bad place; it was rather cute really if you liked loggers, hillbillies, bikers and cowboys all in the one Hotel Bar. We were already a novelty there, being the only two black folks in town. I found the people really friendly, bikers and all. I was a little afraid of them at first until I found out they were just people, and nice enough to show me how to play eight ball pool.

The first weekend we could with time off, we'd decided to visit the cities in that area of B.C. that were within driving distance of Falkland. I

275

was hoping they were nice places and a lot bigger. As soon as we left, I was feeling excited and looking forward to exploring this British Colombia, something like a South American England, if there were such a thing. As we turned left on the Trans Canada Highway, I had the odd feeling of wanting to turn right instead of left to Kamloops and just keep going and see all of Canada, right to Ronnie's Nova Scotia.

I was wishing I could see it all!

Of course we didn't, we headed toward our planned destination. It was an obvious change of scenery again as this area of B.C. is a semi-desert. I thought about desert and Sudan and no water, and as I watched the city grow on each side of a winding lazy river, inside a voice said "nope." Instead I got a picture of beautiful lakes and again felt a small inner excitement grow.

We drove around and everyone felt the same way, '*nope.*' So why waste any more time in Kamloops? It was all right as far as cities go, busy with lots of roads going everywhere but rather an industrial looking place. So it was back down that Number One the way we came and off to Salmon Arm, the second city on my must explore list. It was amazing how fast the scenery changed back to very beautiful B.C. It had nice trees and as we went through the Village of Sorento just before Salmon Arm, we passed Shuswap lake. What was it with my head? Inside I was looking for somewhere with not just one lake but three.

It was like an underlying itch. Salmon Arm was a really nice city and everyone thought this was a possibility All nodded, yep. Better than Kamloops. I was agreeing but inside said, '*nope.*'

Again everyone then started finding things they didn't like and wanted to head for the highway. Yes, Salmon Arm was a very nice city. It would have been a little further to drive to work but it didn't have much in the way of shopping. That's what had decided me. I felt relieved everyone was agreeing. Half the day was gone by and we had spent most of it on the highway. Now we were on the way to Vernon, our third and final choice. We passed several smaller towns like Enderby with a nope. We were moving on.

The next was Armstrong. I had a feeling I wanted to drive in and look around. It looked intriguing, but then again I thought this town could be a mini Brooks. *No Way!* We were quite close to Vernon now and as we came to the intersection that would have taken us back to Falkland, Ronnie said, "well that's the road we'll take to go to work!"

Hearing him saying it that way, I thought was odd. It was like he was saying this is a done deal.

We would be going that way to work every day and I could see it. Then on the right I saw Swan Lake and it came as a very strong *déjà vu. I had the feeling I had done this exact same thing before. I felt as if my long road ahead was finally ending. I had a rush of thoughts. This place was going to take me home. Or, was I home?*

I was almost confused and everyone wanted to talk to me all at once. I couldn't make out a word they were saying. Then the moment passed and left me feeling . . . full. I wasn't hungry, some space had just moved right in. At that point it was as if everyone in the car caught the buzz. "Look Sarah, a great big mall!" As we got deeper into the city, I could find nothing I did not like. Another something popped into my head as I saw a sign that point to Okanagan College. "Oh hey, let's go see where this college is!" We just kept on going on the highway that left Vernon and on the way to Kelowna.

At the top of what is a very long hill we drove past an Army Camp. That was the only thing I wasn't too sure of. Visions of Bilfam swam around somewhere in my mind. We went through one more light and I passed it, everyone telling me so. I was looking to turn around and down in the valley bottom was another lake. OK, two out of three. Where we turned around was a viewpoint and we got out and read the sign, Kalamalka Lake. It was a native name meaning 'Lake of Many Colors'. It was too, the most beautiful shades of moving colour with greens and almost turquoise like hues. I was truly captivated. To the left I could see a beautiful beach full of people that reminded me of Cuba somehow.

We got back on the highway and didn't stop at the College. I only needed to know where in Vernon it was. I was thinking, 'someday I will finish Baba's wishes and go back to school there.' And I did, but somewhat later.

We found a local paper and looked for apartments for rent. One caught my eye right away and I said to Ronnie, 'hey look, let's go see this place. It's called Brookside Apartments." He laughed. It was back to Brooks we went. We were shown a three bedroom place on three floors with a basement. It was perfect for four people; they didn't even ask for references and we rented it right there with a damage deposit on the spot. Wow, two hours in Vernon and we had our new B.C. home. Two weeks later we moved out of the travel trailer and our world moved on.

Over the next four years, many things for me remained only a part of my dedication. That would never change. I was continually working toward making things better. Still some of the things I wanted seemed a long way down that road. I did have the constant connection to Africa and my family by phone. That was a given. It was the emotional constant I relied upon to make me get up every day and face the work that provided the necessities of my dreams. It motivated me to find my purpose, a purpose I really didn't know or understand what it was quite yet. I needed to check off the next thing on the list. Sarah in Vernon was becoming more and more part of Canadian life. In those four years I moved three times, moving up towards this unseen goal.

This undercurrent, and that's the only way to describe it, was a desire for personal transformation shaped by the events of my current life. Part of it was the almost overwhelming desire to become a Canadian citizen. I felt a need to have this connection taking place within me. All that had happened for me to be here, and the way it all took place, had been so well put together and almost seamlessly presented. It was all I needed, even those times when I faced hard thoughts, and struggled to be the Sarah that I am, it was always there, burning behind the scene somehow.

These things were revealed and I'd think about them and then they'd hit my to-do list. Things were now needed to acquire whatever it was I was moving toward. What was it this force that was driving my world through all its changes? Why had I needed to know and love Cuba? Was it to know multicultural interaction, to gain an understanding of the way people need to be engaged with one another equally, without prejudice? Why had I suffered displacement from my homeland, something so close to the very fiber of my being? This love of my Africa was an engine. Some days I wanted to just pull the covers over my head and hide, and it wouldn't let me. I had to have the courage of the lion and face the challenge. I had to carry on no matter what I was faced with. Now four years of this and it was only growing hotter.

This, unreasonable fire...

In the meantime everyday things filled our lives in the passing of time. Life was filling up your car with gas to go to work, making dinners, visiting friends and enjoying a social life. These are all necessary things and the stuff needed to create the life Sarah was living. This aspect of the world at times pushes hard to acquire more and more. It's easy enough to be sidetracked by lovers, friends and obligations that arrive between us as people working our way through surviving. We allow life to push us around and through unbelievable happenstance. At some point we have to decide just what we are to do with our life. This was in me at times almost like a fire out of control. Then at other times it was easy and I'd run down my favorite jogging road, go to the beach at Okanagan Lake and lie in the sun.

Vernon held all these things for me, and more than I could explain.

There was a background of keeping what were the more important parts. They were all being gathered, stored away in my travel bundle. They were no longer buried, but carried with me everywhere. It could be put in one simple word. Hope. Mama packing only the necessary things for us to run was the start. Then I had to acquire the courage to face the impossible and live. It included all my wishes, these wonder places found in the Addis Ababa mansion, my royal fantasies. It was a collection of my most

278

important dreams and aspirations, my dedications, and my family teachings. I believe it was where I keep the best parts of the transformations of my soul.

Meanwhile, in the foreground, there were the daily details of ordinary life and some highlights, both planned and happy happenstance. The work-a-day world consumed the turning of seasons, and I felt I was settling into what was becoming a familiar place. Our small circle began expanding into this community of our choosing. One big step was a change in our living arrangements with more room to move around and our own bathroom for a shower before and after work. Our first home was better than a travel trailer, but it was difficult to have a private life living with four roommates.

There were changes at Medallion as well. Our work hours were cut back and promised wage raises weren't forthcoming. Although Anam Kur, the owner, was a good man, there were obvious problems for the business financially. We stayed on with him for the best part of our first year in BC hoping things would pick up and our earnings improve.

I was able to send a portion of my usual monies to Mama, but the cut backs had me again sharpening my pencil. I was juggling between my share of rent, groceries, car payments, household bills and phone cards. The cards were cheaper than using long distance on our shared phone. All these monthly calculations ruled my world.

One day I was shopping for groceries after pencil sharpening with James. We were standing in the aisle talking about whatever, maybe what brand of cereal to buy. A lady heard us talking in Spanish. She just walked right up to me and introduced herself. She told me her daughter-in-law was from Cuba. That caught my interest right away and James' too. She said she spoke almost no English--I could relate to that--and she needed a girlfriend and was lonely. She asked if I would be willing to call her. Of course, me being me, I said sure, took the offered number and we went our separate ways and back to picking our Cornflakes. This came in the midst of a number of changes.

Ronnie and I had decided to find a place of our own. We had found an apartment I didn't really like at all. It was available right away and the price was right. What had helped force the decision was that other friends showed up in Vernon because we were there. This was due to us phoning friends, talking to family, using our personal grapevine. We were always talking about who, how, where and what was going on in our life. A small migration from cow country was taking place; friends wanted out of Brooks and away from Lakeside. Marco, Andrew and Chino moved right into our Brookside Manor home, laughing how they'd moved from Brooks to Brookside.

So in the midst of all this was Sarah. Dan had moved out, but it was still me and five guys in the house. I was done with all the waiting for the bathroom. I would have moved into an African round house of sticks, to have a place of my own! Changes were all happening rather quickly. A new meat packing plant called Blue Mountain started in Salmon Arm. Bob, who had worked at Medallion, was hired as manager there. He approached us and offered us eighteen dollars an hour, eight hours a day, five days a week and maybe, overtime. Things at Medallion were really slow; we were getting three days work a week if we were lucky.

'OK, moving on!'

It was almost the same distance and I enjoyed the different drive to get there. The new Brooks guys all got jobs at Blue Mountain too. During all this moving about, I called the number given by the lady at the grocery store. Yanerxi Dominquez, what a tongue twister name, was ecstatic and wanted to meet me right away. As she'd answered the phone, I just started talking with her right away in Spanish. This out of the blue call for her was a very happy happenstance. Actually it was for both of us. Until then I had a very limited circle of friends, and all of them were guys. Yanerxi was my first girlfriend in Vernon and what an odd circumstance it was. It turned out she lived in the building I'd just moved into.

Later Yanerxi told me that she felt God had brought me to her. I don't know if that was true or not, but it was a nice thing to say. When we were together we talked up a storm, sharing stories about the place we both missed in our lives, Cuba. This filled a need in me. James and most of the people I knew here had gone to school in Cuba, but we didn't talk about it all that too much. For me, I was seeing Cuba again and exploring it again through my friend, and her very different life there. The more I knew her, the more I saw Yanerxi was really very depressed. We shared a lot of personal things and she opened up almost right away. She was married and her husband was trying to keep up with the bills but she was no longer able to afford the long-distance calls needed to keep contact with her family.

Really her problem was that she was solely dependent on her husband's income. I certainly understood the problem of finding a job with no English. Yanerxi was stuck. I got a brainstorm and asked at work if they'd hire my friend, doing this first before I mentioned it to her. I didn't want her to get her hopes up and it not happen. You could say Bob was skeptical because she had no experience and didn't speak English. I got right on it and talked him into it, promising to train her myself. There was also our Spanish speaking crew that would help. They would also help her improve her English. So it was that my new friend rode with me to work every day.

Yanerxi turned out to be a very fast learner. Bob hired her at eight dollars an hour because of her lack of experience and was rather surprised at her work performance. Shortly after she earned a raise. This helped her get over her depression. She started sending money home again and had the ways and means to meet her bills. I felt really good to be able to help my friend get by her difficulties and move on.

I was growing to love Vernon. It was a place I felt was home. I didn't have to run off to anywhere. Many of my tensions seemed to relax. With the scenery of the valley and surrounding blue Selkirk mountains, with the lakes and just the layout of this city, it was for me a cozy, comfortable bubble.

Until it snowed! I don't know if I will ever truly like winter. The cold and I don't get along very well. Still, it wasn't like the white deep freeze of Arctic Alberta. Winter in Vernon was gentler and really pretty when the first snow fell and, as is the nature of the white stuff, rather horrible when it turned to slush. Even winter was becoming a normal occurrence. My tropical days were now far behind me although never really forgotten. I had Yanerxi there as a constant reminder and only ever a conversation away. When I was lonely for that hot southern breeze and crystal white beaches, I spent my days off inside dreaming of what it was like thousands of miles away.

I was beginning to understand why there were a lot of Canadian tourists in Cuba at that time of year; even two weeks away from the northern deep freeze was pure heaven. I would get to imagining myself on an airplane taking off to somewhere beautiful and warm. One day I realized it wouldn't be Cuba, at least not yet. I wanted to truly go home. This became an idea that wouldn't let me go. I had thought of this before in Brooks when I'd first talked to my parents. I wanted to get on a plane right away.

I really put a point on my pencil then, but it wasn't the right time. I didn't have enough money to carry out my wish no matter how I tried to make the numbers work. One thing I knew; it was a visit I wanted, not a move. Things had been developing in Vernon that were giving me a new understanding of myself. I couldn't see myself going back to Africa to live. My life was here. This wasn't a temporary situation; there'd be no going somewhere else to start over. I had a good paying job and I was going to night school, taking English courses. I was finding a growing Latin community to spend time with when not working. Then I hit another bump.

Blue Mountain wasn't working out. There were plant problems with water and with it came tensions and management stress that filtered down to us on the floor. Bob was unhappy with the way the plant was changing on him. Then, suddenly, everything changed for us yet again.

The owner of Medallion, Anam Kur, and Dennis came right to our apartment one day to tell us their business had picked right up and they were in trouble. They didn't have enough employees to keep up with the demand. It was a little strange as they looked so panicked. They told us how good we were at our jobs and offered us the same wage as Blue Mountain plus overtime. It wasn't that hard a decision; none of us liked Blue Mountain and our crew, plus some of the other people there, came with us. It was back to farmer Falkland with, again, a different sort of drive to work.

That wore off soon enough and became just an everyday chore. Actually, while the work was better, I was wearing out. I was getting to the point of wanting to get out of being a meat cutter. There had to be something else. Just what, I couldn't really imagine. There were two meat Inspectors who came to the plant all the time. I got to watching what they did. I got to thinking I could do that. Debbie and Ruy were very friendly and liked to stop and talk when there was time for it at breaks or lunch time. Debbie actually brought it up. "You should think about becoming a meat Inspector Sarah," she said. They both thought it was a great idea, mentioned it often and showed me more of how they did their jobs. There it was; I could see it. Sarah was going for it!

Chapter 25
Wings of Hope

I made up my mind to apply to the Canadian Food Inspection Agency and a government job. I found the idea really exciting. I had passed my thirty, 'ahem,' something birthday. 'I could do this!' was the constant thought. I was very positive; it all would happen. The salary and benefits were, to me, unbelievable. I had thoroughly checked it out and was planning that someday soon I'd put in my application and do the required tests. Then Medallion went suddenly back to the same cutting limited work schedule, cutting our hours to nothing.

We were all pretty upset. We knew Blue Mountain was totally shut down and we certainly weren't going back to Brooks. Especially me; I never go backwards. No way! I knew I had to give up on Medallion as the promised hours never seem to come about. They were nice people certainly, but I couldn't support all the needs I had with the pay checks I was getting. Dennis was sad to see me go and tried again to talk me out of it. No, I wasn't going to change my mind. I was determined I could find something better as I was on part time and was already receiving Unemployment benefits to make up the difference. Dennis let me go and laid me off officially, hoping I might still come back when their work picked up again. I knew I wouldn't.

I wanted to move forward to a better life, one that wasn't going to kill my body. If I stayed meat cutting for too much longer, it would happen again. It was one demanding job. It wasn't in me to hate anything, knowing that in the end hate can turn into a bitterness that can destroy one's quality of life. At this point I knew it was time to act, before the job consumed me, before I stopped striving to find that place in me that as yet had no name. I only knew I had to go get to it, had to arrive there.

Things were getting really tight financially. Ronnie was in the same predicament at Medallion and was hanging in there. Between us, we were getting by. It wasn't the way I wished it could be, but it was enough to keep our relationship going. I knew I couldn't sit at home on Unemployment and started looking for other work right away. Vernon is a beautiful city, but it has its difficulties. Finding work is one of them. A lot of people were applying for the few jobs that are out there. My short resume was still only about cows.

With that kind of limited experience, all I could find was a part time position at Superstore at minimum wage. I liked it well enough there. I was assisting shoppers buying clothes and that I knew all about. There was that and the store was clean and smelled good and there wasn't a stupid cow in sight. That was the best! It wasn't the wage I needed, but it was extended work experience. As it was part time, I went out and found another part time job at Max Fiberglass making bathtubs in Armstrong. It was heavy work and I could feel my back injury beginning to act up again. I couldn't live with that nightmare again and decided the job was beyond me and quit in only a month. Then I got a cleaning job in the hospitality industry up on Silver Star Mountain Ski Resort. That only lasted about a month as well. It just wasn't my style, cleaning up after other people, especially tourists. They just don't care and were really messy, knowing the 'Maid' would clean up. I was no stupid 'Maid' for anybody... not even Ronnie.

Buddy, clean up your own mess!

When I lived at Brookside it was like that. All the men I lived with found out it was true. I was nobody's maid. We all chipped in and our place was always clean. So that was another job added on to my resume and I was now three months into the superstore part time. They liked me and the job I did for them, but I felt I was getting nowhere. These jobs weren't enough to get me to my goals.

Through the family grapevine I got news that cheered me right up. I phoned Yong to check up on him and hear a voice that was in my Cuba. We always talked a little about how things were going for the country in general. He said actually the economy was improving to a degree. I was happy to know life for the people of Cuba was getting less difficult. I found watching any kind of news program was to see that the world has so many problems. It made it hard to hold hope for our future. At least I would soon have an opportunity to again have a direct connection to my family. I felt we were bettering our world and it made me want to keep trying.

I knew that Yong would be finished his schooling shortly and wanted to know what his plans were. He was excited and had it all arranged. He was already in Ontario and called me from there. I gave him the news that our sister Abany, along with Dunia, were coming to Alberta. Then we really got down to it and arranged for all of us to go to Brooks and meet Anyuon. I was very excited as this would be the first time in a very long while I would see so much of my family in one place.

Finally it was organized. I took a week off work and Ronnie and I left on a trip to Stinkyville, first picking up Abany and Dunia at the airport in Calgary. It was July in the summer of 2006, the hottest time of year when that Brooks smell is even harder to live with. I was never so glad I was no longer living there. You should have seen Dunia's face when she got out of the car. She screwed it up and asked, "What's that smell auntie?" I had to laugh and then tried to explain it to her.

I had last seen my niece in Cuba when she was just a baby and there she was before me already a teenager. It was this really, that made me realize how fast life goes by us. It was a blessing to see how beautiful she was. She tried to be wherever I was, following me everywhere. Not that I minded; she was a pleasure to be with and a lot of mischief and fun for Sarah. Abany too was different in a way. I hadn't seen her for thirteen years. She looked almost the same and very young for her age. Now she was an adult and a well practiced mother; that made a difference.

I teased Abany that I was going to take Dunia back to Vernon with me. I envied her a little really; having a much loved child. I knew I would someday be a mother, but until then, I would just enjoy my role as 'Auntie Acuach.'

Yong was already in Brooks staying with Anyuon. When we all got together jumping up and down with unconstrained happiness, it was like my heart would explode. There was a ton of hugging and deep emotions and leaky tears. The celebration didn't let up for a whole week while we soaked in the limited time we had together.

We had a wonderful party we planned on the spot and more or less invited the whole community. Many of our friends, Canadian, Cuban or otherwise, all came. How can you even put into words the feeling; watching my family mingle with the world I knew; feeling pride, seeing everyone so glowing and happy and sharing food, enjoying the company of invited friends we'd known for years? How can I express my gratitude at how they treated my loved ones with such honour and respect? I could have died and gone to heaven right there and we all danced till the cows came home!

It was a homecoming I will never forget. Through it all I had a vision in my mind what it was going to be like when the real homecoming took place. Right then I didn't know if my heart could contain that joy. Even with just this portion of our family represented, I could feel all of us there. It almost hurt too much to imagine Mama there to see all this. I still held some hope I could have them come to Canada for a visit. Yes, I wanted more than anything to go home to my Africa, to be with my family. But it would be such a pleasure to see Mama and Baba experience even for a short while, the lives we were building toward as potential Canadians.

It was really hard to leave that gathering. There were such raw emotions in the goodbyes as all of us went off to build our lives. It was really a good experience for my family too in the manner in which they accepted Ronnie and my relationship. Of course Anyoun already knew and liked Ronnie, and that helped. Ronnie was a real prince through the whole affair. He spent a lot of time with me and Dunia as well. I had been a little nervous of that and it turned out I had nothing to worry about. All too soon the time came to drive back to our jobs and our responsibilities.

I'd come back from Brooks and one day I went to a gas station to vacuum out Echo. I was pulling in and there was a beautiful chocolate

285

woman doing the same on the other side of the Island. It was a little unusual in Vernon at that time as one didn't see a lot of Black people kicking about doing everyday things. So I just walked right up and got friendly. This beautiful woman, Anne, would become in a very short period of time like a sister to me. It was as if we passed right by the becoming friends part and joined sister hearts. She became my hiking partner, as she just loved to walk in the wilds. All my other Sudanese friends were freaking out, worried that the bears would get me out there in the wilds. They're deathly afraid of the idea of bears.

Anne was good for me. She was a person outside my small community circle, and I could talk to her about anything. I learned Anne was from Kenya. With my family there, I felt we held a lot in common. Anne is very educated and she was really supportive in that as well, helping me to improve my English. For me, Anne was my touch stone, my agent of change. Her attitude was all things are possible if we try hard for our goals and stay positive. There was a whole new avenue of maturity opening up for me.

There are people in any community who have the attitude that things are impossible. I hate to say it, but I think everyone has friends like that and we all fill different roles for one another. I was growing in many ways. For example, I had always gone out of my way for my friends. I just couldn't do enough for them. Anne helped me realize that I didn't have to. "Why do all these things for people Sarah?" she asked. "You are not helping them; they need to learn to do things for themselves." She is very perceptive and knows about how to deal with these ideas. I began to see that in some ways people were taking advantage of a good thing. When I started to back away from them, I realized I was a much happier person. I guess we all have to learn this kind of lesson the hard way. I began to separate some of my world from people and not try to be everything to everyone. I needed time to be me, to do things for myself. Anne taught me this.

There were a number of things about my life I hadn't shared with many people. One day I was invited by Anne and her husband Julius to come to their home for lunch. We got to talking about life and where we were from. I shared a little about my experiences in Cuba and they asked questions. They both were quite interested in my story and brought more and more out of me. I began to actually get emotional and started to cry without feeling embarrassed really. I felt as if I was with family and they were very understanding and supportive.

In time I learned Julius was a writer. With my always sharing my world with Anne, she suggested I should think of writing it all down and make a book of all that had happened to me. I thought about it and it seemed something I should do. Knowing that Julius was a writer, I asked one day if he would help me do this. He seemed interested in helping and said I should try. I was really nervous about how I could do this with my broken English. I could do it in Spanish and thought someone could then translate it. Julius thought that a good idea as well, although he said if I did it that way he wouldn't be able to ghost write for me. He said to write the book that way would be a lot of work. Julius sat me down and told me not to worry, just start by writing down in notes whatever you can remember of those events and that time. The seed had been planted; I just never really got to watering it.

After Julius told me to remember the events of my life, I began to dig around in my memories. I discovered some were really very hard to live through again. Still, they were a part of my world and it wasn't getting easier to talk about them.

I'd become familiar with going to Immigration Canada for English classes and to get help for things I didn't understand: making resumes, writing important letters and such things. I had made friends with some of the workers and sometimes I stopped by for a visit and to say hello. They knew about some of my experiences, my travels and how I'd got around in the world of the displaced.

I got a call from them one day asking if I might be interested in coming to their offices to talk to some students from Fulton Jr. High School. There would be four others who had been asked; five, if I agree. I thought sure why not, and a week later there we were in front of a whole room full of teenagers about the age of Dunia. I was nervous when it came to my turn. I thought of Dunia and that I was telling her these things. Imagining just one little girl I really loved, rather than twenty young people all staring at me waiting to start, seemed to help. I was a little slow to start because I was deciding what part of my world to begin with. Basically immigration had told me they wanted to know how I came to Canada. It was a pretty wide topic.

I introduced myself, said I was born in Sudan, and said because of the civil war we had to run away to Ethiopia. I didn't go into any great detail, but a lot of memories were rolling through my mind. I'd got to Cuba and going to school there and my parents leaving to go back to Africa. It was here they began holding up their hands and asking really tough questions. They wanted to know more about why my parents had to leave me in Cuba. How long had it been since I had seen them? I said it had been eighteen years.

There were a lot of very wide eyes in that room. It was as if they couldn't get their heads around the idea. They asked when I was going to go and see them. I was getting really choked up and was trying to hold back the flood gates. God, I didn't want to start bawling in front of this group of children. I got a little stronger and wiped tears away thinking I must answer this. I gave them the truth. I said I couldn't afford to. I worked at the Superstore for minimum wage. I was sending as much money as I could back to my family in Kenya to help support them. I looked across the room at a sad sea of unbelieving faces. I had been the last to speak to them and I couldn't take it anymore. I ran out of the room, heading for the safety of my Echo.

No one understood me like my car. It knew everything about me and never complained. It was always an accepting comfort, my little red race car. That was where I finally broke down into wailing sobs of 'that was horrible!' Those thoughts of eighteen years of no Mama were too much. It was seeing Mama's sad face before me that had me running for the door. Sitting there behind the steering wheel, I felt raw and exposed, out in public crying in front of children. Now I was in my car where any passerby could see my deepest pain. It was with an almost an angry reaction that I turned the key to start up Echo to get me out of there and home. I had an overwhelming panic seething through my reality.

I started backing out with a veil of tears fogging my vision to a blur, actually not able to see where I was going at all. A man on my right side of the car was waving at me hard and saying something, pointing at Echo. This caught my attention and stopped me backing further into the parking lot. I rolled down my window to find out what he was yelling about. "Your tire, your tire is flat," he said, pointing at my front passenger side tire. It took a second for this to sink in as this was exactly what I didn't want, someone witnessing the tears that damn it, wouldn't stop!

I got out and went around the car to have a look. 'Yep, flat as a pancake!' I turned to the man and said I wasn't far from home; I'd just go as it was. The man was shaking his head and telling me '*I couldn't do that.*' I started feeling a burn of, '*oh yes I can!*' Imagine him telling me what I can and can't do. I wasn't thinking very straight at that point. I just wanted out of there and to go home and hide.

He was a very convincing man. "No no, I have BCAA Auto Insurance." He flipped open a cell phone and called for a tow truck. Well what do you say to that, but thank you.

Meanwhile, there were faces sticking out of Immigration's windows, peering out at the developing scene; my worst nightmare coming to light. I was totally exposed to all of it now, standing beside my poor hurt Echo. I was trying to win a losing battle with water rolling down the embarrassed burning cheeks and runny nose of sniveling poor Sarah. The nice helpful stranger gave me an understanding smile and walked away as Monica from Immigration came out the door. He went up to her to say he was in a hurry and gave Monica his BCAA card to give to the tow truck guy when it was all fixed. What a production this was all becoming. I didn't know what to feel now.

I went to Monica and stood around leaking stupid tears, feeling like what? Thankful I guess, that so many people cared. I think Monica understood what I was going through and didn't say too much. She stood beside me, a pillar of her concern to lean against. It actually didn't take very long and poor Echo was all better. I didn't wait around for any of the wrap up either. I just jumped in and took off. I was relieved it was all over and done with. I didn't live far from there and had a little time to thank God I didn't drive any further. In the state I was in I probably would have gotten in an accident.

I did have time to come up with a total determination. I was going home. Yes right then I was on my way to our apartment. Eighteen years was just too damn long; I was going to go home to Africa! I had no idea how, but it didn't matter. I just had to see Mama. That was it. This was the bottom line and I'd accept nothing less than this. I parked Echo and was walking up to the door just as Ronnie was coming up the stairs from work. I opened the door and he at first smiled at me then look quizzical as he passed into the apartment. "What's the matter Sarah?" he asked. He could tell I'd been crying.

I stood in the doorway with my hands on my hips, staring him right in his by now cringing eyes. They were reflecting his thoughts, '*oh oh, what's this about?*' He could see I was obviously having a bad day. I stated a simple fact; "Ronnie, I'm going to Africa!"

His eyes went all wide and didn't say anything right away thinking hard. Then he blurted out with conviction, "Sarah, I'm not moving to Africa!" He explained himself, "I really like Vernon." I couldn't help it with that tortured look on his face my Ronnie had made his hard choice right there at the door. I just fell down laughing, it was just the release I needed.

To Ronnie's relief I explained I wouldn't be leaving today, or even forever. I told him what had happened and that I just need to see my family in person and not just hear them on the phone. It had been too many years to have this need eating me away little by little. After I told him I had no idea how I was going to do it, he said he would help. He knew how much it meant to me. He too at times missed his Nova Scotia, even though his parents now lived in Saskatchewan. He was always talking about someday going home. He was very comforting and we spent a really nice evening together talking through the details of my now definite plan.

For some time I'd been having difficulty shutting off my mind and going to sleep. There was a feeling building in me that knew changes were coming. More and more I could actually see myself going home. This event with the children had planted that vision firmly in my heart. The reality was different. I was still doing part time work and I felt hope sometimes slip away. I wondered just how the funds would come to allow this wonder to really take place. Fall came and went and the seasons changed, but many things remained the same. Though I love the fall and the changing of the leaves, I always get a little nervous as North winds start to blow and the trees become bare and spindly with no color but gray.

It hadn't taken me long to get involved in the excitement of Canadian holidays with the year's passing. I really love Halloween season even though I didn't get to scare anyone to death that year. Which was rather disappointing. Winter, the season I love to hate, came of course. The one thing I look forward to in that season is turkey. Oh do I love white meat and gravy. Christmas is alright too. Ronnie and I liked to drive around Vernon and check out the houses all dressed up in wonderful lights and decorations. In the past we had gone to Ronnie's parents for Christmas in Saskatchewan. It was a long drive for a short time spent with Ronnie's relations, but it was truly worth it. I felt a really warm sense of family there. Ronnie's family came to our Christmas too in Vernon the year before this one.

That year our Christmas was a little sparse as money was tight. We were saving what little we could for my Africa dream. Of course New Years followed right along in that same week and 2007 opened its doors to whatever might come. No one had to ask me that year what my New Year's resolution would be. They all knew as I talked about it all the time. It still seemed a long way down some impossible road with the monies we managed to save so little. That winter seemed to go on forever.

As spring came knocking on the door, I found a whole new energy that often comes with that freshness, one you can actually smell in the air. The trees are budding and soon the leaves will all burst forth. The tulips are usually some of the first to push their way to the heavens. For me and Anne it was a time to meet and go running, finally able to get out and feel the warmth of the happy sun on our faces.

I got up one morning with a kind of startling thought; making breakfast for Ronnie and me. It was a weekend and we didn't have to be anywhere. I started to run though my years of Canadian memories and Wow, realized nine years had gone by. It was a light-bulb moment to realize that as an immigrant, I only had to wait three years to apply for Canadian Citizenship.

I was past that qualification and then some.

Then I thought of the many times I had racked my brain trying to plan for this trip home. It had been two years since getting the exciting news over the phone from Baba of South Sudanese independence. There was a day for memory. It was for us Sudanese true history in the making. Even before the actual event was to take place, Baba couldn't wait. He was fair to bursting there in the family's Nairobi home. It took a few minutes for me to understand what he was saying because of the speed he was explaining it in Dinka. He started with his ideals and the range and scope of the aims and purposes of the Sudanese Peoples Liberation Movement. He talked about them in the context of his writing his book. He said his book's themes were all coming true.

I was rather puzzled as he was so emotional. He went into his love and relationship with Dr. John Garang and the long struggle with his lifelong goal to have an independent Sudan. It was a very lengthy phone call. I spent a lot of it just listening to the History of Freedom. I heard how the tribes of Sudan could now finally come to a unity of purpose, Baba's greatest hope. This had been a holistic representation of my father's entire life. Given to his daughter. Over the phone. My heart was flipping around in my chest. I had never really had Baba speak with me quite this way. I learned how important John Garang was to all of the peoples of Sudan.

Baba was almost in tears when he spoke of what was coming in the Naivasha Agreement in January of that year. His excitement was in full bloom as he stated to me authoritatively, "Peace is coming Acuach Cor, my daughter. The SPLM is to sign this agreement with the Government of Sudan!" His voice cracked with emotion and I could feel the hot tears streaming down his face as he choked out with passion, "we are going home, Sarah!" Those given words shifted my whole reality completely. It was another of those moments that I wanted to run right out and buy the ticket to Africa and couldn't, and had to suffer through those frustrations all over again. It was still just not time.

How many of those calls I experienced, I could not count. One was when the news came that the family was leaving Nairobi and moving back to BorTown, twenty-three years after the day we ran into the madness. Baba and Mama announced they would be taking the family back to its roots...

BorTown.

Then I heard Baba's heart being pulled from his chest when he phoned with the news of the death in a helicopter crash of John Garang, our former rebel leader; how it was such a blow to our family and all the people of Sudan after being sworn in as vice president just three weeks before. His arrival in Khartoum on July 8, 2005 to take the vice president's post had brought millions of former enemies, southerners and northerners, into the streets in celebration.

He was sworn in July 9 was now second only to President Omar el-Bashir. Baba felt El-Bashir clearly saw Garang as an important partner in sealing the peace. He would ensure the south did not secede and help to repair Sudan's international reputation. The Sudanese state media went from describing John Garang in the darkest of terms to respectfully calling him "Dr. Garang" after the peace deal was struck.

Baba was afraid this was going to spoil all they had worked for because el-Bashir and Garang were planning to set up a power-sharing government. It would have meant elevating Garang's rebel troops to an equal status with the Sudanese military. It would have opened a new chapter of peace and given a chance to resolve other bloody conflicts in Sudan, including the humanitarian crisis in the region of Darfur. Garang was seen as a great hope for peace in Darfur. This, more than anything, concerned Baba greatly. He feared the war would once more escalate.

It was a sad chapter in our lives. For me it was time spent learning more of the father I had missed those many years in Cuba. It was a chance for me to feel what his views really where as an adult, not as a child so enamored with her Baba. I was getting to understand my father and the history of my homeland over the phone, with the always present time restraints of the phone card. That weekend my heart wanted more than anything to call home and tell them I was coming. I resisted the temptation.

I knew it was too soon. I wanted to have definite confirmations for them, not just wings of hope and longed for wishful dreams.

That one lone Sunday I put it all in order, starting with Sarah's plan. I began the to-do list! The 'I'm goings,' one by one. The more I spoke with my friends of my plans as a positive fact, the more and faster came the winds of change. In the next available period, I set out what was needed and received my Canadian citizenship. What a feeling! I woke the next day not really feeling very much different. I was ever still only Sarah, this Acuach Cor, a Dinka child of Africa. But really this step was a much larger deal. As a Canadian with full rights and privileges, I applied for my Canadian passport. Acuach Cor needed a passport to truly leave Canada protected by her Canadian government in Sudan.

To go back to the future; back to *BorTown*.

One by one, things began to fall into place. One of them was a real shock right out of the blue. I got a call to go to work at a job I didn't even remember applying for. There was this voice asking when I could come in and receive my personal interview. Somehow I knew, just by my feeling, I already had the job. And my feelings were right! I went from preparing human food from cows to a dog food plant, Darford Industries. Best of all, it was full time. Superstore didn't mind letting me go. They even said if I ever needed a job, "just come on back, Sarah!" That was a stamp of approval for my resume, and a good referral contact with Superstore Personnel.

My goals were all racking right up! It was just like eight ball pool going down one ball at a time. Next was research for the best possible pre-booked flight. It would be a tricky bank balancing act as my go to funds grew to not reveal anything and still send my family a share of support back to Africa. That in itself was a pile of computer and phone work and advice from many helpful friends like Anne. Her positive support was always there as was Julius's constant advice through Anne on the best times and ways to book the ticket, and where. I found I could make payments with a floating date in order to qualify for the time needed before departure.

Then a strange and touching thing happened, one I never expected.

Allan Gee, the teacher who brought the students from Fulton High, called and asked me out for coffee. I was a little surprised. This is a man I had met only once and had bawled my eyes out in front of his whole class. Well I didn't really think too hard on it and said, "Yes, alright, where?" There was a neat Latin plaza type of coffee house called El Portillo (the portal) and indeed, there he was waiting.

As I walked across the room I had a fair idea what he wanted to talk about. I thought the students might want me to come back to their class and share more about my life experiences. I got a nice big mug of hot tea and just carried right in to telling him more of my life in war time. His eyes went very round in places as I talked about bloody boiling rivers of rolling crocodiles. Allan had young children and he was stupefied really, trying to imagine his children going through that at the same age. And, yes, Allan did want me to speak again to his class.

Then this just blew me right out of the river. He said his class had talked it over, and worked it out with their parents, and wanted to pay for my ticket to fly home! I had to pick my mouth up off the floor. Apparently they were part of a school program called Global Ed that helped people in third world countries like Nicaragua. They had really been bothered by how long I'd gone without seeing my family. This wonderful gesture I had to turn down. I explained to Allan it was a wonderful thing for them to do, and as they had already put aside these funds, I suggested someone else might need it more than me. I said I had to do this on my own and hoped they could understand that. Allan was very understanding and said he would explain it to them.

Driving home it was sinking in; the door of opportunity was wide open. It was hard to comprehend this type of kindness from teenagers. I remembered how mature some of their questions were and how they really did care about what was going on in the world. Not that they would have found out easily. Things very important to me and my country were taking place, but I had hardly seen any reports on the news. When John Garang was killed, I watched the news for a few days thinking I would see something of this mentioned. It wasn't. That's why I think my story is important. Many people have no idea what took place in my country for those twenty-three years. There are now estimates that up to three million Sudanese were killed in the civil war. Many of those killed weren't soldiers, but village People, woman and children left in mass graves, or left to starve to death by the thousands.

Even the people who made it to the refugee camps weren't safe from disease and starvation. It wasn't just the lack of food, but of spirit. A child deprived, or as I was, displaced, will carry scars for the rest of their lives. So, in many ways, this writing of 'My Resilience' is an example, one life out of millions, recounted in detail. In writing it, I wanted to include all my friends and people like these children, so gracious in their offer to help. I had so many friends and helpers in my planning this journey, that in the end I simply ran out of chapters to put them in.

In this, the final push to bring the story home, I had to cut a lot! So I make this statement now, as my story reaches the turning point in 2008. All of the people I had to leave out, if you read my book and wonder why I haven't mentioned you, that is the reason. I will always remember each and every one of you. I think of my extended family of brothers and sisters all the time. My friends and family I carry always in my heart. In so many ways, despite all the difficulties, I've had a blessed life. It's been the support of friends that has got me through it.

To all of you, thank you. With all my love, Sarah.

The time of departure was set for April 12 and the winter was shedding its white burden. The seasons and the counting of years are all in the chapters above. The numbered chapters end here. It is in the end, as it was in the beginning, ever about going home, my memories on an airplane. It's impossible to cover all this in one flight, or one book. These pages will come to a close and one part of my story will be told. Another path will unfold another time.

The answers to questions and dreams, of years piled upon years, were now close to being revealed to me. I could feel it inside me; answers to endless questions in me that ran like a deep running river, starting from the time I stood in my yard, waiting for the rain to come to play mud games, a little girl skipping off happily to school and trusted teachers, and instead...

War came to my backyard.

There were these horrid things I'd seen and had never had the opportunity to sit at Baba's knee and tell him. He didn't know his daughter Acuach Cor had witnessed the tragedies of war without a real understanding of why. I thanked God it was much less than most of my people.

I realized it was a blessing to have been displaced. What an opportunity had been provided in my Cuba. Only six-hundred of us had been brought out, these Lost Children of Sudan, while a whole country suffered so much. They got away so few. I was one of them...

Sarah Gabriel, with a little girl, Acuach Cor, still trapped inside, needing healing.

I came to realize I have a debt to my country that somehow must be repaid. This ideal of coming home to a new Sudan burns bright. We few were given the chance for an education, taken out of war torn ignorance, to make a difference. We are doctors, engineers, agricultural scientists, political analysts, diplomats. Our brain trust is what we owe. What I can offer are the pages of my life as Acuach Cor, a writer, a dreamer, a Dinka child of Africa.

Some of these dreams are so vague I wake to keep them and they run away like the gazelles across the plain. There is one I will always remember. I am on the plain and there are many tiny lions chasing me. I am running and trying my best to fight them off. I am so afraid. It seems as if I am fighting for my very life.

"*Whoa, whoa Sarah. Sarah wake up!*" Ronnie went flying off the bed as I was trying to beat him to death. Man, what that one was about who knows, but Ronnie took the brunt of it.

Other times it's the falling down place and all those faces who had lost hope and the face of death. Was that an acceptance for them? Were they living souls dead already? The worst and most dreadful was the disfigured face of death and all the ugliness of human cruelty it contained. To think of the dishonor of having left this peasant so defiled. I had my fears still about this coming journey. Whatever it entailed, if I could meet this face of death and not lose my mind I could face anything! Still, whatever it was the falling people had run through, I had yet to find an answer to that. Or at least, I had yet to find an answer that satisfied me as a human being.

I felt that if someday I found the answer, that spectre could no longer hang there before my sight. It would no longer haunt me, stalk my dreams, and turn into nightmares with all its many masks. I had no meaning for it. These thoughts and feelings became stronger as I approached April 12. This date was the marker of a crossroad where I hoped to find the purpose, the source of meaning of my existence. it would make firm my values.

I knew it would be a deep revelation and a moving experience, so keeping things in perspective was work. I moved through my days, counting them down and doing the best I could, for my family, my friends and the company I was working for. One couldn't have asked for better people to work for. It wasn't rocket science, but a lot of daily doggy biscuits. Danford Industries was one of the better paying companies in Vernon and it was a fair wage for the basically simple jobs I had to do.

The work environment was what made working there so worthwhile. It was extremely well organized and there were a lot of incentives from management to improve the jobs we were doing. I waited the better part of nine months before I asked for time off to take my trip home. After I got hired, the President of the Company, Darcy Bomford, who was in fact the owner of Darford Industries, as was his way, came by to greet his new employees. I was immediately impressed by how he carried on his business, so polite and professional. He put me at ease right away and made me feel welcome and a valuable resource to the business he operated. I figured out later how they came up with the name of their family operated company, combining the first part of his name Dar-cy and the last of Bom-ford to end up with Darford Industries doggie biscuits producers.

He wasn't without a sense of humour either and fun to work for. If things weren't moving fast enough for him on the floor, Darcy would leave his office and chip in. We knew if Darcy was on the floor packing around boxes it was time to hustle, to pick up the pace. In the end, again, they liked me because Sarah set the pace. It didn't take long for the plant manager to notice and my supervisor was a great individual. The people who worked there were all happy and smiles coming to work or heading for the lunch room for social hour. Lunch was more of a mix and mingle with people talking about things like their day at the beach with their kids.

I was always interested in my friend's children; how are they, were they happy, did they have a good picnic at the lake? As the year moved toward that winter of 2007, I was getting absolutely everything I'd ever asked for. We had been talking for some time, Ronnie and I, about getting out of apartment life. I was almost giggling to myself, thinking of all these wonderful things taking place for me. I picked up the paper and thought, 'OK *Universe, how about a house?*' It was like the ad popped right out at me! In all the time I'd spent in Vernon, I liked the Coldstream area the best. It's right by Kalamalka Lake, at the beach! Life is a beach, and you better believe it. When I was out there lying on my blanket in the hot sand, it wasn't a stretch to close my eyes and be in Havana!

The ad was for a two bedroom older house. It was gargantuan; at least it felt like that to me at first. I fell in love with the yard before I'd even climbed out of Echo. I was totally wowed. I walked up to the door and could already see myself answering the door from the other side. This house had Sarah written all over it. And, I could swear it was beginning to talk to me... "fix me up, fix me fix me up . . . pleeease!

So yep, yep, I promised the house I would. The owners of the house lived close by (I didn't even have an appointment to view the house) and the lady and her husband, who were out in their yard, saw me walking around their property. "Excuse me", the lady called over, "is there something I can help you with?" I said, "Yes, I'm looking to rent this house. Do you know how I could reach the owner?" The woman smiled and replied, "Well little lady that would be me, can I show you the inside?"

What could I say to that, but thank you!

This Old House certainly did have its rough edges. It was obvious some of its renters hadn't taken care of what was really a grand sort of place. It had a family feeling of histories past. I could well imagine the sound of children playing in the yard and their laughter, carried on the wind, or little feet running up and down its once happy halls.

I had already started on a list in my mind of repairs and where I'd start the needed saviour upgrades. In the midst of the tour our would-be landlord stopped and announced there had been a lot of interest in the house already. She said they had a long list of renters to choose from. "So little lady," she looked at me with a sharp calculating eye. "Tell me why you feel I should rent this house to you?" I could see a house such as this would have a lot of renter interest. I didn't even hesitate and it just all came out in a stream. To tell you the truth, to this day I couldn't tell you what I actually said. I just stayed positive, gave her Ronnie and my work history, people she could phone for references and stuff like that. I thanked her, gave her my number and got into Echo (liking his new private driveway) and left for home to tell Ronnie.

A week later the Landlady phoned to say she had chosen Ronnie and me and if we dropped off the damage deposit, we could start moving in right away. That day I was out there in Coldstream driving back to Vernon past the beach. I knew I'd be living there and could see myself walking the few blocks to the beach. I told Ronnie about it. "You just wait and see Ronnie. It's our new home, I can feel it!" He agreed and we up and moved right in! The work plan on restoring this poor old place, was like a jolt of energy for all of us. Our whole group of friends got involved and pitched in with enthusiasm.

With the moving in and all, it took some time to get ourselves settled. I lay in bed at night as our stuff got moved over and dreamt of all the stuff I needed for the fix up job. With Anne I got the to-do list all organized and This Old House got attacked. Things got ripped out that were all old and worn and went on the growing pile in the yard that was no longer part of my home. The carpet was in really sad shape and it all came out as we got ready for repairs and painting. Julius was a great help too and he was busy cleaning and repairing walls and putting a new wood floor in the living room.

On Ronnie's days off, he was all about the yard work and I lost him for some weekends in a row. James and Chino had the first go-round at the overgrown jungle in the yard. We got out the machetes and all our orchard experience came into play. That all got whacked down in a day making more piles everywhere. Somewhere we got a truck and it was all taken to the dump.

The neighbourhood at first seemed kind of standoffish. I'd wave at them when they came home and they wouldn't wave back. I hate that feeling; your hand is half way up in the air and umm, OK, you have to move along with your world. As work progressed and the paint, brush and rollers flew, our landlady would be in her yard watching with a big smile. It didn't take long for her to wave hello and the neighbourhood caught up as our happy house began to get its warm glow back. To my good fortune, I learned while doing this my Sister Anne was actually an interior decorator. Umm, that universe was truly working overtime on details. Again I had that bubbly giggley feeling. In such a short time Canada was becoming a wonder. And Vernon, my paradise was at the end of the road.

It was a long drive, but now things were about to fly. Summer was hot as is always the Okanagan, and I was on my way those few blocks to the beach. I never try to tan, don't need one. People already have a hard time seeing me at night. Instead, I'd watch all those people lying out there getting baked to lobster red. I didn't get it really. I love the hot sand, but from the shade of the big trees that line Kal beach. What really made my beach time so precious was watching the children and how they love the water, the sounds of their happiness, and even their unhappiness, when they're by themselves. There is always a lot going on in summer beach life. And, let's not leave out all those beautiful guys out there.

Scoping all us beautiful girly girls. Well, that makes the world go round doesn't it!

And spring babies come to the hospital, as wedding bells are ringing. Me Sarah, I had a growing ache as I would so love to have my own babies. I had my home now and it was no roundhouse of sticks. This was a marker on that road, my journey. Meanwhile there were new and different emotions to experience as my other plans got all the more real, especially getting the flight plans and tickets arranged for that go fly date.

Another Christmas was marked off the calendar. A short week passed and that calendar was taken down and thrown away. Another year was done. I moved along and lived with the snowflakes till spring. Actually it was Ronnie who came up with the rest of what was needed and said we should book the flight now. One more month and I would be away. My emotions ran rampant.

I was in the almost runaway rush of real preparations, packing bags, deciding which clothes would actually wind up in the suitcases. The phone rang, and rang. Ronnie, I remembered, wasn't home so I answered rather breathlessly. I still had style and clothes on the brain and the number on the phone didn't look familiar. It was the Government of Canada? I took a deep breath; it was my C.F.I.A. Meat inspector position. I was hired and they were asking me to move to Kamloops. I was processing this and the man on the other end finished and waited for my acceptance. I was in a total quandary. I asked when the position needed filling. He said right away. Here I was getting ready for the flight home and this comes up. Kamloops? No way! Like a highway waiting for a truck stop, I had just got my happy home all finished and I was going home! It took all of two seconds to turn that dream job down. There was an almost 'really?' kind of dead air on the other end. Yep, really. I said I wasn't willing to move. If a position became available in the Vernon area I would consider taking it. He kind of sputtered and agreed and that was the end of the call.

I went back to my greater concern, packing!

It was time. All the needing was done. Two days after turning down a job that would have again changed my life in Canada, my life in Canada that had such a solid feeling, I got some phone cards and called Mama. This was the big event I'd been waiting for, to tell my family within the month to pick me up at the Airport in Nairobi. I got Mama in BorTown on the second ring. "Mama, I'm coming home!" and There came a wailing dance around the kitchen, and a space in time, and tears...

I'm on the plane. It feels like my legs are breaking and I'm going to cramp.

The running up and over endless sand dunes would never end.

My greatest fear, pounding through the dunes, was that of a mouse in cat-and-mouse, the cat toying with me. I was at the very end of my endurance and couldn't face looking behind. To my doom! This lion had for some stupid reason, six legs. It was easy enough for him to be running in the sand dunes, but I felt I was running in slow motion through soup. I was going to be eaten, dragged off kicking and screaming.

'Chomp, chomp, chomp . . . *oh dear, Sarah Gabriel just gone!'*

Then came the Déjà vu dream... I ran over the dune and into Yalee, screaming and looking for Chol. I realized it was the dream I kept having over and over, but this time it wasn't the same. I couldn't find Chol anywhere and was sobbing. The Prince of the lions had got my sweet little brother Chol. Where was Grandma? Who were these people hiding in their huts, their wasted houses of sticks? Yalee didn't look right at all!

The lions were all milling around its edges, laughing at my doom. I noticed there were no fires which there should have been. I ran from hut to hut and faces, all wearing masks, were shooing me, the bringer of trouble, away. Why wouldn't they let me in, protect me?

My tribe, my people . . . what was wrong?

My shadow relatives shooed me further into the village with my growing panic. The huge shapes of dark shadows ran between the huts, just outside my vision. They had glowing red eyes smirking, "heh, heh, heh, we're going to get you Sarah... and gobble you right up!"

I was lost in this Yalee that never was, running blindly around a corner. Grandma's hut was right before me and in a running slide, I skidded right under the low arched doorway into Grandmas empty space. There was only one lamp, a gourd of water and Grandma's huge frying pan. I could feel her there with me. But when I went through the hut, none of her familiar belongings were in it. I hadn't found her, but I did find just what I needed.

A weapon!

Hearing the deep breathing huff of the Lion finding me with his nose at the door, I bent down and armed myself with the heavy cast iron monster killer, grandma's weapon, her frying pan. Now Lion man was going to be seeing stars for sure. "Bring it on!" I swayed in a fighter stance, prepared to do battle...

With the nightmare.

I expected the fierce head of the Lion to poke his head through the arch and was in mid swing with all I had. It wasn't the lion, but a Prince, a beautiful man who I was about to mash in his brains! He laughed and showed the most brilliant white teeth set in a face smooth and black as the night sky. My swing went wide somehow spun me in a full circle and I fell before him on my bum. My legs were sprawled every which way. I stared into deep dark pools of his endless soul, and saw reflected twinkling starlight.

Those eyes looked so wise.

His whole aura was shining with love and acceptance. His voice flowed out like water, "you have nothing to fear Sarah." Those startling eyes questioned, "are you thirsty? Have a drink of cool water, won't you?" He motioned a nod of majestic knowing toward the water gourd, there right between us.

I slowly, never turning from those wonder eyes, picked up the gourd and took a swallow of cool sweetness like the nectar of the gods. It spread through me and behind me and out the door to the sky and the galaxies that swooned and sighed in patterns of wheels.

They were patterns that shifted and changed as the eons passed over my Africa.

I was now looking into a room. I opened a familiar door and heard a child softly humming the lion song in a desert tent built in a familiar closet. Acuach Cor and I joined her in my fantasy kingdom in the mansion of Addis Ababa, the city of Fathers. I was dressed as a princess in Mama's best housecoat wearing a crown of tinfoil.

Having tea . . .with Baba.

Chol was bugging me and shaking my shoulder for some reason. I didn't want to leave for the airport. I was thinking how could I leave behind my Africa? I was about to turn to him almost angrily. No, never could I do this thing; leave my Prince, my childhood friend and faithful companion. Always he was there having tea with us at play.

Chol was going to really hear a mouthful from me with this stupid shaking.

"Sarah, Sarah you have to wake up now!"

Chol was a woman in a blue British Airways uniform? Man, I was shaking my head and stopped myself from screaming at her. I realized at some point all my thoughts and fears had dropped off into an exhausted dream. It was now gracefully running its way off into the plains. I hung on to it, trying to keep part of the vision that had my heart madly thumping. I could see a grand lion chase a gazelle into the sun shining though my window. Then it faded. 'Ding, ding, ding' went the seat belt signs lighting up and passengers all around me staring with smiles. 'Why' were we there, I wondered?

"Good morning passengers of flight 435 London to Nairobi." It was the smooth voice of the captain. "We are currently at an altitude of 10,000 feet at 5:25 AM and will be landing at our destination in approximately five minutes. Thank you for flying British Airways." Just as that was registering with a shiver, Wanda, my stewardess, placed an electrifying hand on my shoulder. I looked up to see her, my eyes tearing. "I'm so happy for you Sarah!" she said into my growing confusion. All this was happening all at once. My dream had made me gritty with exhaustion, or had my exhaustion made my dream like reality? An older woman next to me nodded and smiled with real warmth. It seemed all the people around me held some of this afterglow.

Flip, flop, goes my heart and I turned to the window and wiped my eyes. I saw above a canopy of brilliant deep blue, the endless African sky. Below the cushion of fluffy white pillows, below my dreams, the clouds parted and the confusion went away. My carriage was falling back down out of those clouds into my Africa for real. The thoughts of my past were no longer there. The wheels touched down and I was on the ground, I was at the end of my beginning. I was no longer running away . . .

I was about to walk the long and winding road.

Home.

Deplaning, and all that entails, was now familiar to me after loading and unloading at several global Airports. It's all the same; hurry, hurry, hurry, yep, yep, yep and a whole lot of necessary things that give international travelers headaches. I got my carry on out of the overhead bin and pushed and shoved in a stampede to get out of the damn plane you've been stuck in for hours and hours. What can I say, it's a nightmare. I reached the open door and my Wanda life support stewardess, giving her robotic bye byes to passengers, stopped that deal and gave me a hug. I loved it, but people behind were all annoyed that the line-up had stalled.

I arrive at the open door and again stopped the line as I stood at the top of the traveling stair platform now attached to the plane and breathed in slowly. I was taking in all of Africa, in that heart beat, till moans of complaint pushed me down the stairs, across the tarmac and into Jomo Kenyatta Airport's International terminal. I could have just stood out there a while, but like everyone else, found myself moving on. I was moving on to the real deal of the custom agents. These are always really serious folks. There's no joking with these people, I'd tried and failed. The only time they get excited is when they find something wrong. Then watch those folks get into gear. Busting bad guys, they live for that moment to kill the boredom of their job. I don't try to be cute, clear right away and I'm off.

I'm off on the lookout for the luggage routine. There's always the fear it won't be on that carousel ... then what? It would be more airport madness to contend with. There were lineups for every damn thing, but you have to get it all done. I was getting my passport stamped and paying for the visitor's visa. Then I had to run around exchanging currency. I had changed over a couple of travelers checks to cover getting out with my family and the travel into my Africa. I had one more line up to go through and I heard, "*Sarah?*" I turned thinking there are a lot of Sarah's in the world. " *Hi, over here.*" I looked about as it was a familiar voice and found the person it belonged to smile. We were really only a line up away. There stood James my Kenyan friend from Heathrow. We waved and he said he'd find me when we got our stuff done and maybe have a tea.

It didn't turn out that way. That stupid line up was being sent to another for some reason I don't remember. So James decided to chat with me while we waited. It was a nice between type event for me. He wanted to know how I was feeling and if I was still concerned about political things in Kenya going south. At that point, no. I was OK with it. My mind was set on getting this part done, collecting my luggage and finding my family.

James told me a small story about his flight. He said he'd mostly slept through, except when he was woken by screaming! My eyes went a little wide to recall just why I'd been freaking out. Maybe I was just a tad embarrassed to hear I'd woken up the whole plane. He said he had wanted to come and find what was wrong, but the person beside him was asleep and sprawled all over so he couldn't get out of his seat. He looked down the aisle and saw Wanda was already there and whispering to me and how it was settling down to no problems. He figured it was a nightmare, which was the truth, so he and everyone settled down and promptly fell back to sleep.

It was nice, I thought, that James had gone out of his way to seek me out and wish me well on my trip home to see my family. I remembered how much I'd shared with James and realized he knew quite a lot about why I'd come back to Africa. He even came along as I claimed my baggage and began hustling hauling it off in search of Chol. I knew he'd be the only one I'd have a hope of recognizing. I even pulled out his picture and showed it to James. I was standing there, showing him my family, and out of the corner of my eye, I saw Chol and he saw me. At the same time!

I left James there with my pictures and flew to my little brother's arms.

No words can describe that first contact of my heart's desire, the electric shock that permeated my whole being, the flow that came from pure spirit. I could only tightly hang on as the dam broke right there in the airport terminal and the world left me.

Only Chol...

It was a timeless experience. All too soon that world blended back to reality of the greetings of the relatives present. James had moved his way to the fringe of the group with my pictures in hand. He was smiling a fuzzy warmth to witness my reunion. Then it came his turn to meet them all before we were off to locate a taxi.

Chol already had a taxi that had brought them there not fifteen minutes before. We got all my luggage into the trunk and I gave James a fond farewell hug and he wished me well. I looked as we pulled away and James was standing there, still waving, with his beautiful Afro smile brilliant like the overhead sun shining into the back window. I turned in my seat excitedly to see where my journey would take me. First there were a maze of freeways and then we made our way into the warren of what is the ancient city of Nairobi. As we got off the highway, I really wanted to see it all. I couldn't get enough of it. My head was snapping to and fro to see everything passing outside the windows. Even Chol and relatives were laughing with me, pointing things out and enjoying my enthusiasm over what they see every day. Chol was right beside me. I noticed he was studying me, soaking me up and with such love there in his eyes. They were saying, "*yes, this is my sister, my big sister Acuach Cor!*"

We turned a corner and, there at that corner, was a really large church and across from it, an empty deserted school yard. I wondered, 'where are the children?' The answer was not what I had wanted to hear. It was as if the Taxi had hit slow motion mode as I saw a row of burnt out wrecks that seemed to be smashed into the corner of the school. It was as if a bomb blast had lifted them up and tossed them into this twisted wreckage. A feeling of horror instantly rose within me. I had a vision of running to the truck in BorTown again past vehicles just like this. I saw them lifted, twisting through the air in flames as machine gun fire killed my friends neighbors and relatives. I saw people fall down in my streets and die in spreading pools of blood. I screamed in a panic, "*Oh my God Chol, what's happening here?*"

Chol's eyes were now all wide in a kind of puzzled shock. "It was an attack this morning Sarah." I interrupted what he's saying. "*Oh God, oh God Chol the children... were they?*" I couldn't finish the thought. Chol patted my knee, comforting me with sad eyes. I was already dreading to hear the worst. "No Sarah, no one was seriously injured. It was thankfully before the children arrived at school!"

This was my worst fear and what I had been watching on the news in Heathrow. Now here I was right in the middle of all this, all over again. As it had started, it was ending. Had I come back to this place only to die? Chol spoke rather quickly, seeing how I was reacting to this. It was a political group not happy with the government and the result of the recent elections. He assure me that yes, we had to go through this part of the city to get to the Komarock district where we were going. Then I remembered what James had told me about in London as well. You could avoid all this stuff if you knew what areas to stay out of. This area couldn't be avoided. Chol assured me the taxi driver was a friend and knew all the roads that were safe.

I didn't relax for some blocks after this view of what, to me, was war, before I began to feel a little better. I was reminded of the brave driver who had gotten us out of BorTown by knowing the back-roads to safety. For some blocks I again saw us bouncing around in the back of that small truck being punished by passing whipping branches. I remembered wondering what had just happened back there. Were we being punished for some reason? *All these feelings rushed back to the forefront of my remembering and imagination. I'd seen those wrecked cars. I could almost see children turning through the air screaming like little Raggedy Anne dolls to die into horror before me.*

Chol put his arm around me and even in the growing heat of the day, I felt cold and was shivering badly. I could see how my brother's eyes reflected his real concern for me. Later, talking with Chol, I realized he'd been so young when all that happened to us, he didn't have the same vivid memory of the details. Achol, my sister in-law and Deng Did's wife, who had come with us, realized what I was thinking and started to set my mind at ease. She pointed to groups of children now out and about playing. Then, as we came to narrower and older streets, Achol pointed, "look Sarah, here's our market place where we shop daily!"

It was all a bustle and very colorful. Some of the women were wearing dresses that were a riot of different colours and patterns, but most were like anyone anywhere wearing designer jeans. It reminded me a lot of similar markets all over Cuba. They had rice and beans and it was the same at that market. The whole third world it seemed survived on rice and beans, even when it didn't have to.

We got to a small house. It was very neat and tidy inside. Achol began to introduce me to half the planet I was related to. This crowd of relatives was there almost every day of the five days of my stay there. Of course for me, the best part was always the children. They were happy too to find out Auntie Acuach Cor was really pretty goofy and a lot of fun to play with. I could think up a hundred games a day to entertain them with. I just loved to kiss them all up, whether they liked it or not. They got used to it and loved me even more whenever I went to the market and came back with treats for them. I had brought gifts for them from Canada as well and, Wow, they would run right off to show the whole neighbourhood what rich Auntie had brought them from that foreign land.

Chol, it turned out, didn't live with Achol. He lived at my step mother's house a few blocks away. Baba had provided both of these small family homes in Nairobi. After the peace agreement in 2005, Mama and Baba had moved to a property in BorTown that was promised to Chol. This is what I ached for and couldn't wait to see. BorTown was an ever present vibration, my birthright, like a thirst that could not be quenched. I wanted to be able to wander, not run, through the deserts of Eastern Sudan, the ever present sweep of dunes that were always in the back of my dreams. This constant was building. It made it difficult at times in those five days to concentrate. They wanted to show me absolutely everything.

I did see a lot too of their Nairobi life and the places the family had lived after getting away from the refugee camps. It had been eight years since I had gotten my life in order in Canada and made this possible. It began with me and the universe then went to work on everyone. Not that I take the credit for it myself. I'm only the way it began. I felt that was the way it was meant to be. I felt my role was of responsibility for the future of these children here. I was so happy; it made it all so worthwhile.

I would never know how hard that life was, but I could imagine because they seldom ever talked about it. It was always the here and now and what was going on in the present. It was Baba in the beginning who set my priorities into an ordered principle: the family always first, our needs, his needs, our pain, his pain. And, Mama was right behind him. They were working hard in Sudan, maintaining these two homes while BorTown was being finished, so we could all come home. This was my parents dream. Though I wanted that as well, a part of me knew I would always live now in Canada. I was a woman of two homes in one life. I will always do it Sarah's way, or no way! I don't mean the people in my life I love can't sway me. Yes certainly they can when I know it's right and true. Sarah I know can be stubborn; it's Acuach Cor who listens. Man, I was just so gullible. I really got into trouble with that at times. Now I'm Sarah and a grown woman with my own path!

A major alliance came out of this as well. It was one that, over time, had grown on me over the phone. It took a lot of phone cards for me to come to understand the reality of having a step-mom. This was one of those 'no way' deals. The very thought that Baba needed more than one Mama was an alien concept for me in the beginning. In the end, it was acceptance. We are a family all together. I, of course, knew Baba had children with Apajok; this woman who, out of respect, I was to call Mom.

I got there and just couldn't. I avoided any possible scenario to avoid saying this. I would wait till she turned to face me and just began talking. She never caught on either. What really turned me around was meeting for real my new brother and sister, Abany and Yong. Wow, talk about confusion when the family did finally get back together for real. All these people answering to the same name; it was totally an honour and I knew that. Using the same name isn't all that strange in Sudanese culture where there are only so many names to go around, passed down from generation to generation, tribe to tribe. These two were the light of my whole trip, my little darlings. I got over my difficulty with their mom as everyone called her Mama Apajok. One day it just came naturally as her name.

To see Nairobi, it was to see through the eyes of my sister-in-law Achol. It was she I spent the majority of my time with. She was always thinking up places to drag me off to experience. It was truly a marvel going to the local market with her. Here was a woman born to shop! We didn't even need money and she never made me feel I had to spend it. We were true sisters and had a ball together looking at fashion. She would tease me about my blonde hair extensions and silver jewelry. She wanted to make me over and make me jiggle in a big way, "Sarah eat, we have to fatten you up for a man!" Acuach Cor was listening, all wide eyed and imagining myself all plump and precious, imagining me wanted.

Then I had a Sarah thought and remembering my McDonald's attack, and well... no way! Take me as I am. I never ever want a belly that jiggles. What a horror that thought is to me. I was happy and built to be skinny. I was never willing to not be athletic. I am a runner.

For real!

I let Acuach Cor out and enjoyed Achol's makeover. This made her very happy. I gave that to her. She wanted so badly to hook me up while I was there, to find a man. She phoned Mama all excited at the change taking place in her rebel daughter. She thought Canada was wrecking me. This new world of ideas, blondes in Africa, was just not going to fly, even if they were only tied on. And what was the deal with silver? Only gold could show how attractive you were.

Well in Canada the idea of what's attractive is very different. I get my fair share of looks from guys and well, Ronnie, he loves me just the way I am. I was learning to do the same; accept what and who I am because I really do love me. When I think about it, I'm loved a lot, by my family, friends and of course Echo. Then there's my house who tells me all the time how much better it feels now that we moved in. I'm sorry, I'm being silly; it's one of those days. Let's go back to Africa, shall we.

Then there was Chol. I went over Apajok's after my make over. Chol whistled and smiled, as if to say, "much better!" I shrugged and laughed inside. Acuach Cor is just so happy to look upon a little boy now in a man's body. I think I will always see him just that way too. Acuach makes him happy when I smooth a gentle hand on his cheek and pinch them as I'm wont to do. I just can't help myself. Most everyone I love gets that treatment, especially the children. I love them up. At times the adults look at me funny because I'd rather be playing with the children and ignoring gossip.

It was interesting to watch the changes in Chol as well. I think he was trying to act all manly man for me, all suave and everything. I could tell the girls really like Chol; the neighbour girl was chasing his attention constantly. I don't think he was too interested in her though. I thought whenever she was around in those five short days, 'poor girl.' She was all love lost and puppy eyed and Chol's eyes were saying, "God, I wish she'd go home!" It was the little ones, Yong and Abany, I got all goofy around. That's when Acuach Cor comes out to play. The adults really had thought I'd lost it the one day it rained for about twenty minutes. I looked at Chol and he look at me, thinking, "Oh, oh, Acuach has that look and, I'm getting wet!"

He yelled for the kids and ran to his room and came out with a soccer ball. We all ran to the closest empty lot between buildings and it was on... soccer, in the rain. Apajok, for a little while, stood on the front step and watched, shaking her head before going back to a friend inside who was over for tea. Chol and I couldn't shake those kids. They went everywhere we went and Chol didn't mind. He is so good with children, he is worse than me. I could see his little brother and sister loved him to pieces. He would spend every spare moment he could with them, helping them with homework. Then they would drag him away after going into his room to get that soccer ball. "Show me again that trick Chol, bounce it off your head then both knees... pleeeease!" And Chol would add the next impossible ball play.

There were at least a couple of times I got Chol all to myself. This weirded him out just a little because I couldn't stop touching his cheeks. "Ow Sarah, stop that! I'm not that little boy in Havana, anymore." I would say the silliness I always add to such things, "Oooo, *look at you, my little man all grown so handsome.*" I'd try not to tear all up as I still couldn't believe I was actually there. With Chol right beside me, we'd go for a walk and very little serious talking. It wasn't Chol's style.

About the time I was beginning to really enjoy myself with everyone we got a call from Mama. "Sarah," she said in Dinka, "get yourself on a plane and come home my daughter. We are all here waiting. I will die not to see you one more day!" *With that, and knowing I was getting on a plane the next morning, my heart felt like leaping right out of my chest. In a half day, I would be in Juba. One more airport and I would be in Sudan.* Mama and Baba were both chattering my ear off a million miles an hour in a language that was rapidly coming back. I have to admit, I was translating everything for a while into Spanish. I was one confused world citizen. Little Acuach Cor had gone through airports half the way round that world. That thought never ceased to amaze me when I thought back on my life and here with Chol and back further to the beginning with my family. It was all too real. I was thirty something and I'd almost arrived.

I felt with just one more Airport, I was to find me.

Then I would have to face another series of airports and again leave my Africa. I would go back to a life I was building in Canada as a Canadian. I hadn't even been one for long. Only a year ago I didn't have the papers telling me I was from this country. So much of my life was based on documents. So many times I had to tell the world I was a lost child of Sudan. So many people had helped me, like Aragon of A.C.N.U.R. who had gone back to the refugee camps with that list of us 600 to look for our families. He had searched through an endless multitude in seas of displaced souls. He had sought anyone who knew us, so we could have documents to prove we were real and deserved assistance. As we ate grapefruit and cut grass with machetes.

There were so many things I needed to tell my Mother and Father, worlds of a life time I might never be able to get into words. I stayed up those last two evenings with a bare minimum amount of sleep, going through all these life events one more time. I was sorting them, making the Sarah list and knowing I wouldn't need one. It would all just come out, I knew that. This was all such a natural event now. It was like a deep flowing river that carves its own way across the plain. For centuries the Dinka and the Nuer had lived with that rhythm of the Nile's passing. They had paddled their boats out to catch their children's dinner. The hunters had run onto the plains with their homemade weapons of survival. This is what I thought of; how my family was an extension of all of that.

I thought of Baba's parents who I never knew and wished I could have a Grandma in Yalee. I wished I'd had a bond with that grandfather mama's father I never knew. There was so much more I needed to know now, things I might sometime in the future, pass on to my children. I wanted Mama and Baba to know that feeling of immortality, to have the experience of being grandparents to so many of their children, adding to our world. This thirst came again as timeless as the sands of the desert, as many as the grains of sand. These sleepless images were like the night sky and the little glimmerings of my thoughts were like the stars that shine. And the sun rose, my bags were packed and Chol called his taxi driver friend and those deep thoughts faded with the morning sun. All the children had their good bye moments with Auntie Acuach. That was the hardest part, leaving them. I knew I might see them again in Bortown if the family's plans of expanding there came true and I sharpened my pencil. If I didn't see them in BorTown, I would be flying back out of Nairobi anyway.

As the three of us, my sister-in-law Achol, Chol and I waved out the windows at so many waving back, the pressure of the coming flight grew. The thought was roaring around in my mind; one more plane and I'm home. This was to be a very short flight across the border to Juba, a trip of maybe three hours. But how can any flight be short that takes twenty years to complete? There is no way to describe that moment, suspended in air, between one life and the next and the next contained in one life's story. The presence of being filled that plane. It contained an element of grandeur, a soul on my way to a source, a well spring of my coming revelation . . .

(to be continued)